Conversations with Norman Mailer

Literary Conversations Series

Peggy Whitman Prenshaw
General Editor

Conversations
with Norman Mailer

Edited by
J. Michael Lennon

University Press of Mississippi
Jackson and London

Copyright © 1988 by the University Press of Mississippi
All rights reserved
Manufactured in the United States of America
91   90   89   88   4   3   2   1
The paper in this book meets the guidelines for permanence and durability of the Committee
on Production Guidelines for Book Longevity of the Council on Library Resources.

Library of Congress Cataloging-in-Publication Data

Mailer, Norman.
  Conversations with Norman Mailer / edited by J. Michael Lennon.
    p.   cm. — (Literary conversations series)
  Bibliography: p.
  Includes index.
  ISBN 0-87805-351-4 (alk. paper).   ISBN 0-87805-352-2 (pbk. : alk.
paper)
    1. Mailer, Norman—Interviews.   2. Authors, American—20th
century—Interviews.   I. Lennon, Michael.   II. Title.   III. Series.
PS3525.A4152Z465 1988
813'.52—dc19   87-34316
                                                            CIP

Books by Norman Mailer

The Naked and the Dead. New York: Rinehart, 1948. Novel.
Barbary Shore. New York: Rinehart, 1951. Novel.
The Deer Park. New York: Putnam's, 1955. Novel.
The White Negro. San Francisco: City Lights, 1957. Essay.
Advertisements For Myself. New York: Putnam's, 1959. Miscellany.
Deaths for the Ladies (And Other Disasters). New York: Putnam's, 1962. Poems.
The Presidential Papers. New York: Putnam's, 1963. Miscellany.
An American Dream. New York: Dial, 1965. Novel.
Cannibals and Christians. New York: Dial, 1966. Miscellany.
The Bullfight: A Photographic Narrative with Text by Norman Mailer. New York:
   Macmillan, 1967. Essay.
The Deer Park—A Play. New York: Dial, 1967.
The Short Fiction of Norman Mailer. New York: Dell, 1967.
Why Are We in Vietnam? New York: Putnam's, 1967. Novel.
*The Idol and the Octopus: Political Writings on the Kennedy and Johnson
   Administrations.* New York: Dell, 1968. Miscellany.
The Armies of the Night: History as a Novel, The Novel as History. New York: New
   American Library, 1968. Nonfiction narrative.
*Miami and the Siege of Chicago: An Informal History of the Republican and
   Democratic Conventions of 1968.* New York: World, 1968. Nonfiction narrative.
Of a Fire on the Moon. Boston: Little, Brown, 1970. Nonfiction narrative.
King of the Hill. New York: New American Library, 1971. Nonfiction narrative.
Maidstone: A Mystery. New York: New American Library, 1971. Nonfiction
   narrative.
The Long Patrol: Twenty-Five Years of Writing from the Work of Norman Mailer (ed.
   Robert F. Lucid). New York: World, 1971. Selections from thirteen of Mailer's
   books.
The Prisoner of Sex. Boston: Little, Brown, 1971. Essay.
Existential Errands. Boston: Little, Brown, 1972. Miscellany.
St. George and the Godfather. New York: New American Library, 1972. Nonfiction
   narrative.
Marilyn: A Biography. New York: Grosset & Dunlap, 1973.
The Faith of Graffiti (with Mervyn Kurlansky and Jon Naar). New York: Praeger,
   1974. Essay.
The Fight. Boston: Little, Brown, 1975. Nonfiction narrative.
Genius and Lust: A Journey Through the Major Writings of Henry Miller (ed. by
   Norman Mailer). New York: Grove, 1976.
Some Honorable Men: Political Conventions, 1960-1972. Boston: Little, Brown,
   1976. Nonfiction narrative.
A Transit to Narcissus. New York: Howard Fertig, 1978. Novel.

The Executioner's Song: A True Life Novel. Boston: Little, Brown, 1979. Nonfiction narrative.

Of Women and Their Elegance. New York: Simon & Schuster, 1980. Fictional autobiography.

Pieces and Pontifications (Pontifications, ed. Michael Lennon). Boston: Little, Brown, 1982. Miscellany.

Ancient Evenings. Boston: Little, Brown, 1983. Novel.

Tough Guys Don't Dance. New York: Random House, 1984. Novel.

Contents

Introduction

"Most serious readers," Norman Mailer said in an interview published in 1959, "like a writer to be a particular thing. It's important; it's reassuring, somehow. I've noticed that most of the writers one might consider as thin blades, yes? stilettoes, dirks, mmm? end up having a sure critical niche. And there have been a few writers, like myself. . . ."[1] Very few, it should be said. And Norman Mailer has rarely been a particular thing for very long. In the summer of 1948, forty years ago, *The Naked and the Dead* topped the best-seller list for eleven of twelve weeks and Mailer stepped into the klieg lights of public attention. He's still there, of course, although he has not attained a sure critical niche, unless it is that of America's most controversial literary figure. Mailer is embraced and rejected, praised and calumniated, almost according to individual need, it seems. *Esquire* places him in "The Red-Hot Center" of its August 1987 "Who's Who in the Literary Cosmos," but he is still our American scapegoat, "a poor man's Richard Nixon," as he put it recently.[2]

Called "the greatest writer to come out of his generation" by Sinclair Lewis after the publication of *The Naked and the Dead*, Mailer underwent a difficult metamorphosis in the fifties. The shy young writer who told Lillian Ross in 1948, "I have refused to let *Life* photograph me," had by the time of his 1955 interview with Lyle Stuart become a "Marxian anarchist" who said his role was to be "as disturbing, as penetrating, as his energy and courage make possible." The same year, while continuing his experiments with "General Marijuana," he cofounded and named the *Village Voice* and became an "apostle-leader" of the hip underground, as he playfully described himself in a 1961 *Mademoiselle* interview.

The sixties were Mailer's happiest, most tumultuous, and productive years, as he has often said. This was the period when

Mailer could interview himself in *The New York Times Book Review* and say happily that he considered himself "the best candidate around" for the post of "president of the literary world." By the time the decade was over he had been courted and then rejected by the Kennedys, challenged Sonny Liston, been arrested for several alleged offenses (including stabbing his wife, crossing a police line at the Pentagon, and refusing to pay a bar bill at Birdland) and run (and lost) for mayor of New York. In 1965 he testified on behalf of William S. Burroughs' novel *Naked Lunch* at its obscenity trial; the following year he dedicated his miscellany, *Cannibals and Christians*, "to LBJ, whose name inspired young men to cheer for me in public." He was awarded several major prizes in the sixties, including both the Pulitzer Prize and the National Book Award for his 1968 nonfiction narrative of the march on the Pentagon, *The Armies of the Night.* He was elected to the National Institute of Arts and Letters in 1967, about the same time that he was elevated to the status of counterculture hero for his civil rights and anti-Vietnam War activities, as well as for writings like "The White Negro," (1957) that brilliant and frequently reprinted essay, and his novel *An American Dream*, which he wrote under deadline pressure, in eight monthly installments, for *Esquire* in 1964. But Mailer was also criticized for his inability to produce the big novel he had promised years before and for appearing on every available television talk show. In the late sixties he began making experimental movies, an enterprise he described in his 1970 interview with Joseph Gelmis as "a cross between a circus, a military campaign, a nightmare, an orgy, and a high." These movies were not tremendously successful, largely because of technical problems. The audio in his first one, "Wild 90," was so bad, Mailer told Vincent Canby in a 1968 interview, that "it sounds as if *everybody* is talking through a *jock strap.*"

The seventies were not as exhilarating for Mailer. People in supermarket lines were reading about him but his image was getting stale. Looking back on this time in a 1982 interview with Michiko Kakutani, Mailer says, "If you work a muscle hard, it tends to develop; but if you overwork it, it can break down." By 1974, he said, "I felt I had used myself up as a reference." In addition, not all of the tremendous changes that he had heralded and labored for had taken place. The world was still the old world yet. As Robert F. Lucid has put it, "Mailer seemed to his audience to be woefully unsynchronized with the reality of his time, and for this he quite clearly was not to be forgiven."³ Certainly not by the women's liberation movement. After debating several feminists at town hall in New York in 1971 he was tagged nemesis of the movement, a distinction he still holds. And there were other problems. In 1973 he hosted his own fiftieth birthday party at which he announced the establishment of the Fifth Estate, a citizens' project to monitor the FBI and CIA. It failed within a short time.

Despite their number, public appearances were not his chief activity. Between 1965 and 1975 Mailer published nineteen books; a blizzard of occasional pieces—from political reportage and profiles to self-interviews, poems, and dramatic fragments, essays of every kind—appeared in most of the country's leading periodicals. Yet there he was boxing with José Torres on the Dick Cavett Show or bouncing a bourbon glass off Gore Vidal's head at a party. And just when it seemed that he was about to lead a barnstorm tour of the country with Salvador Dali and William F. Buckley, Jr., culminating in an appearance on the Gong Show, he decided, as he told John W. Aldridge, "Well, I want another audience." So he produced a major work of astonishing brilliance, *The Executioner's Song* (1979) for which he received his second Pulitzer. This comeback, his fourth, or fifth or sixth, depending on how one scores them, was even more remarkable in that *The Executioner's Song* (a nonfiction narrative which Mailer insisted on calling a "true life novel") was not the big novel that the literary world had waited for longer than any other (except perhaps Katherine Ann Porter's *Ship of Fools*). The "Egyptian novel," as it was referred to throughout the seventies, finally appeared in 1983 after a tremendous publicity campaign. Somewhat like *The Deer Park* (1955), on which Mailer placed great hopes only to be distressed by a middling success, *Ancient Evenings* received two types of reviews separated only by an abyss. Some of his supporters felt that the huge novel might have done better if the early eighties had not been such a publicity-engorged time for Mailer.

In November 1980 his marital troubles became incredibly complicated and his fourth wife accused him of "trigamy." More trying was the 1981 murder of a young man, Richard Adan, by Jack Henry Abbott, a talented writer whom Mailer had sponsored after his parole from prison. In what was perhaps the most unfair treatment of his entire career to date, the media savaged Mailer for not recognizing the violence in Abbott. He was also treated in rough fashion in 1986 after he invited, in his capacity as president of the American PEN Center, Secretary of State George Schultz to speak at the international PEN conference in New York. And so it goes. As Mailer explained in the Kakutani interview, one pays a price for time spent away from the typewriter. "The price that you pay is that it's harder for people to take you seriously—they're afraid to. They say, 'What is that fool, that flake, going to do next?' "

Although the thirty-four interviews collected here (including three self-interviews) do not reveal a truculent or sour individual, someone it is easy to hate, Mailer seems to arouse this emotion easily and regularly. What Michael Ventura says of the Mailer he saw on stage at Berkeley in 1972 holds true today: "To my knowledge no American writer had yet been assassinated or kicked half to death—not, at any rate, for his writing—but if it was going to happen that year it was going to be Mailer. At every level and in every niche of America, from Nixon to the Underground, *somebody* was pissed at him."

Ventura recalls thinking that night at Berkeley that "if it came to a rumble I was on Mailer's side." Others, myself included, have felt the same. But another cadre of Americans are ready to say the worst of Mailer. There are any number of explanations as to why Mailer arouses such contrary responses. Mine is simple: Mailer is Proteus. He became addicted to magnifying and diminishing, dispersing and unifying, to regularly reinventing himself after the huge success of *The Naked and the Dead,* which, as he explained in *Advertisements For Myself* (1959), was "a lobotomy to my past."[4] Not only have some people found some of Mailer's avatars to be repugnant, but just when they concluded that they had a hold on him, one of his whirligig changes took place. What Mailer told Melvyn Bragg about Gary Gilmore in a 1979 interview certainly applies to him: "He does something good and then he'll do something God-awful right afterwards." Extreme experiences and alternatives and the tightropes between them have attracted Mailer ever since the summer of 1948 when he learned that people were not looking at him but at "the sarcophagus of his legend . . . the living tomb of his legend," as he calls it in *The Armies of the Night.* "Of necessity," Mailer said, part of his "remaining funds of sensitivity went into the war of supporting his image and working for it."[5]

It would be reasonable to assume, therefore, that Mailer would relish the idea of interviews. The number he has given (I am aware of approximately two hundred fifty) would support this view. But in fact, Mailer professes to dislike the form, although his distaste is not conspicuous when he is in conversation. Only before or after, when he is considering the form in the abstract, does he deride it. When he is talking, as several of the interviewers in this collection testify, he is all gusto. In the *Paris Review* interview, one of his three or four finest, he tells Steven Marcus that "the only time I know that something is true is at the moment I discover it in the act of writing . . . you discover it at the point of the pencil." It is clear from many of these conversations that Mailer also discovers some moiety of the truth at the tip of his tongue. The three-way discussion among Mailer, Malcolm Muggeridge, and Marshall McLuhan moderated by Bob Fulford in 1968 is perhaps the most obvious of these truth-discovering sessions. The Eugene Kennedy interview is also notable for the way it shows Mailer in the act of coining new ideas.

Why then has he complained about interviews for so long, and yet given so many? The general answer is that Mailer sees almost everything in divided terms. As Christopher Lehmann-Haupt once noted, Mailer's universe is always in the process of being sundered by his "Manichean ox-team—his God and Devil in harness . . . pulling in opposite directions."[6] But his feelings about interviews are not that stark. He has four specific complaints about the form. First, he believes that writing is revision. Most of Mailer's books have gone through several drafts, and he marks up galleys and page proof with vigor. Uttering his ideas right out, therefore, pontificating, is problematic for him. "Authors in raw transcript," he notes, "can seem as bad on occasion as politicians."[7]

His second reason is that he feels that appearing too often in the public eye can injure a writer's reputation. Given his apparent ubiquity in the media from the sixties on, one could ask how Mailer's reputation has survived at all. But his point is a good one. There is a comparative advantage to appearing not at all. As he notes in the interview with Robert Begiebing, more reclusive authors have generated great interest in their work by staying out of the limelight. Has anyone even seen Thomas Pynchon in the last ten years? Mailer, on the other end of the availability spectrum, appreciates and undoubtedly occasionally yearns for anonymity.

Mailer's third reason for being less than fond of interviews is that over the years he, like most public figures, has been misquoted or selectively quoted many times. "The average reporter," Mailer says in *The Armies of the Night* (1968), "could not get a sentence straight if it were phrased more subtly than his own mind could make phrases. Nuances were forever being munched like peanuts."8 Finally, Mailer dislikes interviews because they are interruptions. They are mood-breakers. And for Mailer, "Mood is a harmony. The harmony of a Gestalt," as he notes in "The First Day's Interview," the first self-interview in this collection. Mailer has railed for decades about the dullness that we all feel because of the disjunctions of technology and bureaucracy. His anger about this matter may seem paradoxical given his unwavering commitment to living in what could easily be called the city of interruptions, New York, but it is nevertheless a genuine anger. Whatever his pastoral yearnings, Mailer needs to be near the center of things, even if the center is crazy.

One reason that Mailer consent to interviews is also found in "The First Day's Interview" where he points out that "an interview is dialectical. Any dialogue between two people is a natural dialectic. Each creates the response of the other. So it is possible that the experience of acquainting oneself with my grab bag of ideas, notions, arguments, examples, and *lapses* (as they are illumined and dissipated by your responses) will provide the reader with a sense of the dialectic that will be better than any exposition of the word by me." Mailer likes to see his own thought notched higher by the sharp questions of an interlocutor (even if the interlocutor is himself). The more challenging the questions, the more Mailer is stimulated. I don't mean crass questions designed to ferret out nuggets of personal information, but thoughtful, informed, tough questions that send the dialectic spiraling upward, to use one of Mailer's favorite images. Indeed, as Mailer says later in "The First Day's Interview," such encounters are existential, "if they are not edited." Here it should be noted that Mailer has edited, before original periodical publication, a few of the interviews in this collection, most notably the one in the *Paris Review* (all interviews have been reproduced here as they originally appeared). As he once explained, "You try to obtain a fair balance between the original tone, and the rights of the reader to respectable syntax."9

Mailer's friendship with an interviewer is another factor in encouraging him to talk for publication. George Plimpton, William F. Buckley, Jr., Jennifer L. Farbar, John W. Aldridge, Laura Adams, Barry Leeds, and Eugene Kennedy were friendly with Mailer long before their interviews took place. But the notion of the interview as an existential challenge is probably what has persuaded Mailer more than any other factor. He thrives in situations where he has to mobilize his energies on the spot. His self-imposed challenge is not just to answer questions well or tell the public about his new book but to alter a mood, shift a perception, locate a new idea, and so create a new reality for the reader. The reward of doing so will be greater if the interruption is particularly onerous and the questions difficult. In his interview Roger Ebert is surprised that Mailer is able to jump into a complex discussion while he is in the middle of directing a movie: "Mailer actually talks this way. He has been up all night for days, and has been working for hours and has stolen this moment to sit in the corner of a favorite bar, and the words and ideas come tumbling out, connections made between Shakespeare, the Mafia and mathematics. I listen fascinated. . . ."

Mailer's power to spin worlds out of words, conjure them almost on demand, demonstrates a Falstaffian prodigality. Part of the pleasure a Mailer interview provides is the satisfaction of our curiosity about how he will handle the questions he is asked. Like the fat knight he will shift and change before our eyes, peppering us with metaphors, conceits, obscure information, and, most of all, new connections. Mailer himself best summed up his protean ability when he said in *Advertisements For Myself,* "I become an actor, a quick-change artist, as if I can trap the Prince of Truth in the act of switching a style."[10]

For providing assistance on this collection I would like to thank the following: Marcia Plasters for manuscript preparation and, especially, for helping obtain permissions; Daryl Shaw for research and manuscript preparation; Ned Wass for helping on copyright questions; Marilyn Huff for general office support; Peter K. Lennon, Robert F. Lucid, and Cheryl Peck for editorial advice; Judith McNally and Gloria Taylor for helping locate several of the interviews and many other kindnesses, and Norman Mailer for his generosity and trust on this and other projects. Thanks also to the interviewers, publishers, periodicals, and literary agents, especially Scott Meredith, who gave me permission to use the interviews in this collection. I would like to thank Seetha Srinivasan of the University Press of Mississippi for her flexibility, advice, and encouragement. Finally, thanks to my wife Donna for her love, patience, and support. This volume is dedicated to her.

JML
November 1987

1. Interview with Richard G. Stern and Robert F. Lucid, reprinted in this collection. Hereafter, all quotations in the text without footnotes are from the interviews collected here.

2. Anonymous, "Norman Mailer's 'Extreme Situations,' " *You (St. Louis Post-Dispatch)*, 30 September 1987, p. 4.

3. Robert F. Lucid, "Prolegomenon to a Biography of Mailer," *Critical Essays on Norman Mailer*, ed. J. Michael Lennon (Boston: G.K. Hall, 1986), p. 176.

4. Norman Mailer, *Advertisements For Myself* (New York: Putnam's, 1959), p. 93.

5. Norman Mailer, *The Armies of the Night* (New York: New American Library, 1968), pp. 5-6.

6. Christopher Lehmann-Haupt, "Mailer's Dream of the Moon—I," *The New York Times*, 7 January 1971, p. 33.

7. Norman Mailer, *Pontifications*, ed. J. Michael Lennon (Boston: Little, Brown, 1982), p. iv.

8. *Armies*, p. 66.

9. *Pontifications*, p. iv.

10. *Advertisements*, p. 18.

Chronology

1923   Norman Kingsley Mailer born in Long Branch, New Jersey on 31 January, first child of Fanny Schneider and Isaac Barnett (Barney) Mailer.

1927   Mailers move to Eastern Parkway, Brooklyn. Barbara Jane, NM's sister, born on 6 April.

1939   NM graduates from Boys' High School, Brooklyn and enters Harvard for the study of aeronautical engineering.

1941   In November, NM wins *Story* magazine's college contest with "The Greatest Thing in the World," first published in *Harvard Advocate,* April 1941.

1943   NM graduates from Harvard in June with a B.S. (honors) in engineering; most of his elective courses were taken in English.

1944   In January NM is drafted into the U. S. Army. In March he marries Beatrice Silverman and is inducted. His novella, "A Calculus at Heaven," is included in Edwin Seaver's *Cross-Section: A Collection of American Writing.* Begins tour with 112th Cavalry in Philippines and Japan as a field artillery surveyor, rifleman, cook, and clerk.

1946   NM discharged from Army in May and begins writing *The Naked and the Dead.*

1947   After completing the manuscript of *The Naked and the Dead* in September, NM leaves for Paris where he studies on the GI Bill at the Sorbonne. Meets Jean Malaquais, a leftist writer who becomes his friend and mentor.

1948   *The Naked and the Dead* is published by Rinehart on 6
        May while NM is still in Europe. The novel tops the best-
        seller list for eleven straight weeks during the spring and
        summer of 1948. Returns from Europe in August to
        campaign for Progressive Party presidential candidate
        Henry Wallace.

1949   In March, NM speaks at the Cultural and Scientific
        Conference for World Peace (Waldorf Conference) in
        New York; he then spends several months writing scripts
        with Jean Malaquais in Hollywood. His daughter, Susan is
        born in August.

1951   *Barbary Shore* published in May.

1952   NM divorced from Beatrice Silverman.

1953   In April, NM publishes "The Language of Men" (short
        story) in *Esquire*, the first of dozens of pieces in the
        magazine he has become most closely identified with over
        the years.

1954   NM becomes a contributing editor of *Dissent,* establishing
        a relationship that continues today. Marries Adele
        Morales, a painter, and becomes associated with
        Greenwich Village life.

1955   *The Deer Park* is published in October by Putnam's, NM's
        new publisher. NM founds (with Edwin Fancher and
        Daniel Wolf) *The Village Voice,* which he names.

1956   NM publishes seventeen weekly columns, titled "Quickly"
        and (last two) "The Hip and the Square" in *The Village
        Voice* from 11 January through 2 May. "The Man Who
        Studied Yoga" is published in *New Short Novels 2*.

1957   Danielle, second daughter, born in March. "The White
        Negro (Superficial Reflections on the Hipster)" is
        published in *Dissent*.

1959   Elizabeth Anne (Betsy), third daughter, born in
        September. *Advertisements for Myself* is published in
        November, preceded by advance excerpts in *Esquire*,
        Partisan Review and *Big Table*, a promotional tactic NM
        continues to use for all his major books.

1960   NM covers the Democratic National Convention for
        Esquire and publishes an article strongly favoring John F.
        Kennedy, "Superman Comes to the Supermarket," in the
        November issue. On 20 November NM stabs his wife with
        a penknife after a party; he is committed briefly to
        Bellevue for psychiatric observation and later receives a
        suspended sentence when she refuses to press charges.

1962   *Deaths for the Ladies (and other disasters)* is published in
        January. NM divorced from Adele Morales; marries Lady
        Jeanne Campbell. Kate, his fourth daughter, born in
        August. In September, NM debates "The Role of the
        Right Wing" with William F. Buckley, Jr. in Chicago. NM
        begins a monthly column, "The Big Bite," in the
        November *Esquire* (through December 1963), and a
        bimonthly column, "Responses and Reactions," in the
        December *Commentary* (through October 1963).

1963   NM divorced from Lady Jeanne Campbell and marries
        Beverly Bentley. *The Presidential Papers* is published in
        November. In 1963 NM publishes a total of thirty pieces
        (poems, book reviews, essays, columns, stories, debates)
        in ten different periodicals, the continuation of a
        periodical blizzard that began in 1959 and continues
        through the mid-70s.

1964   Serialization of *An American Dream* begins in the January
        Esquire (through August). NM's first son, Michael Burks,
        born in March. In the summer, NM covers the Republican
        National Convention for *Esquire:* "In the Red Light," his
        account, appears in the November issue.

1965   *An American Dream,* now revised, is published in March.

NM speaks against the Vietnam War in May at the
Berkeley campus of the University of California. Also in
1965, NM testifies on behalf of William S. Burroughs'
novel *Naked Lunch* at its Massachusetts obscenity trial.

1966   Stephen McLeod, NM's second son, born in March.
          Cannibals and Christians is published in August.

1967   NM's dramatic adaptation of *The Deer Park* opens at
          Theatre De Lys in New York on 31 January; closes 21
          May after 127 performances. Publishes four books: *The
          Bullfight* (January); *The Short Fiction of Norman Mailer*
          (May); *The Deer Park: A Play* (July); *Why Are We In
          Vietnam?* (September). Two experimental films, *Wild 90*
          and *Beyond the Law*, filmed. Premiere of *Wild 90*. NM is
          arrested for antiwar protest at the Pentagon on 22
          October. Elected to the National Institute of Arts and
          Letters.

1968   NM's third experimental film, *Maidstone*, filmed. Premiere
          of *Beyond the Law*. Portions of *The Armies of the Night*
          appear in *Harper's* (March) and *Commentary* (April)
          before appearing in book form on 6 May (twenty years to
          the day after *The Naked and the Dead*). NM covers both
          political conventions and publishes his account, *Miami
          and the Siege of Chicago* in November. *Why Are We In
          Vietnam?* nominated for the National Book Award.

1969   *The Armies of the Night* wins both the National Book
          Award and the Pulitzer Prize. *Miami and the Siege of
          Chicago* also nominated for a National Book Award. NM
          testifies at the trial of the Chicago 7 in January. In April he
          announces for the Democratic nomination for the Mayor
          of New York (with Jimmy Breslin as his running mate);
          comes in fourth in a field of five. Awarded honorary
          doctorate by Rutgers University in June. Covers the
          Apollo 11 mission to the moon for *Life*.

1970   In May NM serves two days in jail in Washington, D.C., for his disorderly conduct conviction for violating a police line at the 1967 Pentagon demonstration. Little, Brown, NM's new publisher, publishes *Of a Fire on the Moon* in December following excerpts in *Life*. Separates from Beverly Bentley.

1971   NM again publishes four books in a year: *King of the Hill* (April); *The Prisoner of Sex* (May); *The Long Patrol: 25 Years of Writing from the Work of Norman Mailer*, edited by Robert F. Lucid (September); *Maidstone: A Mystery* (October). Premiere of *Maidstone*. Maggie Alexandra, his fifth daughter, born to Carol Stevens in March. In April NM takes part in "A Dialogue on Women's Liberation" at Town Hall in New York with Diana Trilling, Jill Johnston, Germaine Greer, and others. A reading of *D.J.*, a one-act play adapted from *Why Are We In Vietnam?*, is given in New York in December, the same month he has his celebrated fight on television with Gore Vidal on the "Dick Cavett Show."

1972   NM begins work in earnest on "the Egyptian novel." *Existential Errands* is published in April; NM covers the political conventions in the summer and publishes his account, *St. George and the Godfather,* in October. NM's father dies.

1973   In February, NM organizes and hosts his own fiftieth birthday party at the Four Seasons restaurant in New York. *Marilyn: A Biography* (produced and designed by Lawrence Schiller) is published in August.

1974   Jack Gelber's dramatic adaptation of *Barbary Shore* opens in New York on 10 January and closes 27 January. *The Faith of Graffiti* (in collaboration with Mervyn Kurlansky, Jon Naar, and Lawrence Schiller) is published simultaneously in *Esquire* and in book form in May.

1975   *The Fight* is published in July.

1976   *Some Honorable Men: Political Conventions, 1960-72* is
            published in April. In September NM profiles presidential
            candidate Jimmy Carter for *The New York Times
            Magazine,* following a visit to Plains, Georgia. *Genius and
            Lust: A Journey Through the Major Writings of Henry
            Miller* is published in October.

1978   A facsimile of the manuscript of NM's unpublished novel
            from the early 40s, *A Transit to Narcissus,* published in
            January. John Buffalo, NM's third son, born to Barbara
            Norris Church in April.

1979   Lawrence Schiller collaborates with NM in conceptualizing
            and researching *The Executioner's Song,* which is
            published in October after advance excerpts in *Playboy.*
            NM meets Jack Henry Abbott at the Marion Federal
            Penitentiary in Illinois the same month.

1980   Within the same week in November, NM is divorced from
            Beverly Bentley, marries and divorces Carol Stevens, and
            marries Barbara Norris Church. *The Executioner's Song*
            wins the Pulitzer Prize. *Of Women and Their Elegance* is
            published in November. NM plays Stanford White in
            Milos Foreman's film, "Ragtime." NM participates in the
            documentary, "Norman Mailer: The Sanction to Write,"
            made in Munich by Jeffrey Van Davis.

1981   NM writes introduction to and helps arrange for
            publication of *In the Belly of the Beast: Letters from
            Prison* by Jack Henry Abbott in June. On 18 July Abbott
            stabs to death Richard Adan in New York. Abbott is
            subsequently convicted and sentenced for the crime.

1982   *Pieces and Pontifications (Pontifications,* edited by J.
            Michael Lennon) is published in June.

1983   *Ancient Evenings* is published in April after advance
            excerpts in *Playboy, Vogue, House and Garden,* and *Paris
            Review.*

1984   *Tough Guys Don't Dance* is published in August by
        Random House, NM's new publisher.

1985   NM's mother dies.

1986   In January, NM chairs the International PEN conference
        in New York as President of the American PEN Center. In
        the spring, "Strawhead," a play adapted from *Of Women
        and Their Elegance,* is staged by the Actors Studio in
        New York with Kate Mailer as Marilyn Monroe.
        Production of NM's film version of *Tough Guys Don't
        Dance* begins in the fall with NM as director.

1987   Premiere of the film *Tough Guys Don't Dance.* NM
        continues working on "the CIA novel."

Conversations with Norman Mailer

The Naked Are Fanatics
and the Dead Don't Care
Louise Levitas / 1948

From the *New York Star*, 22 August 1948, M3-M5.

In the winter of 1943 the Army drafted Norman Mailer, age: 20; residence: Brooklyn; education: B.S., Harvard, '43. The Army got a slight, medium-sized rookie with intelligent eyes in a thin, pointed face—the brainy type, a little incongruous in khaki. "I was," says Mailer, looking backward five years, "an arrogant, nasty young man. I thought I knew everything."

Being drafted suited his plans exactly. Because, as he told his bride of two months, after that he intended to write THE War Novel.

Four years later he finished writing *The Naked and the Dead* which, besides becoming Number One on today's bestseller list, has been hailed as THE novel of our War. But it was not the book of heroic adventures with death that Mailer once had confidently in mind.

Instead, it turned out to be about anxious, tender, uncertain men ground down by the Army's "humbling process," made brutal by terror, sweat-grimed, cursing, and facing death, "with your bowels dropping out of you."

The graphic foxhole minutiae, it was clear when he talked about these things last week, came from his own misery as a Pfc. "To this day I don't like officers.

"I was the third lousiest guy in a platoon of 12—it got so I thought there wasn't anything I could do as well as anyone else."

He smiled in deprecation the way young men do when they can look back and see how much they've learned since a year or two ago. He was sitting in the large, old-fashioned living room of his mother-in-law's home in Boston, a comfortable place with family pictures on the grand piano and tall, awninged windows from which

3

you could see sunlight on the lawn outside. Mailer and his wife, returned from Europe 10 days before, were on a brief family visit. In slacks and a T-shirt, he sprawled on the couch, looking like a collegiate on vacation, but his slangy, Brooklyn-accented talk was, unexpectedly, adult. He was telling how peacetime, 1946 and '47, had affected him while he was writing *The Naked and the Dead*.

"I never even thought of its being an anti-war book, at the beginning. But every time I turned on the radio and looked in the newspapers, there was this growing hysteria, this talk of going to war again, and it made me start looking for the trend of what was happening.

"It seemed to me that you *could* get men to fight again. They came out of the war frustrated, filled with bitterness and anger, and with no place to focus their anger. They would be thinking, 'I don't give a goddam, I'll go into it, at least it'll be a change!' They would start remembering the good things about being a soldier, the furloughs with money in their pockets, how swell it was to be walking around in a uniform in a foreign city, and to be the most important men in that city just because they were in that uniform.

"That really formed the book—the feeling that people in our government were leading us into war again. The last half was written on this nerve right in the pit of my stomach."

Out of that disgust came the sharp outlines of Mailer's General Cummings, the fastidious, dictator-minded intellectual who, while commanding a Pacific island campaign, planned the militaristic future of America.

"The chances are that there's not a single general in the U.S. Army who's like him. But there could be! He articulates a kind of unconscious bent in the thinking of the Army brass and top rank politicians. He's an archetype of the new man, the coming man, the one who's really dangerous. I still think that half the guys in the State and War departments have the same psychology."

Some of the analysis, Mailer confessed, was hindsight, realized in Europe where he had gone immediately upon finishing the manuscript of his book. With GI Bill assistance he and his wife, an ex-Wave officer, had studied at the Sorbonne and then traveled around. In France, Italy, Spain and England, because the conflict of economic ideas was sharper than in the U. S. A., he had glimpsed what the future might hold.

He thought now that he had written his book in a political vacuum. "There's a tendency among too many leftist writers—and I think I'm a little guilty of it in *The Naked and the Dead*—to avoid a lot of the problems. The hero generally functions in a politically colorless frame. He sees only the things that are obviously bad and he tries to correct them. But that's false. Very few Americans live in such a clearly defined world."

The Naked and the Dead, he said, had a negative sort of politics. "I mean I knew everything that terrified me, like Cummings. But at the time I got out of the Army I didn't believe in any kind of collective action, whereas I do now.

"I just had such a fantastic hatred of the Army, I had known that particular organization so damn well, I thought that all organization was bad—political parties, charitable organizations, what have you. Organization brought out the lowest common denominator.

"I thought of myself, naively, as an anarchist—that is, without reading books about it or knowing any other people who were. I didn't belong to any group—political or even literary. I was just sitting in my room in Brooklyn, writing. All I knew was what I read in the newspapers."

Mailer's voice was mellow, husky, rapid and as he spoke he seemed to be aware of so many things at once that his conversation was almost elliptical. His words crowded each other, skipping the usual prefaces, trying to get to the heart of what he really meant.

His wife, a pretty, dark-haired girl, very shapely in a cotton dress and sandals, sat on a footstool as he talked. His mother-in-law, Mrs. H. I. Silverman, came in now and then to listen. She had diligently read *The Naked and the Dead* and had more than a parental interest. Her husband had been in the first World War; and Mrs. Silverman was a past president of the Jewish War Veterans auxiliary.

The Mailers teased her about that. Her young son-in-law didn't hold much sympathy for veterans' groups. He had, as he said, misgivings about all organizations, although he had changed his mind about political ones.

"Granting the corrupting effects," he said, "if you are going to accomplish anything in your framework of time, you just have to work with them."

After he had finished his book, even before he went to Europe, he had joined the Progressive Citizens of America. He is so convinced now of its importance that he is delaying his next novel until after the elections in order to work for Wallace. The fact that there might be Communists in the same organization didn't bother him; he hadn't met any of them in PCA. And what he had seen in Europe gave him a sense of urgency.

"Italy is pretty bad right now, a pretty ugly country. The Marshall Plan definitely is keeping in power the smartest, dirtiest, old-time politicians, the broken-down aristocracy that would normally have been kicked out. Italy would be better off under communism than under the kind of very bad capitalism they have there. You don't have to be a Communist to see that.

"About France and England, I don't know. As far as the countries of eastern Europe go—like Poland, where they had one fascist dictator after another—they're better off. Czechoslovakia—I don't know what the score is there."

As if he were answering an unspoken argument, he added quickly, "The thing is, America is one of the very few countries that has a tradition of intellectual freedom, and that kind of freedom can only exist in a country with a high standard of living."

Beatrice Mailer had been regarding her husband during the conversation, sometimes with solicitude, at times with amusement. Interviews were still rather new. The Mailers had been removed from the fuss that the author of a first novel stirs up. Clippings of the reviews had been mailed to them in Europe. And a cable had brought the news that The Naked and the Dead had reached the Number One best seller spot. "I felt kind of blue the rest of the day," Mailer said. "A lot of people I'd like to like the book are set against it, because it's a best seller."

For a writer, all this fuss could be a handicap, he thought. As an unsuspected, unrespected author in the Army, he had been "a neutral and unimportant guy. It was a marvelous state of writing. I absorbed without having to take too much of a personal role. Everyone acted more directly in front of me. Now people take an artificial attitude."

The week they had spent in New York since their return had been mostly prescribed by Mailer's new status: business talks with the publisher, conferences with Lillian Hellman, who was writing a play based on the book, and the usual literary cocktail party (said Mailer with a grimace) at which he met reviewers.

The clippings he read in Europe had been very favorable, Mailer said, "but for the wrong reasons." He was annoyed by the reviews that discussed the desperate and profane soldier characters as if they were perverts. And by those reviewers who had called his book a documentary.

"I don't think the book is at all a documentary—a piece of realism. For one thing, the number of events that happen to this one platoon couldn't possibly have happened to any one Army platoon in the war." He had made that group of men a composite of all the experiences he had known and heard and felt, not only about the war but about his whole young life.

It was, he thought, a "highly symbolic" book. For example, the mountain behind the Japanese lines which the platoon attempts to climb. "It represents a great many things," he said, "—things like death and man's creative urge and man's desire to conquer the elements, fate—all kinds of things that you never dream of separating and stating so baldly.

"The title I wanted to use for the book—and that I feel very sorry I didn't use now—was *Plant and Phantom.*" This is the title he gave to Part Three of his book. He took it from Nietzsche: "*Even the wisest among you is only a disharmony and hybrid of plant and phantom. But do I bid you become phantoms or plants?*"

He meant it to refer, Mailer said, to the conflict between the animal roots of man and his sense of vision. "*The Naked and the Dead* is another way of saying it—the naked being the fanatics, the men obsessed with vision."

Mailer talked about these things haltingly and with reluctance. An author shouldn't describe his book, he said. "I'm very, very inarticulate, and particularly inarticulate when it comes to explaining this book—I worked on it so long."

It had taken him 15 months to write but, he said, he had really been thinking about it for four years. His wife remembered, smiling. "He used to have fits and conniptions every time another war book came out!"

He hadn't started to write *The Naked and the Dead* until a year after the war ended. Mrs. Mailer had saved all the letters he had sent her from overseas. They contained characters, incidents, the theme of the novel. "I kept my diary writing to Bea. I wrote her four and five letters a week. In the middle of a letter I'd put down a whole page of notes. We were moving around so much there just was no way of keeping it otherwise."

The Mailers had also saved $2000 by then, from his $50 monthly Army allotments and Beatrice's salary as a Wave. "The idea was, we would write until the money ran out and then look for jobs." For Mrs. Mailer was writing a war book too, about her experience with the Waves. Closeted in separate rooms of their two-room Brooklyn apartment, they worked all day, and then read over each other's manuscripts at night.

Mrs. Mailer's novel, in spite of her husband's admiration, was not accepted for publication. "They all said it was dull," she said, and added cheerfully, "I gave up writing. I found out how hard it was."

Before Mailer's novel was accepted by Rinehart & Co., he had to attend a profanity conference. "We agreed that I would cut it to what I thought was the irreducible minimum." This meant taking out perhaps a fifth of the profane words in the original manuscript.

Mailer found this a reasonable attitude compared to previous publishers' reactions. Right after he got out of the Army, he had gone to see an editor at Random House, who had expressed some interest in Mailer when rejecting an earlier manuscript. The young author outlined his plan for *The Naked and the Dead* and this publisher, intending to be kind, said, "Oh, Lord, don't write a war novel! None of us want it."

"So when I started showing *The Naked and the Dead* around," Mailer said, "I didn't think of showing it to him." He took it first to Little, Brown & Co. They held it a long time before they rejected it because of its language. "We just couldn't come to any kind of agreement on what was to be cut out." Soldier talk without profanity, Mailer said, was artificial. "When I start creating characters, I have to believe in their speech as it comes out."

But while Little, Brown was hesitantly considering the book, they sent it to Bernard De Voto for his opinion. He read it and sent it back with a humorous eight-page letter advising against publication. The letter began something like this: "I swear. My wife swears. In fact, my whole family swears. BUT—"

When he grinned as he was telling this story, Mailer looked even younger than his 25 years. His ears stuck out from a head of brown, curly hair. On his face, with the wide forehead, large blue eyes and narrow, sensitive chin, it was still possible to see the traces of an earnest adolescent. How could so young a face have written such a book?

Most of the literary critics have asked that question. *The Naked and the Dead* shows an astonishing versatility, an understanding of many kinds of men from widely different backgrounds. Mailer, when he thought about it, simply considered that he had been very fortunate in his experiences. "I cut across a lot of social groups."

He was born in Long Branch, N.J., but his family moved to Brooklyn before he was kindergarten age. They had a four-room apartment in "a quiet section of two-family houses and trees, a mile from Ebbets Field and Prospect Park. It was the most secure Jewish environment in America. Everybody around us was Jewish."

Mailer's father was an accountant. They lived as comfortably as their neighbors. "During the depression, we were poor; after that, well, it was kind of a squeeze on my parents to send me to Harvard."

Being at Harvard was lucky too, for a writer. "It's an extremely complex place," he said. His fellow students came from all over the country, poor and rich and average, the socially elite, outcasts, giving variety to college life. Mailer was studying engineering science. "When I was a kid, I used to build model airplanes, so I decided I wanted to be an aeronautical engineer. But by my sophomore year I got much more interested in writing than in engineering."

The novels of Tolstoy and Dostoievski absorbed him. He thought *Anna Karenina* was the greatest book ever written. "I took a lot of writing courses at Harvard. I think they can help you. You can learn what not to do."

In his junior year, he met Beatrice at a Boston Symphony concert. That year, at 18, he started his first novel, which he now describes as "very bad." It was about Jews in Brooklyn. He wrote his second novel about an insane asylum where he had worked one summer vacation. "It was a very large and overly-ambitious manuscript; it was supposed to be an anatomy of brutality." Both novels were rejected by a great number of publishers.

Six months after he was graduated, he went into the Army, which trained him to be a surveyor for the artillery. But when he got to Leyte shortly after that, he was assigned to the intelligence section of an infantry regiment. "The night I hit them, we were sent on to the invasion of Luzon."

Mailer's job was at the combat team headquarters, typing reports in quintuplicate. He wasn't a good enough typist, so the Army put him in another office, interpreting aerial photographs.

After the Luzon landing, the fighting receded to a comparatively safe distance from regimental headquarters. Miserable in his clerk's job, Mailer, who had always wanted to experience combat, asked and received a transfer to a reconnaissance platoon. The platoon was attached to a regiment deployed into the mountains as a protecting flank for a division fighting its way into Manila. There were Japanese troops in the mountains, and Mailer soon had reason to regret his transfer.

"Going out on patrol every day in the Philippine sun, carrying a heavy pack on your back, that kind of ever present fatigue and diarrhea and just feeling generally awful, broke down any desire I had for action and adventure. And also the feeling that you're going to be killed—I became emotionally convinced of it, and I didn't care much anymore what happened.

"But I didn't see too much combat—a couple of fire fights and skirmishes." The platoon's most eventful patrol had occurred before Mailer joined them. "They had a three-day patrol behind the enemy lines, and I kept hearing about it the whole time I was with them." Finally transmuted by Mailer's own literary purposes, this patrol became part of *The Naked and the Dead*.

The military action in the book was a composite of incidents he had heard about and those he himself had experienced. "Everything in the book really happened somewhere in the war." The average foot soldier didn't get to know why he was slogging up some mountain trail. Mailer had glimpsed the general's eyeview of what was happening while he was typing battle reports and looking at aerial photographs.

"Besides," his wife said, "he's a natural born military strategist."

"A natural born general," he said, with enjoyment. "My favorite reading during the war was the *Infantry Journal*. That's where you pick up a lot of information about strategy and tactics."

At least half of the characters in *The Naked and the Dead* were taken from men he had soldiered with, although they had become quite changed in the writing. The officers? "Oh, you always get to know them. Working for them—there's no kind of knowledge that can substitute for it. You generally operate on hate, and hate is the best aid to analysis."

He could afford to be grateful now, even for the officers he had despised.

"Most of the guys who wrote war novels were working from the top down. If I had had one of the jobs they had—writing for *Yank* or working in Special Services, taking a quick trip to the front and talking to some GIs and then getting back to a typewriter to write about it—I would have written their kind of book.

"I literally functioned as a GI. I hated officers. I had the holy sense of importance that a GI has." Maybe the bitterness of all his experiences came after the war ended and his outfit was stationed in Japan. In order to get out of the drills and other Army annoyances, he became a cook; and as a cook, he finally made his stripes. He got a T/4 rating.

But in a fight, one day, the newly-made T/4 used a few unprintable words to tell his top sergeant what he thought of him. When Mailer refused to take them back, the sergeant reported the matter to the captain. "The captain ordered me to apologize," Mailer said. "It was just a week before going home. So I crawfished—the way Hearn did in the book." (Lt. Hearn, the general's aide in *The Naked and the Dead*, is ordered by the general to pick up a cigaret butt.)

"So after I apologized, I spent the night crying and angry. I saw how much the stripes had meant to me, just how I had been corrupted by the Army, and how weak I had been acting for a long time. And the next morning I went to the captain and said I wanted to give the stripes back. But, because he was the kind of man he was, he said, 'You're not giving them back. I'm taking them back!' "

Mailer looked uncomfortable for a moment. "I got a kind of poetic punishment which I deserved," he said. "It was good the whole thing happened."

All the humbling experiences that a GI endures were good for him as a writer, he said; but being a writer had increased his troubles as a soldier. "I was brought up on those war hero novels. Of course, all the war ideals you had were quickly lost about a week after you got into the Army. But all the time I was overseas I had these conflicting ideas—wanting, the way everyone else did, to get the softest, easiest job, to get by with the least pain—and also wanting to get into combat and see it. The only time I could make up my mind was the time I asked to go to Recon.

"And it paid off, in a kind of curious way."

Rugged Times
Lillian Ross / 1948

From *The New Yorker*, 23 October 1948, 25. © 1948, 1976 The
New Yorker Magazine, Inc. Reprinted by permission.

We had a talk the other day with Norman Mailer, whose novel *The
Naked and the Dead* has been at the top of the best-seller lists for
several months now. We met him at Rinehart & Co., his publishers,
in a conference room that had, along with other handy editorial
equipment, a well-stocked bar. We'd heard rumors that Mailer was a
rough-and-ready young man with a strong antipathy to literary
gatherings and neckties, but on the occasion of our encounter he was
neatly turned out in gray tweeds, with a striped red-and-white necktie
and shined shoes, and he assured us that he doesn't really have any
deep-seated prejudices concerning dress. "Actually," he said, "I've
got all the average middle-class fears." He thinks the assumption that
he hasn't got them grew out of his meeting some of the literati last
summer when he was wearing sneakers and an old T shirt. He'd just
come from a ball game, and it was a very hot day. "I figured anybody
with brains would be trying to keep cool," he said.

Mailer is a good-looking fellow of twenty-five, with blue eyes, big
ears, a soft voice, and a forthright manner. Locating a bottle of Scotch
in the bar, he poured a couple of drinks. "If I'm ever going to be an
alcoholic," he said, "I'll be one by November 2nd, thanks to the
rigors of the political campaign. I've been making speeches for
Wallace. I've made eighteen so far and have another dozen ahead of
me. I'm not doing this because I like it. All last year, I kept saying that
the intellectuals had to immerse themselves in political movements or
else they were only shooting their mouths off. Now I am in this spot
as a result of shooting my mouth off." In general, Mailer told us, the
success of his novel has caused him to feel uncomfortably like a
movie queen. "Whenever I make an appearance," he said, "I have
thirty little girls crowding around asking for my autograph. I think it's

much better when people who read your book don't know anything about you, even what you look like. I have refused to let *Life* photograph me. Getting your mug in the papers is one of the shameful ways of making a living, but there aren't many ways of making a living that aren't shameful. Everyone keeps asking me if I've ever been psychoanalyzed. The answer is no, but maybe I'll have to be by the end of another five years. These are rough times for little Normie."

Mailer's royalties will net him around thirty thousand this year, after taxes, and he plans to bank most of it. He finds apartments depressing and has a suspicion of possessions, so he and his wife live in a thirty-dollar-a-month furnished room in Brooklyn Heights. He figures that his thirty thousand will last at least five years, giving him plenty of time in which to write another book. He was born in Long Branch, New Jersey, but his family moved to Brooklyn when he was four, and that has since been his home. He attended P.S. 161 and Boys High, and entered Harvard at sixteen, intending to study aeronautical engineering. He took only one course in engineering, however, and spent most of his time reading or in bull sessions. In his sophomore year, he won first prize in *Story's* college contest with a story entitled "The Greatest Thing in the World." "About a bum," he told us. "In the beginning, there's a whole *tzimes* about how he's very hungry and all he's eating is ketchup. It will probably make a wonderful movie someday." In the Army, Mailer served as a surveyor in the field artillery, an Intelligence clerk in the cavalry, a wireman in a communications platoon, a cook, and a baker, and volunteered, successfully, for action with a reconnaissance platoon on Luzon. He started writing *The Naked and the Dead* in the summer of 1946, in a cottage outside Provincetown, and took sixteen months to finish it. "I'm slowing down," he said. "When I was eighteen, I wrote a novel in two or three months. At twenty-one, I wrote another novel, in seven months. Neither of them ever got published." After turning in the manuscript of *The Naked and the Dead*, he and his wife went off to Paris. "It was wonderful there," he said. "In Paris, you can just lay down your load and look out at the gray sky. Back here, the crowd is always yelling. It's like a Roman arena. You have a headache, and you scurry around like a rat, like a character in a Kafka nightmare, eating scallops with last year's grease on them."

Mailer has an uneasy feeling that Dostoevski and Tolstoy, between them, have written everything worth writing, but he nevertheless means to go on turning out novels. He thinks *The Naked and the Dead* must be a failure, because of the number of misinterpretations of it that he has read. "People say it is a novel without hope," he told us. "Actually, it offers a good deal of hope. I intended it to be a parable about the movement of man through history. I tried to explore the outrageous proportions of cause and effect, of effort and recompense, in a sick society. The book finds man corrupted, confused to the point of helplessness, but it also finds that there are limits beyond which he cannot be pushed, and it finds that even in his corruption and sickness there are yearnings for a better world."

Talk with Norman Mailer
Harvey Breit / 1951

From *The New York Times*, 3 June 1951, sec. 7, 3. Reprinted in *The Writer Observed* by Harvey Breit (Cleveland: World Publishing Co., 1956). Copyright © 1951 by The New York Times Company. Reprinted by permission.

On January 31, Norman Mailer noted the fact that he had become twenty-eight years old. "I was a young man in my prime," he said the other day with hardly any irony, "when I wrote *The Naked and the Dead*. The army was the only milieu I ever had. It was like living in a society where rumor has the same validity as fact, like a tight community where you can weep about people you never saw. Like someone says, 'This guy got knocked off in a patrol.' And everyone feels bad."

If there is such an attribute as being restfully intense, Mr. Mailer has it. It is a quality of intensity that is without strain and makes no demands on a companion. Strangely, and comfortably let it be added, while Mr. Mailer's thought and speech have intensity, Mr. Mailer himself—beneath the mind and voice as it were—is perfectly relaxed. It is an attractive paradox that creates intellectual stimulation and physical relaxation simultaneously.

He said, "I wrote *Naked* in fifteen months. The new one, *Barbary Shore*, is half the size and took me three years. I don't think of myself as a realist," Mr. Mailer said after a pause, during which he obviously thought back to his first, and very impressive, novel. "That terrible word 'naturalism.' It was my literary heritage—the things I learned from Dos Passos and Farrell. I took naturally to it, that's the way one wrote a book. But I really was off on a mystic kick. Actually—a funny thing—the biggest influence on *Naked* was *Moby-Dick*."

Had he known while writing it? Mr. Mailer nodded. "I was sure everyone would know. I had Ahab in it, and I suppose the mountain was Moby Dick. Of course, I also think the book will stand or fall as a realistic novel.

15

"I may as well tell you what the title of the new book means," he
said. "It has a double meaning. 'Barbary,' for me, is a very rich word.
One of the meanings is barbarism and the other, not in the Oxford
dictionary, has romantic connotations. You think of the exotic, of
pirates, of romantic things."

Were we coming back to romantic things? "I think the tendency as
you come closer and closer to doom and disaster," Mr. Mailer said,
and stopped and began again. "There is a tendency, given such a
condition, to move closer and closer to amorous wish fulfillments."

How did Mr. Mailer feel about being an author in an age that was
moving, as he put it, closer and closer to doom and disaster? "It is
probably one of the worst periods in history for a writer," he said with
hardly any hesitation. "To be a novelist today is absolutely a bone-
cracker. The knowledge that you are embarking on a novel that may
take ten years of your time is vitiated by what you read each day in
the newspapers. I mean if you are trying to do work of the devotion
of *Ulysses* or *Remembrance of Things Past* or *The Magic Mountain*.
On top of that, the fundamental problem of knowledge is involved."

Mr. Mailer stared fixedly at his companion. "In the past," he said,
"a novelist could create a world view, a whole thing in itself. It is
different today because knowledge is broken down, departmentalized.
Time and time again the novelist louses up his work with jargons and
special knowledge. And yet you can't eschew it. It's better to fail that
way than to ignore this condition and keep on in some little
cubbyhole. If a writer really wants to be serious he has to become
intellectual, and yet nothing is harder. Intellectuality delivers the writer
to self-questioning and to despair at his own limitations; it vitiates the
attempt at large, serious works because you are unable to suspend
the critical faculties even at the times when you should."

Eliot once said perhaps the main difference between the good and
bad poet was not so much one of talent as it was the inability of the
bad poet to be *unconscious* at the right times. Mr. Mailer nodded at
least in partial assent. "I'm beginning to have a pride in writers. They
are radical, always disturbing. What they write has nothing to do with
what they profess, which is usually silly.

"A great writer always goes to the root, he is always coming up
with the contradictions, the impasses, the insoluble dilemmas of the
particular time he lives in. The result is not to cement society but to
question it and destroy it. Faulkner may profess all sorts of things, he

may even be off on a white-supremacy binge, but actually the total of his work has caught the horror at the same time that it has caught the fact that he loves it. A great writer has to be capable of knowing the rot, and he has to be able to strip it down to the stink, but he also has to love that rot. A writer has to have a tough mind, the toughest mind of his time. And he has to have a great heart."

Novels Are Easy
Esquire/1953

From *Esquire*, 39 (April 1953), 15-16. Reprinted with permission
from *Esquire*. Copyright © 1953 by Esquire Associates.

Norman Mailer is a rather mild young man who talks very quietly,
and very fast. And he is, at thirty, one hundred per cent a writer. His
concluding mechanism works simultaneously with his observing
mechanism, so that any small incident expands itself into a broader
principle, and he is liable to talk in symbols. For example, his opinion
of himself as a skier.

"I'm a mediocre skier," he said. "I'm a confirmed intermediate.
Each year I begin at the same place and I get a little better and then I
lay off for the summer and next year I begin again just where I did
the year before. An intermediate skier can't get any better. He knows
it and the instructor knows it, and the class knows it, and everybody
is unhappy."

Immediately after such an analysis, he will deny any ability to
observe. "I know there are a lot of writers who remember specific
things, but I never do. Certain things happen to you, and a long time
later something will occur as a fragment or extension of that thing. As
you write it, it becomes something else, something more that you
never thought you knew."

Thus he arrived at the writing of "The Language of Men," page 61,
a nice analysis of the attempts at adjustment by an Army cook stuck
in the Islands after the war. "I was a cook in the Army myself, after
my outfit got to Japan," he recalled. "I didn't think of all the specific
things then. I just thought of it as a lousy job. But then I started to
write the story, and a lot came back that I'd forgotten; and the
experience of being an Army cook was a lot more real for me while I
was writing than when it had happened."

The same was true of his best-selling novel, *The Naked and the
Dead,* which topped the New York *Times* best-seller list for eleven of

the twelve weeks following publication in 1948. A writer friend, Jean Malaquais, once expressed it for Mailer; "Writing is the only true experience."

"I guess he meant that you only know a thing when you write it."

Unlike many novelists who have trouble with the tight limits of a short story, Mailer finds "stories easier. In a novel, you can make a mistake on a given day—and that mistake can deepen until you're writing a novel entirely different from the one you intended. As a result, you can lose six months or a year. With a short story, if I ruin it, I ruin it, and the worst that's happened is that I've lost a few days or a week."

He is not, however, more relaxed when trying to write a movie. After a winter of skiing and working on a new novel, *Barbary Shore*, in Vermont in 1949, he went to Hollywood and worked on an original script for Sam Goldwyn.

"It stank. It was half-art, half-commercial, the sort of thing you can delude yourself about for a long time. Goldwyn didn't want it, so we bought it back from him and tried to sell it. There weren't any buyers. It took a year before we finally gave it up and came back to New York."

Barbary Shore came out in May of 1951. The book was set in a boardinghouse in Brooklyn Heights, near where Mailer lived after he got out of the Army, and "had the distinction of having the worst reviews of any second novel I can remember. But I don't think it was a bad book. It may have been a bad book, but it was the best of the bad books."

Unmoved by the reviews on number two, he has holed himself up in a barren studio (no telephone, no furniture) in Brooklyn to work on a third book. "I have the first draft finished and I'm kind of sitting on it. It's one of those bad slack times when you can't force anything. I kind of like the book though. It's different than anything I've done before." He wouldn't say how, just different.

For the moment, however, the book could wait, while its author broke away into a cloud of instructor's sad, patient comment during another fling at skiing.

An Intimate Interview with Norman Mailer
Lyle Stuart/1955

From *Exposé*, No. 49 (December 1955), 1, 4. Reprinted with permission of Lyle Stuart.

Norman Mailer's *The Deer Park* is easily the most controversial novel of 1955.

Mailer, the young novelist who blazed to fame at the age of 25 with his first great novel *The Naked and the Dead* was called "The greatest writer to come out of his generation" by Sinclair Lewis.

The Deer Park, a story of Hollywood and sex, of blacklists and beauty queens, is on the best-seller lists, despite weird and angry reviews by many critics.

Expose posed 69 questions to Mr. Mailer. He had agreed in advance to answer ten or twenty of them. He answered all 69.

As with all Exposé interviews, this one has not been censored in any way.

Q: What is the literary situation in America now?

A: I think my attitude will come out as I answer the questions.

Q: Why?

A: Because that is the way I answer questions.

Q: If you were giving advice to a young writer on the brink of fame, what would you say?

A: Try to keep the rebel artist in you alive, no matter how attractive or exhausting the temptations.

Q: Why do you write?

A: I suppose I write because I want to reach people and by reaching them, influence the history of my time a little bit.

Q: Do you believe anybody listens to writers?

A: Yes. But most readers listen with the unconscious ear.

Q: Philip Rodman once remarked that if a writer were very successful, he might reach six people who really understand what he is trying to say. Are you reaching your six?

A: In a certain sense no one can "really understand" what another person is trying to say, not if we take into account the enormous complexity of experience and the greater complexity, if not total uniqueness, of every human alive. But as a practical matter, depending on the artistry of the writer, and in inverse proportion to the difficulty of his style, a sizable number of people can usually "understand" most of what the writer is saying.

Q: What are you trying to say in *The Deer Park?*

A: Everything I know about life at the age of thirty two.

Q: How do you feel about book reviewers in general? (Would you classify them as eunuchs or whores?)

A: Depends on their prose.

Q: Why didn't Rinehart publish *The Deer Park?*

A: Because he was afraid to.

Q: It is really, as some critics charge, a book about sex?

A: Yes, it is totally about sex. And it is also totally about morality. A writer who grows up in this country can hardly write about one without invoking the other. Henry Miller is the only exception I know. And I smell a moralist in him somewhere.

Q: How do you feel about sex?

A: How I feel about it personally is none of your business. How I feel about it as a literary subject is something else. I believe it is perhaps the last remaining frontier of the novel which has not been exhausted by the nineteenth and early twentieth century novelists.

Q: Isn't *The Deer Park* really every young man's dream of paradise?

A: I'm beginning to wonder.

Q: Did you have any censorship problems with your publisher?

A: I had none with G.P. Putnam. The other six houses *The Deer Park* was sent to tried to exercise censorship directly and by the indirect excuse of saying they did not like the book sufficiently.

Q: What is the function of a censor?

A: To retard whatever movement is in the air.

Q: Do you think the current censorship wave will make us a nation of mental eunuchs?

A: The situation is exceptionally complicated. There is not only a wave of censorship but there are counter-waves which are opposed to censorship. I feel more optimistic about the general situation than I have in years. But this may conceivably be no more than a reflection of my present mood.

Q: Is *The Deer Park* autobiographical in that its narrator speaks for you?

A: *The Deer Park* is not autobiographical. No one in it speaks directly for me. I've been writing too long to make that kind of mistake anymore.

Q: Do you know if *The Deer Park* is selling well in Hollywood?

A: I understand that it is.

Q: Isn't this book really a love sonnet directed at the film industry?

A: Let's say a sonnet of love and hate.

Q: If you could be any other living writer but Norman Mailer, whom would you choose to be?

A: I can't imagine. Since I have only my own life, I might just as well put the bet on myself.

Q: Do you write to eat or eat to write?

A: Anyone who asks a question like that knows nothing about writers. Every serious novelist in the world obviously does both. If he ate only to write, he would be merely a poet, a dilettante or a deadly small critic who is kept in a cage until his editor lets him out to devour a new book.

Q: Do you write better before or after sexual activity, or during the periods you deny yourself such activity?

A: I've thought about this a lot, but I don't know that I have any definite feeling about the answer.

Q: How has your social ken changed since you wrote *The Naked and the Dead*?

A: I was an anarchist then, and I'm an anarchist today. In between I belonged to the Progressive Party during the Wallace campaign, and then broke off rather abruptly at the time of the Waldorf Peace Conference in 1949. What followed was a period of political wandering in the small circle of libertarian socialism. I was at the same time very radical and yet half-hearted about it. I've also been a contributing editor on *Dissent*. Still am, of course. This is all very sketchy, but I'm trying to put seven years into a capsule. Let me put it that today I'm a Marxian anarchist, which is a contradiction in terms, but a not unprofitable contradiction for trying to do some original thinking. I suppose part of the change in my "social ken" is that politics as politics interests me less today than politics as a part of everything else in life.

Q: If you were forced to do something other than writing to earn your living, what would you choose?

A: One hundred different things. Just so long as I didn't do any one of them for the rest of my life.

Q: Whom do you hate?

A: People who have power and no compassion, that is, no simple human understanding.

Q: Do you believe socialism or nationalism will ever come to America?

A: Not in the way the words are understood today. Possibly in some vastly complex mutant of one or another of those words.

Q: If you could send a ten word message to every man and woman in America, what would you say?

A: Please don't understand anybody too quickly.

Q: What is your opinion of the current crop of artistic aspirants in Greenwich Village?

A: I have a sincere feeling—perhaps it is no more than a hunch— that more than a few really exciting novels are going to come from there in the next ten years. Provided of course we don't dip back into the cold war again. A cold war is obviously equal to greater censorship, greater censorship is equal to greater fear, especially in serious writers, more anxiety, and hence poorer work generally.

Q: Do you believe that there are good writers unable to find publication in America today?

A: If good writers write novels which are conventionally obscene or exceptionally radical, you can be sure that they would have one hell of a time getting their books published. However there are some good people scattered through the publishing houses, and considering that no two publishing houses are even remotely the same, there is always a kind of chance to get a good but difficult book in bound covers.

Q: Will television put an end to novel reading?

A: It certainly seems to be cutting down on it.

Q: Is there a future for the hard-bound novel?

A: A most doubtful future, I think.

Q: Do you have political ambitions?

A: You can't grow up in America without thinking once in a while of becoming president. But since I'm an anarchist, I try not to think about that too much.

Q: What does religion mean to you?

A: Organized religion has never meant much to me. I do believe in God, but it is a very personal faith and I find in myself, as of this year, no detectable desire to join any church. Too many churches seem like prisons of the spirit to me.

Q: What social problem seems most important to you?

A: That more people do more things their inner nature dreams of doing. In other words that there be less anguish and less depression in the world, for all authoritarian social horrors are ultimately no more than a mirror of the quantity of despair in the world.

Q: Do you believe in life after death?

A: I would have to write a book to answer.

Q: If Jesus Christ were alive today, do you think they would permit him to enter the church?

A: I think I will retire behind the answer Dostoyevski gave in the chapter of "The Grand Inquisitor."

Q: Who is your favorite writer?

A: I have favorites, but they vary.

Q: Are you a Freudian?

A: I believe Freud was a genius, an incredible mighty discoverer of secrets, mysteries, and new questions. But the answers he gave were doctrinaire, death-like, and philosophically most dreary. Of the world's geniuses he strikes me as being unique. He had so little optimism and it is rare to find a genius who does not have even angry optimism. Or, at the very worst—an apocalyptic view of the final disaster.

Q: Are blacklists necessary?

A: They are necessary for propaganda.

Q: Why?

A: Because they give people the idea that an impotent conspiracy is actually potent, and therefore dangerous to fatherland, flag and family.

Q: Have you ever been blacklisted?

A: I think I have been, but of course I could never prove it.

Q: Are people afraid of you because they can't understand you or because they do understand you?

A: I'm surprised that people are afraid of me. What can I possibly do to them? It's a nice question to be asked though.

Q: Was the character of Charles Eitel in *The Deer Park* in any way modeled after Charles Chaplin?

A: Not at all. Chaplin is a genius and I wouldn't presume to write about a genius. Not yet.

Q: Eitel finally did tell. Do you feel that this is the only way the commercial artist can survive—by telling the things Congressional committees want to hear?

A: An artist follows his own nature. A commercial man follows the nature that society exacts from him. So my answer is: of course commercial talents do what they are obliged to do, and say what they are obliged to say.

Q: You precede your story with Gide's "Do not understand me too quickly." Have the reviews indicated that you are understood at all by reviewers?

A: One or two had a vague idea of what I was trying to do. Malcolm Cowley was right on the nose when he wrote that *The Deer Park* was a far more difficult book to write than *The Naked and the Dead.*

Q: Do you think Communism will ever again become an American fad?

A: It may, if some sort of co-existence is settled with the USSR. But it's not the sort of thing I lose sleep over. If it does happen it's likely to attract a new type. The grey flannel suit contingent perhaps.

Q: What quality do you most prefer in a woman?

A: Love, infused with rich sexuality.

Q: G. Legman once remarked that a man is either a sheep or a goat. Which are you?

A: I try to be a man. Why should I take Legman's word for the varieties of human nature?

Q: Is rebellion healthy?

A: As healthy as the sense of life.

Q: Do you find the greatest pleasure in desire or in fulfillment?

A: Both are beautiful. Like most people I've had enough luck to know the advantages and satisfaction of each from time to time.

Q: Ben Hecht and a number of other onetime literary lights have seen the candle of conformity and swallowed it. Do you feel that age will mold you into a high-priced please-the-public author?

A: I doubt it, but I also know that exhaustion of the will can come to anyone.

Q: Do you have advice for your enemies?

A: Yes. In all modesty let them beware just a little of me.

Q: How do you feel about money?

A: I think having money is probably a little better than not having it. Money is one of the things which gives energy to people and I believe that's why most people scramble so cruelly to get it.

Q: About clothes?

A: It's one of the few things I haven't been deeply interested in at one time or another. I probably dress a little better than the average man, at least when I get dressed up. Or is that every ex-rifleman's idea of himself?

Q: How do you feel about Ernest Hemingway?

A: I said what my character, Sergius O'Shaughnesy thought of him in one sentence in *The Deer Park.* If one is going to make a statement about Hemingway it can be done either by posing a riddle or else one has to write at least ten thousand words to say something new in the critical literature. Obviously if I've said this much, it's evident that I think he's been very important as an influence on all American writers, even if like Faulkner they were stimulated to writing in the opposite and possibly greater direction. But just how I rate Hemingway is impossible to answer because each time I think of him—which is not that often—I find that my estimate of him goes up or down a little on the basis of the new thing I've thought. I suppose at the very least it's a sign of some kind of greatness and I would guess right now that Hemingway is going to last for quite some time.

Q: What is happening to the union movement?

A: I don't know, and I don't know that anything much is happening.

Q: Do you think Hitler still lives?

A: No. I don't believe he could ever find a place to hide.

Q: Your General Cummings in *The Naked and the Dead* appears to symbolize the triumph of fascism. Can fascism ever triumph?

A: Fascism is a very vague word. One variant or another of "fascism" may very conceivably triumph. It's one of the possible alternatives, isn't it? If it ever comes to America, it will be a very sophisticated and loose fascism. Or is "loose" spelled Luce?

Q: The lonely mountain in *The Naked and the Dead* seemed to represent the conquest men strive for but never make. Can man ever conquer loneliness?

A: I believe that is at the heart of man's goal.

Q: What can a man believe in?

A: Better to believe in his feelings than in the advice of others.

Q: What is your major ambition?

A: To be a really great writer.

Q: Do you think psychiatry will solve the problems that beset us?

A: It will solve some problems and inevitably create new ones. Whether it is generally a cultural current for good or for bad remains to be learned by the history of this century.

Q: Who will analyze the psychiatrists?

A: The novelists.

Q: Do you believe man will survive the H-bomb?

A: Yes. I really don't believe we're going to destroy ourselves. But we may come very close time and again.

Q: What papers do you read? What magazines?

A: A little bit of everything. The *Scientific American, Cue Magazine,* and *The Commonweal* ought to give a small idea of what I mean.

Q: If you were to be exiled to a desert island and could take only five books with you, what would they be?

A: I wrote two unpublished novels before *Naked,* so in my life I've written five novels. I would take those five novels to a desert island with me because if one is left alone on a desert island it's hardly feasible to learn very much more from books. One can only contemplate nature, become mystic and seek to penetrate more deeply into one's own primitive nature. So, I would take my five novels not because they are so very good, but because they are the best documents I would have about myself with which to take that self-exploratory journey back to the questions of self.

Q: If you could leave a message to a young man who will be your age one hundred years from today, what would you say?

A: I would say: please use your science to discover the secrets of communicating with the dead, because I, for one, would like to know what has happened since I died. That is if I don't really know "out there," and am not really laughing at you.

Q: Are you happy?

A: Every man and every woman has his or her own idea of

happiness. Let people decide for themselves on the basis of my answers how happy or unhappy I am.

Q: How do you feel about Marilyn Monroe?

A: She must be very brave because she has come such a long way. She is one of the few actresses I still have some real curiosity about.

Q: Are you at work on a new novel?

A: Yes.

Q: What is the role of the artist in our society?

A: I think it is to be as disturbing, as adventurous, as penetrating, as his energy and courage make possible.

Hip, Hell, and the Navigator
Richard G. Stern and Robert F. Lucid/1959

From *The Western Review*, 23 (Winter 1959), 101-09.

The interview took place in my [Richard G. Stern's] apartment on May 6, this year. None of the material was re-
hearsed, no questions were written out or thought about
before hand, and there was no warm-up session except
thirty seconds of irrelevant talk which we used for volume
control. The tape [available in the Harper Library of the
University of Chicago] itself is mottled with children's
voices, the zoom of a couple of evening planes, and the
clink of glasses being put down on coffee tables; and these
sounds sometimes form a humorous counterpoint to the
interview itself.

Mailer and I had known each other only a week—he'd
come to Chicago as a Visiting Lecturer in the Department
of English—but we had become good friends, and the
interview was to be a continuation of the many conversations we had had during the week. As readers may
suspect, it is not quite that. We began by expressing our
fear of the tape recorder (not included here), and although
Mailer soon seemed to lose sight of the whirring spools, I
didn't. Secondly there was the artificial urgency to
"produce" something, absent from most conversations.
Thirdly, some of Mailer's responses began to throw me: I
hadn't suspected the intensity and quality of some of the
beliefs he expressed, and I not only reacted—which is
natural—but I verbalized the reactions for the machine.
My expostulations may be taken as testimony to my surprise, and then as testimony to the final "artificiality"
which characterized the interview, my embarrassed consciousness of the role of interviewer, of soliciting gadfly,
and occasionally devil's advocate (or God's perhaps). It
would be hard for me to gauge the extent of my sincerity
here in the interview.

Granted these defects, almost all of them the defects of
the interviewer and his technique—or lack of it—, the

results, it seemed to Mailer and myself are still worth printing. They take off from some pieces alluded to early in the interview, Mailer's article, "The White Negro: Superficial Reflections on the Hipster," which appeared in the Summer 1957 issue of *Dissent,* the exchanges between Mailer, Jean Malaquais and Ned Polsky which appeared in the Winter 1958 issue of *Dissent,* and the piece by Norman Podhoretz on "The Know-Nothing Bohemians" which is in the Spring 1958 issue of *Partisan Review.* The manner of taking off is one which might lead to this piece being called (in the words of a friend) "The Third Testament." This refers to something I was talking about a few hours after the interview took place. I was saying that the group of youngish American-Jewish writers now coming into such prominence might be said to be composing a new sort of testament, a bizarre theology. Bellow's amazing new novel, *Henderson, The Rain King* (which I've read only in uncorrected typescript) expounds a kind of psychological totemism raised magically into believability, at least into the sort of believability usable in fiction; Bernard Malamud's *The Assistant* and some of his stories center about a kind of Essene conversion, though friends of mine have called them "really Christian," or rather resentfully, "evangelical"; Salinger's slightly sentimental variety of Buddhism has, in its drive toward greater explicitness, nearly driven him from the writing of that fiction which was primarily distinguished by its ache for belief. Now, Mailer joins this group—and explosively. Although centuries of epic theological and philosophical finagling seem to have passed him by, he is the most explicit "theologian" of all the writers, a kind of Manichaean whose overlooking of his "heretic" predecessors seems not only forgiveable, but, considering the quality and urgency of his expression, indispensable.

A final note on the rhythm and authenticity of the interview: Mailer talked generally with rapidity, I with hesitation; Mailer with clarity, I with mumbles. Mailer's speech gets more and more rapid and rises to a pitch of excited engagement in the second half of the tape. All in all, there is a kind of music in the tape, and this is nowhere seen so clearly as when our friend Bob Lucid breaks in with a question, an excellent question, but one which comes as a shock to the "sound-spell." I am not suggesting that this "music" constitutes a unique or even an unusual quality, but it does communicate a rapport and ease which will not show up on the printed page, which must of necessity remain slavish to the words as they were said. For with the exception of those few speeches which are starred, this is essentially the interview as it was transcribed by a stenographer. One can even say it is an accurate copy but for the editing of a few false starts, repetitive mannerisms, and an involuted construction or two. The starred speeches were, however, rewritten, since the original remarks in these places were usually too bare and needed expansion. This was supplied separately by Mailer and myself, each of us agreeing to rewrite our own specific remarks in the offhand spirit of the dialogue—if the reader does not notice them, that will be appropriate—they were meant to stand out as little as possible.

Richard Stern: I've been reading "The White Negro" and a fair amount of other material on the Hipster, and I must say that intellectually I resent Hip as much as I can resent anything. Now I wonder about the extent of your allegiance to Hip. Are you using this material for fiction, or are you committed to it as a style of life, one which you want to practice yourself and recommend to others?

Norman Mailer: All right, good. I think the difficulty for most people who are at all interested in my work is that I started as one kind of writer, and I've been evolving into another kind of writer. And since we live in a time of enormous insecurity, what generally happens is that this insecurity is reflected in the critical snobberies of the moment. Most serious readers like a writer to be a particular thing. It's important; it's reassuring, somehow. I've noticed that most of the writers one might consider as thin blades, yes? stilettoes, dirks, mmm? end up having a sure critical niche. And there have been a few writers like myself taking a particular little journey, and this journey consists of losing all the friends that one's found in the past, and not making enough new ones to make it a profitable venture in and of itself. So, I think if I'm going in this direction, it has to be assumed at least from the outside that I'm serious. Now whether I advocate Hip is another thing entirely.

Stern: The interesting thing about Hip is that Hip shouldn't belong to writers. If you're a genuine Hipster you're committed, it seems to me, to a kind of anti-expressionism, Dada, or something like that. You're interested in the quality of the experience itself. If you're a sincere Hipster you shouldn't be a writer.

Mailer: As a writer I'm not interested in less expression. What attracts me about Hip is that it's involved with more expression, with getting into the nuances of things.

Stern: More expression or more experience?

Mailer: The two have an umbilical relationship. What makes a novelist great is that he illumines each line of his work with the greatest intensity of experience. One thing about Hip you have to admit is that the Hipster lives in a state of extreme awareness, and so, objects and relations that most people take for granted become terribly charged for him; and, living in a state of self-awareness his time slows up. His page becomes more filled. The quality of his experience becomes more intense. That doesn't make for less expression; it makes for greater difficulty of expression. It makes for writing more pages about fewer episodes which is certainly not the quintessence of the inarticulate.

Stern:* O.K. You maintain that there is an easy relationship between having experience and expressing it. It seems to me that the Hipster is someone who has a lot of trouble with both experience and expression. His "kicks," his psyche-jogging, might I think be traced to the trouble.

Then there's another thing as far as writing goes. Isn't a novel controlled by some overriding notion, by a kind of fanaticism which organises a great deal of disparate material? In a sense, a novel is like the mind of a madman: everything—casual looks, street signs, world news reports—is charged with meaning. That's why novelists write about ruling passions like love and ambition, passions which put their mark on all they touch, trivial or major. Now I can't believe that Hip allows for such overriding notions and passions. For the Hipster, the cool one, detail is illumined, livid, but for its own sake, unqualified by considerations of any organization, the sort of organization which novels demand. I wonder if such material can be put into fiction.

Mailer: I think it can; and not only that, but I think Hip is particularly illumined by one notion so central and so shattering that its religious resonances and reverberations are going to dominate this coming century. And I think there is one single burning pinpoint of the vision in Hip: it's that God is in danger of dying. In my very limited knowledge of theology, this never really has been expressed before. I believe Hip conceives of Man's fate being tied up with God's fate. God is no longer all-powerful. [Here a phrase was lost to static in the tape.] The moral consequences of this are not only staggering, but they're thrilling; because moral experience is intensified rather than diminished.

Stern: Now that's a fantastic assertion. That really makes me sit up. What is the notion of God behind all this? Do you mean that some kind of personal god is dying with us?

Mailer: Now I only talk about my own vision of it, really, because it's not the sort of thing that you normally talk about with most Hipsters. I think that the particular God we can conceive of is a god whose relationship to the universe we cannot divine; that is, how enormous He is in the scheme of the universe we can't begin to say. But almost certainly, He is not all-powerful; He exists as a warring element in a divided universe, and we are a part of—perhaps the most important part—of His great expression, His enormous destiny; perhaps He is trying to impose upon the universe His conception of being against other conceptions of being very much opposed to His. Maybe we are in a sense the seed, the seed-carriers, the voyagers, the explorers, the embodiment of that embattled vision; maybe we are engaged in a heroic activity, and not a mean one.

Stern: This is really something.

Mailer: Well, I would say it is far more noble in its conception, far more arduous as a religious conception than the notion of the all-powerful God who takes care of us.

Stern: And do you take to this conception for its perilous nobility, or do you take to it because you believe in it?

Mailer: I believe in it.

Stern: You believe in it.

Mailer: It's the only thing that makes any sense to me. It's the only thing that explains to me the problem of evil. You see, the answer may well be—how to put it?—that God Himself is engaged in a destiny so extraordinary, so demanding, that He too can suffer from a moral corruption, that He can make demands upon us which are unfair, that He can abuse our beings in order to achieve His means, even as we abuse the very cells of our own body.

Stern: Is it a person's duty to find out whether he's of God's party, whether he's working with God-beneficent or God-maleficent?

Mailer: Well, look, let's go back; let's go back to something much more modest for the moment which I think may tie this up, to a small extent, anyway. You asked me before why Hip is interesting for the novel. Well, up to now, when a novelist treats someone like a drug addict, the Square way is to treat the addict as a poor sociological cripple who is doomed and damned and goes down to his inevitable defeat. In Hip, which has after all to a certain extent come out of drug-taking (it's one of the elements in the growth of Hip) the attitude would be more that if taking drugs gives one extraordinary sensations, then the drug-taker is probably receiving something from God. Love perhaps. And perhaps he is. Let's just entertain the notion as a rational hypothesis which may or may not be true and let's see how far we go with it. If the Hipster is receiving love from God he may well be draining some of the substance of God by calling upon this love, you see, which the drug releases. And in draining the substance of God he's exhausting Him, so that the drug-taker may be indulging an extraordinarily evil act at the instant he is filled with the feeling that he is full of God and good and a beautiful mystic. This involves new moral complexities which I feel are far more interesting than anything the novel has gotten into yet. It opens the possibility that the novel, along with many other art forms, may be growing into something larger rather than something smaller, and the sickness of our times for me has been just this damn thing that everything has been getting smaller and smaller and less and less important, that the romantic spirit has dried up, that there is almost no shame today like the terror before the romantic. We're all getting so mean and small and petty and ridiculous, and we all live under the threat of extermination. In contrast, the notions of Hip enlarge us, they make our small actions not necessarily large, but more meaningful. If we pick up a bottle while listening to some jazz and we feel each of our five fingertips in relation to the bottle, the bottle begins to have a kind of form for us and we begin to feel each of our fingertips is receiving a different thing from the shape and the structure of the glass, and we then begin to think that maybe the very structure of this glass could conceivably contain some kind of hell within its constitution, some inorganic frozen state of imprisoned being less being than us. I think it's a more interesting notion than just picking up a bottle and pouring out some whiskey.

Stern: It's a very pretty notion.

Mailer: Hip is pretty.

Stern: But it's all action, it's all erectile, isn't it? It's all feeling and taste and touch and smell. Isn't that the trouble with it?

Mailer: The trouble is that it's enormously difficult to return to the senses. We're all civilized, and to return to the senses and keep the best parts of our civilized being, to keep our capacity for mental organization, for mental construction, for logic, is doubly difficult, and there's a great danger that the nihilism of Hip will destroy civilization. But it seems to me that the danger which is even more paramount— the danger which has brought on Hip—is that civilization is so strong itself, so divorced from the senses that we have come to this point where we can liquidate millions of people in concentration camps by orderly process.

Stern: Every powerful and refining force involves danger and waste. Does this divorce from the senses you talk about justify cashing in two or three thousand years of continuous culture?

Mailer:* Well, your argument is moot. It's too vast for this—for me. But let me try to put it this way. If the divorce from the senses I talk about is becoming a human condition, then by all means, yes, civilization must be cashed in or we will destroy ourselves in the cold insensate expressions of due process of law and atomic radiation. On the other hand maybe this divorce from the senses involves just a small part of my generation, and the Square, in contrast, leads a sensuous life with sufficient contentments to keep him civilized (in the good sense) and equable. It is us—Hipsters—who would then be the only ones alienated from our senses. If this be true, then everything I have said is merely an intricate and ingenious rationalization to defend my neurotic . . . perversities, anh? Of course, I don't believe this is true.

Stern: All right, let's grant that it's moot. Now you have a career, a personal career, a career as novelist, and then maybe a career as an apostle of a new creed. Let's leave the last.

Mailer: Yes, let's leave the last.

Stern: Let's even leave the first and just look at the novelistic career. You are a novelist. You conceive of yourself as a novelist, though for the past week you've been saying you don't get much from literature any more. You're looking for something else. But still, you conceive of yourself as a novelist.

Mailer: (*interrupting*): I don't want to be put on record that way. It's more complex than that.

Stern:* All right, let's forget that and concentrate on what all this has to do with you as a practicing novelist. How are these notions going to work for you? I saw them operating in the play version you made of *The Deer Park*. There you had a prologue in Hell, but I think you will remember I thought the Prologue was extraneous to the play. It was as if a critic had watched the play and said, "Doesn't seem like much until I let you in on the secret: These people are in Hell." Wasn't that something you just "put over" on your material? After you had really treated it, finished with it?

Mailer: Well, . . . *(sighs)* when I was doing *The Deer Park* as a novel, characters existed on one level. It seemed to me that putting them into Hell deepened the meaning of their moral experience. That the situation of being in Hell and not knowing it is perhaps the first inversion—no, I don't want to say it that way—it is the first dislocation of the moral space. I find it difficult to express these things—they're terribly intangible for me. It's as if the belief that one exists on one level of being, when in fact—if one could ever discover that fact—one exists on another level of being may literally be the human condition. And so, I didn't do it as a casual or superficial thing. It may be that I lacked enough art to make the prologue work for the play. But I wanted precisely this double state of existence, this existence of a people who are in Hell and did not know it.

Stern: You had a kind of double state in the novel. There it was a natural extension of the fiction, however. You quoted from the memoirs of a French courtier, one who described the rot of Louis Quinze's Court, and I think the idea was to give an extra dimension to the people you were writing about. It was like saying, here's another ash about to fall into the chasm. There you didn't falsify—my opinion here of course—your work, only expanded it. The idea of art seems to me to be to generate emotion from the treated material, not to point out some material and some feeling and say, "Put them together, reader."

Mailer: Well, let me avoid answering you directly. I feel that the final purpose of art is to intensify, even, if necessary, to exacerbate, the moral consciousness of people. In particular, I think the novel is at its best the most moral of the art forms because it's the most immediate, the most overbearing, if you will. It is the most inescapable. One could argue much more easily about the meaning of a non-objective painting or of music, or whatever. But in the novel, the meaning is there. It's much closer; one could argue about ambiguities, but, because one is using words, it's much closer to the sense of moral commandments, moral strictures. And one gets into a particular thing which is terribly interesting, you begin to explore the interstices of moral reaction—which is the first approach to religious experience for many of us, especially since the organized religions don't begin to cover the enormous and terrible complexities of moral experience. It may be that particular people, working in various religions, individually working with particular people in their parish or whatever may bring some good along with a great deal of harm. But institutionally I believe that the organized religions are morally dead, that their net effect is deleterious, if not hideous and horrible. Organized religion is probably becoming one of the great enemies of our time . . . (*reflectively*)—They're murderers of the senses.

Stern: So, as far as a work of art goes, we can work it out and then shove it into any pew or forum we want, all to exacerbate the moral consciousness. We can write a Prologue in Hell—or, how about a Prologue in Heaven?

Mailer: Oh, it would be more interesting.

Stern: More interesting?

Mailer: But it would be more difficult. That was beyond my grasp.

Stern: So for you, actions themselves are neutral. The novelist delivers and then labels them in any way he wants. The belief here is that the actions themselves won't satisfy the reader; he won't be used up, happily cleared of his emotional clots at the end of the book, but will have something left over, will ache for a balm to be supplied outside the novel. Art exacerbates the moral conscience, and then the moral conscience goes out to vote for the reform ticket, and thus eases the ache the novelist has put in it. The novelist's deposit is to be cashed in the world.

Mailer: Well, ideally, what I would hope to do with my work is intensify a consciousness that the core of life cannot be cheated. Every moment of one's existence one is growing into more or retreating into less. One is always living a little more or dying a little bit. That the choice is not to live a little more or to not live a little more; it is to live a little more or to die a little more. And as one dies a little more, one enters a most dangerous moral condition for oneself because one starts making other people die a little more in order to stay alive. I think this is exactly the murderous network in which we all live by now.

Stern: And this is what the Hipster does; he strikes out at others;

he's constantly craving for more. He faces the risk of the extinction of his senses, extinction of his being, extinction of his capacity for making distinctions.

Mailer: He does certain things that are very brave in their way; he gambles for one thing with his soul—he gambles that he can be terribly, tragically wrong, and therefore be doomed, you see, doomed to Hell. Which the churchly people don't do at all. They're thinking of nothing but their own nasty little souls which are being maintained for some careful preservation afterward. The Hipster is gambling with death and he is gambling with the Hereafter; and he may be wrong.

Stern: And the novelist is gambling with his talent as a novelist.

Mailer: Oh, yeah. Yeah.

Stern: The one talent he's got.

Robert Lucid: I can see it with the novelist, but I can't see it with the Hipster. This is what kills me. You presume consciousness, you presume purpose, you presume direction on the part of this class—if that's the word—analogous to the novelist. And it seems to me that the whole notion of Hip is, in fact, unconscious, it is mere action.

Stern: I think it was said that the Hipster risks his personal being— whatever that may be—and that the novelist risks his talents as a novelist. He does it because he has the choice of living a little more or dying a little more.

Lucid: The point is that the novelist consciously makes decisions and accepts the moral consequences. It seems to me the kind of guy we're talking about as Hipster *qua* Hipster is a guy who is, in fact, unconscious of risks of this kind, of the profundity . . .

Mailer: Consciously, he may think he's cutting quite a few corners as far as that goes. What I'm postulating in all this—the notion I've been working with all along that's been tacit to my remarks, implicit in my remarks, is that the unconscious, you see, has an enormous teleological sense, that it moves toward a goal, that it has a real sense of what is happening to one's being at each given moment—you see—that the messages of one's experience are continually saying, "Things are getting better," or "Things are getting worse. For me. For that one. For my future, for my past, mmm?" It is with this thing that they move, that they grope forward—this navigator at the seat of their being.

An Interview with Norman Mailer

Eve Auchincloss and Nancy Lynch/1961

From *Mademoiselle*, 52 (February 1961), 76, 160-63. Courtesy Mademoiselle. Copyright © 1961 by The Condé Nast Publications Inc.

Norman Mailer wrote the great book of World War II twelve years ago. Since then he has written much and though none of this work has had unequivocal success some of his peers have gone on looking to him not only as a major American novelist in the making but as a spokesman of an embattled generation—however antipathetic they may have found his later doctrines. We interviewed him in mid-November. A few days later he is alleged to have stabbed his wife and was committed to a hospital for mental observation. He has since been adjudged sane; his wife is recovered; his future as a writer remains the challenging question it has long been. The following is excerpted from what turned out to be a long, somewhat "existential" discussion.

Mailer: Are we going to chat or are we going to have formal questions?

Interviewers: Formal questions, sort of, which might lead to anything.

Mailer: How long do you think it will be? Half an hour? An hour?

Interviewers: Well, it might be more if we get talking.

Mailer: You mean, just talking and talking? I'd rather not do that. I've noticed that if you know you're going to do a half-hour you do better. It's a bit like the difference of intensity between a canned television program and one where you're on live. If you know a million people are hearing you at this moment it makes you more stuffy or nervous or disagreeable or hysterical or misplaced in one way or another, but you really do feel that every bit of you is going

every moment. And you have an existential situation. What I'm
against in all this just talking is that I'm a terribly slack man. If I'm
given too many allowances, I'll do exactly the sort of charming, thin
thing that's good at the moment but doesn't transcribe. At the same
time, I'm not capable of formal remarks. I don't have that kind of
mind any longer. If we're going to chat I want to chat on a reasonably
high level.

Interviewers: All right. In an article about the Democratic
Convention you recently suggested that Kennedy is a hipster. Why
do you think so?

Mailer: If I say why he is a hipster just head-on, it's going to be
false. It's going to sound very dogmatic. What compounds the
difficulty astronomically is that there is no agreement on the meaning
of the word hipster. You see, to some people a hipster is an
adventurer and to other people a hipster is a rather hideous sort of
evil beatnik. So if I were to say directly that I think Kennedy is a
hipster, to some people this would mean that an evil beatnik is
President of the United States. The possibility this offers of deadening
America's view of its own reality is so bad that I'd rather ignore the
question.

Interviewers: One of the things we wanted to talk about was this
idea that you've written about—that you look forward to a moral and
sexual revolution in this country.

Mailer: Where have I said that?

Interviewers: You said it in *Advertisements for Myself.*

Mailer: Never did I say it that way. Never. I said in *Advertisements
for Myself* something about hoping to create a revolution in the
consciousness of my time. By implication I obviously meant a moral
revolution and a sexual revolution, but I don't think I ever said it
directly because then, you see, it would mean that I'm programmatic
about things that are absolutely alien to program. The difficulty and
the beauty of moral and sexual revolutions is that they are
unpredictable.

Interviewers: What triggers them?

Mailer: What triggers them is the notion that if people became
more authentic the world would be better. And this does have a
rather tender optimism to it. It's like an old joke: "People are no
damn good." If you assume that people are no damn good, then you
need police, you need authorities, you need restraints. But if you

believe that people in their natural state are more beautiful than in their conditioned state, you are optimistic, and you do believe in moral and sexual revolutions. But you don't believe that they are necessarily arrived at by me making statements and looking for planks. It means that you believe in the notion of a hero—a man who will dare the gods . . . and the mass media. . . . Do you have any questions about existentialism?

Interviewers: Well, what about Sartre? You put him on the side of the squares in your list of square and hip.

Mailer: Yes, square, because I think he's programmatic—he tells us exactly what to do. He talks about the authentic but he never gives you any clue to the quality of an authentic moment.

Interviewers: What do you think the quality of the authentic is?

Mailer: I think it's the moment where our aesthetic and theological and ecclesiastical sense of meaning and the beatnik sense of kick, the hipster sense of cool, all come together. It's that moment, the Spanish moment of truth, where one feels that it's no use arguing about anything, because this is the way it is really and this is what we must do. The moment of faith.

Interviewers: Does your moment of faith ever come out of a negative reaction against things as they are? Like morals and sex as they now are? Or marriage?

Mailer: You want me to say something programmatic about marriage?

Interviewers: No, no, talk about it in your own way.

Mailer: You know, I was once on a television show, Mike Wallace. He was trying to get me to say something about marriage and sex and morality. And finally I said with small despair at my dullness— because, you know, when you're on television for half an hour, the things you say have to be said very quickly and with great wit and they must always go to the center, just like an ice pick. And I have a rather dull, slow mind and I talk in private, languorous terms that interest no one but myself. And so what happens is that I very often become strident when I'm in a situation where I have to do things in a hurry. So I became strident. I said, in effect, that I believed in promiscuity. And he said: "What do you mean by that?" (They always say that.) I said I believed in *serious* promiscuity and I thought that no voice could *ever* indicate the wonderful meaning of "serious"—and I did sound terribly dogged and dogmatic—so I added: "I mean joyful promiscuity." Well, what happened is that my wife saw the taped show on television later—we were sitting around watching it. And when that came on she said: "You son of a bitch." And she walked out of the room. And I was caught between all the delights of watching myself, because I was in reasonably good form, and having to go out and make up with her. I have this terrible feeling that to talk about marriage can just, you see, be beyond my means.

Interviewers: Well, you didn't really have much to say about marriage. Does that mean that you don't want to talk about it?

Mailer: Well, can I say that America is about as totalitarian and vicious and—I'm going to coin a word—liquidational about the uses of marriage as the Soviet Union is about the uses of the proletariat. It's been the great scandal of our national life.

Interviewers: Do you think we've made marriage too important a goal? One talks to a lot of college students who say that their primary goal in life is to have a happy marriage.

Mailer: Yes, well, I don't know how to talk to students like that and they wouldn't talk to me. We've nothing to say to one another. If there were a war, we'd be on opposite sides.

Interviewers: You and younger people?

Mailer: No, no. Some of the young. I don't think all students are serious about marriage responsibilities. There aren't too many responsibilities left. I think Eisenhower used them up.

Interviewers: What's taking their place? Or is that programmatic again?

Mailer: Yes, you're right. I was programmatic for the first time. It's not fair to old Eisenhower. Now that he's gone I'm not going to be the first to say he wasn't bad because I think he was terrible. But I think he was really terrible because he never allowed anyone in America to see his charm except the people who were close to him. And this is much too royal for a man who has nothing but democratic notions in his head. Eisenhower was not authentic and this is the tragedy of the man.

Interviewers: Didn't we impose the personality on him?

Mailer: We helped him out to a great extent, but a man of character is able to resist a favorable tide too. He was not a hero finally. He was the Republican Hemingway.

Interviewers: What does make a hero?

Mailer: Courageous moments. It's *not* living in certain courageous moments that gives one cancer. Of course, if it were simple, any time something really big is happening you'd just decide to be brave in order to avoid cancer. Then everyone would be brave. The tragedy of it all is that if you choose to be brave at a certain moment and you fail, that's even more likely to give you cancer than not doing anything at all. And since everyone has lost faith and a sense of certain values nobody acts any more. And more and more courageous moments are being lost all over the world, particularly in this country. And for that reason cancer is spreading. One of the causes of cancer must be the absence of action.

Interviewers: How can one be a real hero? What sort of brave moments *can* we live? It's easy to think of bravery in terms of the bull ring or war, but here in a city it's different.

Mailer: Bravery is doing something that engages grave risk without the certainty that you're going to win.

Interviewers: Without any moral references at all?

Mailer: Look at what I'm saying: Courage is something that engages grave risk without the certainty that you're going to win. If you do this in a vacuum, without moral references, then you are what society calls a psychopath.

Interviewers: You mean a hipster?

Mailer: Well, you would say that hipsters do this in a vacuum. I don't. It's just that a hipster's notion of morality is so complex. A great many people hate hip because it poses a threat to them. They feel that if they admit that I'm right about the hipster, then they have got to go out and become a hipster themselves, which is something I'd *never* ask of anyone. I just ask that the hipster be considered at least as interesting and serious a person as a young congressman.

Interviewers: It's hard to accept the idea of a person who seems to be withdrawn from history, withdrawn from the future, withdrawn from any kind of action.

Mailer: This is the corporation notion of the hipster. I'm a hipster, for example—a middle-aged hipster. I've turned terribly philosophical and mellow but still that's what I am.

Interviewers: Are you naturally a hipster or do you have to work at it?

Mailer: I think you're charming. (*Laughter*)

Interviewers: Will you say just what, at this stage, you feel a hipster is?

Mailer: It's not so important what the background of a hipster is, or their attainments, their education, their station in life. Originally they existed among the Negroes and a few whites. By now I think it's spread out so far, there's been such a promiscuity—let's coin another terrible word—a promiscuization of personality that you find him almost anywhere. A hipster is someone who, no matter how complex or how simple he might be, no matter how good or evil in the old sense of the words (and they never did have any meaning), is still someone who pays more attention to his body than to his mind. He's an existentialist.

Interviewers: Is a hipster competitive in any way?

Mailer: All the time. With everyone, with himself, with every moment, with every nuance of existence.

Interviewers: What is he competing for?

Mailer: For more existence. He's underprivileged. He's a true proletarian, a psychic proletarian. Marx's proletariat has disappeared—they went when the refrigerator arrived—but there's a new proletariat of people who consider themselves good people, who have a vision of themselves, of people they know, of the world, of existence, of eternity. And they feel that their vision is exquisite and extraordinary and they want others to know about it. They want to rule the world, every last one of them.

Interviewers: May not this will to rule be a dead end?

Mailer: Will without tenderness is one of the more dangerous things. Will without the ability to recognize anything but its own will is something that has to be assassinated.

Interviewers: Does the hipster try to kill his will?

Mailer: He tries to keep his will. But he remains tender.

Interviewers: You mean he feels tender as he grinds the heel of his boot into the face of the dying man!

Mailer: May I say this? If we are going to be extreme let's put it on record that you were extreme first! People always think I start these things but I don't. If you're going to grind your heel into the face of a dying man I still insist on the authority of my existential logic: let the act finally be authentic. If you're going to do it, *do it*.

Interviewers: You mean enjoy it?

Mailer: The poor soul is going out of existence. You might as well enjoy yourself! If you're going to grind your boot in his face, don't do it with the feeling, "I'm horrible, I'm psychotic, I should be in a bughouse." Do it. There are very few people who grind their feet into the face of anyone else, because when you get down to it people are much tougher, much more capable of defending themselves than anyone ever believes. And this is the old dim liberal notion of existence. I hate to end up as a liberal but I do think that people are a little bit more resistant than is generally given them credit. . . . Are you really interested in the problem?

Interviewers: Yes.

Mailer: I mean, you've asked me to look into the abyss haven't you?

Interviewers: Don't we have to? Don't you want us to? Don't you think an awful lot of us want to look into the abyss?

Mailer: No, I don't. I think it's very hard. I think people are petrified of it. But if it's gotten so bad that one of America's better writers is talking about somebody grinding his heel into someone else's face, then let us consider this moment. Let's use our imaginations. It means that one human being has determined to extinguish the life of another human being. It means that two people are engaging in a dialogue with eternity. Now if the brute does it and at the last moment likes the man he is extinguishing then perhaps the victim did not die in vain. If there is an eternity with souls in that eternity, if one is able to be born again, the victim may get his reward. At least it seems possible that the quality of one being passes into the other, and this altogether hate-filled human, grinding his boot into the face of someone, destroying that most private part of a person (remember, in the twentieth century one's sexual privates are no longer so private as one's face), in the act of killing, in this terribly private moment, the brute feels a moment of tenderness, for the first time perhaps in all of his existence. What has happened is that the killer is becoming a little more possible, a little bit more ready to love someone. (*Pause*)

Interviewers: To refer to the abyss again, if we don't want to look into it, why do so many people go to analysts, why are so many interested in Zen?

Mailer: Because they *don't* want to look into the abyss. Beg your pardon, but psychoanalysis and Zen, in my private psychic geometry, are equal to nicotine. They are anti-existential. Nicotine quarantines one out of existence.

Interviewers: What do you mean?

Mailer: Whenever one feels an emotion which is a little bit new one lights a cigarette. The emotion is converted into textual material.
Interviewers: What about marijuana?
Mailer: I'd rather not talk about that.
Interviewers: What about your self-analysis?
Mailer: All right. I capitulate. My self-analysis started with marijuana for better or for worse. Whether marijuana is an invention of God or the devil, I really have no idea by now. My self-analysis started with marijuana because I found that, smoking marijuana, I became real to myself for the first time. About five, six years ago.
Interviewers: In what way did you become real?
Mailer: I found that a lot of things I did that I thought were silly turned out to have a reason. If I was crossing the room and I was telling a story in a rather nice way and I suddenly clumsily ran into something and banged my knee, it wasn't because I was neurotic but because I had a profound shame at the way I was betraying something that was true in me in order to tell a good story to people who didn't like me that much anyway. And so marijuana gave me a certain sense of my own importance.
Interviewers: Does it bring out things that are there below the surface already?
Mailer: It's a subtle drug. Most people get almost nothing from it the first time. I smoked it for six months and nothing happened to me.
Interviewers: Why did you go on?
Mailer: I don't know why. I suppose because some tiny part of the drug reached into me and said: There is something here if you want to use it. But you have to be desperate. I was very sick at the time, in Mexico. I really thought I'd had it. I really thought I was going to go, because I had a very bad liver and I was following my doctor's instructions, not drinking, eating exactly what I was told to eat and living a very orderly life. And absolutely nothing was happening. I was just getting sicker every day. And then finally I took it a few more times and it gave me a sense of something that was new. I had a few new emotions.
Interviewers: How were they new? What were they?
Mailer: They were larger than any I had had.
Interviewers: Larger anger?
Mailer: Oh, yes. But also a larger sensuality.

Interviewers: More love too?

Mailer: For a while, yes.

Interviewers: Why does one feel that love is a dirty word nowadays?

Mailer: It's because love, mother and family now belong to the flag and the FBI. There's a war of words going on in America and the difficulty for a writer, precisely for a writer like me, is that I am now forced to use the words my enemies have captured to say anything at all. I have to tie myself in knots not to use the word *love* when I want to talk about love. But I can't use the word because the moment I say *love* or *God* I'd lose three-quarters of the people who might read me. I don't think we can talk about it. I think thirty years may have to go by before one can use the word *love* again without the feeling that one is betraying one's friends.

Interviewers: So what happened when all these big emotions came?

Mailer: Well, what happened is something that one really cannot talk about. That's one thing marijuana did to me—it destroyed my memory in a most odd and disturbing way. I meet someone, I'm talking to them, I like them, I heard their name a half-hour ago—and I can't remember it.

Interviewers: Well, everyone has that problem. But when you talk about your memory being gone, is it just in respect to things like people's names? Or your childhood and the sort of things one might want to recall in great detail?

Mailer: Well, marijuana's terribly personal and it's entirely possible that certain people who wish to recall their childhood will recall it in great detail. I've never had any large feeling about my childhood. I never write about it. But to get back to marijuana, I don't know whether I trust it or not. It did a lot for me, but I may have to pay for it yet. And I don't know that I can recommend it. I think it's far better if these things happen to people without it. But I got to the point where nothing could happen to me without it and so I took it and I got a great deal from it and I lost quite a bit, I think.

Interviewers: Do you still take it? Does it do for you what it did in the beginning?

Mailer: On occasion I give in to it and it does a great deal, but it costs more. It gives me a great day but I lose three or four days—my mind is feverish, disconnected for three or four days afterward and then there's a terrible apathy and depression because I've used up too much for too little.

Interviewers: Which you might have been able to achieve in some other way?

Mailer: Yes, instead of trying to do your best at a time when it counts you just do your best no matter how, because there's so much in you at the moment that you have to give it out.

Interviewers: It's a sprint?

Mailer: Yes, it's a sprint.

Interviewers: Do you think that our society exacts sprints from people? Is that part of the trouble? That people are asked to give too much at a particular moment?

Mailer: Oh, that's an excellent image. People who are ambitious and proud and wish to succeed have to become sprinters. But you don't even win by winning the sprint any more. It's gotten so desperate that you can be the most charming person at the party and the next day people go around saying, "That poor desperate man or woman had to be so extraordinary and why? Because they have no center to their lives." So the ones who aren't charming begin to have an interest in destroying the sprinters and at the same time they are continually electing the sprinters. And so if one's going to keep one's sense that life conceivably has a bit of beauty to it, some way or other one has to enter the underground.

Interviewers: Yes, what about the underground? Somewhere you described it as a concentration of ecstasy and violence that is the nation's dream life. Is it a state of mind or does it exist somewhere?

Mailer: Well, assume that New York had an underground. Would I be likely, as apostle-leader of this underground, to announce where it existed? (*Laughing*) Oh, you're marvelous, kids. I'll tell you this about you: I'd hate to go ten rounds with you. If you were a man and I was a good club fighter, I'd hate to go ten rounds with you. Because I'd win, you know, and I'd get a unanimous decision, but you'd wreck me for my next fight.

Interviewers: We were thinking that it seems from his writing that Mailer has an absolute problem about fatigue!

Mailer: He does. He is tired prematurely. You see, I'm an infantryman. I started as one. And I don't say this with any pride, because it's nothing to be proud about. It's something that's done to you rather than something you do. And I wasn't in a good war. I was in a dull war, in the Philippines. So we just walked off ten years of what was to have been our private lives and when we came out, you know, that fatigue has entered into one. There's a way of walking as an infantryman which is not describable and it never got into any war movie I ever saw. Nobody walks like this in the movies, which is why war movies are so very bad. If they'd just get that for one minute you'd know what war was about.

Interviewers: How do infantry men walk?

Mailer: Without any sense of gesture or pride or individuality. But actors don't have any sense of this because actors are people who don't walk. They are usually carried in the laps of ladies—they are the children of kangaroos. They're carried in pouches until they become men and then they stand up and say a few words and then collapse back into the pouch again.

Interviewers: That fixes actors! What about writers? Let's talk about what you read now, if anything. Or who you think the writers are.

Mailer: All right, the only thing I read is that which is thrust under my nose by people whose quality attracts my fast-dimming attention. So I'll read anything. I think it's impossible to say who's going to be the writer of the ones we know—who's going to come along with something very good. I do think that the one thing that was not absolutely disastrous in the last ten years of our literary history was that we all had enough of a small sense of one another to be able to read one another just enough so that we all did learn from one another a bit. Naturally I learned from my contemporaries and I learned very grudgingly. I mean, I hated their talents. I despised and loathed everything about them that was the least bit good. It killed me every time they did something that I couldn't quite do. I went that way for years. Then I realized that it oughtn't to be that way if I was ever going to grow at all.

Interviewers: How important is style to you?

Mailer: Style? Style's an embrace. If I were to choose a style, I think a man who writes better than I do is William Burroughs. I think he's going to last a long time after me because he's more intense. He's got a quality I don't have. I mean, I write sentences that embrace people. But he writes sentences that stab people and you never forget the man who stabs you. You can forget an embrace.

Interviewers: What do you consider the brave things you've done?

Mailer: The bravest thing I've done? It was the worst piece I ever wrote—"The Homosexual Villain". It was the bravest thing I ever did because it was done out of a dim, dull sense of duty.

Interviewers: What about the piece you did on Kennedy in *Esquire?* Wasn't that done out of a sense of duty?

Mailer: Oh, well, by the time I wrote that I felt, for better or worse, that I was finally a mature artist in command of his powers, doing something willfully. I wanted to accomplish a few things: I wanted to affect the election; I wanted to advance my career; I wanted to advance Kennedy's career; and I wanted to do something reasonably well written. What bothered me was that I felt I could have written something really extraordinary, but I had to rush it. I had only seventeen days. It was excellence of a sort, but I don't think it's going to last as long as *The White Negro*. You see, it's too attractive. I'm not enamored of the piece as much as some people are, because it's the first piece I wrote in my life which was written with deliberate political intention; I wanted to get a man elected and I wanted to warn the Democrats about something that I thought was terribly important. I thought there was a great danger that Kennedy'd lose at the last minute. I think that if the piece had any important effect, you know, on Democrats of some power and influence, it was that they didn't stop working in the last three days. I think they were worried all the way down and it was good that they were worried. I think that if they had eased up a little bit, Nixon might have won.

Interviewers: How are you different from other men?

Mailer: I'm less strong, more fidgety, more determined, more inept, more successful. I don't like myself well enough to follow my instincts as I should. I think I've not had the courage to be authentic . . . but that's enough, ladies.

Interviewers: You have a wonderful way of dissipating . . .

Mailer: Enthusiasm. Yes. Well, if I give something to people, why can't I take it back again? You see, you never gave me a chance to say that *The White Negro* is no longer true.

Interviewers: Isn't it?

Mailer: No. Because what I said then was true as I saw it for the time, but it wasn't true enough. There weren't enough White Negroes around and so the organized world took on my notion of the White Negro and killed the few of us a little further. And I betrayed my own by writing that piece. It's even remotely conceivable I would have done better to have kept silent. I advanced my career at the expense of my armies. As a general, you see, I gained strength and lost troops.

Interviewers: What things in *The White Negro* don't you believe any more?

Mailer: I don't know that I want to lose any more troops. I've said enough. The mood has been marvelous, but it's all over, dear ladies.

The First Day's Interview
Norman Mailer / 1961

From the *Paris Review*, 26 (Summer-Fall 1961), 140-53. Reprinted by permission of the Scott Meredith Literary Agency, Inc.

Sometimes I think my work may be seen eventually as some literary equivalent (obviously much reduced in scale) to Picasso. My vice, my strength, is beginnings. Usually I begin well—it is just that I seem to have little interest in finishing. It seems adequate to start a piece, go far enough to glimpse what the possibilities and limitations might be, and then move on. Which for that matter is close to the discrete temper of our time.

This interview was an experiment. Unfinished one obviously. As an attempt to breach an opening into The Psychology of the Orgy, it has a few charms. It may even be possible to write a good book this way; such a book would be a novel. I can think of nothing very much like it, except perhaps for Gide's *Corydon*, but the difference is most particular. In *Corydon*, Gide stepped aside from his Self, and appeared nominally as André Gide-the-Interviewer speaking to some young talented homosexual artist, a man not unlike the hero of *The Immoralist*. He thus divided his dialogue between two Gides: a young, conventional, severe, most well-mannered and rather agitated young prig, (the "I" of *Corydon*) and the subject, a saturnine, scientifically articulated, rather sinister (in the proper tone of the period) man of talent.

In this fragment—*The First Day's Interview*—the encounter is less narcissistic. The subject is *a* Norman Mailer, a weary, cynical, now philosophically turned hipster of middle years; the interviewer is a young man of a sort the author was never very close to. The vector of the dialogue is therefore opposite to *Corydon*. In that book, Gide appears in a conventional suit and tries to take a trip across the room into himself. He is hoping to seduce his readers. On the contrary, in this piece printed here, the author in full panoply is pretending to travel back to society in order to seduce the brain of the young critic he never was. One might call it a Counter-Diabolism to Gide's method, and be not at all presumptuous—if one managed, small matter, to finish the book.

Interviewer: Is this going to be an important book?
Mailer: Perhaps my most important book.
Int.: Why?
Mailer: Because of its subject.
Int.: You're going to talk about murder in it.
Mailer: As well as a few other things.
Int.: If I may guess from the prevalence of your themes . . .
Mailer: Please do.
Int.: Well, I imagine you'll have something to say about suicide. And perversion?
Mailer: Yes.
Int.: And cancer of course.
Mailer: One shouldn't be flippant about cancer.
Int.: I get the impression that often you are.
Mailer: It's only because I have not been ready to explain what was behind the remark.
Int.: Whereas now you will.
Mailer: A more or less formal attempt will be made.
Int.: I hope so. At any rate let me repeat the list: Murder, suicide, perversion, cancer; thc orgy?
Mailer: Yes.
Int.: Will this be called The Psychology of the Orgy?
Mailer: Perhaps.
Int.: The orgy. That calls to mind some of your declarations about the orgasm.
Mailer: I dislike that word.
Int.: You virtually made it a parlor game to talk about it.
Mailer: If I did, I'm sorry.
Int.: You must have known what you were doing.
Mailer: That's why I'm sorry. I did it to attract attention to myself. Now I pay the price.
Int.: You seem to think you can get away with anything if you tell

the truth about yourself. The fact of the matter is that I for one would like to like you. I like your work. (*Pause*) As a matter of fact I have to admit I like it more today than I did when it came out.

Mailer: Yes.

Int.: But I don't like your aggressiveness. Why can't you let the work speak for itself. Why all these . . .

Mailer: Stunts?

Int.: Precisely. Why must you attract attention to yourself?

Mailer: I'm weary of that now. But at the time I felt as if I were sick, and attention given to me by others was my fastest cure.

Int.: Did it work that way?

Mailer: I don't know. One never knows. I did succeed in getting attention, and everyone takes me more seriously today, but I must wonder if I haven't lost something.

Int.: What might that be?

Mailer: My will to work. It all seems less desperate today. The need to get the work out, I mean.

Int.: I should think so. The rules for literary conduct are the effective essence, after all, of the experience of a good many writers in the past. You break too many rules. I know that people critical of your ideas often advance the argument that you have insuficient respect for the culture of the past.

Mailer: Which is a way of saying, "Insufficient respect for the acquired experience of the past."

Int.: I should think so.

Mailer: I have to agree. It is a lack, and the older I get, the more I come to understand that my talent—such as it is—has been crippled by this lack.

Int.: "Such as it is." You become positively modest.

Mailer: Allow me a convention or two. I would like some of the people who detest my work, and can't bear me, to go a little of the way into this book.

Int.: This interview.

Mailer: This interview. Modesty helps. Modesty is a lubricant for unpleasant intrusions.

Int.: In sex as well.

Mailer: Let's not get into difficulties right away.

Int.: All right. Let's not. You asked me here as a literary referee to help you keep close to your subject. You said you needed that.

Mailer: I do. My mind is as weak as the mind of an old man. It wanders. It dissipates. I cannot finish everything I like to finish. And this subject is too large to wander about in alone.

Int.: Murder and suicide. Cancer and the orgy. I should think so. You want my presence, therefore, as a midwife.

Mailer: I think better when I'm talking to someone. That's the first symptom of a writer who's losing his talent. Writing after all is one of the sublimations of onanism. As one gets away from such vices, one loses one's talent.

Int.: How quickly you sweep over complexities.

Mailer: But that is why I want an interview. I have no patience left for quiet exposition. In conversation you can put writing and onanism in a phrase. People know what you're talking about or they don't. In an essay you must obey formal concerns which I have not the enthusiasm to obey any longer.

Int.: But you cannot do an important work unless you submit to one or another formal discipline. We just agreed on that.

Mailer: I contradict myself already. Except I don't really. It's not a matter of what I would like to do. It's reduced right now to do what I can do. I've tried to command a sustained essay on this subject—I can't seem to get over the first few pages. My style immediately becomes tiresome. It takes on the empty sonorous tones of the kind of writers whose work I despise because they write authoritatively without a full spectrum of experience. They do not know enough about their subject to write a book. Which fits my condition. So my style becomes as bad as theirs.

Int.: I don't want to be tiresome, although I suppose that's my function, but why . . . ?

Mailer: Why write a book if you don't know enough to write it?

Int.: That's what I was going to say.

Mailer: Because what I have to say is sufficiently serious to find a style.

Int.: If you could, what sort of style would you like to find?

Mailer: Something as grand as the style of Karl Marx . . . There! I spoiled the mood.

Int.: I do find Marx unreadable.

Mailer: He's worth the effort. In a way he's a fine test for a literary mind.

Int.: I think he is an absolute bore.

Mailer: People who use the word "bore" usually develop nothing forthright in my associations.

Int.: Some have accused me of being a touch donnish.

Mailer: There is a cloying English simplicity to your remarks.

Int.: The I-am-simple school of Oxford interrogation?

Mailer: There you go. First time I've smiled.

Int.: Good, tell me about Karl Marx.

Mailer: Marx had something enormous to say. And he did the work of preparation. So his style has weight and texture.

Int.: What does that mean?

Mailer: You're right. Weight and texture are dull words. Marx has to be read line by line. He has something to say in every phrase. He knew his subject, knew it as strategist and as tactician. He wrote like one of the greatest generals whoever lived. I like that image. It just came to mind. War is often dull in its details, as is Marx, but the dullness is never flaccid. Marx always has more to say than we can stuff into a sentence, even as a general may have more men and supplies to mount in a major attack than he can ever join onto a given road. The marching may be dull, but one senses as one slogs along that one is obeying the overlying tension of a large mind, the mind of one's general. This mind is bold but it is also enormously tenacious in its grasp of detail. And it does not leave out important detail it has been too lazy to acquire.

Int.: Whereas your mind, by implication, is bold but lazy.

Mailer: No doubt it is lazy first, and merely bold in compensation.

Int.: You will lose the new audience you have gained if you become modest again.

Mailer: (*Gloomily*) It is too late to worry about anything but one's work.

Int.: This is the wrong day for an interview. You are obviously depressed.

Mailer: It is a very bad day, but one must make a start. There will be better days.

Int.: I see the burden of leading this discussion is up to me.

Mailer: For the moment.

Int.: Then to return to your use of military imagery—which parenthetically is psychologically symptomatic—

Mailer: Yes, yes. Militarism, psychic wounds, fears of castration, homosexuality; I'm familiar with the formula.

Int.: Anything to draw a flash of arrogance.

Mailer: Which I never truly possessed.

Int.: Sound like your detractors. (*Holds up a hand*) Enough. The loose associations of your mind seem to be contagious. I will try to get down to punctilio. Let me use the military image. If Marx is a general, and *Das Kapital* the record of a huge and successful war, what do you see this interview becoming if it is successful?

Mailer: An old fashioned cavalry raid with rusty equipment, tired horses, and beat troops which will go out nonetheless into a terrain Marx never dared.

Int.: Never dared, or didn't know about?

Mailer: Perhaps he had intimations. Sometimes I think he saw himself occupying this land as well—if he lived to be a hundred. But of course he would never have cheated the subject by interview.

Int.: Call you to order. Say something decent about the form of the interview.

Mailer: It is natural for our time. We will talk about the kind of things one should discuss on television. We will be superficial but quick. We will not slip into the gulf of unreadable prose. We will be diverting.

Int.: Mann once said, "Only the exhaustive is truly interesting."

Mailer: He was right. But one needs huge loins to be not merely exhaustive but artful as well. I can hope at best to do no more than pass lightly over treacherous philosophical ground. We will discuss in one or another of a hundred contexts the meanings of such resistant words as "dialectical" and "existential." As an immediate illustration of the method, I believe I'll point out that an interview is dialectical. Any dialogue between two people is a natural dialectic. Each creates the response of the other. So it is possible that the experience of acquainting oneself with my grab bag of ideas, notions, arguments, examples, and *lapses*, (as they are illumined and dissipated by your responses) will provide the reader with a sense of the dialectic that will be better than any exposition of the word by me.

Int.: What about existentialism? Is the form of the interview also suited for that?

Mailer: Do you have a comfortable idea of what the word means?

Int.: I've read a smattering of Sartre. I have a dim familiarity with the work of Jaspers and Heidegger.

Mailer: And know a little more about Kierkegaard, Nietzsche and Dostoyevsky?

Int.: Et cetera, et cetera. I admit it. I don't have a comfortable

sense of the word. It makes me uneasy. I use it all the time myself.
Sometimes with authority. I'll say, "Oh, yes, Mailer's trying to become
a Marxian existentialist"—mind you, I don't really talk about you that
much—and I get a laugh I must say. You know I've noticed that one
need only put large words together with authority in the voice and
people will laugh. Let an actress playing a grande dame exclaim on a
stage, "Oh yes, what fearful decoration. *Puerile Baroque*," and
everyone will roar.

Mailer: Most large words remind people of faeces or faces.

Int.: Why do you say that?

Mailer: I don't know. It seems right. I feel the truth of the thing
first, and discover the explanations later.

Int.: Very existentialist.

Mailer: All interviews are existential so far as they are not edited,
and are descriptive of the mood of the conversation. Which is another
argument for trying to express one's ideas in this form. It gives the
reader a sense of the present. That's the first notion to grasp about
existential philosophy. The underlying assumption is that nothing in
one's metaphysical scheme is as important as one's sense of the
present. The truth is found first in the gestalt. Not in the abstractions
of logic.

Int.: I think I have a firm grasp of "gestalt" as a word, but it would
be helpful to those who read this interview.

Mailer: You define it.

Int.: Well, gestalt is context. It's *swarm*, if you know what I mean.
It's the mood, the totality of an experience.

Mailer: Too vague.

Int.: Napoleon lost the battle of Waterloo because he couldn't sit
on his horse. The gestalt would add that he had a venereal disease
which made his saddle an instrument of torture.

Mailer: Well, I don't know. It's still too logical. Gestalt is as bad a
word as existential. Let us say that as we're talking an insect crosses
my field of vision. A brown worm the size of a maggot. I reach
forward and crush it. Nausea turns a small spasm in my throat, but I
go on talking. Can what I say be possibly the same as it would have
been without the insect? No, is my answer. Given the severest
discipline of mind, my words may be the same, my thought may not
waver from its intention but my voice will alter just perceptibly and as
it does, my argument will affect your unconscious more or less

agreeably since the unconscious, unlike the mind, listens not to words, but to the voice.

Int.: I'm going to be literal. Why will your voice change?

Mailer: Because I've just killed something, I have altered the gestalt of the room, shifted the rhythms of life which are present. Gestalt, as I use it, is the harmony or discord of the life present in the context which in this case is you, me, the furniture, the room and the insect.

Int.: Why include the insect? Men are men and insects are insects.

Mailer: But men and insects are not separate if each can give emotion to the other. This, you see, would be one of the implicit logics in existentialism. Existence precedes essence. Emotion determines causality.

Int.: And is causality all?

Mailer: By the style of this logic, it is more significant than lack of causality. Action determines more than sentiment. But we will go back to this again and again. At the moment I would rather not overload my sense of the proportions of this interview.

Int.: And what gives you this sense of proportion?

Mailer: Again you go too fast, too soon. Let us say that my instinct is refined, weathered, dulled and converted by my experience and thus gives me a sense of the moment so far as my character permits my instinct to be heard.

Int.: But that is just *your* instinct, *your* character, *your* sense of proportion.

Mailer: Yes, but I would deaden the life of my argument if I did not obey the knots and quirks of my particular rhythms. I cannot advance an argument which will be vital (read: universal) to my readers until I obey what is particular to me.

Int.: And this is existentialist?

Mailer: Let us say it is true to my mood. I know nothing about Heidegger, but I get the impression from Barrett's book, *Irrational Man*, that Heidegger might argue mood has precedence over matter. I know I would argue that.

Int.: Why?

Mailer: Too difficult to talk about yet.

Int.: Let me be the judge.

Mailer: Mood is a harmony. The harmony of a gestalt. The harmony of the life in the room, or the harmony one senses in a landscape. And harmony permits one to relax. As one relaxes, so new perception comes from the conduits of the unconscious, and one has added one's contribution to the mood which is now subtly different but is still alive in the growing *tissue* of previous sensation, precisely that tissue which was the mood of the previous moment. When a mood is shattered, the life in the room contracts, and a new mood, discontinuous to the last, begins its existence.

Int.: Most sensuous.

Mailer: Now I contract with annoyance. In a second or a minute, depending on your sensitivity you will sense my annoyance and react in turn. A new mood will begin. It will be perhaps less interesting than the last.

Int.: You are annoyed. Why did my expression "most sensuous" irritate you?

Mailer: Because it was obvious. And I was chasing a thought which was just at the end of my limited reach. One does not trap a butterfly by clapping one's hands.

Int.: You are too delicate to live.

Mailer: I may be too delicate to think. (*Lights a cigarette*) All right. Since you bring me to a full stop, I may as well make a confession. My character is such that I must confess a small viciousness in order to prime a new thought. So I will admit I was irritated when you said, "most sensuous," because quite contrary to breaking my mood, you accelerated it, which is another matter entirely. A sexual example came to mind immediately and it was a good one. It would have made my remarks about mood less tenuous.

Int.: Then why didn't you give it instead of abusing me?

Mailer: My ambition interfered.

Int.: Your ambition? Your mind is most elliptic.

Mailer: My ambition at the moment is to seduce all those readers who detest what they think are my ideas. They are the readers I wish to keep.

Int.: I wonder why.

Mailer: Because obviously it is more exciting to capture a hostile reader than tickle a friendly one. And these hostile readers have a preconceived notion of my character which makes it most difficult to talk to them. They see me as oppressive, clumsy, brutal, and mired in the lowest expositions of sex. So my plan was to march lightly for the first few days and reconnoiter no sexual thicket.

Int.: Charming. You'll never get power if you give away your maps before you've begun to move.

Mailer: I don't know if I want power anymore. I think I would rather be clear in my mind. The compromises one has to make in acquiring power dull the brain irreparably.

Int.: Since you are now too pure for power, would you then betray your ambition and give your sexual example.

Mailer: I think I've lost the mood.

Int.: Ugh.

Mailer: You disapprove?

Int.: The mark of a serious man is that he is capable of restoring his mood.

Mailer: I'm no longer as young as I want to be. An abrupt restoration of mood is as punishing to the body as starting an automobile in high gear. It's the sort of thing that brings on a cold.

Int.: Do complaints also prime new thought?

Mailer: They enable me to recover old thoughts. I was speaking of mood as a harmony. You invoked the qualities of the sensuous. So I thought of sex. Of a particular kind of sex. Sensuous sex. The sex of . . . I do not like to use the word "mature." The sex, let us say, of those who have been with sex for more than a little time. They are not young. They do not have that mixture of lust and private fantasy which makes for onanistic heat, for dirty heat, the sex let us say of two adolescents who burst on one another with the excitement of smashing a taboo. No, there is that other sex which comes to people when they are older, a sex of mood. Each one feels the mood of the other, each moves more delicately, aware now that one is no longer altogether attractive, and so one is vastly more attentive to the small offerings and polite withdrawals of the gift.

Int.: I don't want to interrupt.

Mailer: I'm glad you did. The description embarrasses me. It is too chaste. But the alternative is to speak prematurely of the parts of the body, the odors of the act, or discuss such mechanical propositions as the flow of energy.

Int.: Reichian terminology?

Mailer: I'm afraid so. Let us put it this way. Sex-as-mood is a conversation with respect for nuance. Does one raise one's voice to make a point?—one may soften the next remark. Does one wait too long?—the whip of wit must intervene. The dialogue of such sex is tender, it is respectful—it respects the slow conversion of character into mood, it seeks for an artful loss of each separate identity in order to find and give life to the mood which passes from body to body.

Int.: This is the only way sex-as-mood can exist?

Mailer: No. It is only one way. When I spoke of mood as a harmony of everything which lives in the gestalt, I should have explained that not all harmonies are peaceful. There are moods of apprehension, of unrest, excitement, of dread, horror, fear, pending cruelty, whatever one cares to name.

Int.: What separates a mood of horror from a mood which is suddenly shattered and so creates horror?

Mailer: You are close to the difficulty. I don't know if one can explain it. But it may be worth the attempt. Conceive of a landscape which is mysterious. Let me be banal—a landscape which is suggestive of doom. A landscape fit for a nightmare, a dark field across which one must walk. The shadows of the moon are cruel. Now across the field a laugh is suddenly heard, a merry laugh. Does it break the mood?

Int.: I should think so.

Mailer: Not necessarily. The laughter can give new intensity to the mood, offer ironic substance to its shape.

Int.: You speak as if the mood is alive.

Mailer: In a sense mood may be alive.

Int.: Like an organism?

Mailer: You anticipate me. I was about to say that a mood is a psychic organism. Like all living things it reacts to each new breath of the environment. It can grow, be wounded, weakened, changed, colored, fortified, it can adapt itself to many a change or shift in its circumstances. It can also be killed. As a psychic organism, it is obviously more delicate than any other kind of organism, and so it takes very little to kill a mood. But like any other organism, a mood is mysterious, and the most exceptional intrusions can give it life. In my conventional landscape of horror, it may take precisely the sound of a merry laugh to give individuality to the horror. The laughter may sustain the mood just as it was ready to languish, or equally, the laughter may wither the mood by revealing it to itself as absurd. As is true of all organisms, the possibilities are limitless.

Int.: But what is the ground? What is the field, or the seat of the mood? To be literal, where is it located?

Mailer: We must avoid science-fiction. If I start to speak of the air, or of psychic waves, or psychic fields of energy we will both be lost in a terminology for which we have no aptitude and no qualifications. We are literary men, more or less. Let us keep the subject evocative. It may be possible that literature has more to offer on the nature of the universe than the cyclotron.

Int.: The alternative is to leave the reader altogether confused. You cannot talk of psychic organisms without trying to describe some of their properties. Otherwise the suspicion arises that you invoke nothing more serious with your talk of psychic organisms than our old friend, the poltergeist.

Mailer: (*Sighs*) The subject is ineffable. If I try to describe it, I will kill it. There are those who will know what I am talking about and those who won't. I can only hint at the possibility of a new direction or two, for those who know already what I am talking about.

Int.: I thought you wanted to reach the readers who were hostile to you.

Mailer: The irony is that most of the people who are hostile to my work are precisely those people who have the deepest sense of what I am writing about.

Int.: I think you must do better than this.

Mailer: Can we avoid that total worry of where a mood exists? Whether it exists in the separate bodies of the people and objects who make up the mood, or whether it races through the air between them, or envelops all in a cloud, or is all of these things at once. It is enough to say: it exists because I feel it. What it looks like I do not know, but how it feels I am not likely to forget.

Int.: Is that really satisfactory as an explanation?

Mailer: Do you use the word "relationship" in your speech?

Int.: Often. It is a modern word.

Mailer: Do we have a relationship?

Int.: Of sorts.

Mailer: Can you think of a definite relationship you have with someone?

Int.: My wife.

Mailer: What does it look like?

Int.: What does it look like?

Mailer: The relationship.

Int.: . . . . . .

Mailer: Scored a point.

Int.: Yes, you did.

Mailer: Can we keep a side score through this dialogue?

Int.: We'll play Beaver.

Mailer: Excellent.

Int.: Do you feel like quitting for the day?

Mailer: I've never had the sense to quit when I'm ahead.

Int.: Nonetheless, one of my functions is to serve as an aerial editor who cuts so to speak on the fly. And I think we've done enough. What I ask for tomorrow is a presentation which will be a degree more formal.

Mailer: I promise nothing.

Int.: Will we get into murder?

Mailer: That may take a while.

Living Like Heroes
Richard Wollheim/1961

From the *New Statesman*, 29 September 1961, 443-45. Reprinted by permission of Richard Wollheim and the *New Statesman*.

Norman Mailer: What is a free act? It's an act for which there are no guides, when one has to make a moral judgment and there's no preparation for it because the life of the day has become more complex than the morality that covers it. The assumption here is that life always advances far ahead of morality. Morality is a quartermaster corps bringing up supplies to starving soldiers. Right. So the hipster acts and after he acts, he feels that it was either good or not good. He has a sensation which tells him which it was. This sensation is what Hemingway was writing about all the time. Now if the hipster always obeys this sensation, then he follows his unconscious, he acts on the basis of his id. He becomes the creature of the id.

 Richard Wollheim: But how do you get from the idea of the free act to that of a way of life flowing directly from the unconscious? Why shouldn't we identify the free act with the act that results from arbitrary choice?

 Mailer: That's the Sartrean idea, isn't it? Well, I reject Sartre. I don't reject him entirely, because I've not read him entirely. But I think that a Sartrean logic can work psychologically for very few people. There *are* people who can do it. It works for Sartre, but Sartre is so much a man of will that he can literally recreate himself by acts. But most people can't: for most people there must also be expressions of nature which go counter to their will.

 Wollheim: Now this release of unconscious forces is obviously going to result in violence; and certainly in *The White Negro* you don't shrink from the consequences, though I'd say that certain critics make too much of this because they understand violence in too narrow a sense—violence as crime.

Mailer: But the violence must be violence for which full responsibility is accepted, and that's rare today. Today we have the violence of the man who won't look his victim in the face. Take Eichmann. If he had killed 500,000 people with his bare hands, he would have been a monster, but a heroic monster. He'd have gained some of our unconscious respect. He'd have worn the scar of his own moral wound.

Wollheim: I agree that the denial of the existence of aggression is a bad thing in our society. But an ethic of violence, or one that tolerates violence, surely won't reduce anxiety?

Mailer: I think there are two anxieties. The first comes because one contains more hatred than one can express, and one's afraid that it will come out; and there's another that comes precisely when you release it, because when you do, there are consequences.

Wollheim: But isn't there also anxiety that is more directly connected with the release of aggression, that isn't just fear of consequences, but an inherent fear we have of our own destructive forces. That's why hip morality will only increase anxiety.

Mailer: I know it's not easy to release the id. Incidentally I don't like the word 'id.' In America we have a better word: 'it.' You know, 'get with it.' But I don't see the real choice as one between violence and non-violence. It's rather between the violence of the individual and collective violence.

Wollheim: By 'collective violence' you mean the way in which certain aspects of society combine to destroy or deaden personality.

Mailer: Yes, and I mean a literal deadening. I believe there is a way in which a man's personality can die before his time, and that is worse than being killed in a concentration camp because—and this is where I am optimistic—if a man is killed in some most unjust way, then this will be taken account of in eternity; but if one's death isn't dramatic, if one is extinguished day by day by the society in which one lives, then one loses one's chance of eternity.

Wollheim: This deadening of the personality is a great historical theme. But do you think that the method of destruction changes with the different historical phases, so that today we have it in the form of capitalist exploitation?

Mailer: I wouldn't like to say that I'm no longer a Marxist—I don't like the connotations of saying it. And since I happen to have got more from Marx than from anyone else I've ever read, I wouldn't

want to jettison Grandfather. But I'm not orthodox. I don't believe
that capitalist exploitation can be explained entirely in terms like
surplus value. I think that Marxism revisited would have to take into
account something else that goes much deeper than that. Deeper
than the love of property is the fear of the past, the fear of the vitality
of the lower classes, the fear that if all men were to walk the earth
equal, the upper classes would not long survive. I have the
impression that the upper classes of England are superior to the
upper classes of America. For one thing, if they're hypocrites, they're
hypocrites with a certain amount of style; if they're humbugs, they're
humbugs with particularly interesting voices. Just as people there's
something absolutely godawful about the upper classes of America—
they really are horrible people.

Wollheim: But however we think of this exploitation—and I agree
that we ought to see it in part as a kind of emotional parasitism, as
Lawrence did—it exists. Yet hip seems to me to raise what can't ever
be more than a private or at best a minority protest. It demands a
certain sophistication, a special sense of style; in a way it's a variant of
old-fashioned aestheticism.

Mailer: What separates hip from aestheticism is that it's not a man
living in a country house, surrounding himself with the most beautiful
works of art, receiving only those people with manners sufficiently
attuned to his, and savouring every moment of it. Hip is living a little
like a hero in a Hollywood Western. If you like, it's aestheticism with
danger added.

Wollheim: The danger thing seems to show that hip is essentially
an ethic of protest, of rejection. But is it really beyond us to conceive
of, or even bring about, a society in which, though dissent will still be
necessary, protest won't, at least in this total form?

Mailer: Well, this depends on whether one thinks a society can
solve its problems rationally. If one thinks it can, then hip will go
nowhere. But if one thinks it can't, and that barbarism is closer, and
that violence is in the seed, then at least hip introduces the notion of
art into barbary.

Wollheim: And you no longer think that Socialism provides a
rational solution?

Mailer: If anything is to come of Socialism, the existential content
will have to be changed altogether. I've never really been a Socialist,
but I've always thought, 'Better Socialism than anything else—and

what else is there?' The trouble with Socialists, I don't know about English Socialists, but the trouble with American Socialists—and some of my best friends are Socialists—is that they're prigs. They have very often failed to lead interesting lives, and they say, 'My God, I've had a lousy life, and I'm damned if it's my fault. Let's change the world and have a good time.' No, Socialism isn't terribly interesting if it means looking after the happiness of other people for them. And it doesn't solve the real problem. Socialism has never really considered that part of the establishment which puts emphasis on courage, on manners, on physical graces, on wit. I'd be much more excited about Socialism if it contained within itself the notion of the artist-warrior— and I don't mean myself by that.

Wollheim: But why the warrior? It seems to me a historical accident that through centuries of oppression we've come to identify the free exercise of man's powers with conflict.

Mailer: There's a big problem here, one that Socialists won't face. And that is whether the nature of the universe is war. Because, if it is, it's important to have a good war. England had a war that wasn't nearly as good as it should have been, and it paid for it with a terrible greyness afterwards.

Wollheim: You think psycho-analysis has nothing to say on the subject?

Mailer: I see it as an instrument of conformity. Psycho-analysts are sedentary middle-class people, and I see no reason to give nature and the universe over to sedentary middle-class people. In America now there's a new establishment, what I call the establishment of the centre: people who are right-wing Socialists and left-wing—no, that's inaccurate, moderate—Conservatives, who all work together. And their great handmaid is psycho-analysis. It's almost impossible for anyone now to do anything individual without being crucified in those very mediocre and dreary salons which pop up like mushrooms all over New York. I've seen the city dying over the last ten years. There's a psychic poverty in the city today, perhaps in the whole country. The thing that distresses me about America is that for all that country's done, I don't think it's done one quarter of what it should. I believe it was destined, by history if you will, to be the greatest country that ever existed. I don't think it's come near it.

Norman Mailer in Austin
Winston Bode/1961

From *The Texas Observer*, 15 December 1961, 1,6. Reprinted
by permission of The Texas Observer Publishing Co.

AUSTIN: Sweating profusely from the TV lights and the rigors of the
night before, Norman Mailer cocked an eye at interviewer Jean
Covert and said:

"I used to have a saying that all a poet needed was talent but that
to be a novelist you have to have character as well."

Mailer sat with hands folded, legs crossed: a short man with a short
neck and a shock of black curly hair that is slightly graying. He was
dressed as the well-known writer might dress when paying a visit to a
campus: well-cut, rugged-looking coat, dark button-down shirt, tie.

Mailer was kidding himself with his poetry remark. He's a poet
now, at 38, writing a stream of light verse for the Village Voice—"I
guess I wrote 400 poems in six months." Putnam is bringing out a
collection of 200 in February (*Deaths for the Ladies And Other
Disasters*), and it was from proofs of the book that he read to the
students at the University of Texas that night.

Apparently he is some time away from any blockbuster of a novel
like *The Naked and the Dead* that made him famous early. But the
character that is in any major novelist was still much in evidence on
his trip to Texas. Actually, Mailer is at that rather inflamed stage in a
writer's life when one or more big works have established you, when
more might well lie ahead, but when for the present the world seems
to catch you up in cocktail parties, magazine articles, news stories,
and above all—talk, talk, talk.

He is one of the major talkers of our time. On the day he appeared
at the University, he got up for his TV taping after a rousing session at
an old friend's. It is safe to say he had talked a good part of the night.

Before, during, and after the interview Mailer was talking a blue streak in his quiet, controlled, rapid-fire manner. He goes in for no conversational pyrotechnics with words: he uses them well, but he uses them because they carry ideas for him, and because they allow him to communicate with people.

Was there any writing talent around today he admired, came the TV question.

There's one man writing today who is fantastic, he said. William Burroughs.

"He writes incredible prose. He's the only writer I'm profoundly jealous of, nervous about. He's the only addict I know who became a good writer."

Throughout the day, in his hotel room, at lunch, on the stage, Mailer continued to comment, to answer questions—on everything from the Negro to architecture. (One typical evaluation that sticks in the mind: at least with the Baroque Victorian houses on the north shore in Chicago you knew what kind of guy lived there; the blank facade of modern buildings show nothing but a sense of guilt.) When last seen sometime just before the cocks began to crow, he was standing in the middle of the floor, looking students, liberals, politicians, state workers, teachers all right in the eye, listening, then responding.

On the street after his TV interview, Mailer was a little low. "That's one thing I don't like about Texas," he said. "This having to take a BOTTLE into a place when you want a drink . . . Look, perhaps we could do this in my hotel room."

He had little time for another interview. He had to eat lunch, to rest, and prepare his material for the night.

On the way to the Driskill, he talked about the blow up at the Poetry Center in New York when he read his poems.

"They didn't have any words in them that it hasn't been routine to use in poems for years. But I handled it wrong. I held my hand when I was coming to a word. Nobody would have said anything if at the beginning I had announced, 'The esthetic demands of some of these poems have caused me to use certain terms which . . . ' "

In his room, Mailer set out a small leather-covered flask.

He lives in Greenwich Village now. He gets his mail at his sister's place on Bleecker Street. He has no permanent address. He and his wife are not living together.

We talked about how hard it is to avoid mentioning his stabbing his wife when you write a news story on him.

Sitting in an arm chair, he smiled ruefully.

"Yes, I guess I'm going to have to live with that the next 20 years."

We mentioned that one interview after the knifing—which turned out to be minor—had him saying something about people not having the courage to enter new areas of consciousness, of which stabbing your wife is presumably one.

"Yes," he said mildly. "I read that somewhere. Yes, I said it."

We discussed the death of Hemingway.

"I wonder how he and his last wife got along?" Mailer said.

"He called her his vest pocket Rubens."

Brightening, Mailer said: "He did? I should be interviewing you!"

Later, soberly: " . . . I just wonder what effect his father's killing himself had on him. You just must lose some ball from a thing like that. I guess we'll never know. Maybe in 30 years something will come out."

Mailer said Hemingway's death affected him. "I feel a little weaker."

Was he on a novel now?

"Yes, but I've got a long way to go. It's going to be a really big one. I mean like 2, 3,000 pages."

Does he write every day?

"I believe it's good to do that. Like a lot of people's, my life has become complicated. Maybe I'll write five or six days in a stretch."

But after all, he observed, it wasn't so bad making a big hit early, and writing lesser stuff after that. It had happened before. "Look at Somerset Maugham. He wrote one big one, *Of Human Bondage,* then he just kept writing and writing and writing."

Yes, he agreed, age affects a writer. "Being a writer is like being an athlete. When you get older you lose certain reflexes. . . . I always do my best work cold sober. But you can get some fantastic effects when you're high, or have been high. Certain words burst through that wouldn't otherwise. Then you must go back later and edit."

Mailer was a cocky Harvard man and a beginning writer when he was shipped to the Philippines in World War II. He was trained as an army artillery surveyor, but when he got to the islands he asked to be transferred to an intelligence and reconnaissance unit. (Such a unit appears in *The Naked and the Dead.*) He wanted to see action and write about it.

He was 25 when his first novel established him as one of the finest talents in America.

Some people don't make it till much later than 25, we observed to Mailer.

"I don't know," he said. "Sometimes I think it's better to make it when you're 40 than when you're 25. At least when you do make it then, you'll know what it's all about.

" . . . Have you ever heard of Francis Irby Gwaltney?" he asked. "Gwaltney and I were buddies in the Philippines. We went into different companies so we didn't see exactly the same combat. But he wrote a book about the war there called *The Day the Century Ended*. It's interesting to compare the perspectives of the two books."

Mailer went to the phone. Speaking quietly to the co-ed, somewhat like a slightly older fraternity man, he said: "Yeah, Susan, sure. . . . Well listen, how long would it take to get out there?"

The University skydivers had suggested the big kick was to jump out of an airplane. Other students wanted him to see a ranch.

". . . things have gotten a little complicated and I've got to have three or four hours to myself to get ready for tonight. So if we got out there and were able to spend only thirty minutes or so then that wouldn't be so good, would it? . . . All right, Sue."

Standing at the door, Mailer said, "I was really gonna jump!" He gestured, a slight-boned man with large light eyes that peer out from a heavy shelf of brow. He is getting puffy around the middle, and at times gives the appearance of a gentle clothier. "What the heck," he said, "why not jump? All you could do is break your ankle."

At the Texas Union, a thousand students were there to hear him. They filled the ballroom and strained to catch his words over a p.a. system that didn't carry. For one reason or another over half had drifted away by the time he had read from his Esquire piece on the Democratic convention and had answered questions on national heroes and the Kennedy welfare state and architecture.

But there was an unflagging staccato performance of readings, comments, poems—with time out between phases to light cigarette after cigarette.

The tide was in, here in the big smoky hall where students came with dates and with books in their hands: Mailer was part of the stream of voices piped imperfectly from the outside world. The list this year has included Shirer, Bill Moyers, Yarborough; William Buckley due in January, Vincent Price, Hubert Humphrey, Goldwater, Martin Luther King to come.

The voice was passionate but level, detached, analytical:

". . . Liberal Totalitarianism. Curiosity of the age! The concentration camps exist in the jargon of our souls, one's first whiff of the gas chamber in the nausea of cancer's hour, the storm troopers wore tortoise-shell glasses, and carry attache cases to the cubicles in which they work on the Avenue of the Mad."

Mailer was reading "The Blacks," words which he had first given the Village Voice, which from there had been found in Canada by Exchange, a review which noted "in spite of all his wrong doings (Mailer) manages to create the most telling and most explicit picture of the present day life of North America. In our humble opinion, he is the greatest living American writer."

Mailer read on to the students from his comments elicited by the Genet play, in which the blacks (masked as whites) judge the other blacks, who perform their ritual murders and then turn on the jury and condemn it to die.

In his call for a left and a right as opposed to dead center he read: "The liberal tenets of the Center are central; all people are alike if we suppress the ugliness in each of us; all sadism is evil, all masochism is sick, all spontaneity is suspect, all individuality is infantile, and the salvation of the world must come from social manipulation of human material. That is why people must tend to become the same—a bulldozer does not work at its best in rocks or forest. Small accident many of the Negro leaders are as colorless as our white leaders and all too many of the Negroes one knows have a dull militancy compared to the curve and art of personality their counterparts had even 10 years ago. The misapprehension on which they march is that time is on the side of the Negro. If his hatred is contained, and his individuality reduced, the logic of the age must advance him first to equality and then to power (goes the argument) because the Center makes its dull shifts through guilt and through need. Since the Negro has finally succeeded in penetrating the conscience of the best whites, and since the worst whites are muzzled by our need to grant the Negro his equality or sink a little faster into the icy bogs of the Cold War, the Negro knows he need merely ape the hypocrisies of the white bourgeoisie, and he will win. It is a partial misapprehension. In the act of concealing himself, the Negro does not hasten his victory so much as he deadens the taste of it."

Then he tossed the light flies and skinners to his audience. Two lines of verse here, four there, pitched with a smile, with an occasional show of the warning hand. This one might sting a little.

Then he had a small extra, just arrived. John Henry Faulk had told J. Frank Dobie a few days before what Hemingway told the Paris Review what the good writer's greatest gift was. Dobie was moved to write a hearty piece of endorsement.

Therefore, did anyone object to his reading a little obscenity?

Not one single person here objects to obscenity?

OK!

Mailer was last seen by most of us in Austin as he stood in the front room at Roger Shattuck's and talked like an amiable champ.

It was a sort of anti-Goldwater party.

"I challenge Barry Goldwater to a *mano a mano* across Texas," said Mailer. "You can't win every time—it depends on the audience. That's why I want it *mano a mano*. . . . But I don't think he'll accept. I feel about this like Sonny Liston does about Floyd Patterson."

He bent down and tweaked the girl with a toe twist in her back.

A writer in the crowd said he would like to send Mailer something he wrote. "I've got it!" he claimed.

Mailer shot him a quick green glance.

"We'll see," he replied.

Standing with his feet planted, glass in his hand, Mailer had taken on a belligerent, humorous, sly, light eyed look, a squat, curly-haired, Russian look.

As you listened to Mailer then—and as you were to do long after he had gone—you kept getting the shock wave of standards, of impatience for excellence, precision, personal dignity, the thrusting aside of even the half good or the good crust and the rotten center; the feeling of a hard and classical discrimination that derives from the academic and brains and courage and goes past "guts" and "balls."

You thought, it is excellent to be generous with yourself, if you are not just feeding your ego; it is excellent to stir, to cause ideas to begin to squirm under a fatty tissue of getting along. One would almost think if a writer did this he had done enough, had done all anyone could be expected to do.

The only thing is, as you thought of the inflamed endless, all-embracing talk like this—like Dylan Thomas's, like Agee's—you have the impulse, not to be defended by logic, but by something else: What is he doing talking, why isn't he writing?

It is a hard question for a writer to settle, whether he is going to be a popular and sought after conversationalist, a self-revealer and a social critic who writes, or an artist.

It is probable that a writer lives on, and wants only to live on, through what he shapes on paper.

The scene at Shattuck's reminded you that Mailer has considered the issue of the artist in his middle span in *Advertisements For Myself*, where Mailer has considered the problem with the honesty, the familiar, plain-talking lucid bitter self evaluation that comes sooner or later from all good American writers:

"Some of us will probably be launched on a second wave of recognition . . . but what a waste there has been . . . (We) are older than we ought to be, ten years used up in two or three years of war, and another twenty spent in the fourteen years since. When I come to assess myself and try to measure what chance I have of writing that big book I have again in me, I do not know in all simple bitterness if I can make it. For you have to care about other people to share your perception with them, especially if it is a perception which can give them life, and now there are too many times when I no longer give a good goddamn for most of the human race. I had the freak of luck to start high on the mountain, and go down sharp while others were passing me. So I saw their faces as they learned to climb, and what faces they were . . . Still! There is the fault of others, and the fault of oneself, and I have my debts to pay. Fitzgerald was an indifferent caretaker of his talent, and I have been a cheap gambler with mine.

". . . I spent my first thirty years abusing my body, and the last six in forced marches on my brain, and so I am more stupid today than I ought to be, my memory is half gone, and my mind is slow; from fear and vanity, I paid out too much for what I managed to learn. When I sit down . . . to pick up again on my novel, I do not know if I can do it, for if the first sixty pages are not at all bad, I may still have wasted too much of myself, and if I have—what a loss. How poor to go to death with no more than the notes of good intention. It is the actions of men and not their sentiments which make history—the best sentence I've ever written—but I would hate to face eternity with that for my flag, since I am still at this formal middle of my life a creator of sentiments larger than my work.

In closing the section, Mailer added: "the book will be fired to its fuse by the rumor that once I pointed to the farthest fence and said

that within ten years I would try to hit the longest ball ever to go up
into the accelerated hurricane air of our American letters. For if I have
one ambition above all others, it is to write a novel which Dostoevsky,
and Marx; Joyce and Freud; Stendhal, Tolstoy, Proust and Spengler;
Faulkner, and even old moldering Hemingway might come to read;
for it would carry what they had to tell another part of the way."

The next morning after the party he got on a plane and went back
to New York.

Norman Mailer: An Interview
Steven Marcus/1964

From the *Paris Review*, 31 (Winter-Spring 1964), 28–58. Reprinted in *Writers at Work: The Paris Review Interviews, Third Series*, ed. George Plimpton. Copyright © 1967 by The Paris Review, Inc. Reprinted by permission of Viking Penguin Inc.

The interview took place on the afternoon of Saturday, July 6, 1963. The setting was Norman Mailer's Brooklyn Heights apartment, whose living room commands a panoramic view of lower Manhattan, the East River, and the New York harbor. The living room is fitted out with certain nautical or maritime furnishings and decorations, and Mailer, his curls unshorn, seemed at odd moments during the afternoon the novelist-as-ship-captain, though less Ahab than Captain Vere, and less both than Captain Shotover in ripe middle-age. Mailer had recently stopped smoking, and the absence of nicotine had caused him to put on weight, which he carries gracefully and with vigor; the new amplitude of flesh seems to have influenced his spirit in the direction of benignity.

Shortly after the interviewer arrived, Mailer excused himself for a few moments. He wanted to change, he said, into his writer's costume. He emerged wearing faded dungarees and an open-necked sport shirt. His sharp blue eyes sparkled as he suggested that the interviewer keep this fashion note in mind. Lunch was then prepared and served by Mailer in what must be called lordly fashion. In general, he conducts himself without affectation as a kind of secular prince. The interviewer was repeatedly struck during the course of a long afternoon's work by Mailer's manners, which were exquisite. The role of novelist-being-interviewed suits him very well.

Interviewer: Do you need any particular environment in which to write?

Mailer: I like a room with a view, preferably a long view. I dislike looking out on gardens. I prefer looking at the sea, or ships, or anything which has a vista to it. Oddly enough, I've never worked in the mountains.

Interviewer: Do you need seclusion?

Mailer: I don't know if I need seclusion, but I do like to be alone in a room.

Interviewer: When did you first think of becoming a writer?

Mailer That's hard to answer. I did a lot of writing when I was young.

Interviewer: How young?

Mailer: Seven.

Interviewer: A real novel?

Mailer: Well, it was a science fiction novel about people on Earth taking a rocket ship to Mars. The hero had a name which sounded like Buck Rogers. His assistant was called Dr. Hoor.

Interviewer: Doctor . . . ?

Mailer: Dr. Hoor. WHORE, pronounced H-O-O-R. That's the way we used to pronounce whore in Brooklyn. He was patterned directly after Dr. Huer in Buck Rogers who was then appearing on radio. This novel filled two and a half paper notebooks. You know the type, about 7 x 10. They had soft shiny blue covers and they were, oh, only ten cents in those days, or a nickel. They ran to perhaps 100 pages each, and I used to write on both sides. My writing was remarkable for the way I hyphenated words. I loved hyphenating, so I would hyphenate "the" and make it th-e if it came at the end of the line. Or "they" would become the-y. Then I didn't write again for a long time. I didn't even try out for the high school literary magazine. I had friends who wrote short stories, and their short stories were far better than the ones I would write for assignments in high school English and I felt no desire to write. When I got to college I started again. The jump from Boy's High School in Brooklyn to Harvard came as a shock. I started reading some decent novels for the first time.

Interviewer: You mentioned in *Advertisements For Myself* that reading *Studs Lonigan* made you want to be a writer.

Mailer: Yes. It was the best single literary experience I had had because the background of *Studs* was similar to mine. I grew up in Brooklyn, not Chicago, but the atmosphere had the same flatness of effect. Until then I had never considered my life or the life of the

people around me as even remotely worthy of—well, I didn't believe
they could be treated as subjects for fiction. It had never occurred to
me. Suddenly I realized you could write about your own life.

Interviewer: When did you feel that you were started as a writer?

Mailer: When I first began to write again at Harvard. I wasn't very
good. I was doing short stories all the time, but I wasn't good. If there
were fifty people in the class, let's say I was somewhere in the top
ten. My teachers thought I was fair, but I don't believe they ever
thought for a moment that I was really talented. Then in the middle
of my sophomore year I started getting better. I got on the *Harvard
Advocate,* and that gave me confidence, and about this time I did a
couple of fairly good short stories for English A-i, one of which won
Story Magazine's college contest for that year. I must say that Robert
Gorham Davis, who was my instructor then, picked the story to
submit for the contest and was confident it would win.

Interviewer: Was that the story about Al Groot?

Mailer: Yes. And when I found out it had won—which was at the
beginning of the summer after my sophomore year (1941)—well,
that fortified me, and I sat down and wrote a novel. It was a very bad
novel. I wrote it in two months. It was called *No Percentage.* It was
just terrible. But I never questioned any longer whether I was *started*
as a writer.

Interviewer: What do you think were some of the early influences
in your life? What reading, as a boy, do you recall as important?

Mailer: *The Amateur Gentleman* and *The Broad Highway* were
glorious works. So was *Captain Blood.* I think I read every one of
Farnol's books and there must be twenty of them. And every one of
Sabatini's.

Interviewer: Did you ever read any of them again?

Mailer: No, now I have no real idea of their merit. But I never
enjoyed a novel more than *Captain Blood.* Nor a movie. Do you
remember Errol Flynn as Captain Blood? Some years ago I was
asked by a magazine what were the ten most important books in my
development. The book I listed first was *Captain Blood.* Then came
Das Kapital. Then *The Amateur Gentleman.*

Interviewer: You wouldn't say that *Das Kapital* was boyhood
reading?

Mailer: Oh, no, I read that many years later. But it had its mild
influence.

Interviewer: It's been said often that novelists are largely nostalgic for their boyhood, and in fact most novelists draw on their youthful experiences a great deal. In your novels, however, the evocation of scenes from boyhood is rare or almost absent.

Mailer: It's difficult to write about childhood. I never felt I understood it in any novel way. I never felt other authors did either. Not particularly. I think the portrait of childhood which is given by most writers is rarely true to anything more than the logic of their novel. Childhood is so protean.

Interviewer: What about Twain, or Hemingway—who drew on their boyhoods successfully?

Mailer: I must admit they created some of the psychological reality of my own childhood. I wanted, for instance, to be like Tom Sawyer.

Interviewer: Not Huck Finn?

Mailer: The magic of Huck Finn seems to have passed me by, I don't know quite why. *Tom Sawyer* was the book of Twain's I always preferred. I remember when I got to college I was startled to find that *Huckleberry Finn* was the classic. Of course I haven't looked at either novel in thirty years.

Interviewer: Can you say something about your methods of working?

Mailer: They vary with each book. I wrote *The Naked and the Dead* on the typewriter. I used to write four days a week: Mondays, Tuesdays, Thursdays and Fridays.

Interviewer: Definite hours?

Mailer: Yes, very definite hours. I'd get up about 8:00 or 8:30 and I'd be at work by 10:00. And I'd work till 12:30; then I'd have lunch. I'd get back to work about 2:30 or 3:00, and work for another two hours. In the afternoon I usually needed a can of beer to prime me. But I'd write for five hours a day. And I wrote a great deal. The average I tried to keep was seven typewritten pages a day, twenty-eight pages a week. The first draft took seven months, the second draft which really was only half a draft took four months. The part about the platoon went well from the beginning, but the Lieutenant and the General in the first draft were stock characters. If it had been published at that point the book would have been considered an interesting war novel with some good scenes, no more. The second draft was the bonus. Cummings and Hearn were done in the second draft. If you look at the book you can see that the style shifts, that the parts about Cummings and Hearn are written in a somewhat more developed vein. Less forceful but more articulated. And you can see something of the turn my later writing would take in the scenes between Cummings and Hearn.

Interviewer: What methods did you pursue in your next books?

Mailer: Well, with *Barbary Shore*, I began to run into trouble. I started it in Paris about six months after I finished *The Naked and the Dead,* and did about fifty pages. It was then called *Mrs Guinevere* and was influenced by Sally Bowles in Isherwood's *Berlin Stories*. *Mrs Guinevere* never went anywhere. It stopped, just ground down after those first fifty pages. My novelistic tanks ran out of gas. I dropped it completely, thought I'd never pick it up again, and started to work on another novel. Did all the research, went to Indiana to do research.

Interviewer: On what?

Mailer: On a labor novel. There was a union in Evansville with which I had connections. So I stayed for a few days in Indiana, and then went to Jamaica, Vermont, to write the novel. I spent four to six weeks getting ready to begin. I made a great push on the beginning, worked for two weeks, and quit cold. I didn't have the book. I didn't know a damned thing about labor unions. In desperation (I was full of second novel panic) I picked up *Mrs Guinevere* and looked at it. And found something there I could go on with. So I worked on it all through the spring of 1949, and then I moved out to Hollywood for the summer. I finished the second half in Hollywood. *Barbary Shore* is really a Hollywood novel. I think it reflected the impact of Hollywood on me in some subterranean fashion. Certainly the first draft is the wildest draft of the three; it's almost insane, and the most indigestible portions were written in the first couple of months I was in Hollywood. I never knew where the book was going, I had no idea where it was going to move from day to day. I'd wake up and push the typewriter in great dread, in literal terror, wondering when this curious and doubtful inspiration was going to stop. It never quite did. It ground along at the rate of three pages, three difficult pages a day. But I'd get it out. I got a first draft done, and was quite unhappy with it; it was a very bad book at that point. When I rewrote it later, in Provincetown, a summer later, again it went at the rate of three pages a day. This revision was different from the first draft, and I think

much better. But working on *Barbary Shore* I always felt as if I were
not writing the book myself, but rather as if I were serving as a subject
for some intelligence which had decided to use me to write the book.
It had nothing to do with whether the work was good or bad. It just
had to do with the fact that I had absolutely no conscious control of
it; if I hadn't heard about the unconscious I would have had to
postulate one to explain this phenomenon. For the first time I
became powerfully aware of the fact that I had an unconscious which
seemed to have little to do with me.

Interviewer: What about *The Deer Park?*

Mailer: For *The Deer Park* I didn't have much of a method. It was
agony; it was far and away the most difficult of my three novels to
write. The first and second drafts were written with the idea that they
were only the first part of an eight-part novel. I think I used that
enormous scheme as a pretext to get into the work. Apparently I just
couldn't sit down and write a nice modest Hollywood novel. I had to
have something grandiose, in conception, anyway. I started *The Deer
Park* with "The Man Who Studied Yoga." That was supposed to be a
prologue to all eight novels. It went along nicely and was done in a
few weeks. And then I got into *The Deer Park,* and I forget what my
methods were exactly; I think they varied. In the revisions of *Barbary
Shore* I had started working in longhand; as soon as I found myself
blocked on the typewriter I'd shift to longhand. By the time I got to
The Deer Park I was writing in longhand all the time. I'd write in
longhand in the morning, and type up what I'd written in the
afternoon. I was averaging about four-five pages a day, I think, three
days a week; about fifteen pages a week. But I found it an
unendurable book to write because I'd finish each day in the most
profound depression; as I found out later it was even a physical
depression. I was gutting my liver.

Interviewer: It wasn't alcohol?

Mailer: No, I wasn't much of a drinker in those days. The liver,
you see, is not unlike a car battery, and I was draining mine. I was
writing with such anxiety and such fear and such distaste, and such
gloom and such dissatisfaction that . . .

Interviewer: Dissatisfaction with what?

Mailer: Oh, everything. My work, my life, myself. The early draft
of *The Deer Park* was terrible. It had a few good things in it, but it
was slow to emerge, it took years, and was stubborn. It still emerges.
I mean, I could sit down today and rewrite *The Deer Park.* Of course,

what was happening was that this work, such as it was, was continuing to move in a direction which was completely against the grain of my intellect—insofar as my intellect was developed, and had standards and tastes and attitudes toward the novel. I was working toward a novel utterly outrageous to my notion of things.

Interviewer: Say it again?

Mailer: Well, I was a socialist after all, and I believed in large literary works which were filled wth characters, and were programmatic, and had large theses, and were developed, let's say, like the Tolstoyan novel. It's as if, all proportion naturally being kept, as if Tolstoy had sat down with the intention of writing *Anna Karenina* and instead came out with *Crime and Punishment.* Obviously, it would have been intolerable for him, and he would have disliked *Crime and Punishment* very much. That was what was going on with me at a much lower level.

Inteviewer: How does the idea of a novel come to you?

Mailer: I don't know that it comes. A more appropriate image for me might be that I start with the idea of constructing a treehouse and end with a skyscraper made of wood.

Interviewer: Well, how did the idea of *The Naked and the Dead* come to you?

Interviewer: I wanted to write a short novel about a long patrol. All during the war I kept thinking about this patrol. I even had the idea before I went overseas. Probably it was stimulated by a few war books I had read: John Hersey's *Into the Valley,* Harry Brown's *A Walk in the Sun,* and a couple of others I no longer remember. Out of these books came the idea to do a novel about a long patrol. And I began to create my characters. All the while I was overseas a part of me was working on this long patrol. I even ended up in a reconaissance outfit which I had asked to get into. A reconnaissance outfit, after all, tends to take long patrols. Art kept traducing life. At any rate, when I started writing *The Naked and the Dead* I thought it might be a good idea to have a preliminary chapter or two in which to give the reader a chance to meet my characters before they went on patrol. But the next six months and the first 500 pages went into that, and I remember in the early days I was annoyed at how long it was taking me to get to the patrol.

Interviewer: Do you keep notes, or a journal, or diaries, or write scenarios? What's your preparatory material?

Mailer: That also varies with each of the books. For *The Naked* *and the Dead* I had a file full of notes, and a long dossier on each man. Many of these details never got into the novel, but the added knowledge made me feel more comfortable with each character. Indeed I even had charts to show which characters had not yet had scenes with other characters. For a book which seems spontaneous on its surface, *The Naked and the Dead* was written mechanically. I studied engineering at Harvard, and I suppose it was the book of a young engineer. The structure is sturdy, but there's no fine filigree to the joints. Just spot welding and riveting. And the working plan was very simple. I devised some preliminary actions for the platoon in order to give the reader an opportunity to get to know the men, but this beginning, as I said, took over two-thirds of the book. The patrol itself is also simple, but I did give more thought to working it out ahead of time.

Interviewer: People have commented on the pleasure you seem to take in the military detail of *The Naked and the Dead.*

Mailer: Compared to someone like James Jones, I'm an amateur at military detail. But at that time I did like all those details. I even used to enjoy patrols, or at least I did when I wasn't sick with jungle rot and viruses or atabrine poisoning. I was one of the few men in the platoon who could read a map. I was the only enlisted man I know who really cared about reading a map and once I gave myself away. We used to have classes after a campaign was over; we'd come back to garrison—one of those tent cities out in a rice paddy—and they would teach us all over again how to read maps and read compasses, or they would drill us on the nomenclature of the machine gun for the eighth time. One day very bored, I was daydreaming, and the instructor pointed to a part of the map and said, "Mailer, what are those coordinates?" If I had had a moment to think I would never have answered, it was bad form to be bright in my outfit, but I didn't think: he caught me in a daze, and I looked up and said, "320.017 dash 146.814" and everyone's mouth dropped. It was the first time anybody ever answered such a question thus briskly in the history of infantry map reading. At any rate, that was the fun for me, the part about the patrol. I suppose it had something to do with *Captain Blood* and *The Amateur Gentleman* . . .

Interviewer: How much of a plan did you have for *Barbary Shore?*

Mailer: None. As I indicated earlier, *Barbary Shore* just birthed itself slowly. The book came out sentence by sentence. I literally never knew where the next day's work was coming from.

Interviewer: You don't mention (in your description of writing *Barbary Shore*) anything about politics. Wasn't your *engagement* at the time a considerable part of the plan?

Mailer: I think it was the unspoken drama in the working-up of the book. I started *Barbary Shore* as some sort of fellow-traveler, and finished with a political position which was a far-flung mutation of Trotskyism. And the drafts of the book reflected these ideological changes so drastically that the last draft of *Barbary Shore* is a different novel altogether and has almost nothing in common with the first draft but the names.

Interviewer: Did Jean Malaquais (to whom the book is dedicated) have much to do with this?

Mailer: Yes. He had an enormous influence on me. He's the only man I know who can combine a powerfully dogmatic mind with the keenest sense of nuance, and he has a formidable culture which seems to live in his veins and capillaries. Since he has also had a most detailed vision of the Russian Revolution—he was steeped in it the way certain American families are imbued with the records of their clan—I spent a year living more closely in the history of Russia from 1917 to 1937 than in the events of my own life. I doubt if I would even have gone back to rewrite *Barbary Shore* if I didn't know Malaquais. Certainly I could never have conceived McLeod. Malaquais, of course, bears no superficial resemblance whatsoever to McLeod—indeed Malaquais was never even a communist, he started as an anti-Stalinist, but he had a quality when I first met him which was pure Old Bolshevik. One knew that if he had been born in Russia, a contemporary of Lenin's, he would have been one of the leaders of the Revolution and would doubtless have been executed in the trials. So his personality—as it filtered through the contradictory themes of my unconscious—inhabits *Barbary Shore*.

Interviewer: Would you care to discuss what you mean by the "contradictory themes" of your unconscious? Is that related to what you said a little while ago about becoming aware of your unconscious while writing *Barbary Shore?*

Mailer: *Barbary Shore* was built on the division which existed then in my mind. My conscious intelligence, as I've indicated, became obsessed by the Russian Revolution. But my unconscious was much more interested in other matters: murder, suicide, orgy, psychosis, all the themes I discuss in *Advertisements*. Since the gulf between these conscious and unconscious themes was vast and quite resistant to any quick literary coupling, the tension to get a bridge across resulted in the peculiar feverish hothouse atmosphere of the book. My unconscious felt one kind of dread, my conscious mind another, and *Barbary Shore* lives somewhere between. That's why its focus is so unearthly. And of course this difficulty kept haunting me from then on in all the work I did afterward. But it was a book written without any plan.

Interviewer: And *The Deer Park?*

Mailer: That was different. There I had an idea of what I was going to do. I knew it was going to be a story about a most unhappy love. The problem was getting to the affair: I could hardly wait to reach it, especially because the early parts of the novel were so difficult to write. It is truly difficult to trap Hollywood in a novel. Only in the last draft did I finally get the setting the way I wanted it. I think now the setting is probably the best part. In fact I would judge that the first fifty pages of *The Deer Park* are the best writing I have ever done in fiction. But they were the hardest fifty pages of the book to write and certainly took the longest time.

Interviewer: Do you have any superstitions about your methods of work?

Mailer: I wouldn't call them superstitions exactly. I just think it's bad to talk about one's present work, for it spoils something at the root of the creative act. It discharges the tension.

Interviewer: What writers have you learned the most from, technically?

Mailer: E. M. Forster, I suppose. I wouldn't say he is necessarily one of the novelists I admire most. But I have learned a lot from him. You remember in *The Longest Journey* somewhere about the fourth chapter, you turn the page and read, "Gerald was killed that day. He was beaten to death in a football game." It was quite extraordinary. Gerald had been very important through the beginning of the book. But now that he was suddenly and abruptly dead, everyone else's character began to shift. It taught me that personality was more fluid, more dramatic and startling, more inexact than I had thought. I was brought up on the idea that when you wrote a novel you tried to build a character who could be handled and walked around like a piece of sculpture. Suddenly character seemed related more closely to the paintings of the new realists. For instance I saw one recently which had a painted girl reclining on a painted bed, and there was a television set next to her in the canvas, a real one which you could turn on. Turning on the literal factual set changes the girl and the painting both. Well, Forster gives you something of that sensation in his novels. I played with such a concept a great deal in *Barbary Shore* and I began to play with it in *The Deer Park* in an altogether different way. I suppose the concept was parallel to the 'Alexandria Quartet' in its preoccupations. When you tell the same story through the eyes of different characters, you have not only a different novel but a different reality. I think I could sit down today and write *The Deer Park* through Charles Francis Eitel's eyes, and if I changed the names and place, no one might know the new book had anything to do with *The Deer Park*. I suppose what I realized, after reading Forster, was that a novel written in the third person was now impossible for me for many years.

Interviewer: Forster has never written a novel in the first person.

Mailer: I know he hasn't, but in some funny way Forster gave my notion of personality a sufficient shock that I could not manage to write in the third person. Forster after all had a developed view of the world. I did not. I think I must have felt at that time as if I would never be able to write in the third person until I developed a coherent view of life. I don't know that I've been able to altogether.

Interviewer: You know, Thackeray says at one point, that the novelist knows everything. He is like God, and this may be why he could write in the third person.

Mailer: God can write in the third person only so long as He understands His world. But if the world becomes contradictory or incomprehensible to Him, then God begins to grow concerned with his own nature. It's either that, or borrow notions from other Gods.

Interviewer: Have you ever cribbed anything from other writers?

Mailer: Oh, you know, I have such a—what shall I say?—such a stuffy view of myself that I could never *conceive* of cribbing. But I have been *influenced* by—well, Farrell to begin with. Dos Passos, Steinbeck (I am trying to do it chronologically), Hemingway, and later Fitzgerald—much, much later. And Thomas Wolfe of course.

Interviewer: But back to cribbing. Shakespeare cribs, for example. He never invented a plot.

Mailer: No, but my plots are always rudimentary. Whatever I've accomplished certainly does not depend on my virtuosity with plot.

Generally I don't even have a plot. What happens is that my characters engage in an action, and out of that action little bits of plot sometimes adhere to the narrative. I never have to worry about lifting a plot, because I don't conceive of a book that way.

Interviewer: In connection with plot, when did the idea of using a hornet's nest to thwart the climbers in *The Naked and the Dead* come to you?

Mailer: That idea was there before I wrote the first sentence of the book. Actually that incident happened to my reconnaissance platoon on the most ambitious patrol I ever took with them. They sent out thirty of us to locate and destroy one hundred Japanese marines who had gotten behind our lines. Well, we never found the marines, but we did get stuck climbing one hell of an enormous hill with a mean slimy trail, and when we were almost up to the ridge, somebody kicked over a hornet's nest. Half the platoon went tearing up the hill, and the machine gun squad went flying down to the valley. We never did find each other again that day. We just slunk back to our bivouac.

Interviewer: Putting aside the fact that it happened, do you think in fact it was a satisfactory device? It seems to have bothered some people.

Mailer: I think I'd do it the same way again. War is disproportions, and the hornet's nest seemed a perfect disproportion to me. We were ready to lose our lives but we weren't up to getting stung by a hornet.

Interviewer: Would you say something about style, prose style, in relation to the novel?

Mailer: A really good style comes only when a man has become as good as he can be. Style is character. A good style cannot come from a bad undisciplined character. Now a man may be evil, but I believe that people can be evil in their essential natures and still have good characters. Good in the sense of being well-tuned. They can have characters which are flexible, supple, adaptable, principled in relation to their own good or their own evil—even an evil man can have principles—he can be true to his own evil, which is not always so easy, either. I think good style is a matter of rendering out of oneself all the cupidities, all the cripplings, all the velleities. And then I think one has to develop one's physical grace. Writers who are possessed of some physical grace may tend to write better than writers who are physically clumsy. It's my impression this is so. I don't know that I'd care to attempt to prove it.

Interviewer: Well, how would you describe your own style? I ask this question because certain critics have pointed to deficiencies in it, or what they think of as deficiencies. Didn't Diana Trilling, for instance, criticize certain flatnesses in your style?

Mailer: I think that flatness comes out of certain flatnesses in me. And in trying to overcome that flatness I may push too hard in the other direction. Alfred Kazin once said something very funny about the way I write: "Mailer is as fond of his style as an Italian tenor is of his vocal cords."

Interviewer: Have you ever written to merely improve your writing, practiced your writing as an athlete would work out?

Mailer: No. I don't think it's a proper activity. That's too much like doing a setting-up exercise; any workout which does not involve a certain minimum of danger or responsibility does not improve the body—it just wears it out.

Interviewer: In writing your novels, has any particular formal problem given you trouble—let's say a problem of joining two parts of a narrative together, getting people from point A to point B.

Mailer: You mean like getting them out of a room? I think formal problems exist in inverse proportion to one's honesty. You get to the problem of getting someone out of the room when there's something false about the scene.

Interviewer: Do you do any research or special reading to prepare for writing a novel, or while you're writing a novel?

Mailer: Occasionally I have to look something up. But I'm always unhappy about that and mistrust the writing which comes out of it. I feel in a way that one's ignorance is part of one's creation, too. I don't know quite how to put it, but for instance if I, as a Jew, am writing about other Jews, and if my knowledge of Jewish culture is exceptionally spotty, as indeed it is, I am not so sure that that isn't an advantage in creating a modern American Jew. Because *his* knowledge of Jewish culture is also extremely spotty, and the way in which his personality is composed may be more in accordance with my ignorance than with a cultivated Jew's immersion in the culture. So in certain limited ways one's ignorance can help to buttress the validity of a novel.

Interviewer: Have you ever written about a situation of which you have had no personal experience or knowledge?

Mailer: I don't know. Let's see . . . *Barbary Shore,* for example, is the most imaginative of my novels. But I did live in a rooming house for a short period while I was writing *The Naked and the Dead.* I certainly didn't live in it the way Lovett lived in it. I never met an F.B.I. agent, at least I had no sense of having met one at the time I was writing *Barbary Shore.* I am sure I have met a great many since. They didn't necessarily introduce themselves to me. I had never met an Old Bolshevik, either, although ironically, writing about F.B.I. agents and Old Bolsheviks in *Barbary Shore,* the greatest single difficulty with the book was that my common sense thought it was impossible to have all these agents and impossible heroes congregating in a rooming house in Brooklyn Heights. Yet a couple of years later I was working in a studio on Fulton Street at the end of Brooklyn Heights, a studio I have had for some years. It was a fine old studio building and they're tearing it down now to make room for a twenty-story building which will look like a Kleenex box. At any rate, on the floor below me, worked one Colonel Rudolph Abel who was the most important spy for the Russians in this country for a period of about eight or ten years, and I am sure we used to be in the elevator together many times. I think he literally had the room beneath me. I have always been overcome with that. It made me decide there's no clear boundary between experience and imagination. Who knows what glimpses of reality we pick up unconsciously, telepathically.

Interviewer: To what extent are your characters modelled on real people?

Mailer: I think half of them might have a point of departure from somebody real. Up to now I've not liked writing about people who are close to me, because they're too difficult to do. Their private reality obviously interferes with the reality one is trying to create. They become alive not as creatures in your imagination but as actors in your life. And so they seem real while you work but you're not working *their* reality into your book. For example it's not a good idea to try to put your wife into a novel. Not your latest wife, anyway. In practice I prefer to draw a character from someone I hardly know. Hollingsworth came from someone I met in Paris, a vapid young American who inveigled me to have a cup of coffee with him in a cafe, and asked a lot of dull questions. *The Naked and the Dead* had just come out and I think he was impressed with that. Yet, there was something sinister about him. I had met him at the Sorbonne a week or two before and I saw him again just for this afternoon for no more than an hour, but he stayed in my memory and became Leroy Hollingsworth in *Barbary Shore*.

Interviewer: How do you name your characters?

Mailer: I try to let the name emerge, because I've found out that the names of my characters usually have roots in the book. I try to avoid quick or cheap symbolisms. Although, I contradict myself, for much is made in *The Deer Park* of the way the name Eitel is pronounced Eye-tell.

Interviewer: I-tell?

Mailer: Eye-tell. But I became aware of that, believe it or not, only when the book was half done. The original title of *The Deer Park* was *The Idol and the Octopus*. The book was going to be about Charles Francis Eitel, the Director, and Herman Teppis, the Producer, and the underlying theme was the war between those who wished to make an idol out of art, the artists, and the patron who sued art for power, the octopus.

Interviewer: You also called him "Idell".

Mailer: Frankie Idell in "The Man Who Studied Yoga", yes, but there again, I was obviously getting ready for some—shall we say, hankypanky, in the eight novels.

Interviewer: Can you describe how you turn a real person into a fictional one?

Mailer: I try to put the model in situations which have very little to do with his real situations in life. Very quickly the model disappears. His private reality can't hold up. For instance, I might take somebody who is a professional football player, a man let's say whom I know slightly, and make him a movie star. In a transposition of this sort, everything which relates particularly to the professional football player quickly disappears, and what is left, curiously, is what is *exportable* in his character. But this process while interesting in the early stages is not as exciting as the more creative act of allowing your characters to grow once they're separated from the model. It's when they become almost as complex as one's own personality that the fine excitement begins. Because then they are not really characters any longer— they're beings, which is a distinction I like to make. A character is someone you can grasp as a whole, you can have a clear idea of him, but a being is someone whose nature keeps shifting. Like a character of Forster's. In *The Deer Park* Lulu Myers is a being rather than a

character. If you study her closely you will see that she is a different
person in every scene. Just a little different. I don't know whether
initially I did this by accident or purposefully, but at a certain point I
made the conscious decision *not* to try to straighten her out, she
seemed right in her change-ableness.

Interviewer: Is Marion Faye a character or a . . .

Mailer: No, he's a being. Everybody in *The Deer Park* is a being
except the minor characters like Herman Teppis.

Interviewer: Do specific characters reappear in different guises as
the novels appear?

Mailer: To a mild degree. Actually it's easier for me to create a
new character than to drag along one of the old ones. No, I think it's
more that certain themes reappear in my novels, but I'd rather not get
into this just yet.

Interviewer: How did Marion Faye emerge?

Mailer: The book needed something which wasn't in the first
draft, some sort of evil genius. One felt a dark pressure there in the
inner horizon of the book. But even as I say this I know it's not true to
the grain of my writing experience. I violate that experience by talking
in these terms. I am not sure it's possible to describe the experience
of novel-writing authentically. It may be that it is not an experience.

Interviewer: What is it, then?

Mailer: It may be more like a relation, if you will—a continuing
relation between a man and his wife. You can't necessarily speak of
that as an experience because it may consist of several experiences
which are braided together; or it may consist of many experiences
which are all more or less similar, or indeed it may consist of two
kinds of experiences which are antagonistic to one another.
Throughout all of this I've spoken of characters *emerging*. Quite often
they don't emerge; they fail to emerge. And what one's left with is the
dull compromise which derives from two kinds of experiences
warring with one another within oneself. A character who should
have been brilliant is dull. Or even if a character does prove to be
first-rate, it's possible you should have done twice as much with him,
three times as much.

Interviewer: You speak of character as emerging, and I gather by
that that you mean emerging from yourself and emerging from your
idea?

Mailer: They are also emerging from the book. A book takes on
its own life in the writing. It has its laws, it becomes a creature to you

after a while. One feels a bit like a master who's got a fine animal. Very often I'll feel a certain shame for what I've done with a novel. I won't say it's the novel that's bad; I'll say it's I who was bad. Almost as if the novel did not really belong to me, as if it was something raised by me like a child. I know what's potentially beautiful in my novel, you see. Very often after I've done the novel I realize that that beauty which I recognize in it is not going to be recognized by the reader. I didn't succeed in bringing it out. It's very odd—it's as though I had let the novel down, owed it a duty which I didn't fulfill.

Interviewer: Would you say that there was any secret or hidden pattern being worked out in your novels?

Mailer: I'd rather leave that to others. If I answer the question badly, nothing is accomplished. If I answer too well, it's going to discourage critics. I can imagine nothing more distressing to a critic than to have a writer see accurately into his own work. But I will say one thing, which is that I have some obsession with how God exists. Is He an essential god or an existential god; is He all-powerful or is He, too, an embattled existential creature who may succeed or fail in His vision? I think this theme may become more apparent as the novels go on.

Interviewer: When did this obsession begin?

Mailer: I think it began to show itself while I was doing the last draft of *The Deer Park*. Then it continued to grow as a private theme during all the years I was smoking marijuana.

Interviewer: You have spoken so often of the existential view. What reading or individuals brought you to this?

Mailer: The experience came first. One's condition on marijuana is always existential. One can feel the importance of each moment and how it is changing one. One feels one's being, one becomes aware of the enormous apparatus of nothingness—the hum of a hi-fi set, the emptiness of a pointless interruption, one becomes aware of the war between each of us, how the nothingness in each of us seeks to attack the being of others, how our being in turn is attacked by the nothingness in others. I'm not speaking now of violence or the active conflict between one being and another. That still belongs to drama. But the war between being and nothingness is the underlying illness of the twentieth century. Boredom slays more of existence than war.

Interviewer: Then you didn't come to existentialism as a result of some literary influence?

Mailer: No. I'd hardly read anything by Sartre at this time, and nothing by Heidegger. I've read a bit since, and have to admire their formidable powers, but I suspect they are no closer to the buried continent of existentialism than were medieval cartographers near to a useful map of the world. The new continent which shows on our psychic maps as intimations of eternity is still to be discovered.

Interviewer: What do you feel about the other kinds of writing you have done and are doing. How do they stand in relation to your work as a novelist?

Mailer: The essays?

Interviewer: Yes: journalism, essays.

Mailer: Well, you know, there was a time when I wanted very much to belong to the literary world. I wanted to be respected the way someone like Katherine Anne Porter used to be respected.

Interviewer: How do you think she was respected?

Mailer: The way a cardinal is respected—weak people get to their knees when the cardinal goes by.

Interviewer: As a master of the craft, do you mean?

Mailer: As a master of the craft, yes. Her name is invoked in an argument. "Well, Katherine Anne Porter would not do it *that* way." But by now I'm a bit cynical about craft. I think there's a natural mystique in the novel which is more important than craft. One is trying, after all, to capture reality, and that is extraordinarily and exceptionally difficult. I think craft is merely a series of way-stations. I think of craft as being like a St. Bernard dog with that little bottle of brandy under his neck. Whenever you get into *real* trouble the thing that can save you as a novelist is to have enough craft to be able to keep warm long enough to be rescued. Of course this is exactly what keeps good novelists from becoming great novelists. Robert Penn Warren might have written a major novel if he hadn't had just that little extra bit of craft to get him out of all the trouble in *All The King's Men*. If Penn Warren hadn't known anything about Elizabethan literature, the true Elizabethan in him might have emerged. I mean, he might have written a fantastic novel. As it was, he knew enough about craft to . . .

Interviewer: To use it as an escape hatch?

Mailer: Yes. And his plot degenerated into a slambang of exits and entrances, confrontations, tragedies, quick wails and woe. But he was really forcing an escape from the problem.

Interviewer: Which was?

Mailer: Oh, the terror of confronting a reality which might open into more and more anxiety and so present a deeper and deeper view of the abyss. Craft protects one from facing those endless expanding realities of deterioration and responsibility.

Interviewer: Deterioration in what sense?

Mailer: The terror, let's say, of being reborn as something much less noble or something much more ignoble. I think this sort of terror depresses us profoundly. Which may be why we throw up our enormous evasions—such as craft. Indeed, I think this adoration of craft, this specific respect for craft makes a church of literature for that vast number of writers who are somewhere on the spectrum between mediocrity and talent. But I think it's fatal for somebody who has a large ambition and a chance of becoming a great writer. I know for myself, if I am going to make this attempt—that the only way to do it is to keep in shape in a peculiar way.

Interviewer: Can you explain what you mean by that?

Mailer: It's hard to talk about. Harry Greb, for example, was a fighter who used to keep in shape. He was completely a fighter, the way one might wish to be completely a writer. He always did the things which were necessary to him as a fighter. Now, some of these things were extremely irrational, that is, extremely irrational from a prize-fight manager's point of view. That is, before he had a fight he would go to a brothel, and he would have two prostitutes, not one, taking the two of them into the same bed. And this apparently left him feeling like a wild animal. Don't ask me why. Perhaps he picked the two meanest whores in the joint and so absorbed into his system all the small, nasty, concentrated evils which had accumulated from carloads of men. Greb was known as the dirtiest fighter of his time. He didn't have much of a punch but he could spoil other fighters and punish them, he knew more dirty tricks than anyone around. This was one of his training methods and he did it over and over again until he died at a relatively early age of a heart attack, on an operating table. I think he died before he was thirty-eight, or so. They operated on him, and bang, he went. Nothing could be done. But the point I make is that he stayed in training by the way he lived his life. The element which was paramount in it was to keep in shape. If he were drinking, you see, the point was to keep in shape *while* drinking. I'm being a touch imprecise about this . . .

Interviewer: Well . . . what?

Mailer: He would not drink just to release his tension. Rather, what went on was that there was tension in him which was insupportable, so he had to drink. But reasoning as a professional he felt that if he had to drink, he might as well use that too. In the sense that the actor uses everything which happens to him, so Greb as a fighter used everything which happened to him. As he drank he would notice the way his body moved. One of the best reasons one drinks is to become aware of the way your mind and body move.

Interviewer: Well, how do you keep in shape?

Mailer: Look, before we go on, I want to say a little more about craft. It is a grab-bag of procedures, tricks, lore, formal gymnastics, symbolic superstructures, methodology in short. It's the compendium of what you've acquired from others. And since great writers communicate a vision of experience, one can't usually borrow their methods. The method is married to the vision. No, one acquires craft more from good writers and mediocre writers with a flair. Craft after all is what you can take out whole from their work. But keeping in shape is something else. For example, you can do journalism, and it can be terrible for your style. Or it can temper your style . . . in other words you can become a *better* writer by doing a lot of different kinds of writing. Or you can deteriorate. There's a book came out a few years ago which was a sociological study of some Princeton men—I forget the name of it. One of them said something which I thought was extraordinary. He said he wanted to perform the sexual act under every variety of condition, emotion, and mood available to him. I was struck with this not because I ever wanted necessarily to have that kind of sexual life, but because it seemed to me that was what I was trying to do with my writing. I try to go over my work in every conceivable mood. I edit on a spectrum which runs from the high clear manic impressions of a drunk which has made one electrically alert all the way down to the soberest reaches of depression where I can hardly bear my words. By the time I'm done with writing I care about, I usually have worked on it through the full gamut of my consciousness. If you keep yourself in this peculiar kind of shape, the craft will take care of itself. Craft is very little finally. But if you're continually worrying about whether you're growing or deteriorating as a man, whether your integrity is turning soft or firming itself, why then it's in that slow war, that slow rearguard battle you fight against diminishing talent that you stay in shape as a writer and have a consciousness. You develop a consciousness as you grow older which enables you to write about anything, in effect, and write about it well. That is, provided you keep your consciousness in shape and don't relax into the flabby styles of thought which surround one everywhere. The moment you borrow other writers' styles of thought, you need craft to shore up the walls. But if what you write is a reflection of your own consciousness, then even journalism can become interesting. One wouldn't want to spend one's life at it and I wouldn't want ever to be caught justifying journalism as a major activity (it's obviously less interesting than to write a novel), but it's better, I think, to see journalism as a venture of one's ability to keep in shape than to see it as an essential betrayal of the chalice of your literary art. Temples are for women.

Interviewer: Temples are for women?

Mailer: Temples are for women.

Interiewer: Well, Faulkner once said that nothing can injure a man's writing if he's a first-rate writer.

Mailer: Faulkner said more asinine things than any other major American writer. I can't remember a single interesting remark Faulkner ever made.

Interviewer: He once called Henry James a "nice old lady."

Mailer: Faulkner had a mean small Southern streak in him, and most of his pronunciamentoes reflect that meanness. He's a great writer, but he's not at all interesting in most of his passing remarks.

Interviewer: Well, then, what can ruin a first-rate writer?

Mailer: Booze, pot, too much sex, too much failure in one's private life, too much attrition, too much recognition, too little recognition, frustration. Nearly everything in the scheme of things works to dull a first-rate talent. But the worst probably is cowardice— as one gets older, one becomes aware of one's cowardice, the desire to be bold which once was a joy gets heavy with caution and duty. And finally there's apathy. About the time it doesn't seem too important any more to be a great writer, you know you've slipped far enough to be doing your work now on the comeback trail.

Interviewer: Would you say that is where you are now?

Mailer: Let others say it. I don't know that I choose to. The hardest thing for a writer to decide is whether he's burned out or merely lying fallow. I was ready to think I was burned out before I even started *The Naked and the Dead.*

Interviewer: What kind of an audience do you keep in mind when you write?

Mailer: I suppose it's that audience which has no tradition by which to measure their experience but the intensity and clarity of their inner lives. That's the audience I'd like to be good enough to write for.

Interviewer: Do you feel under any obligation to them?

Mailer: Yes. I have a consciousness now which I think is of use to them. I've got to be able to get it out and do it well, to transmit it in such a way that their experience can rise to a higher level. It's exactly . . . I mean, one doesn't want one's children to make one's own mistakes. Let them make better mistakes, more exceptional mistakes.

Interviewer: What projects do you have for the future?

Mailer: I've got a very long novel I want to do. And beyond that I haven't looked. Some time ahead I'd like to be free of responsibilities so I could spend a year just taking on interesting assignments—cover the World Series, go to report a war. I can't do that now. I have a feeling I've got to come to grips with myself, with my talent, with what I've made of it and what I've spoiled of it. I've got to find out whether I really can write a large novel or not.

Interviewer: What have you spoiled?

Mailer: All sorts of potentialities. I've burned them out— squandered them, wasted them. I think everybody does. It's a question of whether I've spoiled more than my share.

Interviewer: You once said that you wished to become consecutively more disruptive, more dangerous, and more powerful, and you felt this sentence was a description of your function as a novelist. I wonder if you still think that?

Mailer: I might take out "disruptive". It's an unhappy word to use. It implies a love of disruption for the sake of disruption. Actually, I have a fondness for order.

Interviewer: Do you enjoy writing, or is such a term irrelevant to your experience?

Mailer: Oh no. No, no. You set me thinking of something Jean Malaquais once said. He always has a terrible time writing. He once complained with great anguish about the unspeakable difficulties he was having with a novel. And I asked him, "Why do you do it? You can do many other things well. Why do you bother with it?" I really meant this. Because he suffered when writing like no one I know. He looked up in surprise and said, "Oh, but this is the only way one can ever find the truth. The only time I know that something is true is at the moment I discover it in the act of writing". I think it's that. I think it's this moment when one knows it's true. One may not have written it well enough for others to know, but you're in love with the truth when you discover it at the point of a pencil. That in and by itself is one of the few rare pleasures in life.

Interviewer: How do you feel when you aren't working?

Mailer: Edgy. I get into trouble. I would say I'm wasting my substance completely when I'm not writing.

Interviewer: And to be writing . . . to be a writer?

Mailer: Well, at best you affect the consciousness of your time, and so indirectly you affect the history of the time which succeeds you. Of course, you need patience. It takes a long time for sentiments to collect into an action and often they never do. Which is why I was once so ready to conceive of running for Mayor of New York. I wanted to make actions rather than effect sentiments. But I've come to the middleaged conclusion that I'm probably better as a writer than a man of action. Too bad. Still it's no little matter to be a writer. There's that godawful Time Magazine world out there, and one can make raids on it. There are palaces, and prisons to attack. One can even succeed now and again in blowing holes in the line of the world's communications. Sometimes I feel as if there's a vast guerrilla war going on for the mind of man, communist against communist, capitalist against capitalist, artist against artist. And the stakes are huge. Will we spoil the best secrets of life or will we help to free a new kind of man? It's intoxicating to think of that. There's something rich waiting if one of us is brave enough and good enough to get there.

Norman Mailer on *An American Dream*
New York Post/1965

From the *New York Post*, 25 March 1965, 38. Reprinted by permission of the *New York Post*.

"For me, reading reviews is a little like a primitive rite. I don't mean it's a test of manhood or courage or an ability to be stoic; rather, it's like a dialogue with the gods, as all very primitive rites are."

So Norman Mailer prefaced his review of his reviewers, (two assailing *An American Dream* for every one that praised it) and started with Tom Wolfe (*Sunday Herald-Tribune*).

"I always thought Tom was a good young promising writer—and I met him once, as a matter of fact, at a friend's house, and liked him and thought he was gentle and sweet. I mention this meeting to underline the quality of my surprise when I read the review. The point is—the review is personally insulting as opposed to critically insulting.

"Now Stanley Edgar Hyman," Mailer went on, "is a real literary critic, and he wrote the worst review (*The New Leader)* of *An American Dream* that I've read so far by a critic who is a professional of the first rank. He said it was 'a dreadful novel,' and yet I read his prose with the greatest delight, because he writes well about literary matters.

"Tom Wolfe was just looking to get attention, and I'll hand it to him—he succeeded, though not in worthy fashion.

"Philip Rahv (*The New York Review of Books*) was the big disappointment for me. In the old days when I was a young writer, I used to quiver like the most thorough-going masochist at the privilege of being flagellated by a fine whip from *Partisan Review*, but Philip's review was a disgrace, because it said nothing I had not heard before, and that is the Old Folks Home for a writer who comes so directly out of the high intellectual grain of the old *Partisan Review*."

As for Granville Hicks:

"One assigns Bobby Kennedy to review a book by Jimmy Hoffa, one puts Governor Wallace in with the *Montgomery News* to give the verdict on Martin Luther King's last speech, one puts Elsa Maxwell in with the Duchess of Windsor. God bless the *Saturday Review*—they put Granville Hicks in with me.

"I'll not insult a nice old man. He has always been honorable, he has always said what he thought, and they should not have made him suffer by being forced to read my book."

Has Mailer always taken bad reviews with such jolly equanimity?

"Of course not," he said. "I think I suffered more over the reviews of *The Naked and the Dead,* even the good ones, than over the reviews for any other book. I wanted to sit down and write a letter to every critic—they had misinterpreted something I said even though they liked the book. It's only after 20 years that you begin to see it as a primitive rite.

"At its best," he added later, "reading reviews (and this is as true for bad reviews as for good ones if they are well-written) is as nourishing as a wild game dinner. I'd never dream of not reading reviews. It's like not looking at a naked woman if she happens to be standing in front of her open window.

"But I must say the nice thing about *An American Dream* is that this very special taste of mine of enjoying reviews no matter how bad they are has been electrified this time out by the extraordinary experience of getting good reviews. I hardly know what to do with such fortune. The gods are up to their tricks, I'm sure of that.

"One doesn't get a good review in *Life Magazine* or the Sunday *Times* for nothing. Yes, the gods are up to some new confidence game. But what guts for Conrad Knickerbocker and John Aldridge to say something nice about my book. There are people thinking now how best to break their heads."

Mailer then answered some questions about the book and the reviews.

Q: What do you say in the face of all this insistence that the book's hero, Rojack, equals Mailer?

A: Well, he never did in my own mind, but I can't pretend to be surprised that so many reviewers made the automatic assumption that I was writing about myself. The point is, I wanted a man who was very much of my generation and generally of my type. When one writes in the first person it's agreeable to have a character who's reasonably close to oneself, let's say as Frederick Henry was close to Hemingway, though certainly not in any manner identical.

But all similarities granted, Rojack is still considerably different from me—he's more elegant, more witty, more heroic, his physical strength is considerable, and at the same time he's more corrupt than me.

I wanted to create a man who was larger than myself yet somewhat less successful. That way, ideally, his psychic density, if I may use a private phrase, would be equal to mine—and so I could write from within his head with some comfort.

Q: How do you feel about the critics who seem to think they know better than you do how you stand in relation to your work? Aldridge and Knickerbocker, for example, seem to center much of their praise around your consciousness of creating a fiction, and the others seem to say that they thought the book was bad partly because you didn't know you were doing this.

A: To begin with, the book is absolutely a myth—I'm trying to create a modern myth. I don't want to be excessively bitchy about this, but nice little Johnny Updike knows the way to make minor league critics happy—you take a certified Greek myth, preferably a touch obscure, build your book within its frame, like a monkey in a cage, season the fodder with Greek, and you're the number one horse on the pole for the National Book Award.

But to get into the serious business of writing a book without a legend, to in fact create a legend about a modern Greek whose heroic conception of existence was formed in his childhood sitting in the caves of the gods watching Hollywood movies is considered so fantastic that the critics who liked my book felt obliged to applaud me for my courage in writing it; whereas the ones who didn't thought I'd lost all sense of reality.

I hadn't. I was merely trying to capture the superheated reality of an extraordinary set of events. In *The Naked and the Dead,* for better or for worse, I showed that I could write a realistic novel. Since then I've been interested in other things. Is it really necessary for me to go back and write a realistic novel in order to prove that I can still do it? Of course I can. Finally they got tired of asking Picasso to go back to his Blue Period.

Q: Do you think it's true, as David Boroff has said, that people will get more out of this book who've read your other things, like *Advertisement For Myself* and *The Presidential Papers?*

A: I doubt it. I think if one has really read these books, yes. But I think most people have a superficial notion of what's in them—and that keeps getting in the way. They assume I'm up to something programmatic, when in fact I'm not trying to peddle any ideas at all.

There are no ideas in *An American Dream*—there are not supposed to be. It's a novel of suspense, not of intellectual action. I wanted an intellectual for a hero who was engaged in 32 hours of continuous action and so did not have time to cerebrate. But the only idea in *An American Dream* (it is the idea which I think makes the book so repellent to some reviewers) is that love is the one human condition we never capture without paying an extraordinary and continuing price. This is certainly not a new idea. But it is desperately out of fashion now, and besides—I did my best to pose this lone idea in as vivid and unendurable a manner as possible.

Q: Would you have felt something was wrong if you'd gotten an overwhelming majority of good reviews?

A: Yes, I would have been upset. I would have wondered if I'd swindled myself in taking the book seriously. Of course my next novel may get unanimously good reviews—and then I'll have to sit down and eat these words.

Mr. Mailer Interviews Himself

Norman Mailer/1967

From *The New York Times Book Review,* 17 September 1967, 5,
40. Reprinted by permission of the Scott Meredith Literary Agency, Inc.

Interviewer: Well, here I am again.

Mailer: Nobody has seen you since *Cannibals and Christians.*

Interviewer: If you want to know the truth, I'm a little annoyed about that. You feel you can call me when you want me, and then need never invite me back for a cup of coffee in between.

Mailer: I want you to learn about social life. It is built entirely on the instrumentalities we offer each other.

Interviewer: Then today it seems I'm of use to you.

Mailer: On occasion, you are of use to me.

Interviewer: Yes, really, you bet. Today! Why didn't you get another interviewer? Someone with a name?

Mailer: Well, you always manage to get my remarks right.

Interviewer: You can also filter and select your questions.

Mailer: Leave me my pride. I am not afraid of questions. A man who can't answer questions shouldn't run for President.

Interviewer: Are you really still running?

Mailer: Only for President of the literary world.

Interviewer: Well, even there you've got a way to go. There's opposition, Mr. Mailer, considerable opposition.

Mailer: Still, I think I'm the best candidate around. It's a modest remark, believe me, because the best isn't necessarily that good. At any rate, I'm prepared to wait for office.

Interviewer: You think you're better than Burroughs or Nabokov or Malamud?

Mailer: They have very large talents, but their nose is not on the Presidency. I concentrate more than they do on that.

Interviewer: What about Bellow and Algren?

Mailer: They are capital fellows. But no one from Chicago can ever become chief executive of the literary world. The East would be in insurrection.

Interviewer: What about William Styron?

Mailer: He's the only Southern writer I know who's the living embodiment of the New York Yankees. I suspect the Establishment would be hopelessly lonely without him, for then they would not have much else but me. And I derive from the Brooklyn Dodgers.

Interviewer: You don't think Styron is a marvelous writer?

Mailer: He has a very fragrant if slightly redolent breath; but so far as I know a dangerous idea has never infiltrated his brain. His mind is happy as a virgin oyster. Oysters taste wonderful if you like them, but they stir no foundations.

Interviewer: Whereas you, sir, are a foundation shaker?

Mailer: I do my humble best.

Interviewer: There are some—I am one of them—who would say that the foundation manages to shake you up considerably more than you shake it. That photograph of you, for example, on the back of your new book, with a black eye as big as a fist on your face— well, you may think it's funny, but there's low appeal concealed in it. What you are really saying is, "Don't get too mad at me! I'm just America's No. 1 literary clown."

Mailer: I didn't see it that way, or I wouldn't have used such a picture. No, I was trying to perform a public service. You see, people go around all the time saying, "That Norman Mailer—I'd like to see him get punched in the nose." Well, it's no good for Americans to walk around with so much anger bottled up. Most charitably, I was trying to relieve them.

Interviewer: Or were you trying to relieve the anger a lot more Americans are going to feel for paying $4.95 for your novel, *Why Are We in Viet Nam?* when it's hardly 200 pages long and has nothing to do with Viet Nam?

Mailer: Do we have to rush into a discussion of my book so quickly?

Interviewer: I would expect you to prefer not to talk about it too much.

Mailer: You dislike it?

Interviewer: I think it's dreadful. It's the most cooked-up phony piece of I don't know what. I hated it.

Mailer: Maybe I shouldn't have called you for an interview. We're a considerable distance apart, and I was hoping I might find you in the middle. You see, there are times when I read *Why Are We in Viet Nam?* and it displeases me too, but there are other times when I decide it's one of the 10 funniest books written since *Huckleberry Finn.*

Interviewer: You are suffering from pre-publication schizophrenia with accompanying megalomania on the manic side of the moon.

Mailer: Not the first author to be so afflicted. Look, I don't know what to say of this book. Sometimes I think it's the best 200 pages I've yet done, the most American, certainly the 200 pages least alienated from genius.

Interviewer: You are daring to say you are a genius?

Mailer: Be careful. This is one of the ways I get my terrible reputation. I didn't say I was a genius, I rather said in effect that the positive half of my pre-publication schizophrenia looked now and again upon this new novel with the sentiment that my prose was here less alienated from genius than in my other works.

Interviewer: What does the negative side of this schizophrenia have to say?

Mailer: That the book was written to fulfill a contract.

Interviewer: You sit there and say you wrote this book to fulfill a contract? Your cynicism would make hardened politicians walk the plank.

Mailer: I wrote the book to fulfill a contract. What's so exceptional about that? My expenses are, to me, huge. I write to make a living. That does not obligatorily inhibit the work from rising above itself. I did *An American Dream* in installments because I was in debt and had to make a small fortune in a hurry. That didn't make it a bad book. I think it's my best book. I confess I still believe sentence for sentence *An American Dream* is one of the better written books in the language.

Interviewer: And *Viet Nam*, which was written in . . . ?

Mailer: Four months.

Interviewer: . . . is thereby twice as good?

Mailer: I started with a cynical motive which was first burned through and then burned out by the rush of the impulse. The pages came to me faster than any book since *The Naked and the Dead.*

Interviewer: But you still have a divided mind on its merit?

Mailer: Some books come to you. As *The Naked and the Dead* came to me. They are bonuses, gifts. You do not have to kill some little part of your flesh to dredge them up. This is a fatal shade mystical, but it is almost as if you are serving as agent for a book which wants to get itself written. So the author never knows what to think of such books when he is done. His real fondness—since writing books is the closest men ever come to childbearing—is more for those books he delivered out of his own flesh, torn and deadened by the process, but able at least to use all art and craft, all accumulated lore. Whereas *Why Are We in Viet Nam?* came through like a storm, writing itself—I enjoyed the work, I was full of energy when I was done, but the work was by the same token impersonal. So I do not know if I love the new novel or am indifferent to it.

Interviewer: Let us go back to the idea that you were serving as an agent for a book which wanted to get written. What then is this book saying?

Mailer: I'm afraid it is saying that America enters the nightmare of its destiny like a demented giant in a half-cracked canoe, bleeding from wounds top and bottom, bellowing in bewilderment, drowning with radio transmitters on the hip and radar in his ear. He has a fearful disease, this giant.

Interviewer: What is it?

Mailer: Greed. Vanity.

Interviewer: What else?

Mailer: The Faustian necessity to amass all knowledge, to enslave nature.

Interviewer: And what is the first vice of this giant who, in your words, symbolizes America, and has now become the metaphor *pro tem* of your new novel, *Why Are We in Viet Nam?*, a work—at last I can get this in—about some Texans who go off on a hunting trip in Alaska. What is the first vice of this giant who symbolizes America?

Mailer: Arrogance. Half the people in this country think they are possessed of genius. It is no accident, you see, that I run for President of the literary world. *(Sighs.)* I wish you liked my book more. Then I could open up and tell you all sorts of interesting little things about it. But as it is . . . oh, well, *(the faintest strain of self-pity appears)* they say Beethoven talked to himself.

Why We Are Interviewing Norman Mailer
Mike McGrady/1967

From *Newsday,* 7 October 1967, 3, 20, 30. Reprinted by permission of Mike McGrady.

Norman Mailer is a writer. This fact is too often overlooked. Even by those who should know better. Critic Wilfrid Sheed calls him that "well-known pitchman and lay missionary" and critic Richard Gilman sees him as "one of the prices we pay for widespread literacy." Critic John Wain introduces the phrase "stunt merchant" and columnist William Buckley says he is "a terribly good measure of the current disturbances in the air, a sort of lightning rod." Sonny Liston has called him, with affection, "a bum," and Norman Mailer has referred to himself, with at least equal affection, as "a slightly punch-drunk and ugly club fighter who can fight clean and fight dirty, but likes to fight."

However, at least one expert on matters literary, Sinclair Lewis, felt that Mailer was a writer, and more than that, "the greatest writer to come out of his generation."

Somehow it remains difficult to place Mailer in the world of writers. The photomontage of his life, the newspaper-eye view of Mailer, reveals another world or, rather, other worlds. Here he is now, arm-wrestling with Cassius Clay beneath a steaming Puerto Rican sun: and again, in the deepest midnight of his life, being escorted into a police station to be charged with the near-fatal stabbing of his wife; again, sleepless, slightly plastered, trading insults with Sonny Liston the morning after a championship fight; then, constructing a scale-model city of the future with $700 worth of toy blocks; and renting Carnegie Hall for a night, advocating regularly scheduled medieval jousting bouts in Central Park as a possible response to the increasing delinquency of juveniles: and showing up with a magnificent black eye after a saloon brawl, then using this photo on the jacket of his book—an insane variety of worlds, of pictures, and when was the last time you saw a photo of Mailer sitting, perhaps reflectively, behind a typewriter?

Which may be why so many people have difficulty approaching a new Mailer novel as something that a writer has done, as a product of a man's craft. It is as though the books came from extraneous worlds, as though they were additional stunts, as though they were not written but ejected, simply tossed out from the whirlwind of his life. And Mailer does little to discourage this line of thinking. He announces that one novel, *An American Dream*, is going to be written under the pressure of monthly deadlines for *Esquire* magazine. And that his brand new novel, *Why Are We in Vietnam?*, was written in barely four months to, in his words, "fulfill a contract."

The critics, unsurprisingly, are overjoyed when Mailer writes or ejects a new novel. It is their opportunity—no, by God, it is their *duty*—to slap his wrists, punish him for his extravagances, for all that time spent in such curious and obviously *non*literary pursuits. Arm-wrestling with Cassius Clay, indeed!

And Mailer, none the worse for wear, comes right back at them with his chin. A recent self-interview printed in *The New York Times* found him announcing once again his candidacy for the presidency of the literary world: "Still, I think I'm the best candidate around. It's a modest remark, believe me, because the best isn't necessarily that good." Critics, of course, take to this kind of thing like a duck takes to oil. And printed directly above Mailer's remarks was a review by Anatole Broyard: "His career seems to be a brawl between his talent and his exhibitionism. Like Demosthenes, who exposed himself during his speeches in order to hold his audience, Mailer has made his life a blurb for his books."

Which seemed to set the tone for many of the reviews. It is, after all, much easier to review a man's life than to review his books. For one thing, it requires less reading. There were some comprehensive reviews of his life (in sum: exciting, reckless, not for the fainthearted) but they ran into some difficulties when they came to the book, *Why Are We in Vietnam?*

"I've given up predicting what they're going to say"—Mailer talking—"I try not to think about the reviews when I'm working; it'd just tighten my hand."

This first meeting of Mailer is more than a small surprise. The suit is pinstriped and there's a vest. The initial impression is one of gentleness and it doesn't go away. He is more matter-of-fact than one would have guessed, more tolerant, quiet without ever seeming subdued. For a man who has spent time on the dark side of the literary moon, for a man who once announced plans "to attempt an entrance into the mysteries of suicide, incest, orgies, and Time," there are no visible marks. At the moment he was talking of critics.

"I know that no matter what I write, I'm going to get mixed reviews. The only question I ask is are they going to be better or worse than the last time."

After the last time—that was *An American Dream*—the direction had to be up. The harshest critic of that novel was Tom Wolfe, a young feature writer who raked Mailer over the coals in *Book Week*, and wound up by comparing him, and not favorably, to the author of *The Postman Always Rings Twice*.

"I never mind a bad review so long as the reviewer stays in bounds," Mailer was saying, "but that one bothered me. When Wolfe started in telling me how to write—when he said it would have been better if I started the book on page 14—well, I objected to that. It struck me as kind of . . . punky, smartass, you know."

A writer's importance is frequently measured in influence, his impact on other writers. Echoes of such stylists as Hemingway and Salinger will be heard well beyond this century. Mailer's style of writing fiction has not settled into any mold; the pattern keeps shifting; there is no trail for the young writer to follow.

His influence as an article writer, however, can be seen everywhere. What he did seems simple in retrospect; he took his considerable skills as a novelist and used them unstintingly in reporting. And what came out was more than facts that can be reduced to numbers. There was background, mood, sound and smell, secondary levels of meaning, ethical considerations, personal insights, all the peculiar truths that a novelist can bring to a work of fiction. His work in this area has made it possible for the best newspaper writers—Jimmy Breslin, Pete Hamill and . . . yes . . . Tom Wolfe—to enter areas that were barred a few short years ago.

"You know, I realize," he said, "that my style of article writing has influenced more people than my fiction style. When I started doing articles, I didn't see why I couldn't use my equipment as a novelist."

What can happen when Mailer uses the equipment was seen in his study of the 1960 Democratic convention, "Superman Comes to the Supermarket," a sustained flow of word and image—

"Yes, America was at last engaging the fate of its myth, its consciousness about to be accelerated or cruelly depressed in its choice between two young men in their forties who, no matter how close, dull, or indifferent their stated policies might be, were radical poles apart, for one was sober, the apotheosis of opportunistic lead, all radium spent, the other handsome as a prince in the unstated aristocracy of the American dream. So, finally, would come a choice which history had never presented to a nation before—one could vote for glamour or for ugliness, a staggering and most stunning choice—would the nation be brave enough to enlist the romantic dream of itself, would it vote for the mirror of its unconscious . . . " and so on, never letting up, all stops out.

Later, a visit to the 1964 Republican convention: "The Goldwater girls and boys were for the most part innocent, and they tended to have slightly protruded jaws, not unlike Big Barry himself, and blue eyes—an astonishing number had blue eyes (was the world finally coming to the war of the blue-eyed versus the brown-eyed?)—and they were simple, they were small-town, they were hicky, the boys tended to have a little acne, an introspective pimple or two by the corner of the mouth or the side of the chin, a lot of the boys looked solemn and serious, dedicated but slightly blank—they could fix a transistor radio, but a word like 'Renaissance' would lay a soft wound of silence, stupefaction in their brain. They were idealists, nearly every last one of them but they did not speak of the happier varieties of idealism; one thought of Lutherans from North Dakota, 4-H from Minnesota, and Eagle Scouts from Maine. Many of them wore eyeglasses."

Through the years Mailer has talked incessantly about a major new book, *the* major new book, the one that would establish him as undisputed president of the literary world, the new post-Hemingway champ, but increasingly his attention turned to more current matters. He started a newspaper (*The Village Voice*), wrote a monthly column for *Esquire* ("The Big Bite"), labored over a long philosophical treatise on hipsterism ("The White Negro") and released a steady flow of articles and essays reflecting the author's deepening involvement in the ailments of our country and our time.

"He's a great reporter and descriptive writer," Malcolm Muggeridge was to observe, "He can be very funny, language is something he manipulates fiercely and masterfully like a lasso. But he's a man of our time: too caught up in life to live . . ."

So embroiled is Mailer in our time, so anxious to identify and diagnose our national ailments, that *the* book has been postponed and postponed again. No sooner is one malady isolated and diagnosed than a new one, possibly cancerous and fatal, appears and he is off again. And, of course, there is a great deal of self-diagnosis going on constantly.

"Yet every year the girls are more beautiful, the athletes are better," he has written. "So the dilemma remains. Is the curse on the world or on oneself? Does the world get better, no matter how, getting better and worse as part of the same process, or does the world get better in spite of the fact it is getting worse, and we are approacing the time when an apocalypse will pass through the night?"

The disease now on the land is Vietnam. And Mailer's *Why Are We In Vietnam?* is his diagnosis. There are some critics who have complained that the title is misleading, that the book is about a hunt for grizzly bear in Alaska, not about Vietnam at all. They feel compelled to point out that the word "Vietnam" was mentioned only twice, both times in passing, both times in the book's final paragraph.

But what then is the book about? The story, told in scatological stream-of-consciousness, consists primarily of the thoughts of a young Dallas boy, named D.J., who is "up tight with the essential animal insanity of things," a boy who feels that, "if the center of things is insane, it is insane with force."

The hunt itself, the heart of the book, is conducted in the modern manner, with the assistance of helicopters and elephant guns. It is comedy, lunatic comedy, and it closely follows D.J.'s definition: "Comedy is the study of the unsound actions of the cowardly under stress just as tragedy is equal study time of the brave . . . " *Not* about Vietnam? It's about, among other things, violence and brutality, fear and power, thwarted and misdirected sexuality, the Texas way of thinking—it is Mailer's attempt to answer the question posed by the title.

Mailer's examination of the problem has nothing to do with territorial disputes, international treaties, deep commitments, conflicting ideologies and all the other phrases so dear to the politician's heart. It is perhaps a more chilling explanation. For if Mailer is right this country needs the assistance of a competent psychiatrist more than it needs a world organization.

He was asked if he was accusing President Johnson of arrogancy and brutality.

"LBJ is an ugly, tragic man," he said. "He's a tyrant enmeshed in the coils of his own tyranny. But I've always felt he was more vain than arrogant. Vanity, that's one of the bad emotions. Being arrogant, that's less bad. Being brutal, that's less bad. But vanity is dangerous. Being vain, he's going to surround himself with people who'll feed his vanity and that's dangerous because it means he's getting worthless information.

"I said this better in a speech at Berkeley two years ago. I think I was the one who first discussed, let us say, the dimensions of LBJ's insanity. My thesis was that Johnson is alienated. When one is alienated he is beset by a host of opposite ideas. No one is more alienated than the adolescent—he feels that he is both very brave and very cowardly, that he is attractive to girls and unattractive to girls; and when one is alienated there is enormous pressure to define one's nature through one's acts. That's one reason alienated nations go to war to define their own nature."

Norman Mailer says this with absolute assurance. It is possible—no, it is more than possible—that he knows a thing or two about alienation, about defining one's nature through acts, about violence.

"I don't like to talk about violence," he said. "I really don't want to. Almost every interviewer tries to get me to talk about violence. It's like putting a sexologist on television and they ask him how does he enjoy making love to his wife and he says, 'Yes, it's wonderful and yes, we have a constructive and wonderful relationship and we make love three times a week and that's wonderful . . . '—you know, and you don't believe a word he's saying.

"I really don't have that violent a life. My 3-year-old son, he has a mean punch. He leans back and . . . *bang, bang, bang* . . . but that's about all the violence in my life now. Look, I'm the father of six kids."

Mailer was pressed on the matter. His thoughts on violence do not seem irrelevant—they would surely be of use to the critic looking for an understanding of either his work or his life. Time was running short, however, and he postponed the discussion until the following day. Then, however, he seemed not reluctant at all.

"I think the reason we're having the war in Vietnam," he said, "is because we need it. We need a war—I'm talking about our country—need a war for our health. And I'm not saying that this is necessarily altogether bad. War is the ultimate extension of The Game and it has a certain primitive meaning. It's a way of resolving the problem of alienation. You can pretend it's a war to save people from communism but there's a profound hypocrisy at the core there.

"I'm not saying it's a good thing. It's no joy to most people. It's a waste. You know, I always seem to get in this position of defending violence . . . what I'm getting at, one has to look into the eye of violence to see its meaning. The meaning of violence is the original desire to master nature, if you will, to create a civilization. I think a civilization is created out of some kind of sublimation of violence. When the violence gets too sublimated, you get a sick civilization. In other words, the problem of civilization is how to have the expression of some modicum of primitive violence. And that's what gets me into all those tangles."

It is possible that violence is a symptom, a surface manifestation of alienation, that alienation itself is a symptom of something else. Mailer's explorations have not led to particularly cheerful conclusions. He once put it into words this way: "Well, it has been the continuing obsession of this writer that the world is entering a time of plague. And the continuing metaphor for this obsession—a most disagreeable metaphor—has been cancer." Last year, during another interview, he switched metaphors: "I think the condition of America is close to the condition of a man who is going to go psychotic in another year or two unless he finds love."

"Yeah, I remember I winced when I read that," he said. "That's a little too oversimple, a little too well-rounded, a little metaphorical. That kind of remark is too overpolished for use. I read that and I thought, oh Christ, here we go again."

Well, how is America psychotic?

"Let's say if a man is . . . no, if a man has got bodies up in the attic and he goes up and chews pieces out of them every night, then he comes down by day and he's a pillar of the town, we'd have to say that guy is psychotic. But what are we doing now? We're not only destroying a country, but we're literally destroying the foliage of that country. We're destroying God's work, not man's work but God's work. And at the same time we're pretending to be the deliverers of civilization. So I'd have to say we are psychotic."

The answer, the finding of love, also seems a trifle pat, a little too well-rounded. And, in fact, Mailer sees no such happy conclusion for the country. He sees the possibility of an end to Vietnam but looks for no miracle cure for the country.

"The insanity of it may begin to affect more and more people at home," Mailer said. "More and more people are beginning to think that it's gone too far, that there's something gravely wrong with it, something psychotic. But I don't think there'll be any huge turnabouts. What might happen, the country might be just a little bit less horrible in a couple of years. Me, I'm going to worry about the air pollution problem for a while."

Mailer, McLuhan and Muggeridge: On Obscenity
Bob Fulford/1968

From *The Realist*, 83 (October 1968), 5-12. Reprinted by permission of CBLT-TV, Toronto, Robert Fulford, and Corinne McLuhan.

Note: Following is the transcript of a program entitled "The Way It Is" which was broadcast recently over station CBLT-TV in Toronto. The panel consisted of Norman Mailer, Marshall McLuhan and Malcolm Muggeridge. The moderator was critic Bob Fulford.

Moderator: Marshall, you said a few minutes ago that obscenity is the way that young people establish their identities. Just what do you mean by that exactly?

McLuhan: Well, rough-house and rushing encounter with rough aspects of life is a great thrill for youngsters because it does help them to get a feeling of themselves . . . an image of themselves . . . body percept. Rough-house and rough language and rough activity . . . this is a great means of self-discovery. One peculiarity about obscenity, if you notice, is that whereas the individual obscene word is very involving, very tactile, very smelly, very rough-textured . . . it is always a part of the human body. It consists in breaking a bit off the human body and this is a bit of violence and roughage just as profanity is a kind of breaking of prayer into bits, into fragments, in order to create this rough thing.

Moderator: But Norman, you actually invented an obscenity or came close to it in *The Naked and the Dead* . . . you used the word fug, F-U-G.

Mailer: Yes, yes.

Moderator: About 400 times in that book as I recall it, and it's become part of the language since then, and there's a musical group called The Fugs.

Mailer: I know, some of my best friends are the fugs.

Moderator: . . . but you're still involved. How, incidentally, how do you like them using your word? I mean didn't you copyright it or something?

Mailer: They're welcome to it. The word has been a source of great embarrassment to me over the years because, you know, Talullah Bankhead's press agent, many years ago, got a story in the papers which went . . . "Oh, hello, you're Norman Mailer," said Talullah Bankhead allegedly, "You're the young man that doesn't know how to spell . . ." You know, the four-letter word was indicated with all sorts of asterisks and, you know, I became a sort of household joke. It was the first of my notorieties. And I regretted it. I was inflamed with Miss Bankhead for years as a result. I thought she should have hired a publicity man who had a better sense of fair play.

Moderator: Yes, that's ah . . .

Mailer: At any rate, the word never gave me any pleasure. I used it because I felt that it was a fair word to use to give the quality of the Army experience, which was not dramatic, which did not consist of breaking things off, of making clubs out of words, it was not used to intimidate . . . it was used to fill certain spaces in the thought waves that you had in the Army. In other words, it really, it was really a way of filling gaps. It was . . . it was used to give a kind of rhythm in speech. It has nothing to do with obscenity.

McLuhan: By the way, there is a peculiar aspect of the obscenity business . . . mainly that nudity is not obscene. And it's only the partial fragmented appearance of the body that is obscene.

Moderator: Or titillating, even.

McLuhan: Yes. Nudity, in fact, in England I believe, Malcolm, they have a strange law that any nude on the stage, as long as it does not move . . .

Moderator: They used to have that law.

Muggeridge: That was the rule, that was the rule, but of course we've moved on a step. It was the rule that if you were nude and kept absolutely still, it was okay. But having reasons why it's difficult to keep still if you're nude. One of them might be because it's cold.

McLuhan: Well, if there's a fly around or something.

Muggeridge: Absolutely right.

Mailer: Well, Malcolm, can I ask a question? What would happen if you kept absolutely still, but conditions in which your nudity was discovered was . . .

Muggeridge: Oh, I see what you're getting at now, exactly. And I think that would have created a special problem but as the people who were nude and kept still were female . . . this trouble didn't arise. I must suggest about this that Marshall was rather suggesting that obscenity is something that the young indulge in; but I should have thought that it was much more the old and impotent who have a taste for obscenity, and that far from seeking an identity, they were in fact trying to compensate for or stimulate appetites that were there.

McLuhan: Or recapture an earlier one.

Muggeridge: Recapture an earlier one, maybe, but I would have thought that most obscenity was in fact for the old and the impotent and often produced by them. I don't think the young produce much obscenity, although they may appreciate it.

Fulford: Well, they use it now. Certainly children use it now as a way of putting on their parents, or getting to their parents. They know if they say certain words their parents will have to pay attention to them. In that sense, you're finding identity, even a nine-year-old or a seven-year-old learns this in our culture.

McLuhan: They're invading a mature world.

Moderator: Yes, but he's establishing himself as a personality who has to have attention paid to him, even though he's . . .

Muggeridge: That's a very ancient thing, isn't it? I mean that famous wall in Pompeii, the obscene words written up there, it's an old and standardized practice.

Mailer: I disagree completely with Malcolm. It's not the old who use obscenity to delight themselves. I don't know any old people who go around using obscenity, getting themselves excited. Oh, maybe some poor old drunken bum here and there; but no, I think it's more . . . I think obscenity is about the last game preserve of class. You'll notice working people use it much more than the middle class people.

Muggeridge: Oh, Norman, you're hopelessly out of date there.

Mailer: Well, I know that's what I'm always, that's what I'm always told; but nonetheless I must persist in my opinions even if they're out of date.

Muggeridge: Cling to your dreams, dear boy. You're a great clinger to your dreams but if you watch the poor souls going into an obscene cinema show you will find that they are most of them well over sixty.

Mailer: You're talking about sexual lucubration. I'm talking about the act of using obscene four-letter words. We're talking about something else.

Moderator: Really two different things entirely.

Mailer: I'm not talking about lucubration now.

Muggeridge: You mean just using coarse words?

Mailer: Yes, yes. Using the four-letter word.

Moderator: It's a working class thing; but it's certainly spread into the middle class today. I mean, those middle class students at Berkeley, California had . . . were putting four-letter words on signs and they had their free speech movement and so on. It's become almost a symbol to a certain kind of young person to use these words all the time and in casual talk.

Mailer: I know, but I think what they feel, I mean I'm presuming to speak for them and I have no right to, but I would just suggest that what they may be feeling is that the reason this is a political move, because we doubt very much if it's a political move, was that these words are used by the working classes who contain the vitality which makes the earth move around. They want to be a part of this working class. They want to get away with middle class hypocrisy. I mean, this middle class hypocrisy is not worth it.

Muggeridge: That was rather the D. H. Lawrence idea, wasn't it?

McLuhan: Yes.

Muggeridge: I think he was the fount for all this rubbish, wasn't he?

McLuhan: And by vitality, let's remember, it is basically tactility and down beat, and these people had never taken the time to specialize their sensory lives by literacy.

Moderator: Malcolm, you said, you said D. H. Lawrence started all this rubbish. I wouldn't have thought it was rubbish at all. I had the idea that there was something in this sexual revolution that was of value.

Muggeridge: Not at all.

Moderator: Nothing, nothing at all?

Muggeridge: Nothing whatever. I mean D. H. Lawrence was just a poor soul. He himself was a well known impotent.

Muggeridge: Working class boy who was mad to cease to be working class and who has provided an alibi for all the middle class people who try to pretend today they're not middle class. I mean he's, in a sense, he's performed a great service, you see. He's given them this tremendous alibi but the whole thing is absolute nonsense. His idea was that this was a sign of virility.

Mailer: Obscenity?

Muggeridge: Yah, well . . . and using these words and all that sort of thing. You know, his gamekeeper. This ridiculous character, Mellors, was a splendid virile man who took girls into the woods . . . whereas poor old Chatterley . . .

McLuhan: Paleolithic man? Hunter.

Muggeridge: Hunter, hunter. Poor old Chatterley had been wounded in an awkward place and therefore was immobilized in ah, in a chair. And this was the image of the middle class. But what's happened is that the book is a joke to Mellors, people like Mellors, but has been fallen on avidly by all the people like Chatterley.

Moderator: Well, of course there . . . they did sell a few hundred thousand copies of it, presumably some of—

Muggeridge: They sold millions in the end because then . . . by that time it had got a sort of reputation of being an exciting . . .

McLuhan: Malcolm, that period was very fond of the word *escapism*—in letters and entertainment—and it is now a word that one never hears.

Moderator: Not very much. No.

McLuhan: The word *involvement* has taken over.

Moderator: It's, it's . . .

McLuhan: . . . and I think this has a lot to do with D. H. Lawrence.

Moderator: Actually, you have a lot to do with that involvement.

McLuhan: Just commenting on it . . . nothing more than that.

Muggeridge: But *involvement* is certainly the word now.

Moderator: It's a very big word . . . that and media. Mixed media. When I hear the word *mixed media*, I reach for my revolver.

Muggeridge: When I hear the word *revolver*, I reach for my media.

McLuhan: Wait. We're—we're exemplifying that mixed media right here by dialoguing in front of the cameras. Ah, you can't get any more mixed than that.

Moderator: Well, that, that's an interesting point you . . . about the use in *Lady Chatterley* of the working classes as vital and so on, but isn't it a very close parallel, Norman, to the White Negro idea that you had in which you saw Negroes in that famous essay of yours as having a certain potency. Isn't the Negro the working class for America?

Mailer: Yah. Well, what I, what I said on the White Negro . . . now, really looking back at it now, was that Negroes are more primitive in relation to life on several counts. One, because he came from primitive culture just a couple of, it was just . . . a couple of years away from primitive culture. But the other was that he says he had none of the benefits of American life, his relation to life was much more primitive in the more general use of the word. It was much more hungry. It was much more vivid. It was much more existential. It was much more naked and therefore, since his . . . he had very few of the sophisticated pleasures of the modern world. He had to go into the basic pleasures if you will of existence such as sex.

McLuhan: Well, ah . . .

Mailer: There's no use getting around it that the Negro's culture has been a profoundly sexual one and it was built on a different premise than the white culture. But I hate to talk like an anthropologist because I'm not one. I'd rather tackle Malcolm Muggeridge on *Lady Chatterley* and obscenity and all these matters because I think that we know . . .

Moderator: You have some disagreement with Malcolm on these points?

Mailer: Oh, well, I have, I have one with Malcolm and that is . . . his remark about *Lady Chatterley* being a work of rubbish. You know, Malcolm's great charm is that he is perfectly capable of taking a beautiful egg and throwing it in the air and he never looks to see if it lands, you know . . . I mean he's extraordinary that way because most people will turn around and look to see what they did to that egg. Malcolm won't. You just took one of my eggs and threw it in the air.

Muggeridge: Norman, you're not seriously saying that you think that *Lady Chatterley's Lover* is a good novel, are you?

Mailer: I think it's . . . it's one of the five or ten greatest bad novels ever written and that's a category I'm particularly fond of, since it's possible I've written a great many great bad novels myself.

Muggeridge: Isn't that what old . . . isn't that what old Sontag is
always talking about?

Moderator: Great bad novels? No. No, I don't think that's it,
although . . . but what you have in mind is a novel with a
tremendous charge in it. A tremendous something in it that does . . .

Mailer: A tremendous flaw.

Moderator: A tremendous flaw which . . .

Mailer: . . . both very very good and very very bad.

Moderator: Yah.

Mailer: I think what's very very bad in *Lady Chatterley* is that
Lawrence just travelled half the road and the other half of the road is
altogether yet to be negotiated—which is, when you have an
extraordinary sexual relationship, the next thing that starts happening
is that you start having an extraordinary violent relation to life.
Women being what they are, sex being what it is—all these things
collapse upon one another and you get extraordinary dramatic . . .

McLuhan: Would you agree, Norman, that the bad novel tells us
an awful lot about a lot of people and the good novel tells us a little
about a few people?

Mailer: No. I wouldn't agree with that at all.

Muggeridge: I'm rather inclined to agree with you there, Marshall.
Once I think that the bad novel . . . you can learn a lot about life
from bad novels. I think that people learn a great deal about this
stupid age from *Lady Chatterley's Lover.*

Moderator: You mean 200 years from now if we survive, they can
look at it . . . very coolly and so on . . .

Muggeridge: . . . but they'll look at it and they'll see first thing is
that there were very intelligent men like Norman Mailer who actually
took this novel seriously, therefore there must be some reason.
That . . .

Moderator: . . . that in itself will be a sense of comedy.

Muggeridge: . . . would be the enormous interest.

Mailer: Why are you curious why I took it seriously? Is it just
because I don't have a rubbish detector in my nose?

Muggeridge: That, that is partly it. Your rubbish detector is not all
I'd like it to be.

Mailer: My education at Harvard was unsatisfactory.

Muggeridge: Yes, I like to . . .

Mailer: Uh, if I'd gone to Oxford would I have a better rubbish detector?

Muggeridge: No. Much worse, much worse. I'm absolutely sure of that. Oxford and Cambridge are the worst . . . the worst possible places.

Moderator: Certainly you don't think at Oxford and Cambridge one learns to find out what's honest and what isn't?

Muggeridge: Quite honestly I don't think you learn anything of any value. I would really be quite happy if they were shut down for a bit anyway to get a sort of pause and for a lot of the Dons to die off.

McLuhan: Surely one of the advantages of those places is dialogue. You do have an opportunity there to converse with an amazing variety of people without the benefit of too many courses.

Muggeridge: You do, but at the same time, it's all set in a certain pattern which makes, in my opinion, what amounts very largely to brainwashing.

McLuhan: Yes, but those who take the exams and curriculum very seriously, they're brainwashed of course.

Muggeridge: But even the Dons, the sort of talk that goes on . . . the talk that goes on . . . I think this is very dubious.

McLuhan: Yes, but there's also an awful lot of talk that goes on about them. You can participate in that too.

Muggeridge: Yes, that is of course to be preferred.

Moderator: Are we facing a situation where Marshall McLuhan is defending traditional institutions? Is this the situation I'm observing at this point?

McLuhan: I'm an alumnus of Cambridge.

Muggeridge: So am I, actually.

McLuhan: Are you?

Moderator: You feel you've cured yourself now, have you?

Muggeridge: Well, I didn't like it there and everything I learned about it since . . . has made me feel that it's a very dubious place to go to. Very dubious.

McLuhan: Would you prefer if you were a young man today . . . you would prefer an opportunity to attend a university in some other part of the world.

Muggeridge: Well, if I were to be very candid with you, Marshall, which I am going to be, I wouldn't be . . . I'm not very keen on

education at all. I mean, I think it's a sort of mumbo jumbo of our
age, you know. It's a sort of . . .

McLuhan: It's becoming big business.

Muggeridge: Big business . . . exactly what it is . . . and as
such . . .

Moderator: Bigger every day too.

Muggeridge: Bigger every day and as such performing no
function that I feel it ought to perform, you see. Uh, it's a sort of, it is
a sort of, as such, religion. It's as though everything that happens,
you know I spend a certain amount of time on these fatuous panels
of the BBC. Did you ever see those when you were in England? You
know, four people sit like this and someone in the audience said, "Do
you think polygamy is a good thing?" and then you sort of scratch
your head and Mrs. Stocks says, "Well, I met some very nice tribes, I
met some very nice tribes who uh . . ."

McLuhan: Do you feel that we are managing to avoid the fate of
those panels that you mentioned?

Muggeridge: A little, a little. Not too much.

McLuhan: Do the universities obtain their relevance from the
culture in which they're placed? And would you say the North
American culture has become the center of the world now?

Muggeridge: Yes I would. Unfortunately, unfortunately, I would
say this.

Moderator: Fortunately or unfortunately, it seems to work that
way increasingly in the arts too. In painting today, for instance, there's
no question of what the capital of the world is . . . New York City. No
question at all.

Muggeridge: The capital will always be where the power is. I
mean that is where the artists gravitate. When we were rich and
powerful, we English . . . we used to be . . . everybody's forgotten
about it now . . . went there.

Moderator: T. S. Eliot went there and people like that.

Muggeridge: For what it's worth.

Moderator: Well, it wasn't worth a great deal?

Muggeridge: I got into terrible trouble, Norman, for saying that he
was the death rattle in the throat of a dying civilization.

Mailer: I'm the death rattle?

Muggeridge: T. S. Eliot is.

Mailer: Oh, I'm sorry. It's my confirmed narcissism.

Moderator: Not to say paranoia as well.

Muggeridge: You're not the death rattle.

Mailer: I was hoping Malcolm would think enough of me to consider me a death rattle. The honor belongs with Eliot much more.

McLuhan: I would say on the whole that Eliot was a pretty festive rattle. A real crackling good rattle.

Muggeridge: He was a death rattle, wasn't he?

McLuhan: No. I wouldn't say so.

Muggeridge: Really?

McLuhan: Oh, for heaven's sake. This present time, we're moving into this electric age, in the dawn of much the greatest of all human ages. There's nothing to even remotely resemble the scope of human awareness, of human greatness . . . at this time.

Moderator: No, no. There we are . . . a value judgment.

McLuhan: Yeah, I'm . . . no, this is quantity. Most people make their judgments in terms of quantity. Now I'm merely saying quantitatively, this is by far the greatest human age. What further evaluations would you wish to have brought to bear?

Moderator: Well, I thought when you said *greatest* that you mean finest. That is, would be more admirable than the renaissance or Florence, or something like that.

McLuhan: We're a thousand times greater than the Victorian age.

Muggeridge: In size.

McLuhan: In size.

Muggeridge: But not in quality.

McLuhan: I don't know.

Muggeridge: You don't know.

Mailer: We may not . . . you know there might be some way of, let's say, if there is a good Lord it's possible He might measure these . . . have a handful of air that appeals to Him. He might take a handful of air in Winnipeg and say, "Marvelous air." He might pick up our air and say, you know, "All the fume exhaust."

Muggeridge: Well, I must say, Norman, if that were being done, contrary to what Marshall has said, I would say that if the good Lord was sniffing a sort of cultural quality of an age that He would turn away with the utmost distaste from the aroma that He'd get.

Mailer: I agree with you. I agree with you.

Moderator: You mean you have . . . you not only can imagine that there is a Lord, but you can imagine that you know His tastes?

Muggeridge: No. I wouldn't say that. I imagine that there is a Lord. I profoundly imagine that but I don't know His taste, but I think that contrary to what Marshall has so brilliantly suggested in all his writing . . . I think there are absolute standards in this thing, culture, in art, and that there are standards you can measure one age against another and that we happened to have lived, no great, no great misfortune really, we happened to have lived in what amounts to the Dark Ages.

Moderator: Well, Norman Mailer is one of the people who is contributing to the Dark, or otherwise, Age we're in and one thing is that film called *Wild 90* and the thing that interests me about it is that it's so obscene that you still think there's going to be some sort of censorship case in the courts.

Mailer: The language in it is obscene. The picture itself is absolutely chaste. My wife is in it, you know. I mean there, as a matter of fact, this picture is probably too chaste to be of interest to most people . . . visually that is. I mean nothing goes on. There are a couple of kisses in the entire picture. That's all. But the language. The language in it is absolutely . . . if people have a taste for obscenity, the language is absolutely sensational. You know there must be something like 500 four letter words used in 90 minutes.

McLuhan: In terms of texture and quality of effect, what is your feeling about this part of the picture? This component?

Mailer: Well, one of the things now . . . it has an extraordinary effect on audiences. The most unusual sort because, first of all, they've never had the experience before. No one in an audience has ever seen a movie which has this much obscenity unless it's some sort of experimental movie. But our movie is fairly conventional. It's about three gangsters who are holed up in a loft and they are seeing other gangsters and people come to visit them, family, police, friends . . . and in the course of the movie, the swearing just goes on and on. It's just one of the elements. It's like the whistling of the wind outside.

Muggeridge: This interests me very much. The tastes that the contemporary bourgeoisie have for obscenities spoken in a public performance. This was the case with Lenny Bruce. You must have been to Lenny Bruce's shows. Anyway, I have. I don't know whether you have, Marshall. The thing about it that struck me was exactly what you say. He was a kind of tragic, tortured moralist, wasn't he? And there was this terrible sort of bourgeois audience, for instance—I saw him in Chicago—waiting for him to use these words, you know, and every time the word came out, giving an awful kind of shiver out of it. I noticed the same thing—I was telling you, this terrible poetry festival that I compered in London two weeks ago—the same thing when these words were used. The audience was absolutely typical, sort of Arts Council audience . . . ladies up from Tunbridge Wells . . . very respectable ladies. They sat there waiting for Ginsberg to use these words. Now there must be a reason . . .

McLuhan: Obscene words are profoundly mixed sensory experiences and they . . . that's why they, empathically, they hit you in the midriff.

Mailer: I've got a few friends who are fairly . . . what I would call guys who are really, fairly tough guys, you know. They love the picture. They laugh and laugh and laugh and laugh, and they laugh because, you see, there's one thing that goes along with obscenity that makes it altogether different from these dances, I think, which is that the dances finally involve a direct sexual provocation, you know, and I say their appeal is slightly below the midriff.

Muggeridge: Of course. It's . . . they're erotic.

Mailer: Whereas obscenity, if we're going to talk about the part of the body, it's the shoulders. For instance . . . (Now, Marshall, let me make this point as it has just occurred to me; I'd hate to lose a point the moment I get it) which is: an obscenity, after all, speaks of people beating you over the back with a club or punching you and the reaction that many people get when they are cursed at is to punch. It's sort of a tension through here you see. What happens is that tough guys after all, I'll use this word, I mean hard guys, whatever you want to call them, walk around . . . they have a great life with their shoulders. They're always moving with their shoulders. No, it's absolutely true.

Muggeridge: I know. It's absolutely true.

Mailer: So what happens is that, therefore, obscenity is one of the ways they have of moving their shoulders. They're always sizing each other up. They jolt each other with obscene talk back and forth and what comes out of it is a whole series of showdowns back and forth because tough guys are always acting. You see, a tough guy isn't always tough. He wakes up with a hangover. He's in love with a girl. He's feeling soft all over. He's his worst enemy. (Marshall, let me just nail this down because I'm really on it now.) And so they have to act and they know more about acting instinctively than most audiences, and so they love, they love this picture with all the sinning going on because we were playing three gangsters who just kept putting each other on all the time, each pretending to be tough and then the other would poke through or not poke through it and so, for them, it was a comedy of manners. Whereas other people in the audience, what it meant . . . people who had a delicate sensibility, what it meant was that this world is really quite horrible and one of the reasons it's horrible is because there's such a marveous logic to this obscenity. It goes on. It's so Laocoon. It is indeed a comedy of manners and this comedy is atrocious.

Moderator: How is it that it is now possible to consider actually showing a movie like that today? I mean six years ago you wouldn't even have thought of making it would you?

Mailer: Well, there's been an extraordinary acceleration . . . This is Marshall McLuhan's field so much more than mine, but there's been such an extraordinary acceleration of environments and one of them has been this, if you will, these permissive environments in the arts. I mean, each shell replaces the shell the year before.

McLuhan: And when you put a new one around an old one, as you're doing right here, you get a new art form.

Mailer: Yes, I think you're . . .

Moderator: I've never been able to quite understand how these permissive shells are created though. Do you know . . . have you any theories on that, Malcolm?

Muggeridge: My feeling about it is completely different. I mean I think this is just what happened to decadent civilizations, you see, and I don't think . . . I think just . . . It's characteristic when a civilization is running down, which I firmly believe our western civilization to be, on the one hand the sort of bourgeoisie, the establishment loses its nerve, is on the run and therefore it wants on one hand, as we were saying about D. H. Lawrence, to try to identify itself with its social inferiors and on the other it's going to get the shock, and it gets the shock out of these four-letter words.

McLuhan: While we are . . . the old one is running down though, Malcolm, we're creating a new one and . . .

Muggeridge: Are you sure, this is perhaps . . . well, Marshall, I wonder, you see . . .

McLuhan: You see the electric age is highly integral. The old mechanical age was fragmented and special. We're a highly integral civilization and this is what distresses people who belong to the old specialist disintegrated one. They can't find a little place for themselves.

Muggeridge: Yes, but are you sure, you see, are you absolutely sure that this is the birth struggle of a new civilization? Are you absolutely sure that it's not just the break-up, not just the break-up. That's what I think is perhaps the whole difference between North America and Europe, really . . . is that you over here do believe that. You do, you do.

McLuhan: You have a bigger stake in the old technology.

Muggeridge: Well, we're inclined to think that all these things you imagine to be of such enormous importance, like for instance, this thing we're doing now on television because there's a lot of people goop at television . . . for hours every day. You're inclined to think that's an enormously important thing. I just think it's a sign of the kind of vacuity that comes when a civilization breaks, like the circuses in Rome. If there had been a Marshall McLuhan then, you see, Caius Marcius McLuhanibus, he would have written a great book about the circuses and he'd have said, "There's this new civilization . . ."

Moderator: There's no medium.

Muggeridge: No.

McLuhan: No. They had no new technology. Ah, the . . . that's . . . Caesar, by the way, educated the Gauls by war . . . this is the approved western method of educating backward areas, is warfare, and Alexander the Great did it the same way. Napoleon, I was reading a book on the Russian revolution the other day in which the author was explaining enthusiastically that the great forward thrust in Russian institutions came from Napoleonic inventions and then from the Crimean War. What is happening in Vietnam now is a great educational forward thrust from us on the war front . . . on the war path.

Moderator: It's very pleasant to think of it that way.

McLuhan: I don't think, I don't . . . I think it's a horribly . . . it's like roast pig, you know Charles Lamb's theory of roast pig . . . "Burn your house down."

Muggeridge: Yes . . . and I'm a bit inclined to agree with you but I don't think it's done consciously. I think that's just . . .

McLuhan: Oh, no, we never do anything consciously.

Muggeridge: No, no, no, but what I mean is this is not, I mean you would see this as the manifestations of some new way of life.

Moderator: Would you say that this North American society is basically optimistic still . . .

Muggeridge: Yes, I would.

Moderator: . . . and European is basically pessimistic?

Muggeridge: In very general terms I would. Here I'm sticking my neck out but I'm going to say this. Marshall may disagree with me strongly but I'm going to say this. That you over here do believe that the environment men create governs their nature and their lives. I don't believe in that. I think that this is only a very small part.

McLuhan: We are of 18th Century origin and it was precisely at the time that Rousseau invented the theory that the environment was the great educator.

Muggeridge: That's right and a lot . . . a load of rubbish it was. Absolute rubbish, which has produced the present chaotic situation.

McLuhan: Nature as a teaching machine is now capable of being programmed by human intentions.

Muggeridge: But these too, in a way, Marshall, are just words. I mean you program it. Men program computers. You mean they put in something and then the computer . . . but you see that is a non-creative process.

McLuhan: But it's like programming lighting levels, sound levels, temperature levels.

Moderator: This is an idea to be welcomed.

Muggeridge: My great point that I'm trying to make is that, that is not life. That's a surface thing, you see, and I think that life is about something much more than that.

McLuhan: It's like saying though, isn't it, that disease is not just a matter of symptoms. On the other hand, if you can get rid of all the symptoms, who cares what disease he has.

Muggeridge: Yes, but the fact is that, the simple fact is, taking that analogy, is that treating the symptoms does not cure the disease. Very often, if you just treat a symptom and get rid of it, you get another. It's the disease itself that matters. In fact, that's very much what I'm trying to say.

Mailer: I think I probably would agree with you generally that the world is an extraordinary bad place right now and it's possible that we're sitting on the last twenty years of anything we know or understand.

Muggeridge: Very likely.

McLuhan: It could be twenty minutes.

Mailer: Well, I know, but quite without any apocalyptic end to the world I think we can sort of poison ourselves.

McLuhan: Do you think with an apocalyptic it's a mere speedup in time? Escalation?

Mailer: Well, whether it's twenty minutes or twenty years, what I'm getting at is, because it is a desperate time, I think that a conservative like yourself has got to regard one possible . . . has got to look one aspect of it squarely in the eye, which is this . . . that they will take extraordinary measures to save this world and that one of the reasons the world got into this impasse is because of a profoundly conservative view of existence which went on for several hundred years and finally failed in a most profound way. Even though it may have been right it may have drawn the line too high. You see, for example, if you go back to obscenity, at least there's a little useful reference as we all know what we're talking about. There's something about obscene language that I find personally offensive. In other words, when I look at this movie sometimes it made my skin crawl. I said, "How the hell could I get involved in a movie like this? I can't bear to listen to it. It offends a good half of me." It did. It was something about the repetitiveness of it. It was obscenity without charm . . . there's not a great deal of wit in it or something. It just goes on. It's like a . . . it's halfway between a leaky sink and a gutter. The language is. All right, one of the things that goes on is, one of the things I'm trying to say is that line about obscenity was drawn too early and too high, you see, and too much of this line was kept out of polite intercourse and because it was kept out it festered and took on anomalous forms and it may be the . . . one of the things we have to do now is we have to dig up all this language and find ways to use it so that there's no longer a ridiculous tension and hypocrisy attached to it. I'm not . . . I'm not saying this is going to save the world. Obviously, it's not, but it's one of the 10,000 things that may have to be done.

Muggeridge: First of all, let me say to you that I am not a conservative in the sense that, let me make it absolutely clear. There's no time in the past that I thought . . . think, was wonderful.

Moderator: But you must think there were times that were a lot better than this one.

Muggeridge: There were times when human society has

integrated and times when it's disintegrated. There are times when
civilizations are waxing and times when they are waning and it's
enormously good to live in all those times. In fact, I seem to detect in
Marshall's writing . . . that point that there's such a lot to be learnt
from a phase of life which may be to you very repugnant. But what
I'm concerned to say only is this, that in this part of the world you are
inclined to say, now as Marshall does, 200 years ago printing was
invented.

McLuhan: Five hundred.

Muggeridge: Five hundred years ago printing was invented. Life
has never been the same since then.

Mailer: Absolutely true.

Muggeridge: I don't agree with that. I think that printing or
television or all these things may affect the surface of men, but the
fascination of life to me is the exact opposite that I find in Socrates
and St. Augustine and all these people who lived before printing.

McLuhan: But not before writing.

Muggeridge: Well, if you like.

McLuhan: By the way, there's a wonderful book called *Preface to
Plato* which just mentions in passing that Socrates' great contribution
was to the dialectic . . . was the ability to say, "Would you mind
repeating that please?" This kind, the Socratic irony, the Socratic
questioning was a playback. With the coming of writing, the
possibility of playback came into human society for the first time.
Socrates was very much a product of technology, new technology.

Muggeridge: I wouldn't dispute that, Marshall. I wouldn't
presume to dispute it but I would say that if you, as far as I've been
able . . . in a very sort of amateur way to read and think about
various contributions to knowledge which have been produced at
different times, the thing that astonished me about them is the huge
area which is the same, which is constant, and how narrow is the
area that belongs to particular environmental changes whether a
civilization is in a very stable or advanced state or whether it's in a
chaotic state.

McLuhan: Remember the phrase "Polite Society" when that
came in? This historically meant a society that established its values
on the word of the behavior that was capable of inspection that
would bear looking at and polite society no longer is with us because
we no longer live in a visual culture, and so the values of polite
society are for the birds and I'm not free of the nostalgic look back at

some of those old values. On the other hand, I can see why they've gone down the drain and I can see why new ones are forming right under our noses and I can see why the new ones create such revulsion, total recoil.

Muggeridge: I think that very often today in the western hemisphere things that seem to me to be surface things are thought of as decisive, see what I mean, and that I think is because of a whole different attitude of mind and philosophy of life if you like. Perhaps you could simplify it. I've often thought of simplifying it in this way, you know. There are two questions that you can ask about life, really. You can ask the question *how* and you can ask the question *why*. But I'm passionately interested in the question *why* and I'm not interested in the question *how* . . . but I think you over here are enormously interested in the question *how*.

McLuhan: What about the matter of appearances . . . do they matter?

Muggeridge: Not terrifically, but they're interesting. They don't matter.

Moderator: What about Norman Mailer's assertion that all this trouble we're in the world now is caused by 300 years of conservative ideology?

Mailer: I didn't say that.

Muggeridge: He didn't say that, actually. He said that this conservatism had existed and had been unable to correct what was happening and he's quite right.

Mailer: I think it's solved the problem too superficially, if you will. In other words, it created a life which worked reasonably well. In fact, looking back it worked very well for a large number of people but it didn't work well enough, finally, for the entire world.

Muggeridge: The conservative has never known what he wants to conserve, anyway. What would you conserve today if it were possible to be a conservative in . . .

Mailer: Oh, I know exactly. I am a conservative. I know exactly what I'd like to conserve.

Muggeridge: What would you conserve, Norman?

Mailer: The trees, first.

McLuhan: It's not a political sentiment.

Muggeridge: No . . . but we may need you to protect them.

Mailer: No, I think that's a very good test of a conservative, which is if you present him with the problem . . . somebody comes up to you and says, "Look, here are five men and here are five trees, which are you going to execute?"—you know, and you answer, you say, "Well, I don't know, let me look at them."

McLuhan: Speaking of this strategy . . .

Muggeridge: . . . but you'd have to execute the trees.

Moderator: Then you are a conservative.

Mailer: No, I wouldn't have to execute the trees.

Muggeridge: Yes, you would.

Mailer: No sir, no sir.

McLuhan: There's a wonderful sign hanging on a junkyard in Toronto which says, "Help beautify junkyards—throw something lovely away today." I think this is a thought that conservatives need to consider.

Mailer: There's a point I do want to make. You know, when you talk, Malcolm, you talk blissfully about how nothing has really changed. We're still marvelous and this is all superficial stuff . . .

Muggeridge: No, I didn't. Norman, now steady, my boy, steady.

Mailer: Alright, alright, I'm exaggerating what you said.

Muggeridge: I said the area of life which didn't change was much greater than is normally supposed.

Mailer: Alright, fair, right. I'm saying that I think you're absolutely wrong on that. I think you're wrong for what particular reason which is what's going on from the birth of writing to the present time is that man has become more and more aware of himself in the superficial narcissistic sense and he's become more and more the instrument of his own will. Every invention you point to, writing, printing, radio, all the means of communication, keep enabling us to become more and more aware of our relation to the universe. In other words, the feedback, as McLuhan is always saying, is really the center of that whole thing, but the more feedback man gets the more he ceases to be man . . . becomes something other and the nature of man is that he begins in the state of innocence.

McLuhan: I'm amazed. I think, Norman, you assume that man is the content of the universe.

Muggeridge: He's not.

Mailer: Well, I think of course . . . I have certain . . . that you won't agree with at all but I think . . . man was the crown of the universe at a certain point. I think he was the noblest invention of God.

McLuhan: But that the universe was in profound sense an extension of man.

Mailer: No, I think the universe at one time was an extension of the Lord.

Muggeridge: Do you think the Lord is gone?

Mailer: Well, I think the Lord, being a sporting gentleman, obviously if he was going to get into any contact with the Devil, it would have to be where he wouldn't have absolute control over the game. You have to start the game on equal terms with the Devil, otherwise there's no real game.

Muggeridge: You see, Norman, it was that Lord . . . the thing . . . the phrase . . . one of the phrases I most chose, you see . . . "As it was in the beginning, is now and ever shall be." It's a marvelous phrase.

Mailer: That makes you much more the conservative than me.

Muggeridge: No, it doesn't make me a conservative. It makes me believe the truth and it was that Lord that you're talking about, you see, and this is really what I'm trying to say . . . that of course, all these things happen . . . of course civilizations come and go. Of course human beings make the most extraordinary inventions, move faster, move slower, have ways of projecting their thoughts, telephone each other, talk to each other.

McLuhan: Speed reading.

Muggeridge: Yes, speed reading, the whole gamut. But still you have it. In all seriousness, what I'm trying to say is, "As it was in the beginning, is now and ever shall be." In other words, there is an enormous area of life which is constant and that is both what has enabled human beings to survive which is an extraordinary thing and out of which also comes their religion.

Mailer: Gentlemen, you must give me the last word. I have just received the signal. I've got to get on my horse and gallop off to the aeroplane.

Muggeridge: I'm sorry you're going, Norman.

Mailer: No, no. I want to get the last word.

Muggeridge: You shall have it.

Mailer: Lord willing that I have a last word . . . I may not.

Moderator: Yes, but you have this microphone problem.

Muggeridge: Yeah, but he's got to keep it on for his last word. I want to hear your last word because I shall cherish it.

Mailer: Well, it seems to me that the only notion of existence that makes for any fun at all, any sense of dignity, is that the universe started not as a noble conception but started as an extraordinary contest. In other words, if you have a God, this God would have to engage evil in order to absorb some of it, so there would be less evil in the universe when it was all done and we of course are the embodiment of that contest between good and evil.

McLuhan: We are the blotter that's to sop up the evil part.

Mailer: Well, no, no, I think it was left entirely for grabs, if you'll forgive that profound vulgarity. It was up for grabs and I think we're losing the game, or at least I think the Lord may be losing the game. I think these are desperate times . . . and on that cheerful note I'm going to grab that plane.

Muggeridge: Yes, it is cheerful note. Goodbye.

Moderator: Actually, one thing that point brings up, it's always astonished me about the climate in which Norman Mailer's novels are received, is that he is a completely religious novelist and the only one in America and it's quite impossible, in fact it's done every year, to review or discuss Norman Mailer's books without discussing religion.

Muggeridge: Of course it is. I have always said to him, he's a Rabbi. He's a Rabbi.

Moderator: I think, I think it's because God is in bad taste in North America now.

McLuhan: I think we're heading into a profoundly religious age.

Muggeridge: I'm almost certain of it.

Moderator: You're certain that we're heading into a profoundly religious age?

McLuhan: Yes.

Moderator: Why is that?

Muggeridge: Well, because I think that this, I mean, I think that human affairs proceed by a sort of *reductio ad absurdium* and I think materialism will reach its *reductio ad absurdium* and in reaching this *reductio ad absurdium* in order that the opposite proposition begins to be attractive. There are very clear indications of this, all round, including evil, this sort of business of, these drugs and things, which in my opinion are very degraded.

Moderator: LSD and so on.

Muggeridge: It's fatuous. Expressions of the desire, but the message of it to me is that, in all of them, is this purely materialistic

view of life is not valid, it won't work. It won't satisfy and therefore
some will turn to it sooner. Sooner or later transcendentalism, in
some form or another, is bound to come as the alternative.

McLuhan: The matter itself has become somewhat porous.

Muggeridge: Certainly. Certainly.

Moderator: So you think the young people who are
experimenting with drugs and so on are groping their way towards
some kind of religion?

Muggeridge: Absolutely. I mean, they are saying in effect that the
materialist Utopias, on which mankind really lived, I mean western
man lived from Darwin onwards . . . no longer interest or attract me.

McLuhan: Consumer's paradise.

Muggeridge: Yeah, they don't interest or attract me. Therefore I
seek some other . . . living in an essentially foolish society, he thinks
that you can swallow a pill or smoke a cigarette and achieve that . . .
of course you can't. But still the impulse is there.

Moderator: What do you think about the young people who are
in this hippie thing? You're one of their favourite people. Are they
among your favourite people?

McLuhan: Well, I can't say that I have given them too much cause
for comfort, or I haven't done very much besides observe what they
are . . . what sort of form their behavior seems to indicate is behind
their life. And, I can see clearly that their desires have a very much
more rich social life, involvement in social life, and the mere finding
of little niches and jobs and so on, will not satisfy them.

Moderator: Aren't they becoming tribalized? You say the whole
world is, and they're actually doing it. And, they even use the word,
don't they?

McLuhan: I don't know, but tribal is not a new form exactly, but
post-literate tribal is a very different matter from pre-literate tribal.
And, we're tribalizing simply by virtue of a much closer family . . . a
sense of the human family.

Muggeridge: This is what I was going to say. This is the thing.
This is the essence also of religion. That it says to man you are not
alone; you are a member of a family.

Moderator: How can you reconcile your idea that this is the end
of a civilization with the idea that we're coming into a great religious
age?

Muggeridge: Supposing we were sitting on this place here, talking at about, in about the Second Century. Alright, I, taking the views I do, would have said—this Roman civilization is absolutely over and done with and can no longer produce any sort of ultimate satisfaction. It is materially successful, it's militarily strong, it's spiritually empty—and you would have said,—well, that's a most extraordinary thing to say. I mean, where's your alternative? Now, we wouldn't have known about the alternative. The alternative were these extraordinary obscure events which took place in a remote part of the Roman empire of which nobody has heard. A religion of slaves. And yet, that was going to produce 2,000 years of high civilization so far known, so that, when I say that I think our civilization is breaking down to something like, the Dark Ages, are descending upon the earth, I'm by no means precluding the possibility or even the probability. Something of that kind will be happening, but we shouldn't know about it.

When Irish Eyes Are Smiling, It's Norman Mailer

Vincent Canby/1968

From *The New York Times*, 27 October 1968, sec. 2, 15. Copyright © 1968 by The New York Times Company. Reprinted by permission.

In "Beyond the Law," his second improvised documentary feature, Norman Mailer, as Police Lieut. Francis Xavier Pope, turns on a prisoner and laments in a brogue that is both mocking and sorrowful: "What's a good Irish lad like yourself doin' becomin' a beast!" The moment produces the kind of "feedback"—the multiplicity of responses—that Mailer says is not only the future of films but also the condition of our times.

The scene has its own reality, like someone who lurches through a subway car wearing a fur coat in August. But it also has another dimension—the Mailer-as-Pope dimension, which, like an old acquaintance, can never quite be forgot, as it wasn't the other afternoon when Mr. Mailer, the novelist-movie-maker-actor, sort of loped through the lobby of the Algonquin Hotel on his way to a luncheon interview.

In that civilized, West 44th Street forest preserve, where people sit—their knees at the knock—around pocket-sized picnic tables, eating peanuts and drinking Bloody Marys, instead of egg salad sandwiches and warm beer, the collected personalities of Norman Mailer seemed completely integrated and at ease. He knows most of the Algonquin's waiters by name, and they know him, and life is perhaps more satisfying for him now than it has been at any time since *The Naked and the Dead* was published 20 years ago.

The boy champ, who was given the count of 10 by many critics for *Barbary Shore, The Deer Park* and *An American Dream*, is back on top. His *Why Are We in Vietnam?*, a beautifully ribald novel, and *The Armies of the Night*, an account of the October, 1967, march on

139

the Pentagon, in which Norman Mailer, in the third person, is the comic hero in history, have been as well received as anything he's ever written. In addition, his "Beyond the Law," which has just opened at the Art Theater on 8th Street, is prompting many movie critics to change their minds about the man whose first movie, "Wild 90," was a catastrophe.

At 45, Mailer is getting somewhat thick through the middle, but he still walks like a boxer. When he talks, he uses verbal italics and sounds a little bit like Don Adams, the TV comedian, imitating a humorous, hyped-up sportscaster reporting the end of the world, play-by-play. At the Algonquin lunch, he was wearing a nondescript gray suit and a white shirt with a gray tie that seemed to have been knotted in the dark. His curly, wiry hair, now quite gray, is long and looks more unpressed than uncombed. The conversation was about movies, Godard's, Warhol's, Lester's and, of course, Mailer's—his own, as well as the ones that have been made from his novels.

" 'The Naked and the Dead' was the *worst* movie Raoul Walsh ever made," he said flatly. "It didn't have enough of *Walsh*, and it *certainly* didn't have enough of *me.*" On the advice of friends he had stayed away from the movie version of "An American Dream." "It's a curious thing, because I'd always thought of it as making a *marvelous* film. When I wrote the novel, I had decided to take a pretty conventional movie story, or movie melodrama, and make it into a realistic novel, but when they made it into a movie, they did some *criminal* things, like filming it in Los Angeles when the *whole psychology* was New York. I mean, a guy just wouldn't push his wife out a window in Los Angeles—for one thing, there aren't that many *high* windows!"

Although he spent a year in Hollywood in 1949-50 (where, among other things, he was working on an original script for Sam Goldwyn "and quit one minute before I got fired"), the novelist did not turn to films himself until recently, largely at the prompting of Jonas Mekas, the movie industry's Savonarola and the guru of underground moviemakers. (Mekas originally called Mailer "the new Greta Garbo," but feels that with his second film the novelist has gone Establishment).

At Mekas's urging, Mailer started attending screenings at the Filmmakers' Cinematheque several years ago to see what was being done by the underground film people, including the pre-"Chelsea

Girls" Andy Warhol. Warhol's "The Kitchen," the novelist feels, "may really be the best film made about the 20th century" and "is almost unendurable to watch." As he describes it enthusiastically: "The camera is locked into position at an irritating middle distance, Edie Sedgwick and some other people are sitting around the table. Edie has the sniffles and keeps blowing her nose and this other guy keeps opening and closing the door of the refrigerator. They talk and you can't understand a word. You almost can't bear it, but . . . when in the future they want to know about the riots in our cities, this may be the movie that tells them.

"I learned a lot from Warhol," Mailer said. "He made every director brave enough to make a slow scene without trying to speed it up."

Slowness was just one of the faults critics found in "Wild 90," Mailer's first directorial effort. Mailer, however, seems to feel that a bad soundtrack was really the main problem with "Wild 90," a one-room talkathon in which the novelist and his friends, Buzz Farbar, Mickey Knox and Jose Torres, played Mafia types. "In the first 45 minutes, you got three guys talking in a room and you can't hear what they're saying," he laughed, and added: "It sounds as if *everybody* is talking through a *jock strap.*

"However," he continued, "the bad reviews were probably the best thing that could have happened to me. I'd just finished shooting 'Beyond the Law,' had gone on the Pentagon march in October, and worked on *The Armies of the Night* in November and December. Then I came to New York in January for the opening of 'Wild 90.' I thought it was going to get a very pleasant reception." He paused and smiled as he recalled his shock. "Instead, I got cockamamied in the alley! *Bam! Boom! Boy,* those *mothers* [the critics]! I found out I was in a tough racket. So I thought, if it's a tough racket, get tough. Stop clowning around. Up to that moment, I'd sort of enjoyed the fact that I was a little bit of a clown."

In getting tough, Mailer spent six months editing "Beyond the Law" with Jan Welt, a young filmmaker whom he credits for much of the success of his second film, along with D. A. Pennebaker and Nicholas Proferes, who, with Mr. Welt, were the cameramen. "It's not that I learned so much, but that I learned where to look for advice and how to take it."

"Beyond the Law" is, in effect, a documentary fiction film, a

feature-length improvisation about one night in a Manhattan precinct
station presided over by Mailer-Pope, a steamy Irishman given to
flights of fantastic lyricism as he and his detectives, Buzz Farbar,
Mickey Knox and others, work over the night's catch. It's a series of
terrifying and funny confrontations with wife-murderers, gamblers,
perverts, prostitutes, pimps and innocents, played by a rare
assortment of professionals, including Rip Torn and Beverly Bentley
(the fourth Mrs. Mailer), and amateurs like George Plimpton, Jack
Richardson, Michael McClure, Edward Bonetti and Peter Rosoff.

The movie was shot in four nights, at the end of which there was
11 hours of film to be edited down to the present 105 minutes.
Because the script existed only in Mailer's mind, the end result is a
kind of psychodrama led by Dr. Mailer-Freud.

"Writing," according to Mailer, "is a very *odd, spooky* activity, and
when you get to filmmaking, you realize that the spookiness is tripled,
especially in improvisational moviemaking, which can't be formalized.
It's luck. What you have in your favor is all the lifetimes of the people
working with you. What you have against you is the fact that you
don't have a script, so you need all sorts of skilled practitioners of
your art besides yourself."

Mailer's moviemaking activities, he says, have had absolutely no
effect on his writing style, except for his decision to treat himself as
the third person hero of *The Armies of the Night*. When he sat down
to write that, he had already edited "Wild 90" with himself as the star
and he had come to see himself "as a piece of material, as a piece of
yard goods. I'd say: 'Where am I going to cut myself?' It's a way of
getting a psychoanalysis, I think."

He also thinks that this kind of improvisational filmmaking could
serve a useful social purpose: "One of my favorite theories is, if I were
king, or *mayor* of New York, or if I had the *ear* of the mayor of New
York, I'd get some people to put a lot of money in movie equipment
and give it to these kids in tough neighborhoods and let them make
movies. Nothing too organized. No scripts—they'd just be a hang-up.

"The blacks, for example, are *absolutely incredible* at
improvisation. They improvise *every* single incident of their lives.
They play *put-ons* like an *88-key piano*. They'd be perfect doing this
sort of stuff. White middle-class people play put-ons too, of course,
but we've got nothing but *felt* on the keys. The song may be

marvelous, but it's so marvelous that if you're not white middle-class, you can't hear *what the hell* is going on."

In "Beyond the Law," Mailer, whose background is New York Jewish, plays the very New York Irish Lieutenant Pope, a kind of middle-aged extension of Sergius O'Shaughnessy, the Irish Mailer-ego figure in *The Deer Park*. At first he seemed a little reluctant to explain his Celtic bag. "I've always loved the Irish and felt very close to them, but I never like to question things that sort of work. If I feel affection for somebody or something, I prefer not to question it, because the affection becomes *calculated*. In other words you're sort of *domiciling* the affection.

"The Irish have always had what the Jews didn't have, and the Jews have always had what the Irish didn't have. The Jews have this *funny knowledge* that if you respect life enough, it's going to respect you back. The Irish have never understood that. On the other hand, the Irish have this *great bravura*, a *style*, an *elegance*. If I were playing a Jewish detective, I could never use the kind of language that Pope indulges. I thought if we were going to do improvisation, the only point is to show what you can do with the *language* of improvisation. An Irishman can say anything he wants at any given moment, and no one is going to argue with it too much. In other words, as an Irishman I can have moral conversations with my prisoners that I could never have if I were any other kind of detective." The novelist suddenly became Mailer-Pope. "What's a fine Irish lad like yourself," he said, rolling his r's out across the Algonquin dining room, "doin' becomin' a beast?"

Mailer, who has just completed his book about the Republican and Democratic conventions and now is editing his third feature, "Maidstone," mentioned the films of Jean-Luc Godard, in particular, his newest one. " 'Weekend,' " he said and smiled, "re-established my modesty. *It just knocked me on my rear!* For the first half-hour, I thought it was going to be the greatest movie I'd ever seen. Then it gets very Godard again—the monologues in front of the garbage truck. He seems to be saying, aghast: 'What am I *doing! Entertaining my audience!*' "

"Weekend," according to Mailer, is very definitely a movie with feedback. "Feedback," he explained, "is when you're watching the kookie girl and the doctor in 'Petulia,' you're also aware that they're

Julie Christie and George C. Scott, and that *enriches*. The awareness
of that extraordinary dolly shot along the highway in 'Weekend' also
enriches. It's totally without bumps or jiggles, absolutely smooth, like
an *angel's flying*. The fact that you're wondering *how* he shot all
these cars and wondering *where* he got them and *what* were his
relations to the French government when he was negotiating to put
all these cars on the highway—that's part of the film.

"I'd go so far as to argue that feedback has become the condition
of our lives. That it's the movies. We've passed the point in civilization
where we can ever look at anything as an art work. There is always
our knowledge of it and of the making of it."

And, Mailer says, an essential part of a movie's feedback is that
provided by the star system. "One of the reasons movies became the
20th-century phenomenon is the feedback provided by the star
system. The star system created the movies, which, up to then, were
just an interesting technological invention."

Asked if he thought of himself as a part of that system now, Mailer
answered: "In a certain sense, of course, I am. Since I've been a sort
of *notorious*—if you will—*character* all these years, it was inevitable
that I should make movies." He laughed fully at the removed, third-
person Norman Mailer. "I wouldn't be *fulfilling my duty* as a . . .
public character if I didn't."

The Latest Model Mailer
Joseph Roddy/1969

From *Look*, 27 May 1969, 23-28. Reprinted by permission of Joseph Roddy.

Of course. Quite a few understand. The world is not ready yet for Norman Mailer. But it will just have to get ready faster. For over 20 years now, the man who thought he might be the dwarf alter ego of Lyndon Johnson has been up there in his pulpit pointing at running sores on the body politic. And still they run. But there is a little more listening in the church now. He doesn't really have to shout so much. And if those he drove out years back with some public outrage or other—my God, but there have been some hard ones to forget, haven't there?—if all those people will just come back again and apologize for their thin souls, the flock (he calls them his troops) will be at least formidable.

At least formidable? That is the sort of WASP-y involutesy way Mailer never puts anything. So let the class take note please, that in this illustrated lecture there will be no scrivening in the style of the old master from the house by the docks in Brooklyn Heights. That vast body of orgasm lore he engendered will be left unalluded to, and the hipster-as-hero will not enter. Many, many things will be left out— most of them important. To soak in every suffering one of them, read the *omnia opera* of the rabbi himself.

You know what he looks like. He's the man at the left in the garb of a fop with a scowl of power coursing about him. He is suffering some holy fool probably, some apologist for the entrenched piety. Or maybe the complainant out there is a wild woman doubting his courage. It is not good for others to question that, but he does it better anyway, and often. This sweaty rogue is the acknowledged free-style champion of broadcasting evangelically and almost steadily all over creation. But he is a big listener, too, even a fearsome one. Don't ever lie to him, they say. And watch your truths, too. So while

145

he listens here, he is probably sizing up his victim for the retort. It might be obscene, it might be epigrammatic, it might be some mad join of the sacred and profane. But most of the world forgives his offenses. It is just the brainy sports who deliver him over to encounters they call existential because no one knows how they will come out.

There are some inspired ones. Long lists of petitioners have made Mailer a candidate for the Board of Overseers at Harvard, where he was graduated in 1943. If elected, he will serve with the likes of Douglas Dillon, Paul Nitze and Francis Plimpton from the peaks of the Establishment. Then those eminences will undergo the existential experience of having among them one who has been clapped in jail for barroom brawls, who put his wife to the knife some years back, and who made his miscalculations anent the plumbing on the men's room wall in a Washington theater into a superb Rabelaisian scene in *The Armies of the Night*. That is a scorching analysis of America's creeping dread. It won the National Book Award.

At Yale, Mailer is already an associate fellow of Calhoun College. When the floor of the Law School auditorium was not big enough for his audience a while back, panting educables ripped doors off hinges to overrun the balconies. The author talked in his brogue, then switched to his cracker demagogue-ese. "You're drunk," one heckler shouted, and another taunted with reminders that he was getting $500 for his performance. Mailer's recurring comeback was . . . you can work it out.

At Notre Dame, Mailer spoke the night after Lyndon Johnson said he would quit, and he liked his President for triggering the hope that he was pulling a gambler's trick—or an existentialist's—to end up niftily reelected. "Better to have a President who is a large and evil man than one who is small and ignoble," he said. He talked eruditely of the overlaps of his existentialism and their Catholicism. Mailer believes Catholic teaching is about right on birth control, and he believes in the very real existence of hell and the devil—hard points of dogma that get a lot of disbelief around Catholic campuses nowadays. The devil and God are at war right now, Mailer thinks, and he is not sure God is going to win. To end up the night, he read from a work of his laced with all the scatology they still try to keep out of South Bend. So much for the Catholics and Mailer.

Now to the Jews. At the end of a long article in *Commentary* recently, on the decline of the New York intellectuals—most of them Jews—Irving Howe points to Mailer as the force they lack the strength to confront. "He is not an easy man to come to grips with, for he is 'our genius,' probably the only one," Howe writes, "and in more than a merely personal way he is a man of enormous charm. . . . What has not been forthcoming is a recognition, surely a painful one, that in his major public roles he has come to represent values in deep opposition to liberal humaneness and rational discourse."

Liberal humaneness is not far from middle-class inhumanity in Mailer's mind. And the rational discourse Howe believes in is, to Mailer, just the language of the techni-structure. Mailer thinks every ideologue finds such tags for him the way drunks find lampposts and dogs get to automobile tires. (The images are Mailer's, of course.) Once at them, every drunk and dog can perform his act because each, if only for an existential instant, has a firm relation to his own past. "By the same token," Mailer says, "the ability to call cops 'pigs,' or for Bill Buckley to get his mouth around 'fight Communism,' or the corporation to refer a new problem to an old committee serves the illusion that one still bears not only some relation to the past, but that the past will provide a guide for the future. It is not that I am against what Irving Howe means by liberal humaneness and rational discourse—as a practical matter he means hardly anything more than courteous manners. But what he is really looking for is a world he has lost, and I would remind him that I didn't kill it. I just saw that it was going because it was inadequate."

Mailer is the large-sculed man of his times who will not stand aside and let inadequacy close in around him without trying to do something large and soulful about it. Again he thinks he has to be the mayor of New York. The first time was some years back. The idea had its run that time as a bold jest at first, then as a yeasty possibility until Mailer's second marriage cracked apart. His lust for public office did not vanish. It was just forestalled by his notoriety, then replaced by his belief that he was really a behind-the-scenes type, a Colonel House or a Cardinal Richelieu, who should have the ear of the man in the White House. The idea of how good that association would be for the U.S.A. came over Mailer back on the other side of the New Frontier. He had satisfied himself that an admiring piece he did for *Esquire* tipped in the few votes that got Kennedy the job. "Right or

wrong, I thought it," Mailer wrote last year, and he still thinks it. All
he wanted was some gratitude, some drinks and dinner and a chance
to preach to the President. After all, he knew what was happening in
the country, and he thought Kennedy could learn.

That chance never came. Mailer thinks he was ostracized for a
burst of candor brought on by a polite note from Jacqueline
Kennedy. She urged him to write some impressionistic history along
the lines of his review of her husband's campaign. "I replied in the
cadence of a Goethe," Mailer wrote, "that while I was not engaged in
certain difficulties of writing about the present, I hoped one day when
work was done to do a biography of the Marquis de Sade and the
'odd strange honor of the man.' "

The Marquis de Sade, by all that's execrable! And for the
edification of the pre-sanctified Jacqueline Kennedy! A mad intention
that. Mailer got no reply, and was refused the next time he asked to
interview the country's last hope for a Madame de Sévigné. But
worse came fast. A string of wrong moves by the President he put in
office saddled Mailer with the conviction that the key to his fellow
Harvard man's success was that Kennedy was simply the first to
detect what this show-biz-ridden country wanted most—yes, a
Leading Man.

A few years later, with that Kennedy gone, then his brother Bobby,
the unconsulted adviser grappled with a larger idea, a really big
existential encounter this time. It was that he, Norman Mailer, father
of six, husband *seriatim* of four, author of much, and, hands down,
the only one around set on forging the uncreated conscience of this
race, that he could be his country's Leading Man.

Why not? A slow transformation of the man's writing stance from
novelist (*The Naked and the Dead*) to essayist (*Advertisements for
Myself*) to journalist (*The Presidential Papers*), and then into a blend
of all three with touches of the allegorist thrown in (*Why Are We In
Vietnam?*) was stripping him of any fears he ever had of winding up
the writer-in-recluse somewhere. He was becoming the writer of
unlimited visibility. Anyone who missed seeing him on panel shows
and the like could still catch him in his poetry readings or his protest
marches, and in his movies. If they hurried. *Wild 90* was the first he
made. It is not altogether good, yet not all that bad for a start.
Beyond the Law followed, and a lot of critics and most of Mailer's
friends thought it excellent. Maybe the rest thought it *Wild 90*

renamed, for they have stayed away in droves, leaving the film to its honor on the college circuits. Mailer, playing a detective in the lead role, evolves into your wonderful neighborhood Irish flatfoot at the end. And the college crowd tells him that is where the movie turns false.

A few words from the novelist on how to make movies: "In the novel, you start with a bag of words, and the way you put the words together has meaning. In movies, you get another kind of vocabulary. You have little bits of film strip, each the equivalent of words—five words or five thousand. But the strips are put together as individual words. Constructing a movie out of the field of experience that you have recorded gets to be wholly fascinating because you are working with a brand new vocabulary. You are putting things together in a way that nobody has ever put them together before.

"What is most interesting about making a film is to start with the idea of making a film. In other words, you have a couple of people in a scene. They don't know what they are going to say next. They do know there is a movie camera on them. That is as much of a sense of reality as any man can have in the 20th century. What you get out of that is a sense of relationships of dialogue and action that offer the possibility of being put together later in such a way that you can get an art work out of it."

So that's the way *Maidstone* was made last summer down at the end of Long Island. It is a film about Norman T. Kingsley's, i.e., Norman Mailer's, campaign for the Presidency. The last scene was made on nearby Gardiners Island. Mailer was on a walk with his wife and the youngest four of his brood when actor Rip Torn went at his head with a hammer. Mailer got a hand on the hammer and a body lock on Torn, who seemed about to choke Mailer, who was biting through Torn's right ear. Mailer's wife and a still photographer pulled at them as the children wailed, for they were eyewitnesses to the strangling of their father. It all ended somehow, with a lot of blood, pain and pieces of ear on the dune grass and with Torn demanding that Mailer admit, for Christ's sake, that he had only done what the film needed. To keep his wife from going for Torn's eyes, Mailer assured her that he understood what Rip wanted to do. "But I never thought you'd do it in front of the kids, Rip. I'll never forgive you for that." The sound track reaches new heights of invective. "You might as well turn off that tape," Mailer says finally. "He's a very dull talker and he'll never stop so long as anything's running." As the National Book Award winner said a paragraph back—". . . there is a movie camera on them. That is as much of a sense of reality as any man can have in the 20th century."

Since Mailer makes movies by putting together strips of film in arrangements that please, you are offered the scenes that follow from the master's life. Think of them as film strips brought back from some war by your dutiful retriever. Arrange them to your convenience, enlarging some, discarding others, referring one or two to the U.S. Senate or your local pathologist. In that way, we may each come to have the Mailer we can live with best.

• We go first to Miami Beach. Mailer was refereeing a match between a hangover and his setting-up exercises. He told his caller he would meet him at noon at Gore Vidal's. At noon, in the entranceway to Vidal's suite, the caller introduced himself to his host, who was even more surprised to learn that Mailer was to be a guest too. Since the caller was in the hire of a magazine, the host hoped he had come to talk about *Myra Breckinridge*. The host was wrong, but still kind. He agreed to talk frankly about Mailer until he arrived. "I don't like him so much as a novelist any more," he said, "but he certainly is a marvelous journalist now that he has turned himself into his own subject. Mailer's writing at the top of his voice now, showing all of himself, and that's bad because a writer needs to keep himself shrouded in some mystery. I do."

Mailer arrived. "You know my friend here who's drinking your liquor?" Mailer asked. Appraisals of stomach circumferences, flesh tones and concupiscences were exchanged before the talk turned to reprint covers, sales (Vidal's) and renown (Mailer's). "As your press gets better, Norman, your sales get worse."

Then Vidal turned to the caller. "Norman's never read any of my books all the way through."

"Oh yes I have. *Other Voices, Other Rooms*. And I'm looking forward to *Myra Breckinridge*."

"As Norman moves more into politics, I move more into sex, where he started. The rest of us follow the formula Norman's given up."

"Whaddya mean, given up? My new movie has a male brothel in it."

"That's just the sort of idea I'd have, but Norman would do. Say, maybe you should direct the movie of *Myra*."

"I'm not ready for it yet, Gore. I should do one other film first."

"Why not start on *Nat Turner* for Bill Styron, then do *Myra* for me. That way, you could do in both of us."

Mailer had seen Vidal and William Buckley go at one another like old biddies on TV the night before. "I wanted you as a couple of club fighters to sharpen up for about three months."

"In doing my show with Buckley, I find that deep personal antagonism helps a lot. You know, Norman, I'm heading for the New Left."

"Okay. But just wait till you have to meet them."

● Thousands of them were in Chicago last summer. So was Mailer. For the deepest possible appreciation of the tiny pleasantry to follow, a close reading and total recall of Mailer's *The Armies of the Night* is assumed. You will remember then the poet Robert Lowell:

> "Yes, Norman," Lowell said, "I really think you are the best journalist in America." . . .
> "Well, Cal," said Mailer, using Lowell's nickname for the first time, "there are days when I think of myself as being the best writer in America." . . .
> "Oh, Norman, oh, certainly," he said, "I didn't mean to imply, heavens no, it's just I have such respect for good journalism."
> "Well, I don't know that I do," said Mailer. "It's much harder to write"—the next said with great and false graciousness—"a good poem."
> "Yes, of course."
> Chuckles. Headmastersmanship.
> Chuckles. Fellow headmastersmanship.
> They were both now somewhat spoiled for each other. . . .

That was in Washington; and now, Chicago. Here is a scene Mailer left out of his account of the Democratic convention. He was at dinner in the backroom of a luxury joint on the near North Side. Abruptly, the service did not exist, and he inquired about the chances for another encounter with the waiter. A higher authority explained that Senator McCarthy and some friends had arrived in the main room and that the hearts and limbs of the staff were concentrating there. So the writer and an attending notetaker decided they would pay their respects to the part-time poet who truncated their dinner. "Why of course I know Norman Mailer," McCarthy said. "YOU ARE THE BEST JOURNALIST IN AMERICA." As Mailer reached across the table, the Senator made no effort to stand. "You'll notice, Norman, that I remain seated because we poets must observe our natural precedence over the prose crowd." A little chirp came out of Mailer then, along with a mock shuffle in his footwork and a lift of the shoulders to protect his chin. Up to a point, Mailer likes to be hit, and here in the first seconds of the opening round, McCarthy had rocked him twice with a neat hook off a jab. The rest you can read all about in Mailer's book.

• Brooklyn Heights now. The house practically hangs over the water. You want to know, do you, what Mailer said there a few weeks ago about abortion? "There, I depart completely from the Catholics," he said. "I always thought abortion was less odious than the pill. And for one simple reason. A woman knows she's killing something that's growing in her. She's killing her own child. She knows she's a murderess. She can't fool herself. And that's terribly important. Take a pill and—there's something slimy. You're working both sides of the street without any clear address.

"Now I wouldn't take away from people who want to kill their own. Why should the state have more wisdom about who should be kept alive than a parent? You hear these incredible things when some parents kill three of their children and then commit suicide. You know, we don't know. There might be some profound statement of existence in that. The parent may just have decided there was something in their strain that was profoundly evil, that did not deserve to continue. It is as ridiculous to consider every human life valuable and worthwhile as it is to consider no human life worthwhile."

• A widely viewed point of view: he should be less a gadabout and stay at his escritoire. Then *Why Are We In Vietnam?* and *The Armies of the Night*, his two most acclaimed works since *The Naked and the Dead*, came forth at the peak of his limelight period. How come? he was asked. The rabbi in him answered: "We can't ever be sure of our moral natures, but we can be sure that we want to confound our enemies."

So let us go back, class, for a lesson by the master. Bellow, Updike, Styron, Vidal and the others are not adversaries, because they are triflers. "I read their books," he said, "from the opposite end. I know these guys. I know them like a detective who knows all those guys are crooks. I just like to know how they are pulling off their latest jobs." Of his own novels, Mailer thinks *An American Dream* is the most skillful. "I don't think the rich have ever been written about with that insight. Scott Fitzgerald was right when he said the rich are indeed not like you and me. Being rich is a problem. How can you know if somebody really loves you or not if you are rich? It's hard enough even for me."

• Back to Miami Beach. The lights went dim in the bar, and the perfumed old lady at the piano left it and engulfed our writer. The scene is not in his Republican convention story. "Harold Robbins puts me in his books, Norman," she said with a whine she thought sexy. "Why don't you put me in your next book?" Mailer studied his drink. The lady kissed him. Earlier, she went on, his mother had been in. His mother told her how Norman got into Harvard when there was a quota on Jews. The lady kissed him. He looked up. "I wrote a poem once that goes something like this: 'The trouble with mothers is they give kisses of congratulations which make you feel like a battleship on which someone is breaking a bottle.' " The kisser was silent for a while. Then she spoke: "That's what you learned up at Harvard, huh?"

• Up to Harvard, where Mailer wrote to his classmates 25 years later: "I notice . . . by the guide of our Sample Lives, that we are encouraged . . . to sermonize on the fruit of our experience, so we'll say it is not impossible that apocalyptic times are upon us, and the Republic will go bust if it don't clean its nose, and stop leaning on committees, corporations, and such ritual activities as the burning of the children of the Vietnamese."

• Let us go now to Toots Shor's in New York, Hemingway's old watering hole. Mailer and José Torres, the ex-light-heavyweight champion, their wives and a few friends repaired there after the Jerry Quarry-Buster Mathis match. "It was the first bad fight of the Nixon Administration," Mailer said on the way. He was in his pinstripe suit with lapels on the vest and he was talking quietly with Torres' wife when a cruising hulk spilled a drink on the table. The hulk saw no reason to care to do anything about it until Mailer suggested that the decent thing might be to call the waiter or some man with a mop. The hulk disagreed. "Who the hell you think you're talking to?" he roared back. "You know what you look like to me? Like some goddamn faggot."

"Outside!" Mailer snapped at him.

The hulk's second came between them, backing his ward off.

"Does that faggot know who I am?" he kept bellowing. Nobody seemed to. Torres stayed at his table, head down, maybe listening.

There is a problem here that recurs. Does Mailer wind up in the papers from time to time because he starts fights? Or are fights forced on him? Or is he just caught in the role Hemingway had—the free-swinging battler that all Americans in Toots Shor's want the novelist to be? They can read about him a lot and they don't have to read him.

• Fast eschatological look-around from the Poodle Bar by the sea in Miami Beach. "Right here now," he said over the Bloody Marys, "we may be exercising some part of a divine scheme much warned against by the devil. You see, don't you by now, that I am as much conservative as Marxist? A conservative, remember, is a man who believes that power resides in God's hands, not in man's."

And did Mailer the conservative leave the power to God alone when he swept into *Maidstone* to—well, just possibly—to advance his own fantasy that he should be the President? "Its time had gone," he said. "If it were there when I started the film, then the hand that held the dagger plunged it into its own back." He looked into the hotel lobby. "Hundreds of people there think they should be President. Probably even Wilt Chamberlain, and certainly John Wayne. Wayne looks at Ronald Reagan, after all, and says, 'I can take him any day, even take his women away from him. So why not me?'

"You see, the only way I can figure out what I really think about anything is to write about it. That is why I wrote *The Armies of the Night*. I was being absolutely honest in a comic vein. If I am *ever* absolutely honest in a tragic vein, then I may have written a great book."

• Let us close on a stick of his verse.

> *I do not think there was an occasion*
>   *in my life*
> *which did not have*
>   *me*
>   *fatally*
> *misquoted*

• But no. Let us close, instead, with his advice to the players of *Maidstone*: "We are trying to find out if an imaginary event can become a real event. And along the way, we will go through some not altogether despicable moments."

Norman Mailer
Joseph Gelmis/1970

From *The Film Director as Superstar* by Joseph Gelmis (New York: Doubleday, 1970), 43-63. Reprinted by permission of Doubleday, a division of Bantam, Doubleday, Dell Publishing Group, Inc.

*"Making a film is a cross between
a circus, a military campaign, a
nightmare, an orgy, and a high."*

Movies were the logical extension of the irrepressible personality of Norman Mailer. How else could he be a Mafia chieftain (*Wild 90*), an Irish homicide squad detective lieutenant (*Beyond the Law*), or a serious candidate for the Presidency (*Maidstone*), except by bankrolling, directing, and starring in his own movies?

The most garrulous, stimulating gadfly of his generation, Mailer became a filmmaker at forty-five with the release of his first film on the twentieth anniversary of the publication of his first novel, *The Naked and the Dead*. The film critics mugged him on the way to the box office.

He suggests that the flaw in *Wild 90* was that the sound was bad—which does pose problems for a film that is nothing but three men playing thugs sitting and talking in one room for two hours. He spent six months editing his next film, *Beyond the Law*, with a young filmmaker named Jan Welt. The film, a kind of staged documentary about a night in a police station, was shot in four nights and was cut from 11 hours of footage to 105 minutes. It impressed a number of critics with its wit and vigor, but it didn't make any money.

Mailer's third film, *Maidstone*, was shot in the summer of 1968 and he was still editing it when we talked in early 1969. It was shot in four working days in the Hamptons on Long Island, with as many as five and six cameras filming at once. In it, Mailer plays a film director running for President during a campaign in which all of the leading

political figures have been assassinated and most of the
fifty contenders remaining are from show business.

Shooting without a script and from the vortex of the
activity, Mailer's unorthodox approach polarizes critics
into those who love him and those who hate him. His casts
are chosen from among his friends who reflect facets of his
persona. His filmmaking could be described by the title of
his 1959 collection of short works: *Advertisements for
Myself.*

Born January 1923 in Long Branch, New Jersey, Mailer
grew up in Brooklyn. He has a house in Brooklyn Heights
overlooking Wall Street across the river ("So I can keep my
eye on the enemy"). He lives with his wife, Beverly
Bentley, an actress, and their two sons. He has four daugh-
ters by three previous marriages. When he isn't performing the Public Mailer role, he is a generous, gracious, warm
human being.

Between the first novel and first movie, Mailer has lived
a Faustian public life as novelist, pamphleteer, mayoral
candidate, para-journalist and participant in events he was
covering (Gore Vidal says Mailer "intervenes in history"),
and neo-Hemingway tough guy who patronizes boxing
and bullfighting and bars.

Gelmis: Why, on the twentieth anniversary of your becoming a
published novelist, did you embark on a filmmaking career?

Mailer: I didn't. I got into it bit by bit. I got into it, I think, the way
some of those old Jewish businessmen became moguls of studios.
Which is, they owned a little theater somewhere that they had taken
over because they tried to put their nephew in business and the
nephew had turned out to be a no-good and a bum. So to keep from
losing a few thousand bucks, they had to take over the movie theater.

And when they took over the theater, they began to see what
people liked. And lo and behold, before they knew it, they owned
twenty movie theaters, because they were very good businessmen.
The next thing was they looked at the product that was coming from
Hollywood and realized it was all wrong for what they needed. So
when they owned enough theaters to command money and
influence, they started making movies in New York to supply product
for their theaters. Then they moved to Hollywood for the sunshine.
And they ended up being tycoons and geniuses.

But they didn't start out with the idea of being tycoons or even being in the movies. They started out with the idea that they were going to give their nephew a job, they were going to buy a little business for him. And at the other end, they changed the history of the western world. I'm not saying that's going to happen to me at all. It's a useful metaphor, though. What I'm saying is that I got into the movies just as inadvertently.

What happened, in brief, was that *The Deer Park* was running as a play and my wife (Beverly Bentley) was in it. And, like any stagedoor Johnny, I picked her up every night after the show. Actors, of course, are all wound up. So about six or eight of us would sit around and drink every night. I got very bored with that. You know, it's very boring to discuss your own play with actors every night for three months. Because actors, particularly stage actors, are extraordinarily literal people.

It's very important to them whether the salt shaker is here or there. After all, a stage actor is a man or woman who is, if you will, the president of an emotional factory which has to produce the same product at the same minute every night. And so they attach all sorts of conditioned reflexes in the gearing of their emotions to the placement of objects.

They may pretend that they want motivation, a reason to pick up a salt shaker. But the fact of the matter is that the only way you can produce a certain emotion a certain hour every night and do it without killing yourself is to set up a whole series of conditioned reflexes. Therefore, just as the dog salivates when he hears the bell ring, so the actor begins to weep as he reaches for the salt shaker.

But the thing is, a guy or woman who works that way and lives that way is not the most interesting person to talk to at night about their work. They're just very concerned with that salt shaker. You know, what happened was that the salt shaker wasn't in place. The prop man left the salt shaker over *there*. And they're having a hemorrhage. So you get into these problems night after night after night. And what you end up doing finally is saying: "Sorry, I'll look into it." And you become some sort of stage manager rather than a playwright, all because your wife is in the play.

Anyway, it was getting pretty desperate. So two of the guys in the play—Mickey Knox, an actor of twenty years and one of my best and oldest buddies, and Buzz Farbar, a pal who had a part in *The Deer Park* as a kind of gag—would go off to the side of this bar where we drank every night. And we began playing this game. We began improvising, to take on parts. I was like the head of a gang, very Mafia. These guys were like my hoods and I was lecturing them all the time.

We had absolutely fantastic stuff going as we were drinking, stuff that was far better than anything we ever came close to in the movie that grew out of those evenings (*Wild 90*). It got so good at a certain point I said, "Jesus, isn't it a shame that we can't film it? All we'd need is a cameraman and a sound track. Warhol is doing this very interesting stuff with his kind of people. And I think it'd be fun to try something altogether different. Instead of being ourselves, let's see what we're like as movie actors."

So Farbar looked around. He was working at CBS at the time. And he happened to run into Don Pennebaker. I didn't know anything about him at the time. We met for a drink. And Pennebaker was sort of intrigued with the idea. He's not only a marvelously gifted photographer but he has an odd, very private aesthetic about filmmaking. He's an innovator and a discoverer. He loves anything that's new, any new way of approaching the idea of a film. Film is almost an object of religious veneration for him. He'd made a number of documentaries over the years and had just finished his Bob Dylan film (*Don't Look Back*), and our project seemed curious to him. So he said, "All right, we'll film for a couple of nights."

We figured out that what we'd do was he'd contribute his services for part of the film and give us the editing equipment and we'd pay for the raw stock, which was supposed to cost about $1000—it turned out to be $1500. At the time I had quite a bit of money, and I thought: "Gee, that's a good way to blow a thousand dollars. Better than going to Vegas for a week." So we blew it. We made the movie.

Originally the film cost $1500. Before I was finished, *Wild 90* cost about $50,000—and *Beyond the Law* has cost about $60,000 to $70,000 by now. Part of it was just waste motion on *Wild 90*. I didn't know what I was doing. It should have cost about $20,000 to make. What happened was that I got fascinated by the film as I saw the rushes. But the sound track is awful. There's not much going on.

So, finally, it can't be a successful movie because you've got three guys sitting in a room for forty-five minutes before anybody else comes in. And if you can't hear what they're saying very well, what kind of movie have you got? But at that time, I didn't know how bad the sound track was going to be, because we had it in double system.

We had a magnetic track. And when you go from double system to optical, you lose something like twenty to thirty per cent of your sound. I almost cried when I heard the sound track of *Wild 90* optically. I didn't know that. People kept warning me. But I didn't really listen. You know, you get in a funny daze when you're making a movie.

G: How serious a limitation are the sound recording techniques involved in low-budget filmmaking?

M: Well, our sound's been getting better and better. We work on it and concentrate on it as we're filming now. Also, I'm beginning to change the way I cut a picture. For instance, often I won't use a scene now if the sound isn't good. I've come to recognize it. You just can't get away with it. You see, my feeling at the beginning was that there's too much attention paid to good sound. You give up a lot to get really good sound. One of the things you give up is the possibility of using people who are not actors. And that's a terrible thing to give up.

What happens is that an actor has a certain kind of psychological structure. Maybe one person in fifty is potentially a good professional actor. But half the people alive are good actors. We spend our lives acting.

Anyway, I spent about six months cutting *Wild 90*. It became my hobby. I'd been without a hobby for a couple of years. I'd put on some weight. I hadn't been skiing for a few years. And I was doing nothing but write, drink, and have a life, more or less. This was really the first new thing I'd become interested in. I just loved cutting. I loved the sort of—if you will—the metaphysical problems involved. The ethical problems. The moral problems.

G: What are the metaphysics of cutting?

M: It's the extraordinary reality. When you cut from one piece of film to another, you are creating a truth. And this truth is intangible, because it's images. By putting images together in one way, you have one truth, and by putting them together in another way you have another truth. I realize that, in a way, it's very much like writing. Getting toward the statement is like writing, in that the same sort of taste could be used. One of the things that's been said about *Beyond the Law* that I think is true in a funny way is they say: "The amazing thing about it is it's as if you *wrote* the screenplay. It's all you." Well the reason it's *all* me, despite the fact that everyone improvised his own lines and there was no script, is that I cut it to my taste.

Granted, I chose people who represented part of my vision. But finally it was in the cutting. Because when I saw the rushes of *Beyond the Law* there was a lot I liked and a lot I detested. Obviously what I liked was the part that fit the particular vision I had of what this reality was. What I was trying to do in *Beyond the Law* was to create the reality, if you will, below the reality, beneath the reality, within the reality of an evening in the police station.

I think that cops and criminals are incredible people. No one's ever begun to deal with how fantastic they are in their love-hate relation. It's like the relation between two linemen in professional football. What goes on between them in the course of a game is closer than a marriage. They know each other in ways that are incommunicable.

G: In *The Armies of the Night* you spoke of them as cops and crooks and then qualified it to "actually detectives and suspects." Why the fine distinction?

M: It's rude and inaccurate to say "cops and criminals." These people are suspects. We don't know whether they're criminals or not. But finally it comes down to cops and crooks anyway. And that's the relation. Because whether you're innocent or guilty, when you're in a police station you're treated as if you're a crook. So existentially you are a crook. At that moment, everything in you is reacting as a crook. You're in trouble. You're now beyond the law.

G: I've heard that you shoot twenty scenes and discard nineteen, rather than shoot twenty takes of the same scene and just pick the one you like.

M: That's true. I don't like to go back. In *Maidstone*, I shot a couple of things twice, just to see. Because you know I feel that if the vocabulary of filmmaking goes from A to Z and people like Bergman and Godard and Antonioni are somewhere between T and W, X, Y, or Z, I've gone from A to C. I mean, it's not a matter of being modest, just a matter of recognizing the simple truth that I know very little about making films. I got interested. They caught me, entrapped me.

G: *Wild 90* was an expensive experiment and unpopular with the critics. Why did you make your second film, *Beyond the Law*?

M: I had already shot *Beyond the Law* before the reviews came out on *Wild 90*. And a lot of people had loved *Wild 90* before it opened in a theater, when they saw it privately and could hear the soundtrack. So when I shot *Beyond the Law* I didn't shoot it as a loser. I shot it as a guy who had found an interesting way to make a film.

G: Was there a particular part of the experience that made you want to continue and to commit months of your life and energies and more of your bankroll to filmmaking?

M: Something in the experience had turned me on. You know this so well, we're writers. So we spend our lives working with words. And once in a while we catch our hand in the act of writing and we're overcome with the mystery of it. It's a mystery. The peculiar power that we have, or the lack of power. The ability to alter reality in other people's minds by the way we use words, by the insertion of one adjective or another, bears such an odd relation to the truth—and what we mean by the truth is just the sort of *feel* of our perceptions. I think it was this mystery that drove Hemingway insane, or partially mad. Dealing with words is a mysterious matter. It's very insubstantial because they're just little pieces of dark curly pigment on a white page.

Well, working with movies, on *Wild 90*, I think I got back to the freshness of it as a kid. I felt the same sort of interest that I felt when I was eighteen and starting to write stories. It was wonderful when I was eighteen and writing. To be corny about it, it was first love. And that's gone. It's been gone for a long time. I'm a professional writer now. I can do a job. And I'm very much like a prizefighter who packs a suitcase and gets on a train or a plane and goes out to fight an opponent in some town. It doesn't matter what the conditions are particularly. I still have reverence for writing. But you can have reverence for something and at the same time not necessarily get much immediate pleasure out of it. I still get pleasure out of writing. But the *act* is not pleasurable. It's hard work. But making a film is a cross between a circus, a military campaign, a nightmare, an orgy, and a high.

G: That sounds like chaos.

M: That's the way I make films. If there isn't chaos in the making of it, then you can't get anything because everybody gets uptight. Because there's no script you've almost got to have a sort of chaos. It's the only way to get people relaxed enough so you can get something out of them.

G: Yet it seems to me that if one doesn't have good footage the best editor in the world can't do too much with it.

M: If you don't have the material at *all*, then you're dead. But the art of cutting is to find material where no one else can find it. It's a little like a detective story. You can cut something out of nothing, almost. In *Maidstone*, we have twelve-minute reels, and these are a unit in a way, because that's what a cameraman sticks in his Arriflex magazine. We shoot until the reel is empty. We look at the reel in the projection room and we all groan. There isn't a thing in it that has any life. It's dead, it's horrible.

Suddenly you take out the sound in a place and then you look at it and it's not a bad piece of film without sound. And then you see another piece five minutes later on which has a relation to this piece. Or you might get thirty really good seconds out of that twelve-minute reel if it's hopeless, and it'll have an artistry and elegance to it. So that afterwards, you'll say: "How the hell did you ever get that?" Where you get it is that you try to create a curious maelstrom in which marvelous facets of people will reveal themselves.

G: To make your cast loosen up, you create a *Mailerstrom?*

M: Oh, wow, stop! I'm not doing it as a manipulator. Because I'm not in command of it, don't forget. I'm no more in command of it than a general is, in the middle of a battle, where he's fighting for his life. The way I make the film, I have to act in it. It's the only way I can direct it. Because there's no script, something has to be going on in scenes. And so there has to be somebody in the scene who really has some conception of what he's driving toward. It's equivalent to—you can't have a party without a host or a hostess. And the host has to be in his own party. He can't send orders down from upstairs. He can, but it'd be a very bizarre affair.

G: How have directors managed until now to make films without acting in them?

M: They have a script. They have professional actors. They have extraordinarily skillful technicians who work generally with fixed cameras. That is, the camera lens may zoom or dolly, but finally the one thing they're obsessed with is: no vibration, no jar. The film image must be rock steady. They spent forty years developing techniques to give them a rock steady image. It's the most important single thing to a distributor. You get some of those distributors, they come to see a movie and the one thing they say is: "I like it so it doesn't shake." We're dead with our movies with the average movie distributor in a small town. He says, "You call this a movie? It shakes all over the place."

That's what we're up against. That's why there are certain

respected film critics who detest my films. Because what I'm doing is going into the church. And we have to face up to the drear eye of the movie critic. And the movie critic is a religious man. Movies are his church. What I'm getting at is that a good film made without vibration has a magnificent quality to it, has the magnificence of a dream. You see, in a dream things don't shake. But the commercial movie, beautifully made, is an abstraction. It doesn't pretend to be life. It says that "we are some weird creature from the netherworld and we are perfect." And that's why it's not a light matter when there are imperfections in films.

It's a sacrilege. I'm committing a sacrilege when I put out a film which pretends to be a major film, a good film, a marvelous film and yet has certain crudities in it that are forty, fifty, sixty years old. For instance, my backgrounds will not be evenly lighted throughout. My camera will not be rock steady. Not every word of my films can be heard. The camera work will be spotty, brilliant at one moment and somewhat disappointing the next. I'll be in and out of focus more than is permissible. These are all terrible imperfections.

It's like that scene in Faulkner, you remember, in one of his short stories where the hired hand comes up to the plantation mansion and walks in over the white carpet with his boots and they're filled with cow manure. And as he walks across the carpet the owner of the plantation is so horrified he can hardly move and he gasps: "See what you've done to my carpet." And there Faulkner symbolized the absolute horror of one part of the south as it saw another part of the south rising.

You know, I've got enormous respect for the beautiful movie as a creature of the netherworld. I grew up with it, as everyone else did. And I love it. But I think there are other kinds of movies possible. And I think they could even transcend this.

G: On this question of imperfect films, don't you think that much of it isn't aesthetic choice at all but a simple case of insufficient funds that makes attention to technical polish impossible? Isn't it a rationalization of the underground to say that anything slick is bad *per se* and thus to institutionalize its shortcomings?

M: Yes, they have institutionalized it. Jonas Mekas, for instance, has certainly tried to legitimize it. And Mekas I find a marvelously interesting critic because he's so passionate. I rarely agree with him on particular things. But while we're on Mekas, I must mention that I

have love for him because he's one of the people who introduced me
to movies, in a funny way.

I happened to see him on the street once and he said: "Why don't
you ever come to see any of our underground films? Do you realize
we're a lot of serious people? We're working very hard to make these
films. And you ought to see them." A year went by. But I
remembered that conversation. So finally I said to my wife, "Let's go
over to the Filmmakers' Cinémathèque." And so I started going to
the underground's showcase. And I saw about twelve or fifteen
underground films in that period. *Scorpio Rising* was far and away
the star of all the films I saw. Technically, it was exquisite. I saw one
Warhol film, *Kitchen*. It was horrible. But it had the horror of the
twentieth century in it. The refrigerator is making too much noise.
The beautiful heroine, Edie Sedgwick, has the sniffles. She keeps
blowing her nose while the hero keeps trying to rustle a sandwich
together out of wax paper. It really had the horror.

G: What was your reaction to the films?

M: Something was going on, but I couldn't dominate it with my
mind. The greatest intellectual pleasure I have is carrying an
experience I can't dominate with my mind. Because I come out of a
tradition of people who are born to dominate life with their minds.
The Jews are the greatest intellectual machines of any species of man
on earth. I think that's really the reason, beyond any other, why the
Jews are next to universally detested by people who don't
understand their fine, warm, tender, loving, and forgiving sides.

The reason why every farmer alive, why every redneck,
instinctively distrusts the Jew is because the Jews are intellectual
machines. And they are, you know, more than anyone else. I grew up
in that tradition. And I had a mind, when I was younger, which was
like an intellectual machine. It wasn't that *good* a machine. In
comparison with certain other machines, it was second rate. But it
was a machine. It had that habit of dominating *every* experience it
encountered. This went on for years.

And I remember that there were certain experiences I had—I
mean, one of the reasons I've always been, in the view of critics,
obsessed with sex is that sex is an experience you can never
dominate. You have to approach it with—dare I use the word
again?—veneration. Bullfighting was something I couldn't dominate
with my mind. It took me about three or four fights to get to like

bullfighting. Once I got to like it, it was a passion. I lived with
bullfights for a year. And the reason was, I encountered an
experience that was larger than my mind. Something was going on
that I couldn't dominate. I couldn't sit down and write a piece, which,
as far as I was concerned, was a definitive piece about it. And I had
to live with it and learn it and recognize that I'd never be able to
dominate it. Boxing is easier to dominate because of the limitations of
it. Boxing you can dominate to a degree with your mind, whereas a
street fight you can never dominate with your mind. The greatest
professional fight in the world is probably not as great a spectacle as
the greatest street fight in the world.

G: Why? Because of spontaneity or improvisation or no rules?

M: Terror. The terror of the audience. What if one of the guys
starts to kill the other guy? Are you going to get in and stop it? Why
do you think that big men always stop other big men from a fight? It's
because nobody wants to face the ultimate chickening-out point.
What do you do if the thing gets out of control? The stronger the
man, the more it worries him. The less he can afford to discover at
any given moment that he's chicken. There are endless codes about
this.

G: Even though I grew up in Brooklyn too, I managed to talk my
way out of most fights.

M: Well, most men do. Who doesn't? You think I don't
intellectualize my way out of most fights? You think I pick up every
fight that comes my way in a day?

G: I think so, but I'll have to find out for myself.

M: Oh come on, come on. I'd have to stay in the shape of a
professional fighter to pick up every small sort of subtle offer of a
gauntlet.

G: Well, now, you've thrown the gauntlet down, because you ask
if I think you accept every challenge. So let me ask you: why do so
many people have the impression that your masculine ego, your
image of yourself as a virile man, is somehow involved in almost
every story you cover as a reporter-writer, as a para-journalist? And
why do some of your projects, like your last film, *Maidstone*, turn into
a brawl, by all accounts, where you and your buddy Rip Torn almost
took each other apart and in another incident a young actor ended
up in a hospital bed? What has that got to do with the artistic process,
the journalistic process?

M: On *Maidstone*, I'm just going to say: "Wait until you see the movie." I can't defend the movie before you see it. You're going to see that film one of these days. And when you do, you're going to walk out to the street and ask yourself the same question in a way that I think will be like a turn of the spiral. In other words, you'll be at the same point you are now but you'll have had an experience which will have you somewhat higher in that blue netherworld of questions. You see, there's the black netherworld of answers and the blue netherworld of questions.

G: And you're concerned wth the blue netherworld of questions in your movies?

M: I think *Maidstone* is concerned with the resonance of questions. A beautiful movie is an experience that you cannot dominate with your mind. That's why you film critics love a perfectly made movie. Because it gives you no opportunity to start ripping the thing apart. When you see a movie that is flawless, one of the wonderful things about it is that you can't get in there and start taking something that was done sloppily and from there make an attack on a picture. Like, you guys are lovers. Everytime a movie critic goes to see a movie . . .

G: What's wrong with beautiful movies, or beautiful women for that matter? Why should we like a movie with problems or blemishes which might have been avoided if the director had $500,000 instead of $50,000?

M: I adore beautiful women. There's nothing wrong with beautiful movies. Every time a beautiful movie is made by commercial processes, it's a miracle. But how many beautiful movies are there? There's *Belle du Jour*. Let's think of another beautiful movie at the moment. I can't think of one.

G: What about *2001: A Space Odyssey*?

M: I thought that was a bold, beautiful, extraordinary effort in a way. But I'm going to tell you something. I slept through half of it. And the reason I slept through half of it was that I hadn't had any sleep the night before. I went there with my children.

G: Now you understand the critic's problem.

M: Yes. But I still liked it. I got involved. But the pace was so slow, it was exactly the pace you would have on one of those interplanetary trips. And what would you do? You would sleep, so I did. I had regard for the film because it was an experience. And I thought it was bold of Kubrick to spend $10,000,000 giving us an

experience that was not on the face of it box office, and then getting
away with it. I think that was splendid.

G: But you thought it was boring.

M: Boredom has an aesthetic, also, in the commercial film.

G: Antonioni proved that.

M: Yes. But I don't think Antonioni's films belong in the dream
factory. I think Antonioni oppresses the critic to the point where you
lose the feeling of splendor and living in another world that exists
nowhere but in the movie. There's a boredom in Antonioni that's
almost physical. It's like dealing with sort of a foreign personality;
there's almost a physical impression there.

Seeing an Antonioni film, I wanted to punch people. I didn't want
to punch Antonioni. I didn't want to punch the actors. I didn't want
to punch the person next to me. I just wanted to take the chair in
front of me and start breaking it because the movie was doing
something to my nervous system that wasn't nice. I'd almost put the
blame on Antonioni. It's half his fault and half mine. The only film of
his I've seen was *L'Avventura*. And I saw it again in the last year or so
and found I just wasn't prepared to accept it.

G: Where does what you are doing fit into the film scene?

M: The way I look at the movie business is that the commercial
directors are mining one end of the tunnel and I'm mining the other.
What they're saying is that I'm crazy and that I'm digging holes like
an earthworm and I'm going to drown in my own stuff. And what I'm
saying is I'm digging in from the other end and we're going to meet
in the center of the tunnel and we're going to come in so close that
we won't be an inch apart. Now if not me, another. What I do know,
and they don't know, is that a movie can be made this way, which is
interesting.

G: How do you feel about the people who had violent reactions
and walked out of Philharmonic Hall when *Beyond the Law* had its
première there during the New York Film Festival?

M: Novels are supposed to hit people where they live. You're
supposed to read a novel and change your life. A movie is supposed
to keep you living. That's why one serious critic said in his review of
Beyond the Law, "Norman, you don't understand the movies. The
movies are not there to hit people where they live. The movies are
there to keep people alive." You go to a movie and you pay your
money and you're supposed to have a good time. The horror of life

should be alleviated for a little while. That's what most critics feel movies are supposed to do. But what I'm saying is that the horror of life has become so completely pervasive that movies no longer enable sensible and sensitive people to survive. It sickens them. The most beautiful movie in the world will sicken you, if you can conceive of a better movie than the one that was there.

G: You were telling me earlier how nebulous your plans were and how you might give up filmmaking if *Maidstone* didn't get a favorable reception.

M: I don't want to load it that way. For one simple reason: I don't trust critics. I think every critic is schizophrenic. On one hand he's a count who's taking care of a mysterious surrealistic estate. And on the other hand he's nothing but a gang bully and a thug who's waiting for the first victim to come down the alley. So if you think I'm going to say for the record that *Maidstone* is going to be the one that proves whether pictures can be made this way or not, you're crazy.

I'll say that *Maidstone* is going to influence my mind to a great degree. I will be either vastly more optimistic or vastly more pessimistic about what can be done by this method of working after *Maidstone* is finished and I see how it's received than I am now. I will be confirmed or denied in my present vision. *Maidstone* is not *necessarily* it. But it is possible that when I finish it, I may say: "This is it." I may say, "Gang, if you don't like this film we have come to the parting of the ways. And I'm going to stop making movies and you'll be the guys who'll be crying in twenty years because nobody makes movies like Mailer any more."

G: Would you make another film before *Maidstone* comes out?

M: I don't think so, for one simple reason. Everything is going into it: money, resources, time. It's going to take six months more to finish it.

G: Let me pursue the matter of cost, which has to be a serious problem in personal filmmaking. You said before that initially $1500 went into *Wild 90* and yet it ended up costing $50,000. Why?

M: Because of overhead. It didn't have to cost anything like that. The fundamental error I made was that I thought it was going to be box office. I knew nothing about the movie business. Never did more of a country simpleton come down the pike than your humble interviewee. To use the army expression we once had, I didn't know a-hole from appetite about the movie business. I still don't, by the way. All I know now is that I don't know a-hole from appetite.

In those days I thought that was the way to make a quick buck, believe it or not. So I thought, "Well, we've got to distribute this thing. We've got something that nobody's ever come across. I mean, this is magical, this is fantastic. We're going to knock the movie business on its ass." So not only were we making a movie, but we were trying to set up a distribution business. We had overhead. It took us six months to make the movie. And all the while it was costing us at least $1000 a week. It was a luxury operation at that time, compared to the small staff we've got working now.

G: How were you financing the operation? From the magazine articles and book sales and the movie rights from *An American Dream?*

M: Right. All that ignoble money I got for *An American Dream,* which I understand, because I haven't seen it, is one of the worst movies ever made . . .

G: Why haven't you seen it?

M: Because I'm close enough to the violent not to want to see it. *An American Dream* happens to be my favorite novel. I think it's my best novel. Most people I know don't agree. They think it's my worst novel. But, either I'm right or they're right. It would be awful if neither of us is right. At any rate, it's not only my favorite novel but also I think it's the only novel I ever wrote that would have made a transcendently splendid movie. So if I go see it and see what they did to it, I'm likely to get violent. And I just stay away from it. It's like an Italian saying, "Don't insult my mudder." Friends of mine said, "Don't go see it." It's the first time in my life I've listened to friends' advice.

G: Would you make a movie of *The Deer Park?*

M: I might. If I did, I'd do it with a script. Because the dialogue is so good.

G: Why make movies which are improvised without scripts, without dialogue written in advance, in that case? Since you're a writer, it would seem a natural thing for you to write dialogue.

M: Well, this is what we're really talking about. The moment you know what you're going to do, you make a preparation. The moment you make a preparation, you're a step removed from the *moment* in life. You see, I'm an existentialist, through and through and through. And I have a certain amount of respect for the moment, because I think the moment is a mystery. The moment that there is not a moment, then you merely have programs. You're bureaucrats. You're bureaucrats of the mind, speaking to one another. You know what you're going to do and I know what I'm going to do and we're no longer talking as men across the table. We're talking as bureaucrats. Then you're concerned with your interests and I'm concerned with my interests. What's been agreeable about this interview up to now is that neither of us has been thinking particularly about where this is all going to go.

Every time I hear questions I feel like a kid who's in the study hall answering exam questions and I get flat and nervous. So, my feeling is that the amount of talent that exists but that's not approached is incredible. One of the experiences that I had in *Beyond the Law* was to see how good my friends were as actors. You know I really think *Beyond the Law* is a tremendous movie. I think in twenty years people are going to go to that movie and say, "But why didn't we see how fantastic it was?" I don't take that kind of credit for it. I didn't conceive it. I didn't direct it that way. I didn't dominate it. This wasn't my plaything. What happened was that these friends of mine suddenly absolutely amazed the hell out of me.

G: Why did you put the dozen newspaper and magazine photographers assigned to cover the making of *Maidstone* in the film as participants?

M: If the movie was the kind of movie that shouldn't have had cameramen there, I would have barred every still photographer from the set. The reason I let all those guys hang around was that this was a movie about a man running for president. So you'd have still photographers in every corner, wouldn't you? Part of the idiom of *Maidstone* is the still photographers clicking away, clicking away, clicking away. We have scenes in *Maidstone* where there are ten photographers visible in panorama.

For instance, we have the candidate throw a big party, a rather mysterious party. All sorts of documentary photographers are making a picture of this man's activities. Everyone says he's presidential material. So what we have is an absolutely wild party with movie cameramen all over the place. Now if it was another kind of party, a quiet tea, I've gotten to the point as a filmmaker where I wouldn't want cameramen all over the set.

I don't want a false myth to start that what I do is to get fifty people together, pull down my pants, do A or B, here or there, and then say: "Let's have some fun." It isn't like that at all. There's an extraordinary amount of work involved. What we were like was a commando team. I had brilliant technicians working with me. The thing is, they may not look like great technicians because they're working under conditions that no Hollywood cameraman would ever go near.

We used hand-held cameras, little hand booms or directional mikes, Nagra tape recorders, and whatever light was available. We worked fast, fast, fast. Each cameraman photographed an average of an hour and fifteen minutes a day during the seven days we were shooting *Maidstone*. That's a hell of a lot of attention to demand of a cameraman. It's the equivalent of a writer, I'd say, writing for ten hours a day.

G: Do you think there's any validity to the nonlinear, nonverbal, nonintellectual aesthetic of movies?

M: Yes. I think movies are in a different place entirely than novels or plays. In fact, my idea for a proper audience for *Beyond the Law* is not intellectual at all, because I don't think it's an intellectual film. I'd love to see *Beyond the Law* played in every slum neighborhood in America. A slum kid would feel about *Beyond the Law* the way I felt about *Studs Lonigan*. I read that and I suddenly realized, "My God, you can write about those things. They're part of art too."

And I wanted to be a writer. Reading James T. Farrell gave me the desire to be a writer. I think that you might get some slum kid who's about ready to blow up something, one way or another—if nothing else, he's going to blow up his own mind, by taking too much of this or too much of that. Maybe he'll see the movie and he'll say, "I've got to make movies." And he's going to want to learn how to read and write and add and measure because of his profound desire to make movies.

These kids should not only make movies but they should cut them themselves. Because as you see yourself in film over and over and over again, you lose all the worst aspects of narcissism. It's really like having psychoanalysis.

G: Do you speak from experience, in terms of self-image?

M: Yes. You come to recognize your relation to others. You recognize that it's not what you thought it was. It's subtly different. In other words, you're not as terrific as you thought you were. It's wonderful that way.

G: What did you think of your performance in *Beyond the Law*?

M: I thought it was good here and not so good there. I thought it was just good enough to create a character that a really good actor like, let's say, Richard Burton, could do fantastic things with. If you took that script that we've transcribed from the screen now and had Richard Burton act as Lieutenant Francis X. Pope, you'd have a memorable performance.

G: What did you think of Raoul Walsh's film version of *The Naked and the Dead?*

M: Considering what they could have had, I think it is the worst movie I've ever seen.

G: Would you like to have directed it?

M: I wouldn't have been able to. Someday, maybe. Someday maybe I'd remake it.

G: If you could write and direct your own scripts, would you work in Hollywood today?

M: I'm not interested in getting a job in Hollywood. I have no desire in the world to write a movie script. Why the hell should I write a movie script? Scriptwriting has nothing to do with writing. The best scriptwriter in the world, ideally, would be a film editor with a novelistic gift. And those are qualities that don't usually go together. But the way things are happening these days, we're going to find some film editor who'll come along and be a born novelist and he'll write movie scripts.

I learned something from the bad review in the *Village Voice* of *Beyond the Law.* I don't have to agree with it. But the fundamental complaint was that I don't go deep enough into the art, that I'm not really willing to give myself to it utterly. What I have learned is that there's no way to get around it, making movies is a religious act. I haven't been a dilettante. But I've just been having an affair with the movies up to now. And if you ask me whether I'm going to be in the film business for the rest of my life or am I not, I'd have to say that sooner or later I'm going to have to make a decision. I'm not giving up writing in a hurry, I can tell you that. Writing may give me up.

G: Would you describe your method of filmmaking?

M: Most moviemakers work off a blueprint. They have a plan, a master plan. They bring in technicians and talent. And whether they're working on a $500,000 budget or a $22,000,000 budget, it works in a corporate fashion. Everything is geared into the blueprint. It's an assembly line. And they can do marvelous work or abominable work, but they work off the plan.

What we do is to work like a military operation. We get a lot of interesting people. Very often we don't know if they're talented or not, but they are interesting. And we get the best technicians we can get who can work in this method, which is very demanding on the technicians because they're terribly orderly people and have to live in disorder. And then we make a raid. We attack a terrain. All right, in *Beyond the Law* what I was attacking was the old terrain of the Warner Bros. gangster and cop movies. I loved that kind of film and I wanted to see what you could do if you shot them in a more realistic vein.

G: Godard said that when he made *Breathless* he was trying to make *Scarface* but it turned out to be *Alice in Wonderland*.

M: In a funny way, I think Godard approaches films in the same way that I do. Which is, he loves these myths. He grew up with these myths. They formed him. So he sets out to make one film and makes another. *Weekend*, which is one of the best films I've seen in years, I think started out to be *Bonnie and Clyde*. Remember, Godard was supposed to do *Bonnie and Clyde* at one point and they wouldn't let him do it. And I think there was a profound fury in his veins which found outlet in *Weekend*. He made an altogether different film, of course.

I think it was a tremendous theme. In a way, what he was talking about was the death of the twentieth century. And he was talking about the fact that we may all perish, that our salvation may be cannibalism. And I would have almost liked a more thoroughgoing treatment of the matter. The only fault I have to find with *Weekend* is that it isn't pretentious enough, isn't grandiloquent enough. The man has a vision. There are parts of that film that to me are like Hieronymus Bosch. I'd never been a Godard lover until I saw that film. It converted me. But I still think there are terrible things in it. I think Godard is tiresome. He delights in boring the very people he attracts.

G: Are you referring to the two men by the garbage truck in *Weekend* who make long Marxist speeches?

M: Yes, one of the worst moments in the history of film. He does it in every film. That's his trademark. It's like saying, "You're *happy*. You're *enjoying* yourselves. You're really *enjoying* my movie. This must come to an end. Now you'll be bored for a while. You have to pay your price for my movie." I'm against that.

G: During your own filming, do you use any kind of outline or notes or script at all?

M: No, none at all.

G: Is it all in your head? Do you know exactly where you are going from beginning to end?

M: Yes. I know where I'm going, more or less. That doesn't mean I'm going to get there. I have a precise idea of where I'm going. To continue that earlier military metaphor: I'm leaving from point A and I'm trying to get to point B, which is two hundred miles away, let's say, across enemy territory. I'm leading a commando raid on fixed positions in certain commercial-aesthetic territory. So I don't get to B. The bridges are blown up. B is no longer there. So I decide, all right, we'll take C, which is fifty miles from there. That's what a commando raid is. A commando raid is not measured by its aesthetic perfection. It's measured by the amount of life it generates, by the amount of stimulation it gives in military history and the amount of time professional soldiers will spend in discussing it afterwards.

What I'm getting at is, supposing I make movies that are only half successful but which stimulate moviemakers who are absolutely dedicated to making movies? What if people who are far better suited to be film directors than I am see *Beyond the Law* and get ideas from it they would not necessarily have had? For instance, I think Andy Warhol is the world's worst moviemaker. But he's enormously stimulating to other moviemakers. He made every director brave enough to shoot a slow scene without trying to speed it up. I think what people will say in a hundred years is: "Warhol made the worst movies in the twentieth century and influenced more people than any other director around."

G: Is there anything in your experience in making three movies that is relevant to young people who'd like to make movies but have been discouraged by the idea that they can't break into the system or raise the money?

M: I think there's at least one thing that's relevant. The less money they have, the more they have to know technically about their subject. If they're serious about making films, then obviously the first thing they've got to do is get their camera one way or another. And they've got to get a good tape recorder, a Nagra, and generally they shouldn't try to do their own sound while they're filming. I think just as a technical matter they should get a good sound man. They've got to get married to a sound man who's terrific. Because that's an art, it's a separate art. Audio is separate from filming. It demands a different kind of athlete, if you will. A different kind of aesthetician. But they've got to find a reliable sound man because sound can make or break their film, as I learned with *Wild 90*.

G: But you found out that there's no viable way to distribute low-budget films commercially even after you've managed to make them.

M: That's a separate problem. That's not really for them to worry about, in a basic way. The only thing they should worry about is making an extraordinary film. If the picture is fantastic enough, they'll find a way to distribute it. If it isn't, then they have a very expensive hobby. And they might eventually get to the point where they work at it and work at it and fail and fail. They're like poets, if you will. How does a poet make a living? The point is not to make a living making films. The point is to participate in the experience, which is an extraordinary experience—filming a movie and then editing it afterwards. Moviemaking is like sex. You start doing it, and then you get interested in getting better at it. I believe that if somebody really wants to make movies, he'll make them.

The Siege of Mailer:
Hero to Historian
Ron Rosenbaum/1971

From *The Village Voice*, 21 January 1971, 1, 38, 40-42, 48.
Reprinted with permission of the author and The Village Voice ©
1971.

"I'm just not tense enough now. How much time is there left? You
know these things are never good unless you go out there tensed
up."

Norman Mailer was sitting on a couch in a dressing room beneath
the stage of the David Frost show. "I'm too relaxed. It's never good
that way, you know. You feel relaxed in here, you step out into the
light and wham the tension hits you anyway. I like to take about 10
minutes before I go on and build up a full head of it, then you can go
out there and you're going the first second."

Someone brought some Jack Daniels and some clear plastic cups
into the dressing room. Mailer came back from make-up and was
thinking about Clay-Frazier. "Boxing is just the opposite of dancing,
you start following a guy, discovering his rhythm, and you're dead.
That's the thing about Clay's style, it's seductive. The fighters get so
fascinated watching him, and then it's too late to get out, and he's got
them."

A studio page appeared: "About 10 minutes now." Mailer left the
dressing room for the taping.

"I'm still not tense enough," he said glumly.

When he talks about writing, the moonshot book, he talks of woe,
and hard work, and the salvation of his soul, and of course he has a
few fight metaphors to tie it all up. "At a certain point in your life you
become a professional writer. Being a professional writer is like being
a professional fighter," he told a luncheon last week. "It means that
someone's started out loving fights in the alley . . . it was a species of

lovemaking for them if you will . . . they'd have eyes with a guy in a bar and they'd fight . . . they got into a fight when they were in the mood.

"At a certain point in their lives a prize fight manager—the man who is the equivalent of a procurer for prostitutes—came along and said, 'You're giving it away, honey, start working, let me pick the guys for you.' "

"So at a certain point this man who loved fighting in the street entered the ring and then developed a secondary ability of being able to concentrate his talent on someone not divinely suited to him . . . "

Mailer stalks out onto the stage of the Frost show, his shoulders hunched, his arms hung slightly forward, lightly hinged at the elbows, hands held apart from hips, playing a heavy from a "West Side Story" street fight or a mean gunslinger from Dodge City.

Frost, who had been staring at the entrance, picked up the gunslinger hint and stalked over to face Mailer, hands ready for a draw, Gary Cooper style.

"Well, if it's gonna be high noon, it's gonna be high noon. I'm ready," he tells Mailer.

The studio audience roars. Frost's move had converted the confrontation—for the audience—into a familiar talk show bit: the Johnny Carson—Jack E. Leonard greeting, the kind where Johnny and Jackie are both mugging frantically and drawing imaginary sixshooters on each other, while the house-band drummer goes wham! wham! wham! and they both clutch their bellies, helplessly laughing. That may have been what the audience was looking for—Mailer is just another talk show gunslinger, right? The Jack E. Leonard of existential combat, right? But Mailer still looked in the mood for a street fight—with Frost, or perhaps with tv—but in the mood.

Mailer calls himself a "professional writer" with an almost belligerent pride—a pro is someone who knows how to work, who can handle any situation, right?—but there is more than a hint of regret evident when he calls himself a professional. Turning professional means more than doing what he's always loved, following his mood, and—how lovely—getting paid for it as well. Turning professional—and the moon book is perhaps his first thoroughly professional major work—means that mood is no longer mistress and muse. It means—to use his metaphors—giving up the improvisatory delights and discoveries of street fighting and lovemaking with an opponent—lover chosen by mood, giving that up for the "secondary" discipline of certain standard combinations and, yes, positions, which work regardless of mood or partner. It means learning to choose good works over profligate grace. It means accepting the idea that he may be the historian of our time, but not its hero.

Who knows whether Mailer began the moon book project as a professional job or an act of love? Yes he needed the money badly, but "secretly the job attracts him" he writes in the original Life version of the story. He has not lost his lust to have his hand "on the rump of history." On the other hand he confesses feeling he is no longer "working for the Lord. Now in fact he was writing for Life, for deadlines, for assignment, for fair fortunes."

This harsh judgment upon himself—in Mailer's cosmology for man to abandon working for God is to condemn God to defeat in his struggle with alien visions—was pronounced in the late summer of 1969 and appeared in the second installment of his Life articles on the moonshot. After a full year more of work on the book, he is less ready to condemn himself for turning professional, and has cut that "working for Life" passage out of the final version of his book. Not only is he less harsh on professionalism, you sense him beginning to wonder if he has not abandoned God, but instead discovered that work may be the only path to salvation for him now.

He is still not comfortable with the idea: "I think that if we could all save our souls through hard work and discipline, then I think we all would," he told the luncheon. "But I think it's more tricky than that. In other words, you may end up saving your soul for too little, end up saving your soul, but my God in terms of Karma you've gone down the elevator."

Mailer has written that there are certain moments in a man's life when he can leap off a building and *know* that his soul will fly up to be welcomed by the moon. Once such a moment has passed any leap will result in both body and soul plummeting to the street. Mailer certainly doesn't want to take that slow elevator down to the street, but perhaps he's wondering if it's better to go that way than to keep trying to leap without hope of flying.

Deciding whether or not one has indeed "turned professional" is a difficult enough decision to make in privacy, having much to do with whether one feels he is selling his soul, possibly selling it for too little, or saving it through hard work and discipline, and perhaps saving it for too little. Mailer's privacy of feeling about the moon book project ripped away from him at the beginning and made a public spectacle a media error which might be called the Million Dollar Misunderstanding.

The Misunderstanding was simple and quantitative, according to Mailer. The Times and the news magazines, guilty of either slovenly or invidious journalism, reported that he had signed a contract with Life to write about the moonshot which would, all fringe benefits considered, bring him One Million Dollars. The facts, according to Mailer, are that he was to get less than $450,000. He points this out in the book itself. He mentioned it pointedly at the luncheon; he brought it up on each of the two tv appearances he made plugging the book, because the Misunderstanding still hangs over him: in the public mind, the moonshot book is still "the one Mailer got a million dollars from Life to do." One Million Dollars is a kind of touchstone number in America: I Wouldn't Do It for a Million Bucks; You'd Have to Give Me a Cool Million to Get Me to Do It, or You Can't Buy It for a Million Dollars. A Million Dollars is not a sum of money, but a Diamond as Big as the Ritz, the price of a very high class soul, the price of It, if It can be bought at all.

What woe for Mailer to discover—just as he's feeling out his new subject to see if love or a cosmic street fight might be in the offing— that as far as American consciousness was concerned, he had already turned into a Professional, one whose price was One Million Dollars. The Life deal was spoken of as if it were The Fall of Man or A Pact with the Devil, a betrayal perhaps of the Vision for which he wanted to be hero.

What woe for Mailer to realize that to save his soul—a soul he hadn't even sold, damn it, but he *was* a public figure and even if it had been sold for him by slovenly journalists, only he could earn it back—to realize that to save his soul he was going to have to conceive and deliver a million-dollar baby of a book from a "sex stripped mystery of machines," the hardest story of all to write.

And perhaps, public misunderstanding or not, Mailer realized privately that this book *was* to be a professional job, and that a part of him, the strict Puritanical taskmaster within him, knew that he still had to prove to himself that he hadn't sold himself, that he could be a

Professional and Norman Mailer, street fighter-writer, at the same time, without needing water-tight compartments to seal the two off from each other.

Mailer and Frost stalk back to their chairs. But they do not sit: they stand facing each other, Mailer still the hunched-over street fighter.

"I'm famous for my apelike propensities," says Mailer in a voice which articulates syllables with Frost's casual precision.

"Well, shall we sit down," says Frost in tones which out-parody any parody of Frost. Mailer explains he's taken a lesson in "voice el-o-cue-shun" today so he can sound like "one of Powell's characters."

"Powell?"

"Yes, Anthony Powell the novelist, your countryman."

"Oh, I thought you meant Adam Clayton Powell," says Frost, managing to score with the audience for his all-American mistake, and perhaps with Mailer by being amused that Mailer could be so naive as to think he, Frost, didn't know which Powell he was really talking about.

It was a silly fight, this exchange of Powell jabs, but by the end of it each one was leaning intently into each comeback, setting it up even if he didn't have anything sharp to deliver.

In the next few rounds Mailer kept jabbing verbally at Frost and Frost held his own, often going for the easy elegant victory of mockery, allowing Mailer, who usually is a counterpuncher, to plunge ahead with his combinations. The lines just weren't coming to Mailer, and Frost was laying back and waiting to prey on his mistakes.

"Have you ever fought with professional fighters?" Frost asked mildly at one point.

"Never, when I could be humiliated in public," Mailer replied with mock gloom.

It was no longer clear whether Mailer still looked on his match with Frost as a good-mood verbal street fight. He was working hard and taking some punishment.

There were moments, Mailer recalls, of "extraordinary woe" in the year-long struggle to write the moon book. "There was a moment of extraordinary woe somewhere in the event when I realized there could be no way I could cover it journalistically, no way I could come back after the event and spend two, four, six, or eight weeks writing hard and come back with something I could accept . . . if you're gonna be paid a huge sum for it, you've gotta come back with

something which will give your ego sleep . . . it was a woe that I had
to work 20 times harder than I wanted to work, and it wasn't the
particular year of my life I wanted to work."

"The kind of woe Cassius Clay felt about the third, or sixth or
seventh round of the Buonavena fight, when he realized he was
going to have to go 15 long terrible rounds and might really lose it
. . . and lose it badly."

Mailer did not look at all bruised in the flesh from his struggle with
the moon book last week. Although the age of Aquarius is now 47,
he looked fit and refreshed. He had just delivered a 55,000-word
piece on women's liberation to *Harper's*—hard work ("I don't think
any man has thought harder about the subject," he said)—but a
labor of love: he was looking forward with the grin of a happy warrior
to the combat which will break out when it's published. In addition
he's looking forward with delight to writing about the Clay-Frazier
fight this March. If he had turned professional, he looked like he was
still doing it for love most of the time.

But throughout his conversation last week—in addition to the
luncheon, I interviewed him the next day and listened to him before
the Frost show taping—there are hints that the woe of the moonshot
book struggle left his vision re-ordered.

"The reason I came on this way is to dramatize to the American
public how important the Clay-Frazier fight is," Mailer told Frost after
a few more sweaty rounds of verbal exchange. "For the first time you
have the matching of the best of two styles. Clay's style, you know,
you can enjoy every minute of it. With Clay you're seduced into
watching it and enjoying it. I came out here tonight like Joe Frazier.
Frazier's just a magnificent man. He's always working."

Work: that's what Clay learned about, in that horrified vision in that
round of the Buonavena fight—that magic and beauty and wild talent
were impotent in the ring with an opponent so divinely unsuited as
the raw-boned, gangly, aggressively inelegant Oscar Buonavena.
(Yes, in the moon book Mailer decides that "America was like a
rawboned lover gangling into middle age, still looking for his
mission.")

In that last fight Clay learned perhaps that the only way he could
survive would be through grim and sweaty punishing work, he could
only survive by abandoning the style which defined him, the
seemingly effortless seductive boxing magic by grace of which he

never seemed to work on, or even to be touched by the other fighter.

Frazier, you sense is someone who has become a professional very, very early—you wonder if he was ever a street fighter—not because of any compromise or fall from grace, but because the agony of hard work is the only form of grace he's known: "every discipline of his moves spoke of grim devoted unrelenting support given to all his body world of muscle . . . a form of grace since the agony of the lungs when straining is not alien to the agony of the soul." Yes, this is Frazier, but the passage is taken from Mailer's description of none other than Apollo 11 Astronaut Buzz Aldrin. (Mailer goes on to tell us he senses deep within Aldrin's "50 psychic institutional casings" of lead a wild streak of radium which can flash into his *eye* at rare moments.)

Given all Mailer's parable-like talk about the fight it will be interesting to discover who his favorite will turn out to be or if he will pull for neither but watch the fight for a Sign.

The instinctive assumption before his experience with the moonshot book is that Mailer will be with Clay. Clay is certainly closer to Mailer's old notion of the hip, existential hero courage, a beautiful "seductive" style, grace, a hint of mystery (that phantom punch), etc., etc., etc. Frazier seems at first less a man of courage than of discipline and efficiency, the courage of a well-built machine, a creation of a punishing work ethic, a Wernher Von Braun among black fighters.

Frazier's courage may reside more in efficiency than grace, but I have a feeling that Mailer has become fed up with the hero who doesn't work. Clay has never had to "work" in the ways that Frazier, or an astronaut, or a clock or a Calvinist seem to work. But for three years he did not work at all—he was idle. The idleness was forced upon him, but in Mailer's metaphysics any failure to continue growing breeds cancer within the cells. And Mailer is filled with a Puritanic rage against idleness these days. You can feel it in his disgust at his friends, his generation, and the generation which followed his adventures with drugs and sex and dread and mystery—they have "fucked out" their creativity, burned out their minds, and squandered their capital of dread. Rawboned gangling America has been looking for a mission, for an adventure for two decades, and his people have been too busy squandering their gifts to offer one. Finally hard-working, machine-like, professional, Faustian NASA offers America-the-gangling lover an adventure, a mistress, and

Mailer and his people have to face the magnitude of their failure, and the consequences.

As hard as it is to envision Mailer adopting Frazier as the hero of this fight, it is equally hard and equally necessary for him to accept Buzz Aldrin—half man, half machine—as a replacement for Hemingway. "What joy in a world with no hope of a Hemingway?" he asks in the moon book; even less joyous is a world with no hope of a heroism at all, so heroism of a kind just has to be found and accepted in astronauts Aldrin, Armstrong, and Collins.

Mailer is both attracted and dismayed by the astronaut, half-machine, half-hero. He admires their "ability to get all that coldness and deadness all together in one compartment, for their job. Most of us have a tendency to let a little coldness and deadness seep into our private lives—we become a little dead at home, a little dead out on the job," he said last week.

Mailer insists the astronauts do have a private "compartment," filled with dread, mystery, and mission, but buried so deep they are hardly aware of it. But the compartmented heroism of the astronauts is not congenial to Mailer because there is little of that constant encounter with "one's portion of dread" (give us this day our daily dread) that has been a quality of heroism for him.

In his book, Mailer offers a nice dialectical counterpart to the half-hero, half-machine astronaut: a belief that deep within the circuitry of the most complex machines secret flickers of consciousness have been kindled, whispers of psyche have arisen within the electronic hum.

Mailer's is not a vision of man versus technology, but of struggles of each tendency—psyche and machine—within man and technology, perhaps the same struggle going on within himself between amateur street fighter and professional.

Hard workers Frazier and Aldrin may not be Mailer's favorite new heroes, but I suspect that given the possibilities Mailer would rather win as Frazier than lose as Clay, that he might rather be on the side of winners like Aldrin than even the most hip of losers, even if it meant compromising his style and locking up his ego.

Meanwhile back at the Frost Show:

"Tell me who *your* heroes are," Frost asks Mailer.

"I'm not gonna tell you . . . that's the kind of thing you keep a discreet silence on . . . things you care about . . . not on tv."

"Why?"

"I hate tv. It makes me feel like I'm in an operating room. The difference between writing a book and being on television is the difference between conceiving a child and having a baby made in a test tube."

"Oh rubbish," said Frost.

Eight hours earlier Mailer had been talking to me about the dangers of tv talk shows: "People are better off walking 10 miles to hear some rotten band play than to hear some incredible stereo. Because they're not really getting what they think they're getting and there's a fundamental, even metaphysical, cheat involved. In other words they may be doing something to the senses that's irrevocable by listening to the fine stereo system . . . you can refine the stereo to the point where the thing sounds better than it does in the concert hall, nonetheless you are not getting the experience you think you're getting . . . you're getting something that has a psychological reality but not an existential reality.

"One example is if you see a tv show at midnight, one of the talk shows that's been done at 6:30 in the evening, there's a subtle distortion of focus that you're not gonna quite pick up, particularly since these shows work to get a kind of midnight atmosphere, nonetheless they're taped in late afternoon, not at midnight, so the people watching are subtly out of phase with the people doing the show and they don't quite know it—they're not in the same scheme of time and when people are not in the same scheme of time I think that subtle psychic diseases, very delicate psychic diseases, get laid in that may not show themselves for 50 years or as much as 100 years."

TV then is the subtle antagonist, the smooth rhetorician serving only the worst tendencies within technology, a disease whose symptoms include the inability to notice that one has symptoms. If there is a villain in Mailer's moonshot book, it is not Technology, which may indeed be at war within itself, but television. In the long central section of the book, Mailer attempts to give the event the reality it *had*, the reality which did not appear on tv, to fill the vacuum behind the tv image. He stops watching the astronauts looking out from the tv screen and attempts to infiltrate himself into the souls of the astronauts to look out upon the phenomenon of the moon voyage from behind their eyes, to see it *with* their eyes and feel the responses of *their* psyche to what is perceived. To begin this attempt at infiltration Mailer first learned every fact he could about the astronauts, their ship, their environment, read dozens of technical

manuals, did an enormous work of scholarship and research. Then,
like all infiltrators, Method actors, confidence men, and some
novelists, he attempted to bracket his own ego, his personal Vision,
and slip into those of an astronaut to taste their dreams, nightmares,
and insomnias.

To succeed too well is dangerous—to become perfectly "objective"
is to lose the self. I don't think Mailer succeeds too well at this (often
he seems to proclaim by mere fiat that things Apollonian are in fact
profoundly Dionysian within) but he does succeed well enough to
make you realize you *were* cheated, that you did have symptoms
without knowing it—to give you an idea of the mystery, heroism, and
dread you were cheated of: the "simple human witness" of the event.
"They killed the greatest week—what did they call it—the greatest
week since The Creation."

If tv is the subtlest antagonist, talk shows are the subtlest of its
subtle killers. The promise of the talk show is that "midnight
atmosphere" of intimacy and disclosure. The promise is that the next
uneasy gap in conversation will not be filled by one more self-
conscious joke about the gap in conversation, but that someone will
fill it with a desperate revelation, or perhaps that the gap will yawn
wider and wider never to be filled, swallowing the utterly humiliated
host and guests. The promise is that after all the jokes about jokes
about jokes-that-went-flat, there will either be some shocking wild
joker of a joke, or everyone will stop trying to be funny. The promise
is that sometime something *really dirty* will slip by unbleeped. The
promise is that some contemporary hero will make a fool of himself
so embarrassingly and so utterly without hope of ad lib rescue, that
he will really have damaged himself.

Talk show hosts are masters of the last minute rescue, masters at
giving you the feeling that things—even boredom—might be getting
out of hand, that genuine horror or shame or wonder might reach
out from the vacuum behind the image and hook you inside, and
give you the feeling that all could break loose because it is happening
live, in the same time scheme as you. Communion as real as trying to
swallow the eucharist offered by hand of a tv priest on your screen.
(Mailer's Stephen Rojack of *An American Dream* was for a time host
of a wild talk show, but under network pressure made a
"professional" compromise, and turned himself into a hip David
Susskind.)

"You shouldn't have said that what *I* said was rubbish," said Mailer.

"Why?"

"Because they'll *believe* you," said Mailer. "They'll hear you say rubbish and they'll remember that and then tomorrow they'll say, 'Yes, Frost really demolished him last night.' "

Mailer had always suspected that God might lose his all-out war with the Devil. But he never suggested that God was capable of making a compromise, a squalid *deal*, just to keep himself alive. Toward the close of the moon book he starts to reconsider his "embattled vision" of God, a vision he "first encountered around one of the bends of marijuana 15 years ago."

What if God, engaged in a combat "just so crude as the counts of point in a contest . . . what if God, aghast at the coming death of man in man-devilled pollution, was finally ready to relinquish some part of the Vision and substitute a vision half-machine half-man rather than lose all?"

Here is something new in Mailer's cosmology! He once was a God constantly being further created or destroyed by the courage or fear we manifest in moments of dread and passion, a God whose ethic is that nothing is won unless you accept the possibility that all can be lost. This is hardly a God for bargaining—the frustrations of compromise, of failure to risk extinction, give birth to cancer in the cells.

But the God Mailer speaks of now is ready to sell half His soul, hedge His bet, silence Himself in order to stow away aboard the Apollo without being noticed—for the astronauts fulfill, indeed embody, that now compromised Vision of a species half-man half-machine, with each half locked away from the other.

Mailer finds "an agony of pain" thinking these thoughts, for "if one held them truly . . . responsibility was then like a burning of the blood."

Why Mailer's responsibility? Well, once he thought he might become a major prophet, that "he had only to get on all the radio and television available and he would be able to change the world." Now he has to struggle clumsily with a subtle antagonist to try to redeem just one tv talk show from its pre-taped time scheme.

Now Mailer is less prophet and more professional. He has not become for the generations following him what Hemingway had become for him. Once he and his friends of his generation had thought they were going to *be* America's next adventure, their lives were going to lead us out on moon voyages; "princelings on the trail of hip, they were so avid to deliver the sexual revolution they had virtually strained on the lips of the great gate." The image suggests premature ejaculation, but the real failure is the consequent failure to *conceive*—to make it past the gate and bring back alive a vision, a mission to deliver to America. One's lifetime supply of—metaphysical—seed is limited, Mailer feels, and his generation has spilled its seed wastefully, fucking away its creativity, without penetrating closer to the center of any mystery.

I asked Mailer if it was this sense of failure of "his side" that had not made him more ready to try to embrace the space program.

"Well, I think what I felt for the first time was a real feeling that the other side might win, which of course I felt all along . . . but I've always felt they were going to win because they were stronger, 'cause they were gonna have it easier, because they haven't been through what we've all gone through, because they're just bigger, and mainly because they were just given the guns.

"But after the moonshot, this was the first time I thought that *maybe* they were gonna win because they *deserved* to win, because they had been working harder at their end of the war than we have.

"Do they deserve to win because they are winning, because they are hard workers, or are they winning because their vision is superior?

"No, I don't have any fundamental belief in them, I think they'll never get there if you get down to it, to that other, unless they learn from us, maybe we're Greeks to their Romans, but if I learned one thing after all these years, it's that they never listen to you."

Portrait of a Man Reading
Charles Monaghan/1971

From *The Washington Post Book World*, 11 July 1971, 2. Reprinted by permission of The Washington Post. Note: Mailer's replies were slightly truncated and paraphrased by *The Washington Post.*

What was your childhood reading?

When I was ten or eleven, I read all the Tarzan books of Edgar Rice Burroughs and they inspired me to write my first novel, about a trip to Mars. I called it *The Martian Invasion*—even then I had some sense of the ambiguities of the English language because the title meant we were invading Mars, not vice versa. The villain of the novel was called Dr. Huer, after a gentleman of the same name in Buck Rogers.

Any other youthful reading?

When I was fourteen, fifteen, sixteen, I was reading my way through Jeffrey Farnol and Rafael Sabatini. Farnol wrote a whole bunch of novels with titles like *The Amateur Gentleman.* He was very romantic about his woman characters—they were all beautiful, noble, and passionate. You can see he influenced me there. But that's about all the reading I did during adolescence, except for *Model Airplane News* and *Spicy Detective.* You can say *Spicy Detective* was an influence on *An American Dream.* When I was going to Harvard, I had to prepare a reading list and had to fake the thing from beginning to end. I put on all sorts of worthy books—*The Rise of Silas Lapham* by William Dean Howells, *The Americanization of Edward Bok.* I don't even know what their first pages look like.

How about your reading at Harvard?

That was what you'd call cultural shock. In my freshman year, I switched from reading Jeffrey Farnol to reading James T. Farrell. If any single event makes you a writer, that sort of shock does. I was fascinated by his books—*Studs Lonigan,* the Danny O'Neill series.

The characters were in an economic group just one notch below
mine and it was thrilling to see how they lived. They made me want
to be a writer. Farrell demonstrated to me that everything in life was
worth writing about.

And there was Dos Passos. I picked up *USA* a while ago and read
one or two chapters—it was just as good as I remember it. It may be
a great novel. I must sit down soon and read it all the way through
again. Dos Passos gave me the strongest, simplest, most direct idea
about what it is to write a great American novel. There is no
replacement for The Great American Novel as an ideal for a writer to
hold up for himself.

Then there were Hemingway, Fitzgerald, Steinbeck, Wolfe,
Faulkner. I read and reread them all through college. Hemingway and
Fitzgerald are important imaginative figures in my life.

How do you think they rank as artists?
Their books stand up as experiences rather than as philosophical
works. Take a marvelous book like Stendhal's *The Red and the
Black*. It tells you so much about the world, about society, about
formal patterns of love—the subject matter is translation-proof. But in
Hemingway and Fitzgerald, it's the sensuous evocation of things. The
effect on the gut is closer to poetry. My new movie *Maidstone* is like
that—more of an experience than a story. Stendhal is a novelist but in
a way he's closer to somebody like Jacques Ellul, a describer of
society. By the way, Ellul's *Technological Society* is very fine, a near
thing to a great book.

What other things did you read at Harvard?
You know I was an engineering major. But about halfway through,
I decided I didn't care about being an engineer, so I took what I
wanted to take—modern art, four writing courses. Stuff for fun. I
guess I must be the most monumental living testimony to the value of
writing courses. But it was sheer idiocy—I was doing the writing
anyway. It meant I didn't have to do any work. By the time a year
started, I'd have about 300,000 words of fiction in the bag and I'd
dribble it out as the year went along.

*You got out of Harvard in 1943 and then there was the Army.
What did you read in those years?*
I had *The Decline of the West* in two volumes in my duffle bag all

the way through the Philippines. It got all mildewed. You know
Spengler had a jewel of a brain. He loves to make remarks that have
a thundering power. Wild comparisons . . . like "One must
remember that the dynasty of Louis XIV is paralleled by the
development of perspective in late baroque art and the early
commercialization of the tin trade from the colonies." That sort of
thing. McLuhan has been enormously influenced by Spengler. The
business of dazzling you with the big statement, that intellectual shell
game, the ideas thrown at you one after another before you have
time to absorb them. Spengler was the same, except that he threw in
names in every clause.

What other reading were you doing in the Army?
Dashiell Hammett, Raymond Chandler, that sort of thing. I read
Anna Karenina on the way home to the States, just before I started
The Naked and the Dead.

After that?
Das Kapital, which I spent about four months reading. I have never
got over it.

Why?
Well, apart from its continuing validity, it is a great portrait of
society, a great novel. The experience of living in a great man's mind
for a few months is irreplaceable. It was similar to the spiritual
experience that a devout young Catholic might get from reading
Augustine. Enlarging your world. In fact, reading *Das Kapital* turned
me toward mysticism. It is such a perfect picture of our social
machine—if it is a machine—that when you try to understand how
such a perfect machine could work, you begin thinking about
transcendental machines, and you get into that most mystical of
notions, the dialectic. Now from Marx we will jump quickly to . . .

*Do you find the dialectic a principle used by other writers you
admire?*
There is no such thing as a real writer who doesn't employ the
dialectic. Henry James never wrote a sentence that wasn't imbued
with the dialectic. He is always reacting to the sentence he wrote
before. That's what good writing is. The beginning of bad writing is
when a writer forgets what he's just written. That's what I'd tell kids if
I ever had a writing class. I'd bang that home.

Can you think of any other writers who employ the dialectic?
Joyce, in *Finnegan,* using the dialectic as an intellectual structure.
Proust—Baron de Charlus is conceived dialectically in opposition to
the narrator.

And from Marx we quickly jump to . . . ?
The Function of the Orgasm. Wilhelm Reich. He was no literary
influence, but he gave me one idea—a man's character is in his
orgasm, a man's neuroses are in his orgasm, everything is in his
orgasm. That idea is in my work and even a pale reflection of it drives
some people into a rage. The Reich I most admire is the Reich of
Character Analysis, a difficult, unreadable book, and *The Function.* I
am not too enthusiastic about his later work—and little orgones flying
around. Organized psychoanalysis drove him mad. In fact, a lot of
ideas taken for granted now in psychoanalysis come from Reich. The
idea that a man's physical posture is his character comes right out of
Reich. After Reich, I guess I stopped reading.

Do you read any poetry?
Oddly enough, I am starting to read poetry. Casually, eclectically.
I'll buy anthologies of American poetry and keep them in the john.
I'm reading the Imagists at the moment—Amy Lowell, Pound, T. E.
Hulme, D. H. Lawrence. I love reading poetry because I don't
approach it critically. To be a great critic of poetry would take a
lifetime of work in poetry. I read it to replenish myself. I was out in
Colorado last year and somebody gave me a poem by Galway
Kinnell about tracking an animal and sleeping inside the skin—which
is much like *Why Are We in Vietnam?* and written at the same time. It
was a magnificent poem. But my tastes in poetry are so catholic—I
like everybody from Lowell to Ginsberg.

Do you like poetry for its language or its spirit?
More the spirit than the language. What poets do with language is
interesting, but I don't stand in awe of them. Pound once said
something to the effect that good poetry must read at least as well as
good prose, and a lot of poets don't write as well as good prose
writers. And of course they're often a marvelous study in sham and
hypocrisy. But the normal poet writes better than the normal prose
writer. You don't get the same shudder from a not-too-good poet that
you do when you're reading a not-to-good novelist.

How about philosophical writing?

I'm an existentialist. Not that I read Sartre and said my God, he's right. I have enormous admiration for Sartre, but his position is that life is an absurdity and we pretend it has meaning. For me life is meaningful but everything in the scheme of things will drive us to seeing things as absurd. We could hardly be more different. He is an atheist and I'm not.

The one I'd really like to read is Heidegger. At one time I literally thought of learning German just to read Heidegger in the original. But if I have any philosophical bent, it will come out in my writing and I don't have to become a flunky for some other thinker.

Essays and journalism?

I don't read much, but Marshall Frady is unbelievably good. His description of George Wallace is unforgettable. That's his best book. Tom Wolfe, in spite of his undeniable excess, is a hell of a journalist. Jimmy Breslin may be the best journalist we've got for a thousand words. That's not to make any invidious remarks about his longer stuff—I haven't read his novel yet. Pete Hamill has more guts than any journalist I know. He takes on the Mafia *and* the police and that takes a lot of guts.

Norman Mailer Talks to Melvyn Bragg about the Bizarre Business of Writing a Hypothetical Life of Marilyn Monroe
Melvyn Bragg/1973

From *The Listener,* 20 December 1973, 847–50. Reprinted by permission of The Listener.

You call your book a novel biography, and you say the question is whether a person can be comprehended by the facts of his life.

I think there are lives that depend entirely on their facts. The life of our President Calvin Coolidge was a life compiled entirely of fact. Even if you take someone like Richard Nixon, it's very, very important, if you're doing a biography of him, not to speculate, to know what the facts are. But that's because they're men who have been forced to be responsible from the time they were children. They think in terms of the facts and they live with the facts. Marilyn, I quickly discovered after I read a couple of books about her and a number of articles, was absolutely protean. In fact, she was amorphous, and you couldn't begin to think about the facts of her life in the same way. Whenever you tried to find out something about it—a particular fact—you'd find two opposite facts. Sexually, for example, you'd hear that she was absolutely fabulous and absolutely frigid. You would almost never hear anything between. What you began to realise after a while was that the particular facts about her life were not important. She was always capable of doing the exact opposite of what she was doing at a given moment. If she was A on one day, it was nothing for her to be Z on the following day. And so the particular sequence in which she did A and Z became less important. And you began to recognise that the people who surrounded her were, most of them, show-business: they lived for legend and loved legend, and were not only not interested in telling the truth about her as they knew it—because, after all, very often they'd been cruel to her and no one is more pious about the past than a sadist—but weren't likely to remember, and in fact disremembered. They'd created so many legends and told them about her so many times that they'd tell you the fiction rather than the fact.

You coined the word 'factoid': for this sort of thing?

No. A factoid is a fact which has no existence on earth other than that what's appeared in the newspaper and then gets repeated for ever after. So people walk around as if it is the blooming lively fact. There is all that about her too. She lived in a swamp of legends, lies and factoids.

So did you say to yourself: I can invent the truth myself? Was it a sort of contest undertaken in your mind?

Well, no. Remember it started as a preface. And the preface got longer and longer, and finally my feeling was: let it be the longest preface ever written. But I could do a book about her, was the confidence I had. There's something I know about her that other people are not likely to know. I know an awful lot about being a celebrity. I know an awful lot about living with one's legend. And I know an awful lot, as a result, about the sort of separation of mind that goes on. I know what it's like to live a little bit on the edge of schizophrenia. I know a fair amount about acting by now. I'd read two fairly good biographies. One very detailed, the other more factoidal, but at the same time full of colour, and they were altogether different in their interpretation of her. Between the two and my own notion of her, and all the movies, and the 14 people I had interviewed before the book was over, I had the confidence that I was in as good a position to say something reasonably definitive as anyone else around. And there were any number of people I didn't want to interview. Joe DiMaggio specifically. I would not have been able to interview him if I'd wanted to. I could have got on my hands and knees and sung 'Mammy' and he would not ever have consented to an interview. And you can respect that. He was in love with the woman, and who wants it to be said: now you were in love with your wife ten years ago—tell us . . . Why interview him anyway? He's not a man who's famous for the precision of his search into his emotional depths. He's not going to tell you much about her that you don't know already. In fact, he's going to take away from you the right to speculate, because if you break bread with a man, have a drink with him, and you interview him, unless you're a case-hardened reporter you have to respect that he gave you his confidences. So I speculated. I know a fair amount about athletes, and a considerable amount about people like DiMaggio getting married to people like Monroe, and I felt that was going to be more interesting and probably truer. In any case, I made it clear to the reader, all the way, that what I was doing, in effect, was showing them how we set out to comprehend the life. And if we try to comprehend the life of some historical figure, we don't interview that many people. In other words, if you have a curiosity about Cromwell, for instance, or—let's take someone living—if you have a curiosity about Richard Burton, but are not going to do a full-scale biography, you may talk to a few people who've met him, but finally your picture of Burton will come from a few books you may read about him and the intense application of your mind to what he's like.

Do you feel then that this book is very close to the fiction you've written?

It's a hypothesis about the nature of her life, and what I've said to the reader is that if it's any good as a hypothesis, the more facts we discover about her, given the difficulty of discovering any facts about her, the more they'll fit this hypothesis. Almost, this hypothesis will become better and better as the years go on. It's a biography which will grow into its clothes.

What did you find out about her childhood?

It depended almost completely on one biographer, Fred Lawrence Guiles, who'd done a lot of very good work on her childhood and gave one a portrait of her. I thought the best way to treat it was to give Guiles's account of her childhood pretty directly, giving full attribution, and live on the edge of speculation. He was rather reticent about his supposings, and I'm not. I thought: I'll just suppose all over the place and I'll explore. So I ruminate and meditate over her childhood—almost in an avuncular position. I kept saying to the reader, in effect: look, either this is true or that's true. Either an attempt was made to strangle her by her grandmother or it wasn't so. All through the childhood and the early years there's so little facts. Yet she began to emerge for me as a writer, and I began to think at a certain point: this ought to be carried over to fiction. We tend to be too precise in fiction: we're too sure of the edges of our characters, whereas in life we never are. We're always adding new things that people tell us about our friends. Sometimes it comes in as certified information. Sometimes it comes in as moot ideas. People travel in a swarm of ambiguity.

This links up with something you said in your essay on the White Negro: that sublimation was no longer possible because things were moving too fast.

I think that sublimation was a psychic state that worked at its best in the 19th century for the middle class, and that Freud may have made the slight error of assuming that it was a universal condition. But sublimation may actually be a luxury, a species of luxury. Maybe there are people who live without sublimation, just as there are people who can live to a certain extent without dreaming. A newspaper reporter, for one. He can see something and write it up the same night. All other sorts of writer usually see something and have to go to bed, for one night at least, and sleep on it before they write, because the unconscious has to work on it. There has to be a certain sublimation of the material—to stretch the meaning of the word just a bit.

Her childhood was almost a total disaster area, and yet out of that quarry she drew things for the rest of her life.

She was brought up by foster-parents. She was illegitimate, and her mother worked for a movie studio: not a film-cutter, but somewhere between a film-cutter and a film librarian. She was foreman over a group of ladies who tacked beginnings and ends onto films. Her mother seemed to have a profound preoccupation, which was to get her child back and raise her. Not that the foster-parents were evil people at all: they were rather God-fearing people and slightly timid and stern, if you will, but not at all terrible people. In Marilyn's family insanity was the major theme. Her mother ended up spending most of her life in a mental hospital, Marilyn's grandfather and grandmother on her mother's side both died in mental hospitals, and her mother's brother died in a mental hospital. There are some fairly good guesses as to who the father was, but she never knew her father, never met him. Marilyn lived with her mother for about a year and a half and then the mother went mad one day and was carried off to a mental hospital. Marilyn never saw her again for about eight

or ten years. After that Marilyn lived with people who took care of her
for a while, but didn't have much money themselves, including a
British couple who were actors. The man used to be a stand-in for
George Arliss. They finally couldn't support her, and had to go back
to England. At that point Marilyn went into a mental hospital—I beg
your pardon, went to an orphanage. The slip is interesting because all
orphanages are a rather drab species of mental hospital. Maybe what
characterises all institutions is that the institutional part of them is
more significant than the specific content. The medium is the
message and the message is institutionality. It's my small thesis—it's
hardly new—that institutions make chronic liars out of people. This has
nothing to do with the meanness of the people who run institutions.
An institution has to function as the machinery that is intrinsic to it,
and this machinery is such that the people who're in it have to fit into
the machinery. So what happens is that the people in the institution
tend to lie automatically, so they won't be the machine—or at least
what the machine's supposed to be. You could do anything in the
Army providing you gave lip-service to the way the idea was
supposed to work. The men who went out on patrols almost never
gave an accurate report on what was happening. We'd say we'd
reached a certain point. We hadn't. We'd looked at that point
through field-glasses a mile away and the sergeant would say, 'Do
you see any enemy activity there?' and we'd say we don't see none.
He'd say: 'Good, I don't see none either. Let's get back.' Then we'd
report it, and it would go all the way up to headquarters. We were
liars. I think the ability to lie enabled her to advance herself in one
way—which was that she was able to tell stories that would really
touch people. There's one story she tells about being raped at the
age of nine. This seems highly improbable. Her first husband states
that she was a virgin when they were married: she married at the
very early age of 16. There are reasons to believe that she wasn't
raped—including the way that she tells the story. She tells the story in
a way that's so patently in the style of a feature-writer that it's almost
as if she had a certain sense of how feature-writers write. She'd tell
stories that would arouse people's sympathy: there are endless stories
that people tell about meeting her and she was such a waif and they
adored her so and such horrible things had happened to her.
Horrible things *had* happened to her. But she sensed there was a
need to dramatise that: I spent 20 months in an orphan asylum and it

deadened things in me for ever, and produced a subtle bitterness that I'm going to have to pay for in 25 years when I'm bitching and poisoning everyone on the set and making life impossible for my co-workers.

Another notion that you draw from her childhood, which is a dangerous notion in a way, is that the small amount of personal identity she had, the narrow sense of her own character, was a great help to her as an actress.

Actors almost always are indignant when you suggest that they might have less sense of personal identity than other people. I think it is generally true. It is my thesis that the foundation stones for the great actor are illegitimacy and insanity.

Tell that to Laurence Olivier.

I hear by now that he's become so splendid one wouldn't dare. The search for identity may be more important in people's lives than any other passion: more important than sex, success or creativity. The centre of their search is for identity: for reasons that almost go beyond the scope of anything one can talk about. It may be that they have souls that are literally looking for some abode. And I think she had this dilemma more than any other actor. Liars always create their own punishment because they travel through unreal situations every step of their lives. So for them a role is superb. A role is a way in which they can be real, because they don't have to lie.

It's a relief.

It's almost as if in every liar there's a closet honesty of intense energies, and those energies go into the role. All the honesty they've been concealing in their lives goes into the role.

You refer in your book to this business of coincidences. She used to boast that her father was Clark Gable, whom she ended up with in her film 'The Misfits' towards the end of her life. And then she was responsible, in a sense, for killing him: he had a heart attack just after that film finished. And people called Baker, which was her real name, making films.

Making her first starring role.

And so on.

I've long had the thought that when you have highly-charged dramatic people engaged in a confrontation—Shakespearian characters, for example—coincidences tend to occur. But then if there's any order at all in the cosmos it's not so exceptional that coincidences occur. In other words, if you have, let's say, a general getting ready for battle, and there are gods and devils surrounding this general, whether this general wins or loses the war will have a certain effect on the fortunes of these gods. They're going to be paying a great deal of attention to this general, aren't they? And the general's going to be paying a great deal of attention to them, insofar as he has any sensitivity to their presence. And such a man's not necessarily psychotic if he spends ten minutes in bed—he won't have the opportunity usually—debating whether to put the left foot down first or the right, because maybe he's calling on whole echelons of gods. And what we can also see is these gods are going to be up to their tricks. They're going to be doing their best to present coincidences, because a coincidence always inspires us with a terror that there's a superstructure about us and in this superstructure are all sorts of agents of a machine larger than our imagination.

It can give you more energy as well.

There are some people who consider themselves favoured by the gods, and they love coincidence. Beautiful women are thrilled and magnetised by its presence.

Can we go to the time when she did a lot of photographs for magazines? She battled through all that, and got herself onto covers, and eventually had her hair dyed blonde and took the name Marilyn Monroe?

It did two things to her. It made her situation better and worse. It made it better because she was now able to step pretty completely out of herself. In other words, external identity had been handed to her. And that external identity moved her a little better through the world. It was more streamlined, it was more efficient. She was now blonde, with all that means. On the other hand, the fundamental difficulty of her life, which was that she was never close to her own identity, was increased. She was now farther away from herself. This alienation from the self is something which at that time was an unconscious theme in American life. It was as if back in the late Forties and early Fifties a great many people unconsciously began to sense that they were getting further and further away from themselves. There was something funny in the scheme of things. The whole apparatus of the buildings about us, the things we read, the things we eat, the things we see for entertainment, the philosophies about us, the faiths—everything was making it harder and harder for someone to have a sense of identity. I think by now it's the collective problem of the 20th century. She embodied that mistiness, that vagueness. Part of her appeal was that she took this theme of the alienation of the self, and the other theme that was coming on, the huge sexual liberation that was on its way, and she embodied them both, so that when you saw her in those films, she was just charged with sex and yet she was so remote from herself that sex was always comic. One of the secrets to the star's great successes is that they embody a paradox within themselves.

You say something very strange: that film is a phenomenon whose resemblance to death has been too long ignored.

There's some reason to believe she had a traumatic experience when she was one: that her insane grandmother may have tried to strangle her. Maybe the baby merely sensed some murderous impulse in the grandmother, who was a very violent woman. But if we ever go through a situation where we're brought half unto death—people who almost drown feel as if they've begun to die—we live in a different relation to death from other people. Hemingway certainly did. Hemingway was wounded when he was a young man and it was as if he was never the same after that. It's almost as if that's what made him the writer he was. Marilyn had this, and certainly anyone who comes from a family that's so insane . . . insanity may bear some special relation to death. It's almost as if part of the mind has gone over. Part of the mind may have died and gone off into some other place. Given all this, I think it was natural for her to live in this funny never-never land between one reality and another. The most spooky thing about movies is that your presence goes into a machine and comes out somewhere else. A savage would look upon it as a situation in which you had died and been taken somewhere else. The peculiar ability she had to engrave herself upon the movie camera, to be more alive in front of the movie camera than anywhere else, bears some relation to this peculiar relation she had to being dead. Why did she take sleeping pills? She used to say that it gave her a womby-tomby feeling. It's as if she took these pills because she had to come back to some twilight land between life and death.

Again there's this terrible business of the sort of pressures on her.

At this stage she's at the studio, she's signed up in some sort of way, and not only is she giving herself to the camera but she's also giving her body away, all over the place.

She certainly wasn't necessarily the chastest movie star that ever came down the pike. And it did a great deal to her. It was terrible. Arthur Miller spoke of the bitterness that was left in her by all these bad men who were using her. She went through a legion of vices, diseases, horrors and what have you. Passing on some of her own horrors, perhaps. And all through this is an extraordinarily beautiful, tender woman, caught up in this unbelievably abysmal life, hardly able to hold her mind together with this absolute intensity of purpose that she was going to succeed, to become a great movie star.

Why, with all this talent and with all this drive, did she have to hang around so long at the studios before they gave her parts?

Well, they hated her. They hated her for a variety of reasons. One of them is that they hadn't selected her. She wasn't an old-school boy. Darryl Zanuck, who was not the stupidest man around, always thought she absolutely couldn't act, she had no talent. And, of course, she bore a particularly odd relation to acting. What she was doing was something that was different from acting. Finally she began to bludgeon her way into pictures. Then she got into a long and serious affair with a very famous agent, Johnny Hyde, and he helped her enormously.

I was surprised, before I read your book, that, in a sense, the marriage with DiMaggio hadn't worked better. He was a star in his own way. He was strong. He was working-class. He was a man's man. He had dignity and money. She might have entered into that world and been the great girl for all the men's men in the bars. She would have been the queen of the working class.

He had no understanding of her profound need to be an actress. He'd grown up in a culture in which, if you were an athletic hero, you got your reward, which was the most beautiful woman around, who would pledge fealty to you. He had the misfortune, perhaps, to meet her at the time when her own career was reaching its peak, and she was not about to give up acting for him. And the worst of it was that his projects at that point were getting picayune. He was no longer a great baseball-player. He'd retired, so his project now was to go out and shoot a round of golf of a morning, and to look into one business

here, another business there. She could hardly be as excited about
the restaurant business in San Francisco as she would about being
the star in a movie called 'Gentlemen Prefer Blondes.'

*So she was successful, she was a great movie star, and the first
signs of breaking up started. Why?*

She'd finally laid down a directive for herself. She'd become the
instrument of her will. And her will said: you will succeed. Whenever
anyone does that, they take everything that's weak in them and they
submerge it, very often for years. All hegemony is given to the
strength. There'll be a much weaker personality travelling with that
strong personality which has its own habits, its own demands, and it
will become more and more inflamed. At the first success there's a
tendency to relax just that little bit, and at that point she would have
to take the pills because there was a part of her which was absolutely
outraged at being killed every minute of her existence: the poor timid
little orphan from the orphanage, afraid of everything. With her, the
thing that's so marvelous is that she had such opposites in herself.
She was so brave, on the one hand, and so absolutely timid, on the
other. When she was a child they called her Mousy.

*But she also turned in revenge, didn't she? In 'Seven-Year Itch',
which she went on to make, she kept people waiting for hours, she
made them do 42 takes.*

It got worse with every film. Miller had a fascinating theory about
it, which was that that was how she got her sociology about the
balance of forces in a studio. In other words, about the time she was
driving everyone out of their mind, she was really seeing where
different people began to crack, or different forces began to splinter:
the boiler would begin to burst and out of all that she would get a
picture of the machinery in the studio. It was part of her relation of
power to the studio. There may have been other elements involved. I
think she was a species of silver witch, if you will: it was almost as if
she had to get her inspiration from near-to-occult places. The image I
used in the book was that just as a medium can't deal with hostile
forces in a séance, it seems as if Marilyn had to wear out everyone
around her, to a point where all the people who were hostile toward
her had died down. They were exhausted. And then her talent could
begin to speak. Very often she was superb on the 42nd take and
poor Tony Curtis, who had been fine on takes one through 16,
began to wear out.

This is about the time of her life when you might have met her.

I came awfuly close during that period, particularly after she was married to Miller. I lived five miles away from him in Connecticut, so I kept waiting for the moment for Miller to pick up the phone and say: why don't you come over to dinner? The call never came. I wanted to steal her from Miller. There was no reason at all why he should have invited me over.

What do you think you would have wanted to bring out in her? What would you have said, what would you have done?

I just would have tried to make her fall in love with me. Anyone who was in love with Arthur Miller was not going to fall in love with me. And I hope that proposition also goes vice versa. But if it had ever happened, I probably would have gotten mean designs. I would have thought of writing a play in which she would star. I think you see the comedy of it. It's a terrible tragedy, in a way. A sweet child of life. Men of considerable integrity. They all want to bring her up, make the most of her. But at the same time they're just human enough to want to do it in their way.

After the Miller marriage she emerges, you say, as a major figure in American life of a new sort: she brought a new force to American life, which has been in existence ever since.

John F. Kennedy brought a new force into American life. Coming after Eisenhower, he was extraordinary—a man handsome enough to be a movie star, with a beautiful wife, and President of the United States: you can't comprehend it instantly or automatically. Marilyn was the same way. So long as she had a career that was going on in Hollywood, she was still a figure who was comprehensible. Suddenly she marries the most celebrated and soberest playwright in American life. A man who physically and personally is the picture of moral probity. For the first time, people are not quite able to understand her. It's the first case on record of a blonde movie star at the height of her career breaking a contract in Hollywood to come East to make films.

That's courage again, isn't it?

Best of all, imagination. It's the same motive that made her say no to Johnny Hyde, when he wanted to marry her. He was dying: she would have been a widow and millionaire all at once. She said no because somehow that would have meant that she was no longer sailing her own boat.

So she and Miller came to England to make a film—'The Prince and the Showgirl'—with Olivier, who shocked her by saying: 'Marilyn, be sexy.'

British actors have to learn that sort of technique or they will get nowhere. By now she's a perfect example of the Method—the feeling that you have to create something analogous to the true emotion in yourself before you can present the part. To Olivier, this had to be the most rotten sort of self-indulgence. It didn't take him for ever on a set to get everything shaped up. And Marilyn, who was described as looking like a slob on the set—her muddy-minded coma had to drive him up the wall. In turn, nothing could have offended her more than the injunction to be sexy, because it implied that this, her greatest talent, was merely some little gew-gaw that she had in her pocket-book and could trot out at will, the way Olivier could trot out any one of 42 different accents. There was more than a clash of personalities: it was the profoundest clash of artistic philosophies—a war of cosmic forces. Is the universe willed or instinctive? They had a terrible time.

There is a feeling that you give her later, that she's running out of energy.

I think she was running out of energy for reasons that are not necessarily so mysterious. One reason was that her marriage with Miller had failed finally. They were married for four years, and the period we are talking about now is after the marriage was over, and by then she had really used up a large part of her fantasy life. When an actor runs out of belief in the marvellous possibilities of his on-going life, then there is a period of collapse. The worse period she goes through is not the period when she probably commits suicide, but a year before that—after her marriage to Miller has broken up. People who described her said she was like a vegetable.

In 'The Misfits' she's got a railroading director, John Huston. She's got the king Clark Gable. She's got Montgomery Clift, who everybody says is a genius. She's got Eli Wallach, who is the complete professional. Miller himself, who wrote the script, is around all the time: he's the poet and he's nursing her.

This, of course, is after the marriage is essentially over, because she made 'The Misfits' after her affair with Montand. The affair with Montand ended the marriage with Miller. So Miller was in the position of being the playwright and, in spirit, the ex-husband. It couldn't have been an easy situation. She was not in good health: she could hardly be in good health. She had broken her marriage with Miller and had this passionate affair with Montand, and Montand had left her for Signoret, so she had to be somewhat obsessed with that. And he was the agent of her defeat, her husband, because the husband is always the agent of defeat in such situations. And here's John Huston, who is the director with more machismo than any other director around. A man who has a fundamental sympathy for the problems of man rather than the problems of woman. Because he knows how hard it is to be a man. He doesn't have a vast tolerance for the fact that she will show up two, three, four hours late on the set. I think she realised that the movie was getting away from her original romantic comprehension of it. I believe she saw this movie as her temple, in which, at last, people were going to accept the fact that she was a magnificent and tender woman. In the early part, that picture *is* a temple to her. But as the picture went along her sense of movie plot told her that this picture was not a movie about woman at all: it was a movie about men. What she realised was that she'd been eunuched out of position.

There have been a lot of controversies about your book, but the greatest is about the Kennedy connection: the definite connection with Bobby Kennedy in terms of friendship and the affection she had for President Kennedy. The Kennedy connection allows you to construct the theory that she might have been murdered by the FBI or by someone to do with politics.

The CIA and the FBI have enclaves in them and people outside the enclaves very rarely know what is going on. It is perfectly possible that in some little right-wing group in the CIA or the FBI, who could be absolutely livid with the Kennedys at that point, because this is just a year after the Bay of Pigs has failed, the thought arose that the Kennedys might be enormously embarrassed. She spoke of Bobby Kennedy as a friend to her intimates, and she always told her intimates who she was sleeping with. So there's no reason to believe that she was sleeping with Bobby Kennedy. But everybody in Hollywood thought she was and the word had gotten out all over America very quickly that she was going to commit suicide because of the White House or Bobby Kennedy, which they might assume would be a source of enormous embarrassment to the Kennedys.

Perhaps not recognising that the Kennedys had their own way of handling things in those days and it was not going to be such an embarrassment. The matter wouldn't even hit the papers that hard. The papers would calm it down themselves. This is a weak and somewhat over-tenuous hypothesis. I put it in only because the explanation of death was not satisfactory. For one thing, her mood had been a little on the up-swing. People often do commit suicide when they are on an up-swing: they're feeling lovely and wonderful, and one little bad thing can knock them down. But the physical details just don't add up. She had a huge overdose of barbiturates in her blood and nothing in her stomach. I've talked to coroners about this, and they've all said that never in their experience have they heard of so high a percentage in the blood and nothing in the stomach, because almost always what you have then is a sludge in the stomach—pills that weren't digested at all, or half-digested pills, pills that had been converted into a solution. There was nothing in her stomach—a teaspoon of a brown mucoid fluid which was never analysed. So the possibility is that she was injected, or a stomach-pump was used, and it seems that the odds against the use of a stomach-pump were great. I did talk to the coroner. He said she definitely wasn't injected. He examined her. So I said: 'How did she die?' I talked to him on the phone: it was a difficult conversation, the connection was poor. He said that it all went to her small intestine. I said, 'How would the small intestine show it?' and he said: 'We didn't examine it.' I said: 'Why didn't you? On the coroner's report you state it was removed for examination.' And he said: 'We didn't have the facilities to examine it.' It's possible that in some mix-up in the department, or some panic, the small intestine got lost. There might have been a suspicion of murder and a panic in the Los Angeles Police Department at this possibility of murder because they'd all heard the rumours too. So they started covering up everything in sight. I felt it incumbent on me to present some of this confusion . . .

You end saying that if she is in another life, then one of the people she should go and see is Charles Dickens, who would love her as a lost child, like many another literary man.

I think he would be absolutely fascinated with her. She's practically out of one of his books: grows up in an orphan asylum and ends up being prime minister of England.

Existential Aesthetics:
An Interview with Norman Mailer
Laura Adams/1975

From *Partisan Review,* 42, No. 2 (1975), 197-214. Reprinted by
permission of Laura Adams and *Partisan Review.*

Adams: Since the late 1950's you've had a vision of God and the
Devil at war for possession of the universe, a vision that has been the
metaphysical and moral center of your work. Has that vision changed
appreciably over the years?

Mailer: I don't know the answer. When you deal with cosmology,
the question becomes on one hand enormous—do God and the
Devil war in the galaxies?—yet is intimate on the other. Since we all
have our own idea of God and the Devil, it's hard for the idea not to
change, even fluctuate. I'd say that over the last ten or fifteen years
I've kept going back and forth in my mind over a notion that's hard
to formulate, and I don't know that I should try—it's the sort of thing
that sounds silly unless you can write a book about it—but for the
purpose of this answer, just let me say that if there is a war continuing
between God and the Devil for humankind, for the *future* of
humankind, then this war is much more complex than a simple
confrontation. We have to ask ourselves what the role of technology
is in all this, and I've had years when I've believed technology is an
instrument of the Devil, other years in which I've seen God in a
Faustian contract with technology. Technology is perhaps some third
force, some element that's come into our universe from other
universes. Now all this is so endlessly and chronically paranoid, that
it's hopeless, I think, to try to talk about it in the form of an interview.
I think you can dramatize these notions in a major novel, but only a
major novel. You would wreck a minor novel by introducing such
ideas. Therefore to talk about it in an interview is hopeless. It leads to
people saying you have a windmill for a brain. Still I can see by the
look in your eye that you're hardly ready to give up.

Adams: Isn't it an obsession, a form of paranoia, or even atavistic to think that there are cosmic forces manipulating us for their own ends?

Mailer: Well, I've never felt we are the simple creatures of these forces. On the contrary, I think they are fighting for our allegiance or even our unwitting cooperation. It isn't only that man needs God, but recall us to the title of that old French movie, "God Needs Men." (Of course you couldn't use such a title today. You'd have to say "God Needs *Persons*.") Here's what I'm trying to say: To the degree I have any intense religious notion it's that when we fail God we are not merely disappointing some mightily benign paterfamilias who'd hoped we might turn out well and didn't. We are literally bleeding God, we're leeching Him, depriving Him of *His* vision. You see, I start with the idea that the explanation for our situation on earth may be that we are part of a divine vision which is not, necessarily, all loving, but on the contrary is a vision which wishes to take us out across the stars—a vision of existence at war with other varieties of existence in the cosmos. Flying saucers may be, or may represent, at least, a certain unconscious human awareness that there is this possibility in the universe, that there are other forms of intelligence which have nothing to do with us. Nothing even to do with our divinities.

Adams: Do you know the Arthur C. Clarke novel, *Childhood's End?*

Mailer: No.

Adams: In it the human race mutates into an essence, a form of energy, that unites with a kind of benevolent Oversoul which, interestingly, has used another race of benevolent beings in the form of devils to prepare the way for the human mutants. It appears that our fear of devils was based on a premonition that they would have something to do with the dissolution of our race. The unconscious awareness you spoke of reminded me of this. But isn't this notion that, as D. J. expressed it in *Why Are We in Vietnam?*, "You never know what vision has been humping you through the night," contradictory to the perception of good and evil in *An American Dream?* There it seemed that good and evil were for the most part clearly demarcated, known to Rojack. Deborah and Barney Kelly were evil; Cherry was good.

Mailer: That was his view of it.

Adams: His view of it?

Mailer: That was all it was—Rojack's view of it. To the degree a reader sympathizes with Rojack, that would be the reader's view of it. To the degree a reader decides that Rojack is an absurd hero, he won't go along with that view. But even assuming that Rojack's view had something to do with *my* view of the characters, I was certainly attempting to make Deborah more complex on any spectrum of good and evil than Barney Kelly. Barney Kelly was supposed to be the focus of evil in the book.

Adams: The Devil personified.

Mailer: Well, the Devil approached, anyway. Whereas Deborah was someone who was, in quotes, "in thrall" to the Devil. But a woman of complexity, not altogether unacquainted with goodness.

Adams: And Cherry?

Mailer: I didn't mean Cherry to be all good by any means. To the degree that she's better than she ought to be, she's too sentimental a character. A gangster's moll is not the simplest kind of goodness we arrive at. But I wanted to indicate some characters had more purchase on good than others.

Adams: Cherry seemed to have a hard kernel of goodness even though she was surrounded by corruption.

Mailer: I think she's finally an enigmatic character. In my opinion, she's the weakest character in *An American Dream*. I think people who don't like the book have their strongest argument starting with Cherry. To a great degree, I'm afraid she's a sentimental conception. We don't really know much about her. We're asked to believe that this goodness exists in her but we don't have any idea of the real play of good and evil in her. She's a shadowy figure. Of course, my cop-out is that she's seen through Rojack's eyes. He's in an incandescent state of huge paranoia and enormous awareness. He's more heroic and more filled with dread than at any point in his life. So she seems like a lighthouse in the fog. What else does one do in such a state but fall madly in love for twenty-four hours and lose the love? It would have taken more wit than I possessed to have made her a character of dimension under these circumstances. Perhaps she did have to appear as a sentimental figure. Still I think there's no getting around it, she's the first weakness of the book.

Adams: But it's a highly metaphorical novel. One of the mistakes many critics made in first reviewing it was to take it too literally. Isn't Cherry seen metaphorically as love, the reward for courage?

Mailer: Well, no. I don't believe a metaphorical novel has any right to exist until it exists on its ground floor. You know I never start with my characters as symbols. I'm unhappy if I can't see my characters. I mean, I not only have to know what they look like, and how tall they are, whether they're good looking or plain, but I also like to have some idea of what they smell like. So I had a pretty good idea of Cherry *physically*, a very clear idea in fact, but I would have been happier if her character had emerged somewhat more. I think Deborah, for instance, is vastly more successful. Deborah is worthy of a book in herself. In fact, at one time I thought idly of doing a book on Deborah, and then chose not to. But how she drew coincidences to herself. One of the things about *An American Dream* that's not often realized is my little theory, if you will, that as events become more dramatic so does the play of coincidence become more intense. You can reverse it. You can say that coincidence may fail to occur unless events are dramatic. I think there's a reason for that. If you believe in Gods and Devils, and I choose the plural because not only is God on one side, Devil on the other but they certainly have armies, adjutants, aides, little demons, angels, well, when important events occur why wouldn't they be concerned? Why wouldn't they be present? Why not try to tip the scales? Why wouldn't God and the Devil have their department of dirty tricks? You know, see them as some sort of sublime extension of the CIA.

Adams: That is why I see the novel as so highly metaphorical. The kinds of experiences Rojack has, the vision of shooting arrows into Cherry's womb while she's singing in the night club, for example, seem to me to exist in a dream allegory but not at the literal level.

Mailer: I would disagree. I'd had the experience of being in night clubs and thinking evil thoughts and really barbing them like darts and sending them to people and seeing them react. At the time I didn't know whether I was profoundly drunk or, you know, was I all alone in the world? But I had to recognize that there was a psychic reality to it. It wasn't just a fantasy. Since then, there's been any amount, my God, there's so much material now to indicate that this is not at all unreasonable. For one thing, we do have telepathic powers, we talk about the human aura, about the ability to send hostile vibrations, everybody uses that phrase, but, you know, if you can send a hostile vibration, which is to say, a hostile wave, why not employ modern theories of light and say hate appears not only in the form of a wave but also as a particle? If you can do it with light, you can do it with hate. In other words, send a damn particle into someone. Why not assume you can sting someone with a thought so concentrated that they'll turn around and rub the back of their neck? Now, I invite people who are reading this interview to try it from time to time. It helps if you're drunk, of course.

Adams: Is that what you've been doing to tape recorders all these years?

Mailer: Oh, I think there's a good reason why tape recorders bomb out on me. Why not assume we have electrical powers—we know there are pictures taken of the human aura in Russia. What is it called, the Kirlian process? Did you ever notice when you're in a real hurry to make a phone call, and you've got one of those button phones where you can dial quickly, that if you dial too quickly with too much desire, you never get your number?

Adams: Yes.

Mailer: Then you have to stop and say, "Okay, I don't really care if I get the number or not," and dial more slowly. Then the phone becomes your servant again. It's as if there's an electrical resistance to your electrical intensity.

Adams: I simply assumed the computer couldn't handle the digits as fast as I could push them.

Mailer: Well, I notice it with a dial phone, too. The phenomenon is not only in the speed with which you dial, but the intensity with which you want to get that call through. It's almost as if there is something in the center of electricity that mocks us. I've felt this with all sorts of electrical phenomena. It's possible I'm more charged, have more electricity about me. I don't mean that as any agreeable or attractive condition, it's bound to be disagreeable, but possibly I could have more effect upon electrical instruments than other people, a little more effect, 10 per cent more, whatever. At any rate, to go back to *An American Dream,* my point is that there wasn't a single phenomenon in that book that I considered dream-like or fanciful or fantastical. To me, it was a realistic book, but a realistic book at that place where extraordinary things are happening. I believe the experience of extraordinary people in extraordinary situations is not like our ordinary realistic experience at all. For example, one of the reasons I've never written about great prizefighters in a novel is that the experience they have in the ring is, I think, considerably different from what we believe it is. More intense, more mystical, more "spooky" if you will, than anything we see on the outside. Who wants to write about a fight the way sportswriters do, or even as fighters discuss it after the fight, "I was waiting to set him up with a good right. He dropped his guard and I popped him." That's the way they talk. Only, it isn't their experience.

Adams: I grant you that the characters in *An American Dream* perceive and experience reality altogether differently from us ordinary folks. Still, it seems to me that their literal reality has a metaphorical level as well, just as your literal realities nearly always turn into metaphorical ones linked to the central set of metaphors regarding the existence of God or the Devil. I've come to see them as metaphors for our moral directions, which in the absence of absolutes become existential, unknowable as good or evil.

Mailer: My metaphors explain more phenomena to me than any theology I can adopt. I was an atheist for years because I couldn't stomach the notion of the all-good, all-powerful God who calmly watched all sorts of suffering which by any extension of our human imagination could not be productive of anything, not even productive of future karma. In other words that whole waste of human possibilities of the most grinding, grim, dull sort. It seems to me that the only explanation is God is not all-powerful: He's merely doing the best He can.

Adams: But how literally does God exist?

Mailer: I believe he exists literally.

Adams: How?

Mailer: It's not for me to know how or where He exists. It's reasonable to assume He exists in a great many ways, in places we can comprehend and a great many where we cannot. All I'm saying is that He does not have to be all-powerful. What is there that makes Him all-powerful? He was powerful enough to have created our solar system, perhaps. And if you ask what are His limits, that might be my guess. But this is babbling. It isn't important where God's limits are. What's significant is the idea that God is not all-powerful, nor the Devil. Rather it is that we exist as some mediating level between them. You see, this notion does restore a certain dignity to moral choice.

Adams: Of course, it does.

Mailer: It becomes important whether you're good or bad.

Adams: In trying to know what is good or evil aren't you in effect trying to take existentialism to its logical end, that is, to end existentialism?

Mailer: Not end it, seat it. Of all the philosophies, existentialism approaches experience with the greatest awe: it says we can't categorize experience before we've experienced it. The only way we're going to be able to discover what the truth about anything might be is to submit ourselves to the reality of the experience. At the same time, given its roots in atheistic philosophers like Sartre, existentialism has always tended toward the absurd. By way of Sartre, we are to act as if there were a purpose to things even though we know there is not. And that has become the general concept of existentialism in America. But it's not mine. I'm an existentialist who believes there is a God and a Devil at war with one another. Like Sartre in his atheism, I offer a statement of absolute certainty equally founded on the inability to verify it. Atheism is as removed from logical positivism as theology. Still, I don't give a goddamn if I can verify this or not. There has to be something out there beyond logical positivism. I want my brain to live. I want to adventure out on a few thoughts. The fact that I can never demonstrate them is not nearly so important to me as the fact that I may come up with an hypothesis so simple, so central, that I may be able to apply it in thousands of situations. If it begins to give me some inner coherence, if I begin to think that I know more as a result of this philosophy, why not?

Adams: But isn't what you've identified as existentialism, extended to its logical end, seeking to know what is finally unknowable?

Mailer: That's not my definition of existentialism. I'd say we find ourselves in an existential situation whenever we are in a situation where we cannot foretell the end. Some of these situations are grave. If you get into a skid on an icy road, at a speed that's uncomfortably high, you don't know if you're going to be able to pull your car out of it without a smack-up. That's an existential situation. When people talk about it afterward they think of that quality of time when it is slowing up. The first time people connect with marijuana,—not the

first or the twentieth time they smoke it, but the first time they
connect with it—they're in an existential situation. It's not the universe
they have been sitting on all the time. It's slower, more sensuous,
more meaningful, more natural, but filled with awe. The light tends to
have a little of the hour of the wolf, a light close to lavender or purple,
that light you get on certain kinds of evenings, or very early on
certain kinds of dawns full of foreboding. But it's—there are all kinds
of situations. A woman losing her virginity is in an existential
situation. Of course, part of the comedy of twentieth century
technology is that it's gotten to the point where a woman can lose her
virginity without being in an existential situation for a moment. It's all
exactly the way she thought it was going to be, she's been so well
oriented.

Adams: I think that assumes that her partner is not also a virgin.
All right. Your basic existential situation is a situation anyone enters at
any moment in time when the end result of his actions is unknown.
But isn't to a larger extent your aim in all the work that you've been
doing to uncover what is essentially good or evil in our natures and
God's nature when that kind of thing is actually unknowable? What I
was going to suggest earlier in talking about the demarcations of
good and evil in *An American Dream* is that you seem to have
become increasingly obsessed since that time with your inability to
know what is good and what evil.

Mailer: You say I'm obsessed, but where would be the literary
proof of that? What books would show that?

Adams: Start with the case of Richard Nixon in *Miami and the
Siege of Chicago* and *St. George and the Godfather:* your inability to
know or to intuit whether Nixon is basically good or basically evil; to
know, in *Of a Fire on the Moon,* whether our space program will
carry God's vision to the stars or the Devil's; to know in *Why Are We
in Vietnam?* whether America has made a Faustian compact with the
Devil or whether God is using us for evil ends; whether or not our
national leaders and events win or lose us ground in this divine battle.
It seems to me that you lead us to this question, with increasing
desire to know the answer, in every work.

Mailer: Well, it could be said that all I'm doing is leading people
back to Kierkegaard. I'd remind you I've written this several times:
Kierkegaard taught us, or tried to teach us, that at that moment we're
feeling most saintly, we may in fact be evil. And that moment when

we think we're most evil and finally corrupt, we may, in fact, in the eyes of God, be saintly at that moment. It's a Dostoevskian, Kierkegaardian notion. Its first value is that it strips us of that fundamental arrogance of assuming that at any given moment any of us have enough centrality, have a *seat* from which we can expound our dogma, or measure our moral value. So we don't have the right to say Richard Nixon is: A. good; B. evil. I might have my opinion of Richard Nixon, but I don't have the right to say that man is evil, any more than I have a right to say he is good.

Adams: Do you have a clear notion of the good?

Mailer: No. But I have, if you will, I have and I submit to the force of this word, I have a fairly well-formed cloud of intuitions about the nature of the good, and, like a cloud, it has to a certain degree a structure, and yet the structure is capable of altering quickly, depending on the celestial winds blowing and the less celestial winds. A cloud changes shape quickly but it remains a cloud. It's not just simply an unformed chaos.

Adams: You've said that an evil person is someone who has a clear notion of the good and operates in opposition to it.

Mailer: Therefore by my own definition I'm definitely not evil.

Adams: All right, but are you wicked?

Mailer: Unquestionably wicked, yes.

Adams: By your own terms, which is not knowing what is good or evil in any situation, but upping the ante each time.

Mailer: Upping the ante, yes. I'd say I may be one of the most wicked spirits in American life today. Maybe. America may be changing faster than I am.

Adams: Is it fair to say that your existentialism is leading us to know the nature of good and evil?

Mailer: It's leading us to—well, let me take a detour. People who submit to logical positivism, and go on from there into philosophies as difficult as Wittgenstein's, will answer if you ask, "Why go through these incredible disciplines in order to verify the fact that you're able to verify the wing span of a gnat but not of an archangel?" They will answer, "Well, it isn't what we are able to verify that is interesting, so much as that we go through a discipline which enables us to think cogently. We're less likely to go in for sloppy thinking thereafter." That's the value of it. I'd say by going in for my variety of associational, metaphorical thinking (which is, of course, the exact opposite) I may be able eventually to think speculatively without feeling philosophical vertigo. You see, it doesn't take any more illogic to posit that there's a god or devil than it takes to say there is none. The latter statement is absolutely as potent an act of faith. There's a marvelous line in *Jumpers,* the play by Tom Stoppard, to that effect. I paraphrase: "Well, maybe atheism is that crutch people need to protect themselves against having to face the enormity of the existence of God." You know, once you contemplate the notion that there is a God and this God may be embattled, the terror you feel is enormous.

Adams: It's a terror, but isn't it also paranoia?

Mailer: No. The terror is not that some force is working on you to ruin you. It's another kind of terror: It's that nothing is nailed down. That we are out there—that our lives are truly existential. That we're not going to end up well, not necessarily. You see, there's always been this sort of passive confidence implicit in Christianity, the confidence that things are going to work out all right. One does have to die, that's true, but if one keeps one's nose reasonably clean, one is going to heaven. That gave security to everybody. The ship of state was built on that security. The ship of state was nailed down. It didn't travel the stormy seas. Rather, it was carried by the strongest pallbearers of the nation. And what's happened now is we're entering an existential period in our history where nothing is nailed down. All the American faiths, one by one, are being exploded. We lived for too long in a paranoid dream world that believed communism was the secret of all evil on earth because it was the social embodiment of the Devil.

Adams: That's paranoid.

Mailer: That's paranoid. But I don't believe the Devil is the secret of all evil on earth. I believe something more complicated than that. I think God might be the source of a considerable amount of evil. Because if God is embattled, He could fail to take care, much to His great woe, of people who are devoted to Him, in the same way that a general might have to surrender soldiers on a hill. And those soldiers could give up with great bitterness in their hearts.

Adams: You've talked about evil in one sense as God's shit, God's excrement.

Mailer: Where did I say that?

Adams: It comes up in "The Metaphysics of the Belly." A

colleague of mine once remarked that it's but a step from scatology to eschatology and I've often thought of this remark with regard to your work. Now I'm interested in the relationship between excrement and eternity. If God's shit is evil, but shit is associated with the Devil, doesn't this imply that God creates evil?

Mailer: There are references in my work to the idea that shit and the Devil have an umbilical relation, but it's not my idea after all. Luther had a few notions about it.

Adams: As did Jonathan Swift.

Mailer: It's an idea that goes—it starts with the most primitive peoples. It goes all the way. There's a reason for it. Shit is what we reject, at least to the degree that the shit felt it deserved a better end for itself. In other words, a lot of our shit has nutrients in it, worth in it. It's just the body couldn't take it, and so passed it out. Some of the best of the food goes out with the shit as well as some of the worst. That's what I said in "The Metaphysics of the Belly." All right. To the degree that we can loosen our imagination to assume this stuff might have a soul, after all we're beginning to discover now that plants have feelings and souls, so it may be that food, even though in a peculiar relation to life, not as alive as a plant, let's say, or as an animal, but still alive to a degree, has a mood, has a spirit, has something. If food feels it has been violated, suppose it can die with a curse. Of course, the Devil loves to be around and pick up those who die with a curse. Malcolm Muggeridge once had Sister Theresa of Calcutta on a television show with him. Muggeridge, who is by any measure a devoutly religious man, had just written a book about Sister Theresa and obviously revered her. He told me what she used to do in Calcutta. Her order of nuns would take people who were dying on the street and move them into her convent where they'd die anyway a few days later—they didn't begin to have medicine to take care of them or anything like that—but her notion was, and Muggeridge was moved by this, and I agree that it is a moving idea, was that she didn't want them to die with absolutely nothing. She wanted them to be able to come in and get a little attention before they died so they wouldn't go out with complete bitterness in their hearts. Now that is a religious woman. The recognition that one not die with a curse is fundamental to any inquiry into what could be the possible nature of God and the Devil. If God is embattled, and can't give fair justice to all, then what of those who do not achieve what they saw as their own

fulfillment and thereby become spiritual material for the Devil, if not
in this life then in another? We haven't said one word about karma,
but my first idea these days is that any attempt to speak of these
things makes no sense unless you take into account the peculiar
calculus of karma. We may have to recognize that we're not only
acting for this life but for other lives. Our past lives and our future
lives. Paying dues, receiving awards. Reducing the cost of future
dues, for example, by certain acts of abnegation that make no sense
to us or our friends, yet ready to dare, on the other hand, sometimes
desperate activities because we *are* desperate. The condition in which
we live is hurting our karma.

Adams: Karma is a word you've used increasingly in the last few
years. It's a term that you did not use in "The Metaphysics of the
Belly" or "The Political Economy of Time," but which you could
have in describing the nature of the soul. Is this something new in
your metaphysics or is it a term for something that you've already
described, like the way in which the soul exists, in "The Political
Economy of Time"?

Mailer: I had come across the word in books but never paid any
attention. In about 1953, I think it was in Marshall, Illinois, I went out
to visit Jim Jones in his colony and he was talking about karma and I
said, "What's all that?" So he gave me the standard explanation
which is that we are not only reincarnated, but the way in which we
are, is the reflection, the judgment, the truth, of how we lived our
previous life. If you exist in a simple form of karma with no
interference by Gods or Devils, a natural flux of karma, then to the
degree you lived a life that was artful, your reincarnation was artful.
To the degree you lived a life that destroyed the time of others and
dredged up all the swamp muds, so you are a creature of the swamp
in your next life. The beauty of this may be that there is now good
purpose to the swamp. (This isn't Jones' talk any longer, just a more
general explanation of karma.) At any rate, Jones went on about it
and I said, "You *believe* in that?" Because I was an atheist and a
socialist in those days. He said, "Oh, sure. That's the only thing that
makes sense." Well, the line rang in my head for years. "The only
thing that makes sense." I thought about it over and over and in the
last three or four years I began to think, "Yes, that does make sense.
Jones was right."

Adams: Let's move from metaphysics into your views of your work. In *Advertisements for Myself* you stated that you were "imprisoned with a perception which will settle for nothing less than making a revolution in the consciousness of our time." In terms of that ambition to alter the consciousness of our time, how would you evaluate the relative effectiveness of the various forms of your work for that purpose: the novel, the novel-history, the novel-biography, film, politics, the Fifth Estate?

Mailer: I'm not the sort to look back. So long as you keep working it doesn't make much sense to rank your own performance. None of my work may have influence for all I know. How can you measure it? Some of the ideas I had on how to make movies, for instance, might seem important in 15 or 20 years—maybe they'll make a few movies that way. The ideas I had when Breslin and I were trying to take New York in the mayorality—some of those ideas have come in. More will. People may yet say, "Oh, those guys—that was an interesting campaign, intellectually speaking." It may even prove a fruitful campaign. Or I might have influence through some of the ideas I had in things nobody ever read. If we go off into the most religious and extravagant kind of existentialism, the ideas in "The Metaphysics of the Belly" may have the most future interest to people. I would say one place I have not had influence, up to this point at any rate, is in the novel. Obviously my novels have been conservative in terms of form—

Adams: Not *Why Are We in Vietnam?*

Mailer: No, *Why Are We in Vietnam?* has nuggets. There are formal ideas buried in *Why Are We in Vietnam?*—I suppose I trusted metaphor in that novel to a degree I've never trusted it before. I worked on the assumption that if I had a metaphor where I might, for example, mix electro-magnetism and pine sap in a tree, that there was something there. Something scientific yet to be discovered. But I don't know if I'm interested in the question. Where do *you* think my influence will be?

Adams: I think it will be in works like *The Armies of the Night, Maidstone,* and *Why Are We in Vietnam?* which pushed back the existing limits of genre, form, and language, and ultimately, perhaps, it will be your style which will have the most influence. I think that you've abandoned the novel in recent years, even though you still consider the novel the highest form of art, of communication, because you see that it's out of the center of history, and that what you've done since *Armies* is to try to move into the center of history and stay there, to try to impose form on things that are moving so fast and appear so chaotic that you not only are present at the making of history, but you're making it over.

Mailer: Well, certainly in *Armies* I was trying to, I was trying to bring a consciousness to America about the war in Vietnam through personifying one reasonably complicated middle-aged man caught up in the peace movement and not altogether willingly. I think the effect of the book was to make resistance to the war in Vietnam a little more human to people who were still supporting the war. So, yes, I think the book did have a political effect. Maybe it tended to strengthen the side opposed to the war in Vietnam. OK, but, you know, that's not going to mean much in 30 or 40 years.

Adams: Not the subject but the form you impose on the subject, the style. That is what I am saying is the significant thing, although you have been criticized of late for this very thing. Critics say that you have an interlocking system of metaphors that you impose on all of your work; that everything you write about now is seen in terms of this metaphysical war of God and the Devil for possession of mankind and that instead of allowing your style to arise from your subject you impose your style on the subject.

Mailer: I think that is their profound resentment that I have a philosophy which is coherent, and they don't. I think that is what they hate. If I were a Catholic, if I were Graham Greene, and a devout and somewhat troubled Catholic, and everything I wrote revolved around Catholicism, nobody would argue for a minute. They would say, "He is a Catholic," so why can't they say of me, "He is an existentialist"? I mean, I don't know Graham Greene, but I would like to think it is possible my ideas are as deeply imbedded in me as his faith is in him. Is that wholly inconceivable?

Adams: That's a rhetorical question. But doesn't there need to be a dialectic going on between your vision and the subjects to which you attach it, namely the major political events of the 1960's and 70's?

Mailer: But I don't write about everything in politics for just that reason. Not everything appeals to me equally. I spent last summer down in Washington going to the Senate hearings. I thought maybe I

would do something for *Atlantic* on Watergate—we had a loose
working agreement that I might do something. At the end of the
summer I called Bob Manning and said, "I don't know if there's
anything I can bring to it that would be mine." You see, I don't want
to get into situations where I start dominating material, just for the
sake of dominating it—which is, of course, what I'm accused of
doing. I only move toward material which makes me feel I have
something to bring to it. I did this last book on graffiti* because I
looked at pictures of subway graffiti Larry Schiller showed me that
Jon Naar had taken and thought, "Something is going on there that's
interesting." Interesting to me, obviously. So I wanted to write an
essay on it and did. But what I'm getting at is I don't think the history
of our time is any more apt for me than any other history.

Adams: I see what you are doing in light of some lines from "The
Political Economy of Time" in which you said, "Form is the record of
every intent of the soul or spirit, its desire to reveal the shape, which
is to say the mystery of the time it contains in itself." It seems to me
that you have a vision and that you perceive certain events of
national importance in terms of your vision, choosing the ones that
have most significance to you, but writing about them in those terms
rather than being the relatively passive observer most other working
journalists are.

Mailer: That could be true. But, if so, a price is paid for the
philosophy. There's always the loss of a sensuous perception of the
event if one is thinking in categories as one perceives the event. That
can happen if one has a coherent philosophy. On the other hand,
you could say that you end up writing best about those historic
events which have a magnetic relation to your own ideas and tend to
write less well about situations where that doesn't occur. I think, for
example, *Miami and the Siege of Chicago* is probably a better book
than *St. George and the Godfather.* For a number of reasons
including the fact that the conventions themselves were more
exciting, but also because there was a polarity in '68 more congenial
to me than in '72. Still, I didn't warp it, I didn't go around violating
what I saw, did I?

Adams: It's not a criticism but an observation: you act upon
opposed forces, becoming the opposing force yourself if necessary, in

---

*The Faith of Graffiti: New York: Praeger, 1974.

order, it seems to me, to create a synthesis, an altered form, not simply to control these forces but to move us toward that alteration of consciousness we spoke of earlier.

Mailer: Maybe the question is how to verify the observer. What are my passions, prejudices, and particularly my infirmities? It's terribly important who the observer is. That's why I always try to put myself into these works of journalism so the reader can have his sense of me. It's important to be able to decide whether I'm perceiving well or where I'm perceiving badly. Whereas, if I attempt to present to readers what I consider the end-product of objective truth, it's likely to be nothing more than the harshly digested conclusions I came up with in my somewhat unbalanced soul. (What else is most journalism?) Whereas I believe the fun in reading comes from observing the observer. After all I did have that happy streak with *The Armies of the Night*. There was fun in that book, but the fun was to observe the observer. An ideal example of the technique. It doesn't always work that well. Still, there's a lovely remark of Trotsky's I go back to over and over again. He said sometimes the only way you can tell the truth is by a comparison of the lies. If you're listening to two liars telling tales, you may never be able to find out who is lying the most. But you can come closer to a sense of reality by the relations between those mysteries. You see, we may never know, for instance, what the truth of one human is, or another, but we can know a lot about the relations between them. We may be confused by two terribly complicated people but we are able to say with greater certainty, "They hate each other," or "Isn't it extraordinary how they love each other?" because we can feel the relation between the mysteries. So, by the same token, when I write, I try to do that. I try to set up a relation between mysteries where I am that relation as the writing voice.

Adams: This is why I think, although you probably won't agree with me, that the kind of work you've been doing outside of the novel per se, which would exclude the novel-history and the novel-biography, is more significant in terms of your own ambitions than the novel.

Mailer: No. Maybe not for the future. You know there was an unhappy newspaper story which had just enough truth to be awful, that I was getting a million dollars for a novel, do you know about that?

Adams: The Little, Brown contract?

Mailer: Yes. Well, you know, everybody said, "Isn't that shameful. Ridiculous the way publishers are agreeing to the prices." So forth. No one takes into account that Little, Brown is one publishing firm that has been around for many years. The contract is for a novel large in scope. The writing is going to take anywhere from five to seven years and I'm to deliver anything from five to seven hundred thousand words which may end as one novel or can break down to two, three, four, or five novels. We don't know at this point. What Little, Brown is doing, which I think is exceptional and splendid for a publisher to do, is they're giving me a chance to try to write that big book I've been braying about to America for the last fifteen years. And I'm going to find out. I can promise you that I've rarely been as scared in my literary life. Finally I will have no excuse. I'll either be able to do something that's large and good, it should be, you know, given all this hoopla, be halfway as good as *Remembrance of Things Past* if it's going to be any good at all. In other words, we've set the bar high.

Adams: I hope it's not as dull as *Remembrance of Things Past.*

Mailer: That isn't too dull a book. I'd settle for it to be as good and as dull. At any rate, I'm so much involved in the problem of writing a novel now that I think about it all the time. Coming back to the novel after all these years, the difficulty is as fresh on me now as it was when I started writing. I mean when you get down to it, it is an extraordinary business to say you're going to write a novel. You are creating a world. When you've been writing for as many years as I have, and know the responsibility of being a writer, the God-like assumption of writing a novel is almost impossible to surmount. How do you open the door? To become the prime mover of your own little world!

Adams: I don't think that for you it's just writing a novel. It's writing *the big* novel. Until recently, when I knew that you actually had the novel in progress, I was thinking of the novel that you promised us as a metaphor, and saw what you have been laying before us for the last twenty-five years as a novel. It's art as process rather than a series of products.

Mailer: I think you could take all my work up to now and say, if you want to extend the meaning of a novel, that all this makes up one book or is equal in its impact to one huge novel. I wouldn't run away from that. I would hope it's true. I mean, suppose I get hit by a car tomorrow. Will people come along and say, "Well, he's never written his novel, but he sure did write a novel of sorts." No, I don't argue with that.

Adams: I think that you have been staking your reputation on this big book and that you've considered that the work you've been doing since *Armies* is less significant, is easier. "Journalism is chores," you've said, but isn't it really in terms of altering the consciousness of our time more significant than even maybe the big novel might be?

Mailer: It could be, but you can't measure that. You can't also say that the sum of my ambitions is that one sentence, effecting a revolution in the consciousness of our time. You can't measure these things. *Finnegans Wake* has apparently had little influence on the consciousness of our time, but we don't know. Its influences are subterranean. Besides, we don't know what its influence is going to be a hundred years from now.

Adams: But it hasn't been widely read.

Mailer: Suppose a hundred years from now people are talking in three or four or five languages at once. The fact that this book *Finnegans Wake* exists is going to be incredible then because it is going to accelerate the consciousness of that time, and yet one man will have done the work a century earlier. Then the book will come into its own. Maybe he forged the first link in something that is going to be tremendously important. The fact that the link is there will serve as a crystalizing force for speaking in tongues. This is an extreme example of what I am trying to say, but we can never be certain of how well we are succeeding in a mission once we've assigned ourselves that mission. All we can ever know is whether we have worked as hard as we can.

Adams: Some of the forms you've created, like the novel-history and the novel-biography, seem to have more effect on those who are reading and experiencing them than the novel.

Mailer: There's no question that there's more immediate impact.

Adams: More widespread, too.

Mailer: It's a fashion, an intellectual fashion for a year or two. Maybe it affects people's minds to a degree and then something comes along which is the opposite of what I've done and changes their minds back. So that, in effect, I'm out there pushing the waves in one direction and other people are pushing the waves in another direction. If you transcend that, if you end up with an absolutely remarkable work which may not have that much impact in the beginning, it's still possible that you will at least have nailed down your points in such a way that people can't keep using the same arguments. I mean, the most disappointing reaction I find in my career is that the criticisms made about me today are so close to the criticisms made ten years ago. It's as if I never reached certain people at all.

Adams: Can you be more specific?

Mailer: Oh, well, the attacks on my ego. I mean, you'd think if a man has been carrying on about his ego for ten years that finally they'd say, "All right, he's got an ego and his ego gives me a pain in the ass. But let's see what he's doing." Can you read a review about me these days that doesn't start with those predictable first 150 words about my character, my nature? Did it ever occur to them that I have less nature by now than they do? That I'm just a serious, hardworking, somewhat dumb professional?

Adams: There are those to whom you're a living legend.

Mailer: There are days when I say to myself that I have to be the second most unpopular man in America. Richard Nixon first and I'm second. Who's more unpopular than me, really, leaving good Richard out of this?

Adams: You can't ask a midwesterner that.

Mailer: It's true I have no existence in the midwest. Nine out of ten people in the midwest never heard my name. That's certainly true.

Adams: That's right, unfortunately. I've been spreading the word but it hasn't reached quite enough of the population. Perhaps you have a less well-defined identity than we imagined; perhaps you have more in common with Marilyn Monroe than Ernest Hemingway, which is why you can view yourself as a literary character and have used so many personas.

Mailer: I think Hemingway also had a gamut of identities. It was just that coming from the midwest, he was considerably more focused in his attempt to build one identity. That is, he didn't try to go from A to Z like Monroe or myself, he kept it pretty much, let's say, between J and K on the one side and P and Q on the other. He worked that middle. But I certainly think Hemingway was forging his identity every day of his life, more than myself as a matter of fact. I don't think there's anything so awful about that. It's not comfortable, but I think most artists have this problem. Or let's say at the least, there are two kinds of artists, those who begin without a sense of identity and those have it from the start. Many young writers right now have a sense of identity. That's the first thing you notice about them, George V. Higgins, Richard Price, any number of good young writers of genre coming up now. James T. Farrell years ago was a perfect example of someone who started with a sense of identity. And then there are the writers who start with other kinds of talents and are always forging their identity.

Adams: You've said a number of times that your public personality bears little or no resemblance to your sense of your own identity. Isn't that the sign of a weak rather than a strong ego?

Mailer: That's a midwestern notion, weakness and strength in the ego. Ego, it seems to me, is many things, but the first is the ability to bear various kinds of pain and discomfort in order to carry out your project, whatever that is at a given moment. In other words, ego is the ability to bring oneself to focus for the situation. Now, ego is therefore not the same thing as predictable character at all.

Adams: It isn't one's sense of oneself?

Mailer: I'd say rather than a sense of oneself, ego is awareness of one's will. Knowing at a given moment what you want to do. At least the kind of ego I'm talking about is that. I once said at the beginning of the piece on the first Ali-Frazier fight that ego is the ability to move with certainty into matters about which we know very little. Now, if you accept that, there's no reason to assume that you have to have a sense of self. What you need is a sense of your will. Monroe had a huge ego considering how void she felt of identity.

Adams: To return to your new novel for a moment, if you can write it as you now conceive of it will you consider it your greatest achievement?

Mailer: Well, I'm at the beginning of it and nothing's more dangerous than to talk about what I think it's going to be. Still, it wouldn't be much fun to write an enormously long book that isn't very good, that just is fairly readable and slightly less good than the other stuff I've done. Of course, says the practical voice, the publisher might do better with that than if I do something really good. But if I can bring it off roughly the way I conceive of it, I think I'll have something pretty good, pretty interesting. Then after that—I don't look beyond. There might be all sorts of things to do. I'm going to be a lot older. The shock right now is that I probably know what I'm going to be doing next year. In previous years I never did. That was fun, not to know what one's future was.

Adams: Isn't the plot of time that Little, Brown has bought you what you've been looking for so that you don't have to do two or three months' work and get a big chunk of money so that you can get back to the novel?

Mailer: That's what I wanted the contract for. I kept making these big chunks of money for quick books, but they would take enough out of me so that I didn't gain time. I kept thinking I might, but never did. Now I can work at a steadier rate, and less on a collision course. The question is, however, have I kept enough of myself intact to do this book? We're going to find out. That's existential.

Crime and Punishment: Gary Gilmore

William F. Buckley, Jr. and Jeff Greenfield/1979

This is a transcript of the "Firing Line" program taped in New York City on 11 October 1979 and originally telecast by PBS on 4 November 1979. Copyright © 1979 by the Southern Educational Communications Association, P.O. Box 50,008, Columbia, S.C. 29250.

Mr. Buckley: Norman Mailer's new book is judged by most of the critics a masterpiece. Whether it is that, only the unseduceable judgment of history—that moves as slowly as a federal agency—will say. Whatever the final judgment, it is a remarkable book, not only for what it accomplishes—the transcription of the life and death of Gary Gilmore, murderer—but for the way in which it is done. Suddenly one of the most rococo writers of the 20th century sounds almost like Dashiell Hammett or Ernest Hemingway. As critic James Wolcott observed on picking up *The Executioner's Song,* "I assumed that Mailer would use the occasion to unveil his own Psychology of the Hangman, turning Gilmore's life into a crime and punishment saga seething with blood, madness, nihilism, damnation, blank cartridges, and beggarly redemption. Once again Norman Mailer would roll out the Dostoevskian cannons and leave the landscape covered with smoke." Nothing of the sort, as you will discover, has happened. This is not a book about Mailer; and not a book, were you to pick it up not knowing the identity of the author, would lead you to guess his identity. You would, however, know instantly that you were in the hands of a master.

Norman Mailer is the most prominent living American novelist. In addition, he is the most notorious American novelist, devoting his time equally to literary production and self-abuse. He has tangled with the Pentagon, feminists, the critical establishment, booze, prizefighters, presidents—and me. He went to Harvard and fought in Asia as an infantryman, and gave birth to *The Naked and the Dead,* becoming a lion at age 25. He was co-founder of the *Village Voice*, he ran for mayor of New York, he won the National Book Award and the Pulitzer Prize, and he has been at work for 30 years on the great American novel. And there are those who believe that in *The Executioner's Song*, he has, in fact, written it.

The examiner will be Jeff Greenfield, about whom more in due course.

I should like to begin by asking Mr. Mailer whether he intended that his book should be adopted by fundamentalists on the subject of capital punishment.

Mr. Mailer: I had no— Well, how to put it? I found in writing this book that I've put away just about every attitude and stance that I'd developed over those 30 years of writing, and part of the pleasure and part of the difficulty of the book was that it was a matter of surveying unfamiliar ground. So I discovered that I had very few attitudes by the time I finished. I started the book with a great many ideas. When I began the book, I thought I would probably do an essay on the nature of capital punishment, on what to do with our prisons, on why people murder, on karma, on a dozen different things. I was drawn to the book because Gary Gilmore embodied all these questions. And I discovered as I wrote it, and as the material came in and as I went out and got more material—because the book is based upon hundreds of interviews—that I knew less and less. Or let me put it this way, I knew more and more and I understood less and less. And I finally found myself in the position of a man who, let's say, has been married to a woman for ten, 20, or 30 years, and knows her inside out—knows every last single thing that she'll do— but doesn't understand her at all—that is, doesn't understand her in the sense that he doesn't know if her moral nature is superior to his or his is to hers. By the same token, by the time I finished the book, I didn't have a clear feeling about capital punishment. I could give you less of a firm idea of what I think about it now than when I started.

Mr. Buckley: I think you struggle very successfully throughout the book not to weight it. However, during the execution scene, it seems to me that the writer of those words is empathically there with the friends of Gilmore rather than with the executioners of Gilmore. And there is a sense there in which there is a poetic disturbance. Now when you discuss the victims of Gilmore, you take some care to give their background so that the reader feels a sense of identification with them, but not quite in the way in which he feels an identification with Gilmore towards the end, which is why I pause to ask you that question. Now you tell me that you left the book without any commitments on the question of capital punishment.

Mr. Mailer: Yes, but to answer your objection, which I think is a legitimate one, there is next to nothing about the executioners in the last part of the book—

Mr. Buckley: Well, not the actual three guys, but I mean—

Mr. Mailer: Five guys, Bill.

Mr. Buckley: Well, there were three shots—there were supposed to be four shots—there were four bullets.

Mr. Mailer: One bullet is a blank and there are four real bullets, and three shots were heard because apparently two guns went off at once.

Mr. Buckley: No, I'm not suggesting you—I mean executioners broadly speaking: the warden, the prosecutor, the various people of the 50 people there who were more or less in sympathy with the operation.

Mr. Mailer: The reason is simple. I built the book on interviews, and I was determined to be scrupulous to the interviews and to be fair to everyone. I think in a funny way—this is stretching the meaning of the word—but I think when you interview someone there is a faint suggestion of the sacramental about it, particularly if you break bread, if you're eating with someone while you're interviewing them. In fact, I don't even like interviewing people, because I feel once I've interviewed someone, it's much harder to write critically about them unless you bring up every critical feeling you have in the course of the interview.

Mr. Buckley: Yes, I noticed that about Jimmy Carter last time I saw you.

Mr. Mailer: Yes, it's very hard to— (laughing) It's that left jab of yours that'll do me in. Tonight I expect to feel a small headache in the back of my head. But leaving Jimmy Carter out of it for the moment, if you don't mind— What if I did that to you and brought up a subject from the moon—like Jimmy Carter. (laughter) But going back to this, I wanted very much to interview the executioners. There were practical reasons why you couldn't reach them. One of them is that it is terribly important to the state of Utah to keep their identities secret, and for good cause from their point of view—because anybody who

has been an executioner gets put on a convicts' hit list. Now that
doesn't mean that convicts are literally going to get together and once
they get out of prison they are going to make it their business to find
that guy out and shoot him. But after all, nobody wants to live with
that tension; it's one more care that you carry around with you. And
so the state was very careful to keep the names of the executioners
secret. That was one part of it. And then the warden, Sam Smith,
refused to be interviewed. He had had some bad experiences with
Truman Capote, and then he'd had some bad experiences with Larry
Schiller, and by the time I came along, he didn't want to talk to me at
all. That was a great loss. I think the book would have been better if I
could have gotten into the warden's mind. But I wasn't going to make
up what was in anyone's mind in this book. I thought I had
discovered a method that was most interesting, which was to be
absolutely scrupulous about what people told me to the best of my
ability. You try to be absolutely pure—you're doing remarkably well if
you can be 99^{94}/$_{100}$% pure. I discovered that invention is a natural
faculty of man, like wiping one's mouth after you eat.

   Mr. Buckley: Truth is asymptotic.

   Mr. Mailer: Asymptotic—what does that mean?

   Mr. Buckley: It's that curve that gets closer and closer but never
quite reaches. Like poverty.

   Mr. Mailer: Yes, yes.

   Mr. Buckley: Take a second before we go on, if you will, to tell
the audience, whose memory is short—even though the events of
January 1977 were awfully vivid at the time—what it is that Gilmore
was executed for, because it will help, I think, to understand the
discussion more fully as we move. Would you mind doing that?

   Mr. Mailer: Gilmore murdered two people on July 19 and 20 of
1976, and he was captured on the second night and was brought to
trial in October and found guilty and sentenced to death. And then in
November—I think it was the first of November or the third of
November—he said that he did not wish to appeal his sentence, and
he wanted his execution to take place as it was scheduled. At that
time the execution was scheduled for November 15th. And what
happened is that some people began to appeal—people began to
appeal from all over. Various social groups appealed the execution,
Gilmore's mother appealed it, and before it was all over there were
many delays, there were many stays of execution, and Gilmore was

finally not executed until January 17th, which was something like half
a year after he committed the crimes. That, I think, is a summary of
the events, and we can talk much more about them as we go along.

Mr. Buckley: Well, I think there is something about the distinctive
nature of the murders that figures here. It was, in every sense of the
word, wanton murder, wasn't it? He had gotten the money, no
resistance, and then just shot them more or less as a formality.

Mr. Mailer: It was a motiveless set of crimes, the two crimes. He
didn't know the people. So far as we can find out—and we really
tried very hard to find out if he ever met either of the two men—he'd
never met them. And he didn't really do it for the money, because
there was very little money involved. He got $100 one night and
$125 the next. He said himself that he really didn't do it for the
money. In fact, he could have had a defense which—He could have
probably gotten life imprisonment if he'd wanted it, by saying that he
did it for the money and shot these men in the course of committing
the crimes, because if you kill someone in the course of an armed
robbery, you are much more likely to get life than the death
sentence. But he didn't even want to do that in his defense. They
were peculiar crimes, because he was a very intelligent, although
somewhat tortured man, and the crimes just made no sense. There
was no sense or any way you could understand it, except that, as
Gilmore said to many people afterwards, he said, "If you want to
understand murder, don't look for a motive, look to the idea that a
person gets so full of rage that they commit murder, that it's a way of
opening a valve." And he spoke of his murder in that way, as a
matter of venting tension. So in that sense they were motiveless
crimes. The question we are left with is—well, you've got this
enormous tension, a tension so great that you have to commit
murder; what is the thing that is even worse than the murder? I
always work on the assumption that people do the best they can do
under the circumstances. You know, we are always trying to do the
very best we can do. Sometimes that behavior might seem absolutely
bizarre to other people—

Mr. Buckley: What was Hitler's alternative?

Mr. Mailer: That is the perfect posing of the question. What
would have been worse than the— But of course, I think with
Hitler— Let me amend my first remark. If we're in a bad situation,
we do the best we can do. I don't think Hitler saw himself as being in

a bad situation. I think he saw himself as a world leader, obviously, and he thought that he was bringing some kind of salvation to the world. So my remarks really wouldn't apply directly or head-on to Hitler. They would apply only to the last month, let's say, of Hitler's life, when he obviously was in a deteriorating situation and even had to know it himself. But as far as Gilmore goes—Gilmore was in a situation I think we all understand, which is that he felt he was in a box and he couldn't get out of that box. He'd left prison, and he had to feel to a large extent as if he were still in prison, as if the habits of his life and the circumstances of his life were such that he just couldn't get out and become what he wanted to become—if you will, he couldn't express the fantasies that he'd had while he was in prison of leading another kind of life. So under those circumstances, the tension increased and increased in him. He also had had a love affair with a girl, he was very much in love with a girl and she finally left him because his habits were so bad. And when she left him, he went slowly crazy over a week—not crazy in the sense of being committed to a mental hospital, but crazy in the sense that this tension, this unendurable tension, got greater and greater and greater in him and finally it erupted into murder.

Mr. Buckley: Well, let me ask you this. I'm uncomfortable with the terms—in part because of ignorance and in part because they seem to be infintely inscrutable—but suppose we use words like psychopath and neurotic to describe Gilmore. What is it that drew you to try to probe the character of somebody who is almost by definition inscrutable?

Mr. Mailer: Let me say that if I had been writing a more conventional novel—because I do call this a novel, for reasons we can discuss later—I would have made every effort to get into his mind, and I would have attempted to explain him. And I would have had my explanation. Before Gilmore—who as I say was a relatively intelligent man, a man who was by turns surprisingly intelligent and surprisingly disappointing; and I found as I was doing the research on him that some of the time I'd come across turns of mind in him that were startling and impressive— And then just about the time I would begin to feel I was really dealing with a man who is possessed of, let's not say superior intelligence, but certainly good intelligence, he would say or do something that I thought was so dumb that he would be disappointing. He was very much like someone you know in life, who is alternately pleasing you and disappointing you all the time. But if I'd written it as a novel, I would have made every effort to understand him and to explain him to the reader. I began to feel that it was more interesting not to. I began to feel that I had to change some of my ideas about what literature should consist of. I've always leaned on the side that literature, finally, is a guide—that it explains complex matters to us, it gives us a deeper understanding of our existence. And I felt that maybe the time had come—at least for me in my own work—to do a book where I don't explain it to the reader, and in part I can't explain all of it to the reader. I can merely make the reader tremendously familiar with material they usually don't encounter.

Mr. Buckley: But that doesn't make you disinterested, does it?

Mr. Mailer: It didn't make me disinterested at all. I'll probably think about Gilmore for the rest of my life.

Mr. Buckley: Right. Now, would you say, for instance, that by contrast, Truman Capote did try to explain the motives of his killers, that he attempted something more conventional?

Mr. Mailer: Well, I think he did try, and I think Truman succeeded in understanding his killers, and I think he did a— I think *In Cold Blood*—and Truman and I are not just washing each other's hands—I think that's a wonderful book. But one of the reasons that *In Cold Blood* is a wonderful book is because I think the characters he had there, those two fellows, were essentially pretty dull fellows. In prison terms, they were punks. Gilmore was a real convict, using the prison term. To prisoners the word convict is a term of approbation. It's the equivalent of a good soldier.

Mr. Buckley: Right.

Mr. Mailer: Any man who is a good soldier in the army is a complex individual. There's no such thing as a good soldier, I believe, who is a simple man. And I say a complex individual because to be a good soldier you've got to have abilities that are opposed to one another. That is, you've got to be very disciplined on one hand and very spontaneous on the other. In the same way that artists come out of opposites, so good soldiers do. And I'd even go so far as to say good convicts do. Because they have to have a sense of justice and they also have to have a great command of violent techniques and what-have-you.

Mr. Buckley: Which in a way accounts for Gilmore's acquiescence in the penalty that he suffered, right?

Mr. Mailer: There we get onto very tricky ground, because I think most convicts would feel—they would question what Gilmore did. I can't speak for convicts, I wouldn't attempt to. But from my understanding of how, let's say, these men I call convicts as opposed to inmates or prisoners would feel, I would expect that there would be a great division of opinion among them whether Gilmore did the right thing or the wrong thing. Because part of the mentality of the convict is that whatever society does is wrong. They see themselves as an army opposed to society, after all. I mean, their pride is that society has not been able to break them, that they remain men, that they're not broken, so—

Mr. Buckley: But isn't my understanding of a convict in the professional sense in which you use it, somebody that understands that society has its own resources and its own rules and does not question the enforceability of those rules— That is to say, typically a convict will only plead not guilty as a tactic.

Mr. Mailer: Yes, a convict certainly has a, if not respect, he certainly has a great sophistication about the power of society to enforce its rules. He also has a great sophistication about those ways in which he can beat society—it's their life study, after all. I mean, a man who has been in jail more than half his life gets to know an awful lot about how to manipulate society. And in that sense they would respect Gilmore, because they would see it as a vast and mighty manipulation, and certainly from Gilmore's point of view, it was a huge—whatever else his motives, one of his motives had to be that he wasn't going to go out quietly. This was going to be an extraordinary manipulation that he could put upon the normal social procedure, which by that time, of course, had been that when a man was sentenced to death, he put in an appeal, and pretty automatically his death sentence was commuted to life imprisonment and so the machinery of the law turned. In other words, a death sentence was really just a formal sentence in the sense that they gave people death sentences, but they didn't execute them.

Mr. Buckley: Oh, we should mention that this was the first execution in ten years.

Mr. Mailer: Yes.

Mr. Buckley: Now you were pursuing the difference between the killers in Truman Capote's book and yours—yours being a convict and his being sort of—

Mr. Mailer: Punks.

Mr. Buckley: Punks—extemporaneous no-goods. There was a sort of a hard consistency in Gilmore's attitude, who had been more days in jail than out of jail at age 34—35?

Mr. Mailer: He was 36.

Mr. Buckley: Yes, 36. Now many people who have read your book seem to be making heavy weather over the setting—the Mormon desert, the experiences of people who had settled in that area. Is there a sense in which you intended to conjoin the history of Utah or Mormonism with this black theatre? Is there a sense in which they were made for each other or is it just coincidental?

Mr. Mailer: Again, it's one of the unanswered and deep questions of the book. A lot of people thought that Gilmore selected Mormons to execute. Parenthetically, one reason the book is called *The Executioner's Song*—and I realized this only after I'd finished it and the title had been there for a long time—is that Gilmore is also the executioner, in the sense that this is the story of an executioner who, in his turn, is executed. But the question is whether Gilmore was executing Mormons as such. There is much evidence for it, but at the same time it remains speculation and supposition. It's very easy when you're in Utah to spot a Mormon—it's not hard. I mean, half the people in the state are Mormon, and they have a look. You know, they're immensely religious people, and particularly active Mormons—which is the word they use for devout—just have a certain look. They have a missionary look. They look a little bit like Jehovah's Witnesses in New York. They stand out. You can see they lead very clean lives. I mean, Mormons—

Mr. Buckley: You think the gasoline attendant was instantly the Mormon to Gary Gilmore when he pulled up there?

Mr. Mailer: Oh, I would think so. Let's put it this way—

Mr. Buckley: Tall and square and—

Mr. Mailer: You could be wrong, but you wouldn't be wrong more often than one time in ten. I spent time in Utah for the first time, and after I'd been there for a couple of weeks, it was very easy for me to be right on who was a Mormon and who wasn't nearly all the time. And Gilmore after all had a mother who was Mormon and he'd spent some of his boyhood in Salt Lake City. I don't think it would have been hard for him to spot a Mormon. So he may well have chosen to murder Mormons as such.

Mr. Buckley: And the motivation for that would have been what?

Mr. Mailer: I think finally an intangible motivation. We were talking about this immense rage that he felt, that had gotten to the point where he couldn't control it. I think he saw— The Mormons after all are tremendously social-minded people. If we're going to talk about society, Mormons epitomize society. They epitomize society with a great emphasis on cleanliness, order, discipline. And to Gilmore, his getting out of jail and finding it very hard to live in the square world, the Mormons would have been his new jailers. So that would have been part of it. There were also old family resentments. His mother, who had been a Mormon all her life, lost her house, and she went to the Mormon church at one point to ask them to save it for her—it's a very complicated business—but finally they didn't, and Gilmore was not necessarily a man who would look into all the niceties and the nuances of a complex situation before making up his mind. There's reason to believe that he was furious at the Mormons, at the church for having let the house go. They were factors.

Mr. Buckley: I won't reveal the conclusions you drew to the extent that you drew them, but is that why he elected to have a Catholic priest at his side when he was dispatched as a sort of a continuing rebuff of Mormonism?

Mr. Mailer: Here again— You know, I find when I talk about him— You know, when you invent a character, you can always explain everything about him. But when you're dealing with someone who lived—And I know him better than I know most of the people in my own family by now—but I find I talk about him the way I would talk about someone who is in my family, because I don't understand the people who are in my family inside and out—I can merely speculate about them. I think Gilmore loved playing games with the people around him. So it was very much in his character to have a great friendship with a Catholic chaplain and with a Mormon chaplain and to play each of them against the other, and to use them to the hilt, and at the same time—since he was a man who had surprising veins of compassion or real feeling along with large areas that were absolutely unfeeling—there would be moments when he would have genuine relations with the Catholic chaplain and the

Conversations with Norman Mailer

Mormon chaplain. And it may have come down to no more, I think, than that the Catholic chaplain was very concerned with being close to Gilmore at the end; and the Mormon chaplain—who, if anything I think in this situation, loved him more than the Catholic chaplain— was the sort of man who hated a show of feeling. So there might have been something where the Mormon chaplain might have been saying to himself, "My God, just look at that Catholic chaplain getting near to Gilmore." And the two chaplains might disagree about what really happened in terms of who was closer at the end. Gilmore spoke snidely about both of them from time to time.

Mr. Buckley: Yes. What was the point that you sought to stress when you devoted as much time as you did to the kind of macabre curiosity that the public developed about those last days—the effort to film him going from the truck into the cannery where he was executed, the helicopter that flew over there, the number of press who wanted to examine the chair to which he was attached for the actual execution. Did you intend that censoriously or were you simply saying that's the way human curiosity is?

Mr. Mailer: I got fascinated at a certain point in drawing an objective picture of American society using the thread of the story. I found that—while one didn't go from the very depths of American society to the absolute heights—one did cover quite a spectrum of American society, from people who were relatively poor and powerless to people who, while they weren't running the state of Utah, nonetheless they were fairly high up in the functioning of the state of Utah—the governmental apparatus of Utah. So it was a social drama. It was fascinating to me to see the relation of the media to it. The media was like another wheel. In other words, the true gears were operating. Gilmore's fundamental battle was with the powers that would and would not execute him—those huge social powers that wanted to execute him and those huge social powers that wanted to change his sentence to life imprisonment. The media came in, almost like a helicopter, if you will, and hovered all over the place. It never truly exercised real power, but it kept affecting and distorting and changing everything that was going on. And I had so much material to draw on in writing this book, that I thought this is part of this invaluable material—the material seemed invaluable to me—I thought, I'm finally getting some picture of how American society works. It works so much better and so much worse than I'd always thought it did. It was interesting to me to see the way American society was in some ways a more efficient and effective social machine than I had expected. There was a little more fairness at certain levels than somehow I'd thought. All that was interesting to me, and—

Mr. Buckley: The decisions were more thoughtful than you had expected.

Mr. Mailer: One of the things I discovered while writing the book is I began to think that there is such a thing as the American character. At one point I almost called this book "American Virtue," believe it or not. I was terribly tempted to, because I thought that was the true title. But I then decided that it would be impossible, because everybody would see it as a sardonic title, and that what I was saying was that American virtue does not exist, and I could just see how the French would see that title and so on. So I thought to hell with that, and I'll keep calling it *The Executioner's Song.* But I learned something about Americans in this book that I'd never quite put into words myself before. I think in America we are all enormously concerned with being virtuous. It doesn't matter what we do. We can be anything from a drug pusher to a clergyman. We measure ourselves by our virtue. You know, the English might measure themselves by the quality of their manners, the French might measure themselves by the amount of security that they establish in their lives and how well-nourished are the roots they put down. It's a game you can play—you can talk about different nationalities in those terms. But it seems to me that there's one thing that characterizes all Americans, and that's that we want to be virtuous. We are obsessed with it. And so what I've found is that in the working of a social machine you find people who may play a very small part—in the execution of Gary Gilmore—yet they thought about it a great deal and they worried about it. It was terribly important to them that this was the right thing and not the wrong thing.

Mr. Buckley: The cousin who turned him in and that kind of thing.

Mr. Mailer: Yes, but all the way down to people—say some clerk in the judge's office who might have made a small error on some form that was filed would stay up at night to change the form. I'm making up an example, but— Everybody wanted to do the right thing, and I thought that it might be that rather than that society is evil, maybe what it is is a sad comedy. One of the things that I found is that people on both sides— I met people who were absolutely decent on both sides who were really working might and main to accomplish their ends. I became fascinated with lawyers who are devoted to their clients and see the other side as evil and—

Mr. Buckley: And you don't draw a distinction between those whose devotion led them to desire the execution of Gilmore and those whose devotion led them to want him to have a commuted sentence.

Mr. Mailer: Well, I thought the balance was close to perfect here. I would confess that if you had a convict who wanted to appeal his death sentence, who didn't want to be executed, my sympathies would probably fall to the side of saying don't execute a man who doesn't want to be executed. It's a large question, and we can get into it if you wish. But in this case, where he did want to be executed, then the question got truly interesting, because does society in a way have the right to insist that a man stay alive who does want to be executed?

Mr. Buckley: Which, as a matter of plain dumb fact, is over the long term impractical. He tried to commit suicide, after all, and presumably one of those times he would have succeeded.

Mr. Mailer: Yes, but, you know, it's different—

Mr. Buckley: The question of course, is whether the State should be an accomplice in a suicide.

Mr. Mailer: But that argument—which was raised by the people who wanted his death sentence commuted—the argument that the liberals brought was: Gilmore really wants to commit suicide.

Mr. Buckley: Let him do it.

Mr. Mailer: Let him do it, and don't let the State be dirtied with this terribly unpleasant, disagreeable, and perhaps sinister process of executing a man socially, impersonally. Execution is the key to it there. But I've thought about that a long time, and my own opinion, for what it's worth—as I say, I kept my opinions to the side while writing the book—is that there's a great difference between committing suicide and being executed. I think there's a difference in one's moral center, if you will, at the moment it happens. For people who believe that death is death and that there's nothing to be said about it, that after you die you're gone forever—

Mr. Buckley: Well, it's a basic theological distinction and it has been forever, so I think it would be hard to disagree with you on that. The fact that people who were violently opposed to his execution were indifferent to the question of whether he committed suicide oughtn't to surprise us. Whether they would facilitate the suicide, i.e., by not inspecting his cell every day to make sure that he hadn't had an accumulation of Seconal, is a question somewhere in between.

Mr. Mailer: No, there I think—

Mr. Buckley: You may remember that when Goering committed suicide, giving rise to that marvelous lead sentence in the UP dispatch, "Herman Goering cheated death tonight by committing suicide—"

Mr. Mailer: Well, he cheated execution, for sure.

Mr. Buckley: Well, sure—

Mr. Mailer: It was a bad headline, because—

Mr. Buckley: Well, the point is that the distinction was sharply drawn. They wanted judicial vengeance, judicial vindication. When Pierre Laval was dragged out to an execution in 1945, he had taken these pills, and they pumped his stomach and so on and so forth all for the purpose of keeping him alive for an extra 15 minutes so that he could be properly shot. So there is a tremendous symbolism that is vested in that distinction.

Mr. Mailer: Well, I think execution is double-edged. That is, if a man doesn't want to be executed, but tries to escape it—

Mr. Buckley: Yes, it's different. That's different.

Mr. Mailer: Then society does get this enormous urge to carry out the act. In this case, I think it's different, because if a man says, "I did wrong and I want to be executed—"

Mr. Buckley: Which Gilmore wouldn't do.

Mr. Mailer: —that's different from committing suicide.

Mr. Buckley: Which Gilmore wouldn't do.

Mr. Mailer: Yes, he did do that.

Mr. Buckley: He wanted to be executed, but he was never contrite.

Mr. Mailer: Oh, I see, you mean to say, "I did wrong,"— I think he was not contrite. I think what he was, he felt that he had used up his chances.

Mr. Buckley: Yes, he was fatalistic.

Mr. Mailer: More than fatalistic, even. I think he had ultimately a certain contempt for people who finally had not done what they were supposed to do with their lives and therefore, from his point of view, the only dignified thing to do at this point was to be executed. But I think also it was terribly important to him, given the way he'd lived his life, that he be able to face his executioners. He had a set of choices. His first choice was freedom. Therefore, he tried to escape the night before the execution. His second choice was execution. His third was suicide. It was fascinating to me, the way these were definite steps to him.

Mr. Buckley: His fourth was life in jail. That was the worst.

Mr. Mailer: That was the worst.

Mr. Buckley: The fact that we can talk, or at least that you can, as interestingly about his motives now, and that so many people on reading your book will be invited to speculate on his motives and on the motives of the people who are major characters in it suggests at least at one level the utility of this new form of yours. Let me ask you this. Do you think of it as a paradigm, and if so, what would happen to, say, *Crime and Punishment* if one were to undertake to rewrite it accepting all of the inhibitions that you accepted in this book.

Mr. Mailer: It would disappear. It would not be a good book. I hold no brief for this method. I don't feel that I've now discovered a— First of all, I didn't discover it, but apart from that I don't feel that I have a unique or that a few of us have a unique way now of writing a book which will do away with the old novel. What I felt is that this story had certain qualities that just begged—

Mr. Buckley: Lent itself to it.

Mr. Mailer: —to be done this way. One thing was that there was an enormous amount of material. I mean, I had a great deal of good luck. I happened to have an interviewer before I even started the book. There were 60 interviews to look at and they were done by one of the people who is a character in this book, Larry Schiller, who had bought the rights to Gilmore's life. Now he happens to be an excellent interviewer. And one of the things that was particularly good about it from my point of view is that his point of view and his style of interviewing is altogether different from mine. So before I even started the book I had an excellent interviewer working, let's say, from another place doing interviews.

Mr. Buckley: But you went back and interviewed those same people.

Mr. Mailer: Well, I had to, because I was interested in other aspects of them than he was. Nonetheless, I started with a great deal. I was able to see the story before I began it, and that gave me the feeling that this method would be ideal for this book because there was so much material. And the story was so good. You know, I could spend my literary life working to get a story as good as this one. If I had ever invented a story as good as this, I would have written a novel. I had never written a novel like this before because I'd never got that good a story. But you know, when you don't have quite that good a story, what you have are other qualities you can bring to a book. There's every reason to keep writing novels. It's just that this particular one, I'm happy with the way it was done. Because what I wanted to do with it, and what I discovered at a certain point—and I think this is really the core of it—is I thought, I can write a book that will really make people think in a way they haven't quite thought before. This material made me begin to look at ten or 20 serious questions in an altogether new fashion, and it made me humble in that I just didn't know the answers. I mean, I've had the habit for years of feeling that I could dominate any question pretty quickly—it's been my vanity. And it was an exceptional experience to spend all these months and find that gently but inevitably, I was finding myself in more profound—not confusion—but doubt about my ability to answer, to give definitive answers to these questions. But what I had instead is that I was collecting materials that I would think about for the rest of my life. In other words, I was getting new experience. I thought it might be very nice for once just to write a book which doesn't have answers, but poses delicate questions with a great deal of evidence and a great deal of material and let people argue over it. I feel there are any number of areas in this book where there are people who have better answers to give than I have.

Mr. Buckley: You said a moment ago that if I wanted, we would touch on the question of why you novelized—no, you didn't novelize it—why you called it a novel, and the answer is yes, I would like to go into that.

Mr. Mailer: All right.

Mr. Buckley: Did this make those questions stand out more sharply than otherwise they would have, or what?

Mr. Mailer: I think of nonfiction as living on two stomachs, like the cow. In other words, the material is eaten, it's partially digested, it's regurgitated and then it's digested again. In other words, in a book of nonfiction, there is a tendency in nonfiction to present the author's conclusions to the reader, and while this is not true for all works of nonfiction I think it's true for most of them—most serious works of nonfiction. You read it because you want to know what the author thinks definitively about a subject, and the author will present his thinking process to you sometimes—sometimes he doesn't. But he literally digests the material, and when he does present a scene, it's as illustrative material to make a difficult passage more simple. And the one thing that nonfiction calls for is understanding—clear understanding of what's being said. It's hard to think of a good book of nonfiction whose waters are not clear. Whereas I think in fiction, what we want to do is we want to create life. We want to give the readers the feeling that they are participating in the life of the characters they're reading about. And to the degree that they're participating in it, they shouldn't necessarily understand everything that's going on any more than we do in life. Maybe they should understand somewhat more than we do in life, but not everything. The moment we understand everything in a book, it can't possibly be fiction, I'd say, by the way I'm defining it. Now the fact that these are real people and I attempted to be as scrupulous as I could to what happened—subject to the limitations of journalism—means only that this is a novel which is not an imaginative novel, which did not come out of my imagination. But I wrote it as if it had.

Mr. Buckley: One is not entirely clear what you're saying here. You say you wrote it as though it had—are you simply referring to things like sequences and liberties with the chronology and that sort of thing.

Mr. Mailer: No—

Mr. Buckley: Or are you saying that there are actually exchanges that were invented by you and put inside quotation marks?

Mr. Mailer: No, there's very little invention in the book. I would not say that every single line of dialogue in the book literally came out of an interview, but I think the amount of invention of dialogue is very small and almost always it was functional—sometimes you just have to end a scene, and—

Mr. Buckley: Sure, someone has to say goodnight.

Mr. Mailer: Out of respect for the reader, if you will, sometimes you have to turn a scene and just leave it with a little flourish or something, just for the reading of the book. But what I meant is that when we pick up a novel and we read it, we say, "I'm having an experience—I'm reading a novel." And I wanted the reader to have that experience, because I wanted a reader who didn't know anything at all about the source of this book, who the author was and how it came to be written or anything like this—to pick it up and think they were reading a novel. It's just a matter of style, if you get down to it. You know, you could just give the book to 50 people who knew nothing about it and you could say to them, "What is this?" and they'd say, "This is a novel." I wanted it to read like a novel, and so I used my skills such as they are over these 30 years, to write it as a novel. But it is accurate. That was the requirement. Because, you know, I had to overcome 10,000 habits—intimate habits—in the course of writing it. I'd create certain people—see, I say create; they're real people, but as you're writing a book you feel you create your characters—and then they'd meet. And they'd be two people I was interested in, and I knew the reader hopefully was interested in them. And I thought, well, when they meet what I want is to have a very good scene between them—as I would if I had been writing the novel. But in fact they met and not that much had happened. It was sort of a disappointing scene. So I felt bound to stay with the disappointment of the scene and have half the scenes in that book a little less than they ought to be.

Mr. Buckley: Because they were transcriptions.

Mr. Mailer: Because they came from the interviews, and the interview— What happened when those two people met was that it wasn't as interesting as everyone thought it would be. But what I also thought was that after awhile it began to add its own flavor. Ideally, if it worked it would add its own flavor. It would make the book even more lifelike—because life is like that. Half the meetings we have prove to be less than we expected. And very occasionally when we are least ready for it, something very interesting can happen. And I thought the book, in a way—because it didn't have just my mind working out a form, but because it came out of all the people who in one way or another contributed to the book—I'd think it was a little closer to life than anything else I've worked on before.

Mr. Buckley: Mr. Jeff Greenfield, who is familiar to viewers of this program, is a graduate of the University of Wisconsin, a former aide to Mayor Lindsay and Senator Robert Kennedy. He is an author, is engaged in regular television work and screenwriting. Mr. Greenfield.

Mr. Greenfield: Thank you. I cannot resist the temptation to pose one of those great questions that you have said that you are used to dominating, with full recognition that you came out of this book uncertain as to your attitude toward capital punishment. But to pose it in its baldest form, do you believe there are people whose deeds render them unfit to live?

Mr. Mailer: If you're asking as a matter of personal belief, yes, probably. Probably I do.

Mr. Greenfield: Let me take it the next step. I apologize. I know this is literal— That's a law school education for you.

Mr. Buckley: No, but you see, people would be sore if those questions didn't get asked here.

Mr. Greenfield: Yes, that's— I was being unnecessarily humble. Do we as other people have the right to make that judgment? Now you say as a matter of personal belief, you believe that you can say some people commit deeds that render them unfit to live. Do we have the process—the criminal justice system, I suppose—to turn that judgment into reality? That is, by condemning people to death?

Mr. Mailer: Well, that is where the question gets immense and probably unanswerable. Because I would be highly suspicious of any group of people, no matter how well-intentioned, who take on that right—because, you know, the more we know, the more we know how imperfect we all are. And also the key question is this: for every murderer who commits, let's say, an absolutely abominable crime, for every hundred murderers who commit an absolutely abominable crime, how many of them are finally unredeemable—unredeemable in any way at all? The number may be very small. There's where the ability to be certain of oneself begins to falter. But then on the other side, you have this other terrible practical problem, which is when you have men who are the worst kind of murderers—the kind who seem absolutely unredeemable—when they're in prison for many, many years, they become virtually depraved animals, some of them, because they're living on death row. And they can poison the very inside of a prison. They certainly take the general level of life in a prison and they lower it.

Mr. Greenfield: I guess to violate the intentional fallacy, one more time, when you'd gotten finished with *The Executioner's Song,* I wonder whether there was a moment that never made it into the book when you said to yourself either "I'm glad he's dead," or

"What a horror that this man died." It seems to me that there would have had to have been some kind of moment when you stopped up short and had to confront how you felt about Gilmore.

Mr. Mailer: Oh, I lived with it, after all. I found something a little close to the sort of experience that you might have in life, let's say, if you had a relative who had an incurable illness, and you really spent a lot of time virtually hoping for their death because they were in such pain and it was just so awful. And at the moment they died, a part of you was very happy and yet another part of you felt a tremendous sense of loss. That might be analogous to some of the things I felt about Gilmore. Because on the one hand, having gotten to know him that well, you did have to sympathize—at least I did—have to sympathize to a great extent with his desire to be executed the way he saw it. I thought in a funny way that this man, who had done all these terrible things and had had all these incredible frustrations in his life, was now finally having an ultimate frustration, which was that he couldn't even die in that way he had chosen, which was his last attempt by his own life to find some odd kind of dignity. And so in that sense I sympathized with that desire up to a point. So that when he was executed, there was a certain feeling of, "Yes, at last." On the other hand, I suddenly thought, "My God, this man, with all, he had none." This tremendously complex and somewhat talented man, this tortured man, this man who was not without compassion, this man who was certainly—by any measure you couldn't say he was wholly unredeemable. He was too complex to say that quickly about him. This man was dead, and he was truly dead. That's why I took the execution right through the autopsy—because that was something that I wanted the reader to feel. That's what it means when we kill a man. That even this man who wanted to die and succeeded in getting society to execute him, that even when he was killed, we still feel this horrible shock and loss. And I wanted the reader to live with this incredible complexity that's involved in—not just the process of execution, but with that most mysterious fact that we live and then we die. You know, one babbles as one speaks about it, but there's something profound in the recognition of it. I don't mean by my effort—I mean when we come face to face with it, it's awesome.

Mr. Greenfield: Bill, could I ask you— It's a question that I've always wondered about the realtionship between the conservative philosophy and the support for capital punishment. Let me just

phrase it as briefly as I can. I can understand theoretically that there
are people who commit deeds that render them unfit to live. I think,
the way that Norman Mailer just described it, that one feels that
about people—that these people have forfeited whatever
membership in the community of people they had by what they did.
What is difficult for me to understand is how, given an attitude of
mind which recognizes how frail the instruments of public decisions
are: government, the criminal justice system, the bureaucracy—we
can't mail letters, we can't get social security checks to old people,
we can't tear down the right buildings—how one is willing to place
sufficient faith in any instrument to say, "Look, we know we are
imperfect, so we will run that risk when it comes to putting someone
in jail," but given the finality of death, on a practical, not theoretical
basis, how do we say that we have that much faith in the institution of
criminal justice that we trust it to put people to death?

Mr. Buckley: Well, my own feeling is that you've swallowed a
beam and strained on a gnat. Because I would disagree with both of
you that there is anybody who is, "unfit to live," because I think that
the word unfit is much more difficult to define than the much simpler
question is it possible to codify the social will on the matter of an
appropriate punishment. I think for certain crimes the death sentence
is appropriate. And—

Mr. Greenfield: How do you make that judgment if you don't say
that person has forfeited the right to live?

Mr. Buckley: And the fact that the federal post office cannot be
trusted to deliver my mail in time is, I think, a dodgy comparison for
the kind of attention we give to matters of guilt and innocence. Now I
wouldn't say that Gilmore was, "unfit to live," but I would say that
the sentence of execution, given what he did, justified draconian
punishment. I believe that, as Walter Burns explicated so well in his
last book, in his book on capital punishment, that a society not only
has the right, but the obligation to punish, and that it's a copout
simply to assume that punishment belongs in another world.

Mr. Greenfield: Excuse me, but that is the copout. Because that
whole argument inevitably blurs the distinction between the case for
punishment—which I think is quite sound—and the case for what
kind of punishment. I mean, what I think, and what Mailer was
saying, is that when you look upon death as opposed to any other
kind of sanction, you are dealing with something very different. I

mean, the Spenkelink case, which was the first man executed against his will—he was executed under a Florida law which specifically said execution is to be done only for especially heinous murders. His murder was the firing of a bullet into his sleeping companion who may or may not have terrorized him, while murderers in Florida who had tortured people, who had done things infinitely worse, didn't receive it. What this goes to is not the validity of punishment, but whether we believe our system can properly weigh this question when the punishment is this final. Isn't that what we're talking about?

Mr. Buckley: An argument against the arbitrary administration of justice is not an argument against punishing that person against whom you move arbitrarily—

Mr. Greenfield: It is when the punishment is death.

Mr. Buckley: It's an argument over irregularity.

Mr. Greenfield: No, no.

Mr. Buckley: If you catch only one person who is speeding at 100 miles an hour and let 99 people go, it's not an argument against stopping the one you caught.

Mr. Greenfield: And you keep evading the point. Of course we have to have an imperfect system, because we're not perfect, of any kind of punishment. It seems to me that that is what defines, that is what settles the question of capital punishment. You keep talking about speeding tickets, whether we should punish them—nobody disagrees with that except three people who are on government grants. The question is death.

Mr. Buckley: If capital punishment is the only apposite punishment for certain kinds of crime, then that you should execute Spenkelink—who, by the way, shot somebody in the back of the head and also participated in digging an axe in his skull and sat on his carcass and drank a bottle of vodka with his companion and toasted to their accomplishment—that there are other people who, as you put it, committed equally heinous crimes leaves you over at that end of the horror spectrum in which your resentment is over the sluggishness of the processes of justice, not over the execution of Spenkelink.

Mr. Greenfield: Let me go back to Norman Mailer, if I could, just for one second. Did you find when you were immersed in this book that the mechanics of the criminal justice system—that is to say, the mechanics of appeal or post-conviction judgements—in a way were almost rendered—I'm trying to think of the right word—rendered sort of trivial in comparison to the question that was at hand here? Did the spectre of death in a way make these processes to you seem almost bizarre and banal by comparison?

Mr. Mailer: I think the process has to seem bizarre, because the law is designed in most cases to deal with— I mean, anyone who has ever had any experience with the law knows how irritating the law can be, because the law is not interested in the nuances of anything. You know, facts have to be established, and on the basis of facts being established a ladder of logic is built, and on that ladder of logic, the two ladders cross one another at some point and whoever builds the better ladder presumably wins the case. Now it's more complicated than that, but one of the maddening things about the law is how factual and exact you have to be and how you have to establish this apparatus of this factology, if you will—this ladder. And of course when you come to death, the law, by its nature, tends to break down. It can codify punishments, but the law is not equipped, emotionally speaking, if you will—or the people who exercise the law, are not equipped by their training to deal with this very delicate question which comes up one time in 100,000 or a million cases. So it's going to look bizarre. It's going to look absurd. You can almost take it for granted. You know, if you write a war novel, obviously war is going to seem, in some of its aspects, hideous. You don't write a war novel to show that war is hideous. So I don't write this book about capital punishment to say that the law is absurd. I took it for granted that it was going to look terribly absurd in it. What's surprised me in a funny way is that, given all the absurdity of the way people were acting, given the fact that Gilmore finally made his point—which was the law had to be bent and tortured in order to get him executed on schedule, which in a way was one of Gilmore's revenges on the law—nonetheless I was surprised at the amount of real feeling on the side of the executioners. Because they took their role very, very seriously.

Mr. Greenfield: I have to ask you one question about style, because it has become such a remarked-upon fact, that this is such a spare narrative—spare in the sense that one is used to a Norman Mailer striding through the pages, if not at the center then certainly very close up there. Was there a temptation for Aquarius or Norman Mailer or whoever the persona was at any point in the writing of this book to break the rule? I mean, was there a point, was there a scene, was there a thing that happened where you said, "I want to be there."

Mr. Buckley: Aquarius had an Alfred Hitchcock cameo role, didn't he?

Mr. Mailer: I was never going to use Aquarius, but when I started the book, I thought, "I need some ironic framework to deal with the book." And I was going to create a character, a movie-writer, a middle-aged movie-writer whose marriage had broken up and he was living in Paris and he was miserable, just a big, ungainly man with two huge suitcases, sort of a figure in the Latin Quarter and everybody would wonder, "What is this man with the two huge suitcases doing?" Well, they happened to be all the interviews of the Gary Gilmore case, and he was going to be writing a huge treatment for someone like, let's say, Francis Ford Coppola, who said to him, "Put everything in, don't leave anything out. I want to know all about this man Gilmore before I make the movie." Well, that was going to be the means by which I was going to be able to comment on the action.

Mr. Buckley: And surface occasionally.

Mr. Mailer: And surface not through myself but through this fictional character.

Mr. Buckley: Was there a draft that actually had that?

Mr. Mailer: I started the book that way, and then at a certain point, I said, "This is ridiculous. You just have to bite the bullet. You have to be brave enough to write this book without putting yourself in it at all."

Mr. Buckley: Thank you Mr. Mailer; thank you, Mr. Greenfield; thank you, ladies and gentlemen.

A Murderer's Tale:
Norman Mailer Talking to Melvyn Bragg
Melvyn Bragg/1979

From *The Listener*, 15 November 1979, 660-62. Reprinted by permission of *The Listener.*

Norman Mailer's apartment is on the crest of Brooklyn Heights. From his window there is a view of Manhattan which is so spectacular it looks unreal. Forbidding formations of skyscrapers float across the Hudson. Helicopters cut back and forth across the panes like windscreen wipers. Out there is Wall Street, the Staten Island ferry, Ellis Island which digested and disgorged so many immigrants at the beginning of their American dream: Mailer has welded himself to the contemporary consciousness of his country and there it is outside his window in all its fantasy, greed and glory: facing him.

He doesn't let you down. There's the battle-scarred warmth which unpretentiously welcomes the crew as they clamber all over the furniture and set up lights, mikes, cameras.

'How could anyone so Jewish look so Irish?' Kenneth Tynan once exclaimed, and there is that bitten-in charisma—fatal, Kennedy word—about him. It's been double-edged. For many critics and literary scavengers he's long been a sitting duck to be nipped and gnawed at will. Friends and defenders admit that he's written as many bad sentences, indeed bad books, as most good writers. But he has been good and in the first half at least of *The Executioner's Song** he is as good as he has ever been.

He tells the story of Gary Gilmore, the man who demanded that the state shoot him for the two meaningless murders he committed in a small Midwestern Mormon town. Gilmore was 35 and had spent 18 years in prison.

Once he had declared his intention of being shot, the media moved

The Executioner's Song. By Norman Mailer. Hutchinson £8.85

in. Leader of the pack was photographer and film producer Larry
Schiller, who bought all the rights to Gilmore's life story. He
interviewed Gilmore, the relatives who had stood by him, his
girlfriend, the wives of the victims . . . he built up a vault of tapes and
then called in Mailer to turn it into a book.

Mailer was 800 pages into a novel and wanted some quick cash
and a break. And, like most of America by then, he was curious
about Gilmore, who refused the thousand and one chances offered
him of dodging the firing-squad. Mailer came for a swift essay and
stayed to produce a book as long as *War and Peace*. He, too, went
on the interview trail; he read letters, legal documents, files, papers,
and finally decided on a panoramic documentary form which, in its
scope and large cast, echoes the 19th-century novel.

The result is a scan which picks up scores of contemporary
Americans—lawyers, perverts, workers, prisoners, reporters,
housewives—and deals in detail with the squalor and despair of a
criminal who started to 'grow' (Mailer's word) only under the
sentence of death. The circus provoked by his decision to be shot is
also described at length—not as successfully, in my opinion—in the
book and Gilmore becomes notorious, even a 'star'.

My first worry, though, was to do with the morality involved in
writing at such length about such a man and it was there, burning
lights on to balance and block out the outside light, that we began:

*Were you worried that you were merely glorifying somebody who
would be better not glorified, by taking on the Gilmore book?*
I've got to confess, and this may be shocking to some people, that I
worried about that to the greatest degree because I thought it would
affect the fortunes of the book. You know I naturally, like any other
author, want my books to do well and I thought this is the hurdle. An
awful lot of people are going to resent this book and they're going to
say there's something just swinish about glorifying a two-time killer
and a bad man, and I'm not certain that you can defend yourself
against that absolutely. There's no doubt in my mind that if you write
a book, particularly a long book, about one person you've affected
their place in history. You don't even have to be a terribly good writer
to do that. Once that much space and time is given to one person,
and there's that much reporting in the media about what's been
done, you've altered the nature of that man's life and that man's

record. He is taken more seriously. On the other hand, I wasn't personally troubled by it because one of the feelings I've had for a long, long time is that, you know, righteousness and self-righteousness have absolutely no place in literature—obviously they don't.

And Gilmore, I thought, was an absolutely fascinating phenomenon. Apart from anything I might have felt about him personally, I couldn't remember a time when a man insisted upon his own execution and then proceeded to carry it out. Died. I mean there are people who say I want to be dead. There are people who are capable of saying: 'You're accusing me of these crimes and you've convicted me and sentenced me—execute me.' That's one thing. There are any number of criminals who can do that and any number of condemned men who can do it. But Gilmore then proceeded over a period of three months to carry it out as if he were a general carrying out a campaign, and the impulse of his campaign—and his idea of victory—was his own execution. That's going beyond normal suicide. This goes beyond normal criminality. It goes into some of the deepest questions.

You know we've been sitting smugly on Freud and Jung for 70 years but we don't know a damn thing about human nature, and Gilmore poses questions that psychologists and psychiatrists can't answer; and that's why I'm fascinated by him and that's why I think he's worth the attention.

The media moved in very heavily on Gilmore: did it change him— do you think it changed him? Did you discover a different Gilmore afterwards? I mean, when he was sentenced to death for murdering two men in cold blood there were fewer than 20 people in the court. Then he insisted on being shot, and it's boom, isn't it?—'Playboy' interviews and various television stations get their cameras out, fighting for the rights . . . Now did Gilmore change in that process? What did that do to him?

Well, it changed him, yes. Whenever the media attach themselves to anyone the challenge implicit in it is will they collapse? After all, even Presidential candidates have collapsed under the pressure of facing the media constantly: they make one remark that's ill-chosen and they lose their Presidential chances. It's happened to a couple of them along the way. Gilmore of course didn't have to worry about that—he could make a thousand mistakes with the media and it hardly mattered that way—but what was involved was that his own importance, not only to others but to himself, kept shifting at a vast rate as an immense amount of money relative to what he'd had before began to come his way.

Here is a man who never started smoking and the reason he gave for it is that he had no money in prison and no one in his family had any money. And he just didn't want to get into a situation where he wouldn't have the money for cigarettes and would be craving them. Here's a man who had that little money and now he's gotten $50,000 and he's given $2,000 to one old friend and $3,000 to another and he just throws his money away and is giving it to people in huge sums. A girl writes him a nice sexy letter from Honolulu and he sends her $300—that sort of thing. So there are these changes in his life.

The man's had no attention and no money and now he's got both to a great degree. He also started having relations with people of the sort he'd never had before because by the time he was executed he had two lawyers, the same two lawyers for a period of almost two months, and they were both Mormons and both well established small-town lawyers. That means they were very dependable, very regular, very decent men more or less—I say more or less because it's hard to think of a lawyer as being *very* decent . . .

He goes through many changes that way. He also begins to be put into the position of a Solomon. He has to make all sorts of decisions and choices about what is going to be done with the parts of his body—which parts to give to charity, which parts will be cremated. He also has to make all kinds of decisions in relation to the legal processes because there are people who are trying to keep him alive against his will and there are people who are trying to carry out his will—quite independently of him. The state wants to execute him on time. They can't bear the circus that has suddenly descended upon Utah. They want to be rid of Gilmore. Gilmore wants to be rid of Gilmore. The American Civil Liberties Union and various liberal forces are coming in from all over the country to try to save Gilmore's life—not because they are tremendously enchanted with his life but because finally they were afraid that his execution might kick off a wave of executions all over the place. So all these forces start to impinge on him and . . .

And fan mail of about 40,000 letters?

Altogether yes, about 40,000 letters. So he's reading. There are scenes where various chaplains come in on him and he's sitting on the floor with a blanket and letters all around him and he just picks a bunch and says, 'Here, read these.' And he hands them a bunch and says, you know, 'If you see any interesting ones pass them to me.' He's become a movie star in effect but a movie star on the rise of popularity, and with it all he grows. I mean he still shows all the difficult, knotty, unpleasant sides of his nature over and over and over. It isn't as it he suddenly becomes a wonderful fellow, far from it. But what you do see is, yes, the man does have a capacity to grow. He's not simply that habit-ridden petty monster that he was in the early stages who arouses our compassion because he's so trapped. He's even capable of kissing good luck on the mouth.

You know, he begins to rise a degree in stature. He begins to assume some part of that role that history has given him and that is almost awesome. To see the growth of a man. As I say, it's a partial growth and it's not at all a straightforward line. He does something good and then he'll do something God-awful right afterwards. He'll make a very wise decision and then he'll be so petty and so childish the next moment that you just throw up your hands. But slowly you see the man moving towards this idea he has himself that he wants to die with dignity, he wants to carry it through and he wants to establish a few simple things about himself. One is that he is serious about his death and for reasons you almost can't begin to name. You see, you can't begin to say at this point why is he a man of such pride—of the kind bred after 20 years in prison where you weren't broken—and finally he has set this bluff up. It's a poker bluff and he will carry it through until he's killed.

You see, by now there's no doubt at all that if he just says 'I will appeal' he could stay alive for years now, if he wants to, because all the appeal machinery is open to him if only he'll take it. He can stay alive for the rest of his life in prison. He can probably get his sentence commuted to life imprisonment. There were probably a few irregularities in his trial. There are any number of things he can do if he wants to; but, no, he keeps forcing this issue. 'The state said I was guilty and sentenced me to death. Let the state carry out its sentence.' And he forces his own death and of course all the people who are opposed to the execution are saying the man's mad. He's suicidal—the state is collaborating on a suicide—this is heinous, this is monstrous.

And he does attempt to take his life?
He attempts to take his life twice . . . He's all alone and through it all he moves towards the day of his execution with this kind of implacable will. It's exactly like a general who's decided that a certain mountain must be taken on a front. That hill must be taken at all costs: we are going to take that hill and nothing will stop us. It's exactly like the general whom people come back to with reports of this front collapsing, and that flank in terrible trouble, and he says 'No matter, we go forward.' Really this is the way he handles the lawyers. They come to him with what's going on and he gives them his reaction of what to do. Sometimes he's as intelligent as hell; sometimes he's silly. But you begin to see that he is working very practically and quietly and efficiently for his own end and, you know, it's off the normal spectrum of human behaviour completely and yet he's not the least bit insane . . .
And that is the part of karma that I think will always prove indigestible to civilised society. Because the idea that there is something more important than the life we live on this earth is anathema to civilised society. Civilisation is built on the firm premise that we have one life and one life only and that if we waste this one life there is nothing worse we can do. Gilmore runs counter to that, which I think is one of the reasons that he arouses this intense antagonism in many, many people where it's almost surprising. I've seen people who are perfectly pleasant liberal people who practically gnash their teeth when they hear about Gilmore because he cuts at the very ankles of every liberal premise.
I think somewhere between 80 and 90 per cent of the people who live in the highly civilised urban society believe when people start talking about death that they are a little flakey at least. It's very hard to talk about death. At the least you're accused of being morbid and at most the general assumption is that there's a touch of insanity present. Gilmore—I suppose one of the reasons I kept saying what a marvellous character, when I was reading about him in the newspapers long before I got near the book—was I thought that, well, now, here's a man who's got a preoccupation with death that is obviously right on the hook and at least the equal of mine and

probably more. Or, rather, here's a man who has certain ideas about
death and he's willing to die for them. And his ideas about death
come down to the idea that the hold that we have on life is karmic.
The man had a firm belief in karma, and karma, as I understand it, is
a belief that the meaning of the events in any given life can't be
comprehended entirely by what one's done in one life.

When outrageous things happen in a life then it's reasonable to
assume that they are payment for outrageous things that were done
in another life. Now, it's not hard to have this as an idea you can talk
about in the living-room or on television—you can say 'Oh, yes, I
rather believe in karma,' and it can seem rather interesting and
something to deal with. But what fascinated me about Gilmore was
here was a man who obviously has this belief that this life is one of
several continuing lives and who also believes that the way in which
you die is therefore immensely important: you can die well or you
can die badly and it will affect your karma incredibly. This man had
this passionate belief so he worked concertedly to be executed by the
state rather than be sent to jail for 20 or 30 years, as if his karma
would be spoiled irreparably if his soul had had to slowly expire in
jail.

In other words, I think that in some almost incredible way Gilmore
was not a religious leader but he was the stalking horse or the
vanguard of something that is going to be immensely more important
in 50 years' or 100 years' time. I think Western civilisation is going
around a tremendous bend and we're approaching Eastern concepts
of reincarnation and karma and what have you, and the next great
religion of the future, which will probably be some new form of
Christianity, if you want me to speculate wildly, will have implicit in it
notions of reincarnation that we just don't begin to have today. At that
time Gilmore will be almost a symbol of this period—no, not a
symbol but the first man who could be an historical figure at that
point.

*When you started this you were a long way through a big novel
that I take it for granted means an enormous amount to you, a huge
work of fiction. You were 800 or 900 pages into it, and you explain
the reasons for taking this—you were quite straightforward about the
financial reason you took it—and you thought it would be a quick
job. And you obviously could have done a quick job, but you*

haven't; you've been drawn into it and the thing has become an
immense book and, from my reading of it anyway, an immensely
powerful book where you're attacking the character of not so much
one man as of a society, and of a society that represents various
contradictory forces and is stalemating itself all over the place: always
through character in the way that the 19th-century novelist did. I
mean, the comparison that I would draw would be with 19th-century
novels.

It's fascinating that you say that because, you know, it's been one
of my thoughts that the documentary novel as such goes back to the
19th-century novel, in many ways, including the fact that usually in
the documentary novel you have almost no sex. After all, if you're
interviewing people, they're normally not going to tell you about their
sex lives. In this book there is the exception of Gilmore's girlfriend
Nicole, and a few other people are quite frank about their sexual lives
for various reasons. But, normally, there is no sex in these books and
so what you get is a study of people in society with their character
impinging on society. Society impinging on them. It's very 19th-
century with all the virtues of a 19th-century novel too, which is that
you can have a large panorama and you can have an omnipotent
God-like 'I' observing everyone's mind and all that.

Well, you had all that because the range of characters is enormous
and I mean you take it into the background, you literally do tell us
how people were born, where they went to college, what their
degrees were, in American terms what their income is, their lifestyle,
lawyers, small businessmen, policemen, perverts, drug addicts,
college students—a whole range of people and you're taking it on in
a bigger way than I can think of any contemporary American writer
or British writer doing in that way. It's a huge swathe across society. Is
this the kind of, I presume unexpected, land that's drawn you into
writing at such length and so excessively about it?

I think what drew me in is that ever since *The Naked and the Dead*
there's always been a part of me that's been a social novelist and I
have become more and more frustrated over the years because I
never found a way to write a large social novel. I always wanted to
and I just never found a story as simple as that, that lent itself
naturally to a large social novel. Now, that big novel I'm writing is
going to be the attempt to write a large social novel, but it's terribly

complicated with other things as well. It's not really a social novel; it's more something else I don't want to get into now. I found here the perfect social novel and, as Kissinger once said, 'It has the added advantage of being true.' Oh, and ever since the Sixties in America I decided that God is a better novelist than any of us, because none of us writing in the Fifties would have dreamt of writing about the America that took place in the Sixties. It was beyond our imaginations, it was more dramatic, more surrealistic, more fanciful, more incredible, more vivid, than anything we would have dared to write about.

Are you implying that these great fictions and panoramic fictions—in which you introduce a huge number of people in society—can't exist any more out of a current imagination? That they've got to be found, they've got to be given by documentary events or something like that?

I think that it may be that we will go through a period of documentary novels in order to learn how to rethink the problem of a novel. One of the feelings that I had after writing this is it will be much easier for me now to write a panoramic novel because what it's opened up for me is how much I've been missing. One of the reasons I have not been able to write a panoramic novel is that I haven't had enough curiosity—I haven't looked into enough corners when I'm looking at a large situation. One of my flaws has been that I've always tended to focus upon the main character and not see the secondary cast and how important they are. So working on this book was the only way I could approach the main character from the secondary cast. I kind of realised that a novel, a panoramic novel, has to have immense roots. And, for what it's worth, I think if I ever do such a novel again—as a complete fiction, not based on something—this book will have been an incredible help for it.

Maybe the same will be true for other novelists; in other words, this may be a period, I'm just guessing, when a good many novelists may start to do documentary novels as a way of relocating their craft.

Why do you think fiction is so important?

Oh, because I think it's the place where art and philosophy and adventure finally come together. For me there's nothing more beautiful than a marvellous novel. I love the idea of a novel; to me a novel is better than a reality. I mean as good as this book may become—and I hope it becomes a very, very good book—it can never be as good as a novel, to my mind. It could be better than a novel in a lot of ways but it could never be as good. I mean there's something so beautiful about one mind being able to come up with a vision that's not Godlike but close enough to the Godlike to give us a vision of how marvellous the Lord's mind might be. You know, when we read Proust or the best of Maugham or Stendhal or Joyce or any of the great novelists. We could name 20 of them, say, who give us this idea of God's mind being something like that. Don't you get that feeling when you read Proust—that one side of God's mind is like Proust? And that's the challenge.

An Interview with Norman Mailer
John W. Aldridge/1980

From *Partisan Review*, 47 (July 1980), 174-82. Reprinted by permission of John W. Aldridge.

Much too early one morning last summer on Nantucket, a large and heavy box was delivered to our door. It contained the longest typescript I had ever seen, 1681 pages of *The Executioner's Song*, Norman Mailer's book about Gary Gilmore, the Utah murderer who sought and finally won the right to be executed by firing squad. I read the manuscript through in just three days, and when a short time later, I sat down with Mailer in New York to talk about it, I told him I had been held every step of the way but that there were certain points I hoped he would clarify. For example, why, out of the many executed murderers of our time, was he particularly attracted to Gary Gilmore? Because Gilmore wanted to die? Because he was interesting as a personality?

Norman Mailer: I have to go at this on two levels—the aesthetic and the cynical. We may as well start with the latter. I've had money troubles the last ten years—lately they've become so pressing that I can't really think of taking on any book unless I see some real possibility of earning at least as much money during the time I write as it will cost me to stay afloat. You just can't go along and be married as many times as I have, have as many children, live in a time of inflation, without discovering to your horror that even though you're going along by your own lights modestly, you're still spending a huge sum in a year, and therefore, you have to earn a huge amount. When you pay the IRS their sizeable tithe, it becomes a double enormous amount. You're always thinking about money. You know, when I was young, I used to meditate about literature, now I think about money. I never dare to consider a book any longer just because it appeals to me. I've forgotten what it's like to be drawn by a theme. I've become a commercial writer. I say it with woe, because there's no fun in being that. You start writing with the idea that you have a talent, maybe it's a large talent, or maybe if you work very hard at it, you will make it into a large talent, and then suddenly, you see yourself in the last third, probably, of your productive career, measuring everything by its economic potentialities. That is depressing.

John W. Aldridge: So you thought of Gilmore at least initially as a commercial property?

NM: Well, as I said, yes, I think of commercial possibilities. But, obviously, it's important not to take a book on just because it promises money. You can go down the tubes very quickly by that route. After all, it's bad enough that one's working as a *semi-*commercial writer. Once you're *wholly* commercial, once you take on a job merely because it'll pay the bills, and you have no interest in what you're doing, you're in terrible trouble. So if something appeals to you and also promises money, that gives it charisma. Gilmore, ergo, was a marvelously appealing character to me. By that, I don't mean he was someone I necessarily would have wanted to be close friends with . . . he appealed to me because he embodied many of the themes I've been living with all my life long before I even thought of doing a book on him. I knew just by what I read about him in the newspapers that I could write a 20,000-word essay on the man with no trouble, and have a lot to say. Before I wrote a thing about him I felt here's a perfect example of what I've been talking about all my life—we have profound choices to make in life, and one of them may be the deep and terrible choice most of us avoid between dying now and "saving one's soul"—or at the least, safeguarding one's soul—in order, conceivably, to be reincarnated. Maybe there is such a thing as living out a life too long, and having the soul expire before the body. And here's Gilmore with his profound belief in karma, wishing to die, declaring he wants to save his soul. I thought, here, finally, is the perfect character for me. So I was excited about the book.

JA: Did you feel you understood him thoroughly by the time you were finished with the writing?

NM: No, I felt I didn't understand him at all. I knew him by then better than I knew a lot of my relatives and friends, but I didn't understand him. It's analogous to the way you can be married to a woman for ten years and know her very well, know exactly what she's going to say, what she's going to do, what's going to make her happy, what's going to get her drunk, yet, fundamentally, you may not know whether she's good or evil. You don't perceive the source of her, if you will, of her *moral* inspiration. Does she worship the same gods you do, or are they alien? That's what you don't get near. So I was left at the end of the book with a sense of ambiguity about Gilmore that you can only feel about someone you know very well. I don't want to falsify the issue, or sentimentalize it. Gilmore was fond of saying that he was a very bad guy, and he was in a lot of ways. He had a lot of very bad, dull habits. He had a terrible temper, he was unspeakably selfish, and he had absolutely no desire to see other people's needs unless he chose to. He was terribly private, even secretive, and everything had to be done his way, or he wouldn't play. Yet, to be fair—I think it's fair—one could speak of Gilmore as having a quality that was almost saintly. He was certainly capable of rising far above the situation he was in and looking at it with the kind of extraordinary detachment very few people have. Since it involved his own death, I think he was doubly remarkable that way. I say saintly, but, of course, such powers are also Satanic. It's possible he was a very evil man. So by the end of the book we know him well, even intimately, but his moral personality beneath the man we know is considerably more saintly or malevolent than I can pretend to tell you.

JA: That suggests something else I wanted to get at. The narrative method that you've adopted here, as far as I know, is entirely new to you. It's one of extremely detached and impersonal documentation of every last detail that seems pertinent to the case. And you go on with this documentation to very great lengths because the manuscript runs to more than 1600 pages and it gives me the impression of being a sort of immense prose photograph. Now, I wonder, is this method meant to express the meaning that the Gilmore case came to have for you finally? In other words, does the huge quantity, the sheer mass of this material and your close documentation of it—are these somehow essential elements in creating the quality of the story that you had to tell?

NM: I'd say I made a literary decision to do the book this way. I was starting with a story about a man who, to a certain degree, is a talented artist, has been in jail all his adult life, comes out, meets a beautiful girl, and has a passionate love affair that almost works, then is very unsuccessful. They break up. It's so intolerable to him that a week later he murders two men on two successive nights. Once he's back in jail, he and the girl fall in love again. It is then he comes to the conclusion that it's hopeless to stay alive in such an incarcerated existence and so they must commit suicide together. Indeed they make a serious attempt to commit suicide, and failing, are separated forever except for their more or less profound belief in reincarnation which he finally takes with him to his death. Now I thought these elements of tragic love were so operatic for the modern temper that they're almost unbelievable, unless you nail down every detail. Let's put it this way: it's as if there's a wind blowing so fierce and you're dealing with so large a tarpaulin, that unless you tack down every square foot of it, it's going to whip all over the place. Besides, I also felt that if I wrote it in my own style, the style that we're lately used to, no one would believe the book for a minute. They would say, "Oh, there's Mailer taking this very average, ordinary, dull punk killer and inflating him." They would have said I was working away on my bicycle pump. So, I thought, no, I'll stay out of the book entirely, I won't use anything that doesn't come from interviews or documents.

JA: Of course, if you had been much more Maileresque, you would have ended up writing a different kind of book.

NM: Maileresque is your word, not mine.

JA: Okay, it's my word, but you don't show in this book any of the characteristics associated with your past writing. Because the style is a great departure from what you normally write—it's very simple, unadorned, unmetaphorical. Also you never once make use of one of your favorite dramatic devices, and that is to extrapolate from the experience being described to some kind of large generalizing statement about the implications of the experience. For example, in *The Armies of the Night*, you start out, at one point, with a physical description of the marshals who try to keep order during the Pentagon march, and you go from that to a meditation on the small towns of middle America—the barely controlled fury, the pent-up rage of the people who come out of that experience—the small town. And that leads you to very large questions of mystery, dread, finally Christianity in opposition to technology—it's all a marvelous and complex network of associations and references. Now this you scrupulously avoid in this book. You don't allow yourself any of these flights at all. Is that because you thought that the story of Gilmore in itself, narrated at great length, without any speculation or editorializing, would convey its own message, that it is itself a sort of metaphorical, or if you like, a metaphysical generalization about the nature of evil?

NM: No, I felt something else. The more I worked, the more I began to feel I didn't have the right to generalize on the material. In the past, of course, I always have. I usually had more in me to say than proper material with which to express it, so that it was natural to overflow into essays. But, at this point in my life, I thought, well, the people who have chosen to listen to what I've said have registered it, I've sort of used up my audience, and I thought, well, I want another audience. I want those people who think I'm difficult to read. And I must confess, there was also something else. I think we can name twenty American writers who each believe secretly and not so secretly that he or she is the best American writer living. I'll confess I'm one of those twenty. And I also know I can write in a number of styles—that is one of my talents, at least. All proportions kept—I don't pretend I'm one-hundredth as important in the cultural scheme of things—but I wish a few critics could see that I may feel a legitimate kinship to Picasso's need to keep changing his style. Preserving one's artistic identity is not nearly so important to me as finding a new attack on the elusive nature of reality. Primarily, one's style is only a tool to use on a dig. Of course, with such an attitude, you have to be able to mimic other writers. I've always been amused by people who say, "Oh, well, Norman Mailer can't write a simple sentence." I'm the guy who started by writing simple sentences. There's nothing easier than to come full circle and write a book with prose even simpler than *The Naked and the Dead*.

JA: I think it's the simplest prose you've ever written.

NM: There is real amusement in that, you know. I think of all those constipated, stingy writers who stick to a simple style all their lives and claim that's the only kind of prose worth doing. What nonsense. It's harder to write in a good baroque style than good simple English. For one thing, it takes a lot less time to write good and simple. That doesn't mean it's easy, and available to all, but it's not, you know, all that hard. Besides, the material called for such prose. The book has so much going on that its novelistic nature is rich without language. There just wasn't space to take an interesting character, and, make the room in which he is sitting equally interesting. In the past, I always liked long descriptions, but in this book there's just enough to keep the background from blurring out. A minimum of description is, of course, perfect for Utah. The variation from town to town is not great, and the variation from living room to living room is rarely striking. Even variations of income are not that dramatic. If people have a great deal of money, they usually don't show it in Utah. And if people are poor, they may live in a shack, or a sleazy two-story apartment building, but there's a beautiful mountain on the horizon. So I eschewed description where I could. I wanted to get 3000 pages of material into half the space. I wanted my story to *move*.

JA: It's really crowded with material. That brings up another question: how did you get together this great volume of information? I mean, were you on the scene during the whole of the last days, the last weeks before Gilmore's execution?

NM: No. In fact, I read about it in the papers, like everyone else, and was equally fascinated. I felt I might just understand what Gilmore was doing. But I didn't think about it anymore than that. Then after, oh, a month after the execution, Larry Schiller called me. Now, Schiller and I worked together on my book *Marilyn*, closely at one point, and very badly at another. There was a period when we didn't even speak for six months. After that, we did a short book on graffiti together. As with *Marilyn*, he got the photographs and I wrote the text for it. Our relations became friendly again. Now he called me to read an interview with Gilmore that he and Barry Farrell had done for *Playboy*. I thought it was the best interview I'd ever read. So I got the idea it would be nice to direct a play out of that dialogue. Schiller said, "You can, but first you have to write the book." I was going well on my Egyptian novel at that point, and didn't really want to give it up. He sent me more material and then Warner Paperbacks offered a good sum, and I thought: "I can do this book in six months. It will give me more time to work on the novel." Of course, once again, six months took two years. Make such an error in estimate on two books, as I have, and you are seriously in debt. But to do the job in six months would have slaughtered all the possibilities of doing something exceptional. Schiller had been doing a lot of interviews before I came in, and I spent the first six months wandering around in bewilderment trying to put people and events together. I really had to work it out. Try encountering a hundred names at once. It's like looking at the laid-out pieces of a clock.

JA: So you essentially drew on the material that Schiller had already gathered. He had first rights, didn't he, to all the stories of almost all the principals?

NM: He had acquired rights to the principals. Also, he had done about sixty interviews before I came aboard. After that, he did another forty or fifty. I probably did almost as many. A lot were follow-up. I had the advantage of reading the initial interview he'd done, and he's a very good interviewer. But I must have collected a hundred interviews on my own. Then my secretary, Judith McNally, proved to be a marvelous interviewer and she talked to a lot of people toward the end, a lot of lawyers—she has a fine legal mind for a layman—and much of the jurisprudence in the book comes from her research. I'm considerably in debt to her for that. Altogether there may have been as much as 12,000 pages of interviews. At the place where we stopped counting, there were 6000 pages of transcript and we more than doubled it after that. Schiller and I often went out together to interview, and we must have looked like two detectives on the fat side, not one but two Continental Cops, side by side. I remember we interviewed a woman once, and after we left, were driving along and suddenly, Schiller, who has a passion for verification, started pounding the wheel and said, "She's lying, she's goddamn lying!" Part of figuring out what happened was living with these interviews long enough to compare them to other interviews until you felt you could decide what probably did occur in a given situation. Then, of course, there were also the transcripts of the trial, and press clippings, and a great many psychiatric reports by the various doctors involved. Oregon State Prison was also a huge help. The Warden, Hoyt Cupp, had a 200-page summary of Gilmore's prison record prepared. A lot of material was there that never even got directly into the book. A lot of marvelous prison stuff from Gilmore's years in prison that just didn't get in. There were people who knew him when he was an adolescent. We had long interviews with them. They didn't get in for two reasons: one, it would have been another 500 pages, and, also, I hated to break the unity of *The Executioner's Song*—those nine months from the time he left jail until he was executed.

JA: There were moments, I thought, when you were strongly tempted to make some kind of comment. For example, where you had this marvelous interview with the lady who turned out to be one of Nicole's neighbors. In the scene I'm thinking of, she is being interviewed while her small boy keeps coming in and bothering her about the peanut butter, and she's telling a story about one of her husbands who pulled a butcher knife and killed himself right in front of her. She's telling this horrendous story interrupted from moment to moment by yells at the kid . . . "Get the hell away from the peanut butter jar!" And it struck me that this was marvelous material for some sort of comment about the kind of world that Gilmore came out of—where the women could be so indifferent to violence and so concerned with the trivia of the peanut butter jar without at all seeing the incongruity.

NM: I was thinking about painting as I worked on this book. That particular interview was like a found object. You know, it was lifted almost verbatim from the original transcript.

JA: It's one of the few times you do that.

NM: It's the only time in the book where I literally do that, where I just take an interview and put it in the book. It was a found object. You know, a painter may find something on the street that he thinks is incredible. Sometimes he'll glue it right into the painting. It becomes part of the work. In *The Executioner's Song*, newspaper stories became part of the painting and part of the transcript of the trial—a lot of found objects. I felt acted upon, in a funny way, while doing this book, by painting terms. It was as if I'd shifted from being an expressionist, not an abstract expressionist, but an expressionist—like Munch, or Max Beckmann . . . those kinds of painters who worked with large exaggeration and murkiness and passionate power—into now being a photographic realist, even a photographic realist with found objects. The reason, I think, is that a painter like a writer sometimes gets to a point where he can no longer interpret what he sees. Then the act of painting what he literally sees becomes the aesthetic act. Because what he's seeing is incredible. It may or may not be possessed of meaning. Reality, itself, closely studied is mysterious, and it's elusive.

JA: So you simply presented it.

NM: Sometimes you just have to. This, I think, is the place painting has gotten to . . . paint this realistic scene as it is, because in the act of presenting it, you will underline the mystery. That's why you show it with no decoration and no interpretation—for just that reason. The aesthetic imperative, if there was one, finally came down to: let this book be lifelike. Let it be more like American life than anything that's been done in a long, long time. I don't think good writers often have this kind of opportunity. Usually, material this good gets chewed over by journalists and bad writers. There are probably a few exceptions, but I can only think of *In Cold Blood*.

JA: I wanted to ask you about that because a comparison is bound to be made.

NM: Well, I think Truman's book and mine are formally similar, but vastly different. Obviously, I'll be the first to state that if he hadn't done *In Cold Blood*, it's possible that I wouldn't have thought of doing *The Executioner's Song* this way. It's perfectly possible. It's also perfectly possible that there's something about *The Executioner's Song* that called for doing it this way. I might have gone the same route in any case. Besides, its total flavor is considerably different from *In Cold Blood*. Truman retained his style for *In Cold Blood*, not the pure style—he simplified it—but it still was very much a book written by Truman Capote. You felt it every step of the way.

JA: It also novelizes much more.

NM: Yeah, he novelizes more, where I was determined to keep to the factual narrative. I wanted my book to read like a novel, and it does, but I didn't want ever to sacrifice what literally happened in a scene for what I would have liked to see happen. Of course, I could afford to feel that way. I had advantages Truman didn't. His killers were not the most interesting guys in the world, so it took Truman's exquisite skills to make his work a classic. I was in the more promising position of dealing with a man who was quintessentially American and yet worthy of Dostoevsky. If this were not enough, he was also in love with a girl who—I'll go so far as to say—is a bona fide American heroine. I didn't want, therefore, to novelize a bit. Dedicated accuracy is not usually the first claim you wish to make for books like this, but here it became a matter of literary self-preservation. I wanted people to believe me. What I had was gold, if I had enough sense not to gild it.

Before the Literary Bar
Norman Mailer/1980

From *New York*, 10 November 1980, 27-31, 33-36, 38, 40, 43-46. Reprinted by permission of the Scott Meredith Literary Agency, Inc.

Prosecutor: Your Honor, our first and only witness will be the defendant, Norman Mailer.

The Court: He has waived his rights?

Prosecutor: Yes, Your Honor.

The Court: All right, let's put him on.

[*The defendant is sworn*]

Mr. Mailer, I will remind you of the charge. It is criminal literary negligence. On this charge, the court may find against you for censure in the first or second degree, or for reprimand. You may also be exonerated.

Mailer: I am aware of the charge, Your Honor.

Prosecutor: Mr. Mailer, I am holding in my hand a work entitled *Of Women and Their Elegance*, which has your name on the cover as author. Would you describe it?

Mailer: It is a book of photographs by Milton Greene, with a text of 50,000 words by myself.

Prosecutor: Fifty thousand words is the length of the average novel?

Mailer: Maybe half to two thirds the length.

Prosecutor: Would you say this work presents itself as an autobiography by Marilyn Monroe?

Mailer: Originally, I wished to title it *Of Women and Their Elegance, by Marilyn Monroe as told to Norman Mailer*, but it was decided the title could prove misleading to the public, who might think the interview had actually taken place. I suppose it would be better to describe the text as a false autobiography. Or an imaginary memoir, since the story, but for a few recollections, only covers a period of three or four years in her life.

271

Prosecutor: It is made up.

Mailer: More or less made up.

Prosecutor: Could you be more specific?

Mailer: Much of the book is based on fact. I would say some of it is made up.

Prosecutor: Are you prepared to offer examples of fact and fiction as they occur in your pages?

Mailer: I can try.

Prosecutor: Let me read a passage to the court, written in the first person, which purports to be Marilyn Monroe's voice. The Amy she refers to is one Amy Greene, Milton Greene's wife. I will enter it as Exhibit A. It is taken from page 24 of Mr. Mailer's book.

The Court: All right, go ahead.

[The prosecution reads Exhibit A, page 24]

I went out shopping with Amy. She took me to Saks and Bonwit Teller's, and people lined up to look at me as soon as I got spotted. Women were ripping open the curtain in the dressing room, which was enough to do Amy in, if she hadn't been made of the toughest stuff. First, she discovered I wear no panties, and to make it worse, a bit of my natural odor came off with the removal of the skirt. Nothing drives people crazier than a woman with an aroma that doesn't come out of a bottle. Maybe I should use deodorant, but I do like a little sniff of myself. It's a way of staying in touch.

Anyway, Amy turned her head at the sight of my pubic hair, which is, alas, disconcertingly dark, and then the curtains flew open, and shoppers gawked, three big mouths and big noses, and a tall, skinny salesman came over to shut the curtains and croaked, "Miss Monroe!" and disappeared forever. I had to laugh. I knew I'd changed his life. I think, sometimes, that's why I do it.

Prosecutor: Now, Mr. Mailer.

Mailer: Yessir.

Prosecutor: Did this scene occur?

Mailer: Yes. Mrs. Greene told me that hordes of shoppers did indeed gawk at Marilyn.

Prosecutor: And ripped open the curtain to the dressing room?

Mailer: It is my recollection that Mrs. Greene told me something of the sort.

Prosecutor: In a tape-recorded interview?

Mailer: *[Pauses]* Perhaps, in casual conversation. I am old friends with Mr. and Mrs. Greene, and we have had many unrecorded conversations about Marilyn Monroe as well.

Prosecutor: And you drew your impressions of Miss Monroe from these conversations, recorded and unrecorded?

Mailer: Some of my impressions.

Prosecutor: So Mrs. Greene told you that Miss Monroe was wearing no panties on this occasion?

Mailer: I don't recollect that Mrs. Greene told me that.

Prosecutor: Then how did you arrive at such a conclusion?

Mailer: On the basis of many conversations with many people who knew Marilyn Monroe, it seems to be established that Miss Monroe did not like to wear panties.

Prosecutor: So you took the liberty of deciding she was wearing none that day?

Mailer: It seemed a fair assumption. You try to be fair.

Prosecutor: You weren't just trying to sell copies?

Defense: Objection. The witness is being manhandled.

The Court: Overruled. I want to hear the answer.

Mailer: I wasn't trying *just* to sell copies, although I didn't think the description would hurt sales—I'll give you that much. What I was trying to do, however . . .

Prosecutor: We're not interested in what you're trying to do, Mr. Mailer, but in what you did.

The Court: Let him give it.

Mailer: I was trying to get across Miss Monroe's sense of fun. She may not literally have been wearing no panties on that day, but it was in her nature to have been wearing none. I think she could certainly have been engaged in such a scene and have enjoyed it. So I chose to write it that way. It seemed right to me. That is what I must go by.

Prosecutor: I will continue with Exhibit A, page 24 to page 26.

[*Reads*]

After two days of such shopping, Amy said, "That's it, kiddo. From now on, we stay in the St. Regis and have everything brought up." I began to see how it worked. Some designers came by, friends of Amy's; I could tell by the way she said the name of one that it was another case of Laurence Olivier, Milton Greene, Joe DiMaggio, Arthur Miller, or Elia Kazan. First in category. So I said, "Oh, yes, Norman Norell, greatest dress designer in the world." And he had a couple of the second-greatests with him—George Nardiello, John

Moore. They were the nicest men. It was not only that they were well groomed and slim and fit into their clothes like a beautiful hand has gone inside a beautiful glove, but they were so happy inside their suits. It was like the person within themselves also had a good suit which was their own skin. Moreover, they liked me. I could tell. Oh, I felt open as a sponge. I knew they were going to help me. Norell said, "Marilyn, everyone has a problem. I have a friend who's very ugly and she's the princess of fashion in New York. She takes that ugliness and makes it dramatic." Yet, he said, after she was done with her dress and coiffeur, she looked like a samurai warrior. You couldn't take your eyes off her. Besides, she was smart enough to wear jewelry that clanked and gonged with every move she made. You could have been in a Chinese temple. "Her little beauty tricks, if tried on anyone else, would have been a disaster," Norman Norell said and gave me my first lesson in style. "It's not enough to find the problem," he said, "and avoid it. Elegance is magic. The problem, *presto*, has to become the solution."

Sure enough, Norman Norell got around to informing me very kindly that my neck was too short, only he didn't put it that way. My neck, I was told, wasn't that long. I wouldn't be happy in a *Vogue* collar. Ruffles were death. "Let me," he said, "show you a shawl collar."

I got it instantly. A nice, thin dinner-jacket set of lapels and a long V-neck. Society cleavage. I felt as if I had spent my life until that point being sort of very fluffy à la Hollywood. Now I could see the way Amy saw me with my head sitting on my shoulders like an armchair in the middle of a saggy floor.

Prosecutor: Mr. Mailer, would you say your account of conversations between Miss Monroe and Mr. Norell is factual?

Mailer: Miss Monroe met Norman Norell, he designed dresses for her, he had many conversations with her. I attempted to capture the flavor of those conversations as they might have occurred. They are imaginary conversations, but, hopefully, not too far away in mood from what was said.

Prosecutor: Not too far away in mood. But not in fact. In fact, they have no relation to what was said.

Mailer: Most conversations are lost. We reconstruct the past by our recollection of the mood fully as much as by our grasp of fact. When facts are skimpy, one hopes to do well at sensing the mood.

Prosecutor: I will continue Exhibit A, pages 26 and 27.

[*Reads*]

Of course, this new interest in clothes had all started on the trip to
Palm Springs, when I told Milton I wanted to be immensely respected
and he told me, "First step: Don't act like a slob." He held up a finger.
"Be a woman."

"You say, 'Don't look like a slob.' "

"That dress you're wearing," said Milton. "It's a *shmatte*."

"A what . . . ? No, don't tell me." I once saw a guy in a delicatessen
spearing kosher pickles out of a barrel. That was what Yiddish
sounded like to me. One more pickle on the prong.

"You want to be the greatest actress in the world," said Milton, "but
you're exhibiting neither class nor taste. They call you a dumb blonde,
and they are getting away with it. You have to carry yourself different.
Don't walk around like you're nothing. Never forget you have
something fantastic on the screen."

That was now prominent in my thoughts after meeting Norman
Norell. I felt as if I was getting out from the carpet I had been living
under all my life. I was beginning to see that class was not beyond me,
nor was I beneath it.

Prosecutor: Would you say Miss Monroe's conversation with
Milton Greene is also based on skimpy facts?

Mailer: Less skimpy. I take it from Mr. Greene's recollection. Of
course, his conversations with Miss Monroe were held more than 25
years ago. In my case, I am not trying to delineate a boundary line
between fact and fiction here. In this book, I want to explore the
elusive nature of a most talented woman and artist.

Prosecutor: Let me now conclude Exhibit A with the rest of page
27.

It was the scene in *The Seven Year Itch* where I stand over a subway
grating and my skirts blow up. Now I guess the studio had given me a
white *shmatte* that night and tight white panties, and my hair had a
hundred marcelled waves, and I certainly had no neck and lots of
back and shoulders, where I was pleasantly plump, to say the least,
but I paid no attention. I threw caution to the winds, which is one
cliché I could die saying and hold it in my arms, I can't help it, give me
a ton of caution to throw to the winds. There were 2,000 people on
the street, watching, and they had a million whistles. All the while Joe
D. was on the outskirts of the crowd dying because he knew the secret
of acting. Maybe it was because he was a ballplayer, but he knew it
didn't have to be false when you acted that you were in love;
sometimes it was real, and when that happened, it could be more real
than anything else. So I guess he knew—no secrets between husband

and wife; that's what the ceremony is for—guess he knew I was feeling a little moist every time my skirt blew up. Immortality would be immortalized if I ever took those white panties off. It's true, I wanted to throw myself to the crowd.

Prosecutor: Mr. Mailer, did your researches bring you to ask various friends of Miss Monroe's if, on this occasion when her skirts were flying, she wanted, and I quote from your text, "to throw myself to the crowd"?

Mailer: No, I asked no one.

Prosecutor: To your knowledge, she told no friends of such a feeling?

Mailer: No.

Prosecutor: Never mentioned it to you?

Mailer: I never met her.

Defense: Would the court instruct my client that he need only answer the prosecutor's questions. He does not have to add supplementary information.

The Court: Mr. Mailer is now twice instructed.

Prosecutor: Norman Mailer, you never met Marilyn Monroe?

Mailer: No, but I sat behind her once at Actors' Studio.

[Laughter]

Prosecutor: On the basis of the firm insight you gathered from having once sat behind her, you presume to write of Marilyn Monroe's inner physical condition. You declare that she wanted to throw herself to the crowd.

Mailer: Yes.

Prosecutor: Would you call this a fair conclusion?

Defense: Objection. The prosecutor is trying to make my client characterize his replies.

The Court: Sustained.

Mailer: I wish to answer anyway.

Defense: Please obey the court.

Mailer: Your Honor, with all due respect to my own attorney, I wish to say that such perceptions and such liberties as I took on trying to enter Miss Monroe's mind are considered fair in literary practice.

Prosecutor: Objection. I think this ought to be cut off.

The Court: You started it. Let him go on.

Mailer: I have been thinking about Miss Monroe's life for many

years. I have already written one other book about her, called
Marilyn, and in that work did not enter her mind once. It was out of
respect for the intricacies of her mind. I only dare in this case because
I believe I know more about her by now. The experience of looking at
Milton Greene's photographs of Marilyn Monroe over several years is
part of that greater knowledge. Sides of her nature are revealed by
Mr. Greene's photographs that I do not find anywhere else. I would
also submit that I have been fair to Miss Monroe in my heart. In fact, I
find her charming in those passages you read, and not at all
maligned. She is a humorous woman.

Prosecutor: Mr. Mailer, concerning Exhibit A, which has just been
read, you say you do not malign Miss Monroe but find her charming.

Mailer: Yessir.

Prosecutor: I will not argue your conception of female charm. I
will ask you instead to read aloud from Exhibit B, pages 83 and 84.
May it please the court, Exhibit B is selected from a later part of the
work but is concerned with earlier episodes in Miss Monroe's life
when she was still in Hollywood. I believe this comes under the
technical heading of "flashback."

Mailer: You could call it that.

[The defendant reads Exhibit B, pages 83 and 84]

Now, of course, even in those days I had a sheltered life. I wasn't
respected, but I was sheltered. I might be considered the property of
the studio and so be sent at a moment's notice with ten other girls to
Denver or Modesto to help out with publicity, knowing full well that in
such situations, the studio liked to hold the broadest view of publicity,
that is—breed a little goodwill. I wasn't being sent out in my sweater
to strew ill will. All the same, it was a sheltered life. I might have to go
through certain experiences with a big laugh when I was actually
feeling a little queasy inside, but, still, who ever had to be afraid of a
local movie reviewer or a small-town theater manager? Most of them
didn't have poison in their system. In fact, they were really grateful,
and some of them were nice people. Anyway, back on the studio lot, I
also had to keep appointments. One day I saw three executives on the
half hour—2:30 P.M., 3:30 P.M., and 4:30 P.M.—before going off to
acting class in the evening, although, of course, those kind of
assignments only took five minutes. "How are you, Mr. Farnsworth,
how nice to see you again," and he had you behind the desk.
Sometimes he never got out of his chair. Sometimes you never got off
your knees. I knew the pleats on some executives' trousers better than
their face. All the same, most of such people were not that rude, and I

had an orphan's philosophy: Cheer up, it could be worse. They could take off their socks and ask you to kiss their feet.

The key thing, however, was that I was on contract at the studio. A girl might have to do one little despicable deed or another, but you were not out there where you really had to know how to protect yourself. You were sort of more in the very bottom reaches of the middle class. You had to be obedient, that's all.

Prosecutor: Mr. Mailer, thank you for reading from your work. Would you summarize for the court your sources for this material.

Mailer: I would say it is based on general knowledge. I have read many books about Hollywood, I have known many people who lived and worked in Hollywood, I spent a year there myself in just the period of which the exhibit speaks, and have also drawn on many stories I heard about Miss Monroe's life during that period, or, for that matter, the life of many other starlets on studio contracts. I believe I can say that the scene described is not exceptional but common to life in Hollywood in the early fifties. It was well known that Miss Monroe had such a life during that period, and the scars of it were probably responsible in part for her future personality. I am trying to explain a woman of angelic appearance who, by the end of her career, was notoriously difficult to work with. Such scenes help me to understand her.

Prosecutor: Still, you are taking liberties with the facts.

Mailer: I would say this excerpt is factual. I can't certify it as a fact, but I believe it is a fact. She had the life of a stock girl on contract in Hollywood studios in the fifties. Her drama coach, Lee Strasberg, who is one of the beneficiaries of her will and had the highest regard for her talent, did say, "She was a call girl . . . she was on call for things the studio wanted." Arthur Miller once wrote, "She was chewed and spat out by a long line of grinning men! Her name floating in the stench of locker rooms and parlor-car cigar smoke!"

What is poignant about Marilyn is that all her life she wanted to become a lady. Elegance was as elusive and fearful and attractive and as awesome to her in these somewhat sordid early years as the hidden desire to be macho can feel to a young and wimpy intellectual.

The Court: Would Mr. Mailer define "wimpy"?

Mailer: Muscles like cold spaghetti might do it, Your Honor.

The Court: You are saying that women feel about elegance the way men feel about machismo?

Mailer: Well, sir, I would say many men decide to reject machismo. They see it as a trap that can dominate them. I expect many women feel that any undue longings toward elegance might direct them from more individual solutions to their lives. Nonetheless, I expect no man puts down machismo without a little uneasiness, and I think it is the same for women and elegance. The rejection of elegance can be haunting. Miss Monroe, having her voluptuous figure and no neck, was not free of the desire to be elegant. In fact, I think it was a major force in her life, a true source of motivation.

The Court: Hmmm.

Prosecutor: Mr. Mailer is doing his best to be his eloquent best. Still, you are saying, if I may dare to summarize, that your imaginary autobiography wishes to study her desire to rise above sordid beginnings, to become elegant.

Mailer: Something of that sort.

Prosecutor: Please forgive these inelegant expressions of your elegant intentions.

The Court: Will the prosecution forgo this? The prosecution is elegant enough for all of us.

Prosecutor: Thank you, Your Honor. Mr. Mailer, if I understand you correctly, you are saying that every excerpt read in court until now can be justified by you, whether factual or not, as material that can reasonably have occurred in Miss Monroe's life.

Mailer: Yes.

Prosecutor: Not literally true, but aesthetically true.

Mailer: Yessir. Well put.

Prosecutor: So you believe that up to here, through the exhibits cited, you have not maligned Miss Monroe's nature nor denigrated her character.

Mailer: I believe that.

Prosecutor: Even though you mix the real and the fictional, you have succeeded in giving a portrait of her that, hopefully, is more true than fact itself.

Mailer: Yessir.

Prosecutor: Would you also agree that when a portrait cheapens a character, the portrait can hurt the reader's mind, that is, injure his future powers of perception?

Mailer: Yessir. There are some who would say that is what the moral nature of literature is all about.

Prosecutor: How then would you characterize our next excerpt? Please read Exhibit B, page 88 to 91.

Defense: Before Mr. Mailer begins, would the court again instruct the witness that he need only reply to the prosecutor's questions. He does not have to expatiate on them.

The Court: Maybe Mr. Mailer thinks he is being paid by the word.

[The defendant reads]

We passed through several rooms, and one had knives and guns on the wall, and another with zebra stripes for wallpaper, and then a room with nothing but filthy pictures all nicely framed, and the last room was big and had a photograph and a table with drinks, and a lot of couches on which guys and girls, and guys and guys, were lying around in a very dim purple light, just enough to see that there was a lot of purple nakedness in this neck of the woods, worse—I couldn't believe it. This was the first Hollywood party of the sort I'd grown up hearing about. I was used to walking in on a roommate who was under the covers with a fellow, but never anything like this. There were twenty people.

Then I saw our host. Bobby was naked except for cowboy boots and a Stetson hat, and he was walking a Doberman pinscher on a leash around the room, a huge female I suppose, because she had a diamond collar around her neck. But as the dog came up to one couple, it tried to mount, and I saw my mistake. She had a lot of male in the rear. Bobby was giggling like a two-year-old, because the dog kept jumping forcibly into all these lovers' midsts, if you can say such a thing. There were screams and shouts galore—"Bobby, get Romulus away! Bobby, you're a madman."

I would have thought our host was horrible, but when he came up to me, he gave the sweetest smile I'd seen in a year, as if he'd spent his childhood eating nothing but berries and grapes, and when he kissed me, his mouth was tender. I couldn't get over that, his mouth was as good as Edward's, who had the best mouth I'd ever kissed, but Bobby was also strong. I'd never been introduced to a man who was naked before, you learn so much that way, and his skin felt smooth as a seal and terrific to the touch. I couldn't keep my hands off. It was as if he was one boy who everybody had been rubbing love into since he was a baby. Oh, did his lower lip pout.

"Come on," he said, "you and me are going to leave these people."

He handed Romulus's leash to Rod and took me down the tunnel

to a room at the other end that turned out to be another apartment. I
didn't have time to look around; it didn't matter. We were on the floor.
I was embarrassed for a little while, for I reeked of Rod, but Bobby de
P. loved smells, I think he had a nose instead of a brain, and besides,
he had his own aroma, as I have said. Maybe something in him had
the answer to my secret, or maybe I had just been prepared for Bobby
by that crazy ride with Rod, and so had kept nothing, absolutely
nothing, with which to protect myself, but it was as if the very inside of
me was pushing to get over to him as desperate as the feeling you
know in a dream.

We went on all night. Somewhere in the middle I said, "Oh, you're
the best, I never knew anything like this before," and I hadn't, I felt
things start in me and go flying off into the universe or somewhere,
they were sensations going out to far space, so I meant what I said,
except even as I opened my mouth, I knew I had always had the same
thing to say to any fellow who was any good at all, in fact I had said it
to Rod as soon as he could hear me after the motorcycle stopped. I
had even been tempted to compliment Mr. Farnsworth (after all,
Farnsworth would say to himself, "Nobody sits in a chair like me!"), it
was exactly the remark to make if you wanted to keep a fellow happy
and on your string. I once had eight great lovers on eight strings.
Three more and I would have run out of fingers. Saying it to Bobby
was true, however, I meant it, maybe I meant it for the first time since
I'd begun to say it, and Bobby just roared with a crazy kind of
laughter. Then we just started reaching into one another as if we were
really going to catch something never caught before.

After a while, we moved over to the bed, and later he even turned
on the lights, and there were a lot of mirrors. The room was full of
antiques who sat there like rich and famous people, and I could see
the Persian rug we had been doing it on, red and gold and purple and
green. The bed was the largest I'd been in till then. We must have
used every inch of it; he was one rich boy who wouldn't stop. All
through the night, there were knocks on the door and people yelling,
"Bobby, where are you?" or "Join in the fun, for God's sake," but in
the morning, when we wandered out (and by then I was so
comfortable I wore nothing but high-heeled shoes, and Mr. de P. was
back in his Stetson hat), we came to the dead smoky smell of old
reefers and cartons of cigarette butts in ashtrays and nobody around
but the dog. Romulus was lying in the middle of the floor with his
diamond collar gone and his throat cut. His eyes were open, and he
had the peculiar expression of a young pup learning to sit on his hind
legs. A simple dog look. Plus all that blood on the carpet which you
couldn't see at first it was such a dark carpet.

Bobby started to blubber like a five-year-old kid. He cried and his belly shook a little and his big jaw looked really prominent the way a five-year-old kid with a big jaw can impress you with how mad they are going to be when they grow up. Then he came to a stop and knelt by the dog and got a little blood on his fingers and touched it to himself and to me, but so softly that I wasn't offended, as if that was a nice way to say goodbye to Romulus, and then we went back to the bedroom and made love, which turned out to be sweeter than anything because it was full of sorrow, and I cried for the baby in my stomach who would soon be gone and the dead dog and for myself, and felt very sweet toward Bobby.

Later that day I asked him, "Do you know who killed Romulus?" and he nodded.

I asked, "Are you going to do anything about it?"

"You bet," he said.

Prosecutor: We would like Mr. Mailer to continue directly to Exhibit B, page 92 to page 95. May it please the court, the new excerpt concludes the description after skipping over a brief account of the household of this Bobby de P., and his business connections, and his family.

[*The defendant reads Exhibit B, page 92 to page 95*]

Then I began to have this ferocious headache. When we weren't making love, I felt nauseated and wondered if it was morning sickness, and slowly, day by day, Bobby de P. and me began to fight. Except they weren't quarrels so much as savage displays, you might say, of bad nerves, after which we'd be off once more. All the while we'd talk about getting married. Only it was like we were flipping a switch. Maybe it was the benzedrine. He kept feeding us pills until I couldn't sleep, and every time I came near to something fabulous, my chest also came near to exploding.

On the fifth day Bobby said to me, "You want to get married?"

"Yes."

"Well, I'll get married."

"Let's," I said.

"We can't," he said. "I'm married already," and he bit me on the lip. I flung him off. "You said you were divorced."

"She won't give it."

His wife was living with Rod. Rod, he told me, had killed the dog and then stole the collar. Of course, that diamond collar had used to belong to Bobby's wife, except that Bobby had taken it back from her the day they broke up and put it on the dog.

"Rod is away now," he said, "on location in Utah. Let's go over and visit my old lady."

"And tell her you want a divorce?"

He squeezed my arm so hard I could feel the bruise instantly. "No," he said, "we'll finish her off like the dog."

What I couldn't believe was the excitement it gave me. I was nearer to myself than I ever wanted to be. I saw inside myself to the other soul, the one that never spoke. It was ready to think of murder. In truth, my headache went away.

"Let's drive up to her house," he said. "I'll do it and you watch. Then we'll come back here. If we stick together, nobody can prove a thing. We can say we were in bed."

I could see us looking at each other forever, one year into the next. I could see my pictures in the newspapers. STARLET QUESTIONED IN MURDER CASE. The pictures would be printed in all the newspapers over the world. A candle could burn in a dark church at such a thought. The idea that everyone would talk of me was beautiful. Killing Bobby's wife felt almost comfortable. Maybe if I hadn't seen Romulus with that funny expression on his face where he was dead but still seemed to be learning to sit on his paws, maybe if I hadn't seen something in that animal lying there so calmly after his throat was cut, I might have worried about Bobby's wife, but now I just felt as if it was all fair somehow. Maybe Bobby would even let me keep my baby. I remember thinking of how I felt when I first saw my face on film in *Scudda-Hoo! Scudda-Hay!* and decided I was very interesting, except I had what you might call a space in my expression. There was something in me that didn't show itself to others. Like: I'm ready to commit murder.

We got into Bobby's car and drove across Bel Air into Beverly Hills, and in one of the houses off Rodeo Drive was where she lived. It was dark, and there were no cars outside, and the garage was locked, so Bobby and I went to the back of the house. He found the wire to the burglar alarm and cut it and cracked the latch on the window. There we were standing in her kitchen. He looked in the rack for the carving knife and found one. Then we went up the stairs to her bedroom. I remember it was on the side that would have a view of the hills above Beverly Hills, and all the while he was doing this, despite the benzedrine, I never felt more calm as if, ha ha, I was on *This is Your Life*, and they were talking about me looking for the woman's door. I even held Bobby's hand, the one that did not have the knife.

There was no lock to the master bedroom. By the light of the street lamps coming through the window, we could see that there was also no woman in the bed. The house was empty. We went through every room, but it was empty. Bobby's wife must have gone on location with Rod.

We went home. Before the night was over, Bobby beat me up, or at least he started to, but he was too drunk to catch me. I was awful sick of sex. I grabbed up my clothes and ran out the door and had the luck to find a taxi on those lonely streets and went home to Hollywood. I didn't even cry in the back seat. It just occurred to me that Bobby didn't even know my phone number or address, or even my last name, just my first, and maybe he would never try to find me, and he never did.

Two days later, I had the abortion. Whenever I looked into my mirror now in my apartment in the Waldorf Towers, on the 37th floor, I could still see how something ended in me that day, I don't know what, but it is still in my expression.

Prosecutor: Mr. Mailer, concerning these last two excerpts, what percentage of fact and fiction would you estimate are there?

Mailer: I would say those passages are fiction.

Prosecutor: This Bobby, as he is called, he is based on no one?

Mailer: No one.

Prosecutor: His wife?

Mailer: She is imaginary.

Prosecutor: The man named Rod?

Mailer: Equally fictional.

Prosecutor: Do you have knowledge that Miss Monroe at any time in her life made a compact to help a husband murder his wife?

Mailer: To my knowledge, she never did.

Prosecutor: There is nothing on record anywhere that she ever contemplated such an act?

Mailer: Not so far as I know.

Prosecutor: Did anyone suggest this possibility in an interview?

Mailer: No one.

Prosecutor: Yet, in a fictional situation, you make Marilyn Monroe accomplice to a conspiracy to commit murder.

Mailer: I suppose that's the legal description.

Prosecutor: How can you ever justify yourself? If Miss Monroe were alive, she could sue you for libel. And win.

Defense: Objection.

The Court: Prosecution knows better than to draw conclusions.

Prosecutor: Forgive me, Your Honor. I consider the action of the defendant outrageous.

Defense: Objection, Your Honor.

The Court: I'm putting the prosecution on notice.

Prosecutor: You wrote Exhibit B, page 88 to 95, knowing there was no basis for them?

Mailer: No factual basis.

Prosecutor: What makes you think there is a fictional basis?

Mailer: I'm not sure a fictional basis is possible. I'm not even certain Marilyn Monroe could have gotten into such a situation, fictionally speaking, and still be Marilyn Monroe. I've pondered the question. All the while I was writing this book, I kept asking myself, Is this true to Marilyn?

Prosecutor: Are you telling us that you doubt your ethics?

Mailer: I call them in question.

Prosecutor: You think yourself guilty of literary malpractice?

Mailer: I hope not, but it's possible.

Prosecutor: We rest our case.

The Court: Let's take ten minutes.

[Recess]

Defense: Your Honor, while court was out, I discussed his testimony with Mr. Mailer, and he has made clear to me again that he is not interested in an adversary proceeding so much as to ask the court for a discovery of his motives. That is the legal position out of which my questions will be asked.

The Court: You want to let us know where your questions are coming from.

Defense: Yes, Your Honor.

The Court: I hope they are not coming from left field.

Defense: It is my fervent hope, Your Honor.

The Court: Please proceed.

Defense: Mr. Mailer, when you conceived this work, did you plan to have such scenes with the character named Bobby as are described in Exhibit B?

Mailer: I can say that I planned to have such passages, yes. There is a period in Marilyn Monroe's life about which very little is known. I would locate it during 1948, 1949, and 1950, sometime after she became a model but before she made *The Asphalt Jungle*. In those years, she was one of many girls around Hollywood, and there is no telling what kind of adventures she got into, or with what sort of men she went out, other than a few movie people we know she knew. So I thought I would try to invent some episode that might, in a few pages, capture the impact and probable horror of those years upon her.

The Court: Mr. Mailer, how did you form the conclusion that those years from 1948 to 1950 were horrible for Miss Monroe?

Mailer: On the basis of her later life, Your Honor. The tragedy that surrounds Marilyn Monroe is that as her career succeeded, so did she begin to come apart. It is tragic to be destroyed in the years of one's success. Right when she was most happily married is when she became most unhappily married. There is no simple explanation for such matters. We have to assume there are buried matters in the psyche.

The Court: Does that justify endowing her with murderous instincts?

Mailer: It is my understanding of Marilyn Monroe that she was murderous. I would say she was a killer in the way most of us are. On the set, she killed time and slaughtered expectations. She wore people out, she chilled their talent. Finally, with her husbands, she exhausted their hopes. She left not one death but a thousand little deaths in many of the people around her, nice people and awful people both, at least by her measure of nice and awful. When we slay indiscriminately, I think it is a sign we are trying to hold off our own doom. Any portrait of Marilyn Monroe that restricted itself to showing how attractive she could be in the panoply of all her tender wit had to be an untrue portrait which would mislead the reader.

Defense: We wish to point out that the prosecution has offered excerpts that show Miss Monroe only in an unattractive or controversial light. Such passages are but a small part of this book, *Of Women and Their Elegance*, and give a distorted portrait.

Mailer: Yes, most of the time, in fact, since Marilyn Monroe is telling the story in her own voice, I did my best to show her as quintessentially charming.

The Court: Mr. Mailer, would you care to define your use of "charming"?

Mailer: Unpredictable but positive, Your Honor. We don't know how we'll get there, but we're looking to find our way to someplace nice. Miss Monroe is presented in most of my pages as nice.

Defense: Exhibit C, page 96, may be an example of this, Your Honor.

[Defense reads]

I didn't like television because it made me want to burp. On the other hand, it was a little like having another person in the room. Nobody impressive, of course. Somebody who was pale and had a lot of stomach noises. Color TV was like they were putting makeup on that pale person. A very unhealthy person with a wheeze in his lungs and a twitch—if you got to know them well they would tell you about their operations. So I used to think TV was ridiculous. The entertainment industry, instead of understanding that they had this unhealthy individual who could only do a little bit, had it out instead working hard. Maybe one year it would come down with some awful disease, but in the meantime they were giving it dancing lessons.

Defense: We will also offer Exhibit C, page 33, as typical of characteristic aspects of this work.

The Court: Do you object? I see you are standing.

Prosecutor: We will not object. Our case does not rest on the presence or absence of agreeable passages concerning Miss Monroe. It is based instead on one outrageously unfounded presentation of her character.

Defense: I proceed to read Exhibit C, page 33.

[*Reads*]

Once in a while, to put myself to sleep, I would think of Amy's underwear, which was not only immaculate but color-coordinated. If she was wearing a purple dress, why, she would also put on a purple bra and a purple girdle and a purple half-slip. "Why?" I asked her. "People can't see what you have on underneath."

"I like the feeling of being altogether in the color I wear." I got it. She did everything for the inner feeling. I was so impressed.

"Besides," said Amy, "if my husband comes wandering through while I'm getting dressed, I want him to see something pretty. Why should I show Milton cotton underwear? With his eyes!"

Her lingerie cabinet was like a rainbow. All those colors arranged in a fan. When I thought about it, going to sleep, the lingerie gave off sounds like organ pipes. I felt so much love for Amy because we could be friends, she who had every color of the rainbow for her underwear, and I who never wore any.

Defense: Would you say, Mr. Mailer, that it was to balance such favorable impressions of Miss Monroe that you invented the scenes concerning the imaginary man named Bobby?

Mailer: No, not to balance the portrait so much as to disturb it.

The Court: To disturb it?

Mailer: Yes, Your Honor. I did not wish to add to Miss Monroe's legend but to shock its roots. So I decided to take a chance.

The Court: Can you expatiate on this chance you were taking?

Mailer: One reader, close to me, so hated the section in question that it spoiled the manuscript for her. She is a practical woman, just the sort of levelheaded reader one looks for, and I knew her reaction would be common to many. Yet I felt no desire to remove that part—indeed, I knew I would keep it. For to contemplate my book without such a passage is intolerable. The work would then present Miss Monroe as sweet, charming, madcap, a natural soul. That could only deepen the confusion surrounding her life and her legend. We would be farther away from understanding how it is that someone so attractive could end so badly.

Defense: Yet the prosecution has asked in effect why you chose the explanation you did.

Mailer: That still bothers me. The tone of the episode itself. There may have been a failure of invention. It is not easy to conceive of one powerful dramatic episode that will substitute satisfactorily for the sum of a thousand smaller episodes.

Defense: Yet, what is this sum—to use your word—that you are trying to show the reader?

Mailer: It is Marilyn Monroe's unrecorded years in Hollywood. They must make up a large-size bag of foul encounters and small ruthless impulses that wakened in her one by one. In later years, I believe they were like a psychic cyst within her. Memories so bad cannot be called upon. It is exactly the memories we cannot face that destroy us. We are always carrying them uphill.

Defense: So you felt it was fair to invent this extraordinary episode at the home of Bobby de P.?

Mailer: Yes. Fair to the reader, that is. I wanted the reader to be jarred into comprehension of the size and spectrum of a movie star's soul. There is more to a movie star than we think, not less. I wanted to deepen the legend of Marilyn Monroe, not sweeten it. I thought it would be better for our comprehension of many things if we understood that art comes out of more contracts than are written, and the artist's inner negotiations with evil are often as comprehensive as the generosity of the artistic offering. So I do not think I was unfair to her at large. I expect the total of the little horrors she committed in those years would equal the one large horror I gave her. But whether I caught the taste and tone of her personality by that episode, or lost the flavor of her voice for a little while, is another matter.

Defense: We rest.

The Court: A question. How would you feel, Mr. Mailer, if some other author were to characterize you in such extreme fashion after *your* death? Let me say I do not wish to rush that occasion. Still, how do you think you would feel?

Mailer: Your Honor, I have already been characterized in many books as if I were dead. Jacqueline Susann, from what I am told, depicted me as the improbable and repulsive villain of one of her novels. Mario Puzo once portrayed me as a fat man who smoked cigars and strangled a poodle with his bare hands on an airplane. That sounds more like a description of Puzo than myself. I also resent what Puzo's fiction had me doing. I owned a standard poodle once, and he was a great dog and lived to be eighteen years old. I do not go around killing poodles. Another writer gave one of his characters my name, literally!, and then had him drop his pants obediently at gunpoint, for which compliance, he—I should say I—was shot in the anus and killed. There have been other such portraits. I do not say that because I have been, on occasion, poorly treated in print I have a right, therefore, to distort Marilyn Monroe's life. I say, rather, that I think uneasily of her opinion, and I hope she accepts, wherever she is, the equation I drew between her many lost episodes and the single one I gave her. For if I have been unfair to her, as I believe those authors have been unfair to me, then I must shift uncomfortably before any bar of judgment, since I know how deep is the contempt I hold for authors who would write about me and yet do not have the imagination to come up with some equivalent of my life that may be extreme but is fair. I would not like to think Miss Monroe feels an equal contempt for me. I guess that is all.

Defense: Can we ask for an immediate verdict of exoneration?

The Court: Some might think your client lucky to escape hanging. I am going to take this under advisement. There is a lot to mull over here, and I am hardly going to let you off on the spot. I will say that I have read the book and consider it a serious enough work to give Mr. Mailer a fair opportunity of avoiding outright censure. But there is no escaping the conclusion that what he has done is downright dangerous. He almost certainly will be reprimanded for making up false and sordid episodes concerning public figures. What if a lot of bad authors were to act as Mr. Mailer has?

Defense: They have, Your Honor. Ever since Gutenberg.

The Court: Well, I'm going to have to live with this for a while. Let me tell you that once again Mr. Mailer has done his best to take over my weekend. I'm going to close this court for now.

[Adjournment]

Mailer Talking
Michiko Kakutani/1982

From *The New York Times Book Review,* 6 June 1982, 3, 38-41.
Copyright © 1982 by The New York Times Company. Reprinted
by permission.

"There was that law of life," Norman Mailer wrote in *The Deer Park,*
"so cruel and so just which demanded that one must grow or else
pay more for remaining the same." Clearly it is a sentiment taken to
heart by the author himself. Now 59, Mr. Mailer has fashioned a
career in which he has continually reinvented a style and a self, using
his own personality as a kind of index to discover how the world has
changed. The polite young Brooklyn-born, Harvard-educated author
of *The Naked and the Dead* evolved, through the 50's and hectic
60's, into the blustering protagonist of *The Armies of the Night—*
"warrior, presumptive general, champion of obscenity, embattled
aging *enfant terrible* of the literary world"—and surfaced again in the
less flamboyant 70's as a "modest and half-invisible Aquarius."
Indeed, the self-portrait that emerges in Mr. Mailer's new collection of
short work and interviews from the 60's and 70's, *Pieces and
Pontifications,* is that of a writer who has traded his egocentric
concerns of the past for a new objectivity, his prodigality of emotion
and rhetoric for more modest satisfactions.

"By the end of the 60's and into the 70's," Mr. Mailer said in a
recent interview, "I felt more and more that I was no longer
interesting as a subject to myself. In a way, I was no longer perceiving
things through my self. I was beginning to look at the world more
objectively, and I think my work turned around a bit in other
directions."

Given the shape of his own career, he tends to think of his life in
terms of decades, and those decades are as distinct to him as
"separate countries; the difference between the 40's and 50's is the
difference between France and England." The 40's were a "simple

time, a time when I knew what I was doing." He married his first
wife, went off to war and then wrote his first novel, *The Naked and
the Dead.* The book was hailed by one critic as "the greatest war
novel produced in this century," and the consequences of that early
success were to be profound indeed. Not only did his new celebrity
cut him off from his own past, but it also made the sort of detached,
novelistic observation of the American scene that Mr. Mailer then
aspired to more difficult. The observer had become the observed;
and he soon learned, as he wrote in *The Armies of the Night,* to "live
in the sarcophagus of his image."

"I think," Mr. Mailer says, "for anyone who's become an author
early and has had a good deal of success, as Capote did and Vidal
did and Styron did and I did, it's not automatic or easy afterwards to
look upon other people with a simple interest because generally
speaking they're more interested in us than we are in them. This has
nothing to do with character, but with the social situation—I am more
interested in Marlon Brando than he is interested in me—and it has
an immense impact when you're young. You become a mirror and
the only way you can perceive events is through the mirror of your
self."

So for the next two decades Mr. Mailer tried on and discarded a
variety of roles, including Greenwich Village bohemian, talk-show
guest, film maker, self-proclaimed hipster and would-be politician.
During the 50's, he willfully collided with all that was conventional
and established, experimenting with drugs and alcohol and what he
once called "the psychology of the orgy." By the 60's, his public
inventories of his life had calcified into a kind of legend; he had
succeeded in creating a life that personified the popular image of the
decade itself.

Certainly, such forays into public life as running for Mayor of New
York and marching on the Pentagon provided Mr. Mailer with raw
experience to write about, and they also helped him, he says, to
understand "how the world works." The tireless self-dramatization,
the courting of public exposure and ridicule—the need, as he writes
in the preface of his new book, to "be there to speak to one's time"—
also seemed to serve as a sort of "psychic housekeeping," a means of
testing his convictions in the open marketplace.

"If you want to know why I do these things," Mr. Mailer says, "I do
them for myself. I'm old enough now as a writer to enjoy old lines of

mine and there's a line in *The Deer Park* I like— 'experience when it is not communicated to another must wither within and be worse than lost'—and I think that's true. I think that when we keep inside us something we think is true and don't speak out, it does bad things to us."

Still, if the rewards of leading so public a life have been considerable, the costs have been high as well. "You're in the position," he says, "of a poor, good-looking kid who decides he's not strong enough, not tough enough to get all the women he wants in the whole world. So he decides to become a boxer, and he goes into the ring and becomes tougher and tougher and tougher, and by the time he's at the top and gotten really tough, he's also so ugly that the women still won't look at him. So you're out in the world and you learn a great deal as a writer, but it's also very punishing."

"Take running for office," he goes on. "On the one hand, I learned an awful lot about the political process, so I'm not so paranoid about it as I was and, parenthetically, I also ended up with a little more respect for politicians. But in the course of learning this, I ended up making eight speeches a day for three months, and I'm sure I did something to my spontaneous gifts of oratory forever—which has to bear some reflection on your power to form sentences in the loneliness of the room in which you do your work. You know, I'm possibly a less polished writer as a result of running for office and making all those damn impromptu speeches. It ages the brain a little."

Of course, time spent making speeches or advocating causes or going to parties is time spent away from the typewriter; and whether or not the seriousness of one's work is actually affected by such nonliterary diversions, the public's perception of the author often is.

"The price that you do pay," he says, "is that it's harder for people to take you seriously—they're afraid to. They say, 'What is that fool, that flake, going to do next?' and they feel somewhat vulnerable if they like your work. [Today] buying a hard-cover book is a sacramental act, and when people have to pay that much money for something they have to have a certain respect, even a touch of awe, for the author. And if you're unsavory in public life and everyone knows your name, you're not going to sell thousands of hardcover books. The people who sell lots of hardcover books are usually not in the public eye—Saul Bellow, John Updike, John Cheever—and very few people can break that law. Capote's broken it successfully. Vidal's broken it successfully. But I certainly haven't."

Whether it was the literary and psychic consequences of maintaining his self-generated myth, the fact that he felt increasingly out of step with the 70's—a period, he says, characterized by "the lack of ideas that anyone was even remotely willing to die for"—or simply a weariness with self-scrutiny, Mr. Mailer began to turn away from himself as a subject. Biographies of Marilyn Monroe, Muhammad Ali, Henry Miller and Gary Gilmore replaced autobiography. And the famous Mailer narrators—the "psychic outlaw," the "generous but very spoiled boy," the "criminally egomaniacal" writer—gradually disappeared.

"Writing is a way of using up anything that's good and bad in you about a subject," Mr. Mailer says. "It's supposed to be famously known, for instance, that pornographers end up impotent. It's probably a myth that has a certain amount of practical application. If you work a muscle hard, it tends to develop; but if you overwork it, it can break down. I think something of the same sort is true of the psyche. If you force an aspect of the imagination, it can come to the point where it ceases to return anything at all, and I think I probably got to that point by the time I wrote *Of a Fire on the Moon.* I liked the book in a lot of ways, but I didn't like my own person in it—I felt I was highly unnecessary. And in *The Prisoner of Sex,* I felt my attempt to do something with my own personal relation to things was the least thought-out aspect of the book. I felt I had used up myself as a reference, though I tried once more in 1975 with *The Fight,* and that was wholly feeble."

"What actually happened," he continues, "is that I began to get interested in other people, and this sounds like an extraordinary remark for a novelist to make, but in truth we really write novels out of two impulses. One is to understand ourselves better as we write, and the other is to present what we know about others. And more often it's impossible to truly comprehend others until one's plumbed the bottom of certain obsessions about oneself."

Alternately charming and combative, earnest and sly, Mr. Mailer is well practiced in the subtle arts of literary gamesmanship, as well as in the art of the interview, and he points out that there was also a certain amount of calculation in his adoption of a more objective style.

Piqued by critics who have tried to pigeonhole his work, he says he has tended to "start off in a new direction" with every major book, and in that respect, *The Executioner's Song*, was written partly tongue in cheek.

"By the time I started that book," he explains, "I'd probably been nettled by people saying, 'He can write about nothing but himself,' 'He can't write objectively,' 'He can't write simply.' *The Executioner's Song* was my way of saying, 'Hey, look, it's very easy to write simply, it's very easy to write objectively; if you know how to write, you can write anything and you can write in any style.' Style is merely a reflection of deeper talents that one hopes to possess."

For Mr. Mailer, the finest fiction serves to intensify "the moral consciousness of people," and for many years he argued that "a writer of the largest dimension can alter the nerves and marrow of a nation." During the 70's, however, he "lost all the easy optimism about how quickly one could affect things in the world as a writer." In part, this was a reflection of his sense that he was growing older, that "the audience was further away, that I was no longer speaking to my own time," and in part a reflection of his belief that today's cultural milieu has diminished the importance of the novelist.

"They're all highly accomplished and skillful and talented and artful," Mr. Mailer says of such contemporaries as John Updike and Saul Bellow, "and they're craftsmen to a degree that Hemingway and Faulkner weren't. But I don't think they're as great because greatness doesn't just depend on the author; it also depends on the time. If someone who writes in the equivalent of a Hemingway style came along today, it wouldn't move people as profoundly—their senses are too dulled by TV and their higher senses are too diverted by film. In fact, if I were coming along at this point, either rightly or wrongly, I might be more attracted to writing films or directing films than writing novels."

Given such doubts about a novelist's possible influence, Mr. Mailer says that during the 70's he started to withdraw from the world. "As you get older," he says, "you realize that what's important is to do one's work and do one's best work and be serious about it. It's not that you're retreating completely—you're just saying, "It's too much, I abdicate, I resign, I will cultivate my own garden.' You say, 'I will work on that garden on the assumption I will produce an herb that will change all that is before us.' In other words instead of seeing yourself as the embattled artist, you begin to see yourself as the alchemical artist. Art as magic rather than art as war."

The particular garden Mr. Mailer is referring to is his Egyptian novel, which he has been working on since 1972. Part of a trilogy— the second part is to take place in the future; the third will have a contemporary setting—the book is set in the reign of Ramses IX, a pharaoh who lived around 1130 B.C., and for half its length is told from the point of view of a 6-year-old boy. Unlike most of his work, Mr. Mailer says, the novel "has nothing to say about America today"; rather, his intent is "to create a consciousness that's so different from our own that we read it in wonder as if we were reading about Martians."

It is nearly two decades since Mr. Mailer first began to talk about writing a "big" novel, and both the stakes and expectations for this new book, a first draft of which he recently completed, are high. He has described it as a "novel which Dostoyevsky and Marx; Joyce and Freud; Stendhal, Tolstoy, Proust and Spengler; Faulkner, and even mouldering old Hemingway might come to read," and it is sure to affect his literary reputation. "Unless it is very, very good indeed," he says, "it will be like having spent 10 years with the wrong woman. I think if you spend 10 years on a book and the book is not good, you lose just as much as any man or woman spends being married to the wrong mate. You lose a piece of your life."

Why has it taken Mr. Mailer so long to complete the novel? Why has he taken time out for *The Executioner's Song* and the odd journalistic assignment? Family responsibilities and financial pressures—alimony and children's tuition, the aftermath of five previous marriages—have been factors. And there are also the special problems faced by established authors late in their careers. The youthful need to articulate new ideas and tell one's story, the drive of early ambition, the joy of "scoring rich allusions"—these incentives gradually dissipate with time, and, as Mr. Mailer notes, "a writer who's been around for 30 to 40 years is, in a certain way, a battered case."

"That particular insensitivity you have to build about yourself in relation to reviews doesn't do you much good as a writer," he says. "So anyone who has kept working has found ways of renewing his desire to write. And we no more question it than we question our sexual desire. You don't say, 'Why do I have sexual desire?' You're quite content to have it.

"What gets easier is, because one's been through that literary mill so many times, the fears are less and one's professionalism increases over the years. By professionalism I mean the ability to work on a bad day. There's nothing glorious about being a professional. As you become a professional, you become more dogged. You almost have to relinquish the upper reaches of the mind to do your stint of work each day, because being a professional means being able to endure a certain amount of drudgery and the higher reaches of the mind are not enthralled by dull work."

In Mr. Mailer's own case, he says that most of the ideas he possesses today—his theories about violence and God and art, for instance, as well as his vision of America as a kind of spiritually impoverished Cancer Gulch—developed during the 50's, when he found himself opposing the dull repressive mores of those years. Today, it seems, he is engaged in "less of an exploration and more of an occupation of territories I reconnoitered years ago."

"What happens is you become the hat on your own head," he says. "You're not having the pleasure of enjoying your own mind the way you used to when you were young, but you have the product of your mind to work with. You know, I ran into Henry Kissinger years ago and I asked him if he enjoyed the intellectual stimulation of the work, and he said in effect, 'I am working with the ideas that I formed at Harvard years ago. I haven't had a real idea since I've been on this; I just work with the old ideas.' I certainly know what he means now—I think there are just so many ideas you can have in your life and once you have them, you have to develop them."

Along with consolidating the past, there appears to be, on Mr. Mailer's part, a certain chastening of ambition, a diminution, however slight, of expectations. In a 1963 interview he spoke of "a vast guerrilla war going on for the mind of man." "The stakes are huge," he observed. "Will we spoil the best secrets of life or help to free a new kind of man? It's intoxicating to think of that. There's something rich waiting if one of us is brave enough and good enough to get there." Today he is a more cautious man, less assured of the possibility of coming up with a "vision that would comprehend everything," though also unwilling to relinquish all his youthful aspirations.

"My ambition," he says now, "would not be any longer to try to reach Americans with a book the way Hemingway could reach them with a book, because I believe that's beyond my powers. Hemingway's style affected whole generations of us, the way a roomful of men is affected when a beautiful woman walks through— their night is turned for better or for worse. Hemingway's style had an ability to hit young writers in the gut, and they just weren't the same after that. That would not be my ambition—I don't have that kind of talent. But to give up the ambition entirely is another matter. No, I won't give it up entirely."

Unbloodied by the Critical Pounding, Norman Mailer Defends the Egyptian Novel that Took a Decade to Write

George Plimpton/1983

Since its publication last month, Norman Mailer's *Ancient Evenings,* a story of Egypt in the 13th century B.C., has drawn the kind of critical fire that only a major writer could expect or endure. Reviewers attacked it variously for its ponderous length (709 pages), its scatological content, and an overall lack of coherence. Nonetheless, Mailer, 60, who calls the book "my most ambitious work," has reaped rewards; his publisher, Little, Brown, gave him a $1.4 million advance, the paperback rights fetched another $500,000, and *Ancient Evenings* has been consistently on the *New York Times* best-seller list. Mailer would like this, his 22nd book in a 37-year career, to achieve a stature commensurate with the labors of imagination required to produce it. He spoke of the novel's decade-long creation with fellow author George Plimpton.

Given the severe criticisms, would you consider changing Ancient Evenings, *had you the chance?*
I'm not sure that I'd change it much. I spent four months last fall going through the book and I took a hundred pages out. I didn't go in for any major surgery. The length is necessary; slowness is important to give a sense of the pace. If you speed the book up you gain a quick readability, but you lose the pace of ancient Egypt. Also, I was working with the vanity that this was the nearest I was ever going to come to the possibility of writing a great book.

299

And that's what you were trying with Ancient Evenings?

Whether the book is great or a disaster—and it's been called both already—my attempt was to create a new psychology, a new consciousness. After all, the Egyptians had a psychology that existed long before Freud. I was trying to write of these matters from the perspective of those times. One of the conceits of this book is that it's an *Egyptian* novel, and since there are no others, it's *the* Egyptian novel. I mean if one supposed—which of course is impossible, given the culture of the time—that one rather talented young man had written a huge novel about Egypt, this would be it; it would have come down to us as an extraordinary work out of the past with no tone of the present.

And with no attempt in it to establish a metaphor between Egypt and America?

No. Indeed, exactly the opposite. I know that Harold Bloom in the *New York Review of Books* said I was writing about America. He may be right, but at least that was not my conscious intent.

Wouldn't it then follow that you'd have to keep yourself—the contemporary Norman Mailer and his distinctive sensibilities—out of the book?

One of the big problems certain people have with *Ancient Evenings* is that they keep thinking of me as they read. They find that they can't concentrate; it's distracting; it's a great pain in the neck. That's obviously a problem if you're a well-known writer. Thomas Mann had to face it when he wrote his famous *Joseph* books about Egypt. Of course, his problem was larger—he was by far the most famous writer in Germany and had an immense international reputation. Mann could not write a book about Egypt in which he didn't appear. So he *did*, very correctly, in there to mediate for the reader, saying, in effect, "Look, we can't really understand Egypt, but I've been studying these people for a very long time, I know as much as my novelist's brain can contain, and I will, in effect, be your guide." As he told the story he kept stepping in and saying, "Now what's going on here is most peculiar. It's very hard to understand what their motivations were right here, but let us assume that possibly *this* is so. Whereas in this other case, I must confess I will leave it to the reader."

The reader, in consequence, was comfortable because Thomas Mann was there. On the other hand, I felt that one doesn't *want* to be comfortable with Egypt; therefore I kept thinking of Mann, for whom I have immense respect, as being nonetheless the model to avoid. What I hoped to do was capture a culture in a way that would make the reader feel right in the middle of it, and so look up in shock and say, "My God, where am I? I'm not here; I'm in Egypt." Such total disorientation would be quite an aesthetic experience.

But surely your voice, your preoccupation with odor and ordures, for example, gives the game away.

I didn't see any way to write about Egypt without entering a few unhappy subjects. In Egypt, given the Nile flooding its banks and turning villages into islands in the river, with detritus everywhere, animals living in the houses, everyone huddled together, one knows that it was an incredibly fecal place. I dealt with it because there was no trying to avoid it. *If* I did, I was not going to get to the heart of my theme, which is that the Egyptians have much to tell us—precisely because they came before the Judeo-Christian era—about power, wealth, sex and death, and right in there is waste, excrement. That's one of the fundamental factors. It's no secret that Freud gave us a firm set of connections between anality and power . . . and what I learned about Egypt seemed a kind of confirmation.

What about your famous nose? Did you smoke at one time and then quit?

I smoked an awful lot. *An American Dream* is the first novel I wrote during my attempts to stop, and, of course, one's sense of smell is incredibly acute at such times. It certainly turns up in the writing. By 1966 I quit smoking forever, and that faculty, though not as strong, has continued. My eyesight is not that good. Writers with marvelous eyesight tend to show that in the writing. I don't think Hemingway's got three smells in all his work.

Did your editor make any firm suggestions—perhaps that you were going on at too great a length—in Ancient Evenings?

My editor, Roger Donald, was very high on the book and still is. We agreed, pretty much, that the chances had to be taken. He is one brave editor.

Might it not be difficult for an editor to press his views on an author of fame and distinction?

The editor is there to be a great and noble blocking back and keep people from wrecking your mood when you're at work. But to name one's peers—Vonnegut, Pynchon, Updike, John Irving, Bellow, and so on—if I were their editor, I'd hate like hell to tell them, hey, I think you're too long here. That'd be an enormous responsibility to take. When you get to the place where we all are as writers, you're supposed to be able to do your own editing.

What do you think are your major weaknesses as a writer?

I could list about six or seven but I don't think I will. They'll be thrown at me in later years—"Mailer himself admits that he's no good at . . ." But mind you, authors tend to make a weakness a virtue. For example, I doubt that Hemingway was capable of writing a long complex sentence with a lot of architecture in the syntax. So he turned that inability into the virtue of writing short declarative sentences and long run-on sentences connected by conjunctions. Faulkner was not capable of writing simply without personal pain. He turned that into a virtue and as a result you get this extraordinary mood out of this writing. Henry Miller couldn't really tell a story with any pleasure. He preferred his excursions away from the story, and those excursions are what make him a great writer.

And you won't say what you've turned into a virtue?

I'd say I have most of my problems with plot. The moment I think of a good plot, I find that the book is almost impossible to write because I know I won't believe in it. Life consists of people plotting all the time, and the plots never coming through. We always say, I'll make this or that out of my life, and then life confounds us. I like a plot that develops during the writing. I don't like one that moves ahead of my characters, because then my characters don't live. You can do the same thing to characters by allying them to plot that we would do to our children if we very carefully picked out their colleges, their wives, installed them in the proper job—well, you know what happens to kids like that. The same thing weighs on characters in a novel if they never get to fulfill their capabilities; they never come alive. The development slowly comes into focus as I work. Bill Buckley is wonderful at plots—his mind works that way—but nobody lives and breathes in his books with any more three-dimensionality than some passing movie star who can't act.

How did you begin Ancient Evenings?

With the Egyptian burial customs. Then at a certain point—about 100 pages into the book—I had to emerge onto terra firma . . . from the Land of the Dead to the land of the living—the fanciest literary transition I've ever gone through.

Working on the book off and on for more than a decade, how did you keep track of where you were?

I reread what I'd written, revising as I went along. There were ways to get psyched up, certain books I'd read. I never could have written *Ancient Evenings* without the 10 volumes of drawings in Lepsius Denkmaeler. These extraordinary books were printed around 1850—really at the birth of Egyptology. The pages are of very thick paper, almost like papyrus, so when you turn a page it's like a great sail flapping in a lull, and sometimes if you are able to do it neatly it's equal to a sail jibbing. I'd spend hours in the New York Public Library just peering at these incredible drawings of the temples and the tombs. Aside from this, the research was also a matter of endless reading until one had digested the material. A lot of it was contradictory. The 20th-century Egyptologists have a very different view from those of the 19th century.

Did you see any scholars?

I just read books. I was scared of going to Egyptologists. It would have taken another 10 years. My conscience was also gnawing at me that I should learn hieroglyphics. I was awfully tempted. I finally decided not to, because I felt it would be a self-defeating study. When you're past 50, one's memory isn't good enough to learn a new language. But actually most of the clues I had about life in those times came from language—a two-volume hieroglyphic dictionary by E.A. Wallis Budge. In it, you begin to discover the extraordinary puns and contradictory meanings that the Egyptians put on words. The word for "oil" is the same for "helplessness." The word for "think" or "ponder" is nearly the same as the word for "anus," and that also means "the moral of the tale." The word for "radiance" can also mean "conceive." The ancient Egyptians were a tactile, sensitive, visceral people.

What effect do bad reviews have on you?

I treat them like a politician running for office. A couple of friends called up after the bad review in the Sunday *New York Times* and asked, "Are you all right?" I'd seen it a week before, so any unhappiness I'd had about it was now digested. I said that it was like realizing that the county chairman in Schenectady is deciding against your candidacy. But to lose Schenectady doesn't mean that you stop running. It isn't my ego that's hurt, it's my damn pocketbook. Getting a bad review in the *Times* hurts you as much as any single review can.

Over the country as a whole (I'm beginning to sound like a theatrical producer), 15 out of 25 reviews have been very good. The prediction that I would catch the very best and the very worst has been true.

Have you ever taken it out on a reviewer personally?

When I was younger I used to consider a bad review a personal insult and would consider a guy who wrote it evil. In fact, I have never actually punched out a reviewer, which I say with a certain amount of wistfulness. I once sat next to Philip Rahv after he had written an atrocious review of *An American Dream*. Philip Rahv had his virtues, bless him, but physical courage was not one of them. So I made a point of sitting next to him at a party, and while I smiled at him, I kept my body firmly pressed into his, leaning into him, while we had a long 30-minute conversation about something else altogether. I was perfectly pleasant the entire time and everything seemed all right except that we were both tilted alarmingly from my leaning into him. He was in an absolute panic, waiting for me to strike. It must have seemed an odd sight from the other side of the table: He was a heavy man, and the two of us must have looked like two doughnuts crushed together in a box.

How has your immediate family reacted to the fortunes of Ancient Evenings?

I've always kept my writing separate from my kids. They're interested in a lot of things, but not in my writing. Of course, they're loyal. Their feeling with a bad review is, "Oh, that bastard, how dare he"—just a good family reaction.

Did you ever think of doing Ancient Evenings *as nonfiction rather than using the novel form?*

Never. Of course, nonfiction is much easier. Endlessly easier. It would have been no problem at all to write such a book. I could have done it in a couple of years at most—a series of essays on the nature of Egypt—and they would have been fascinating to readers and a lot more agreeable to some. But it never crossed my mind. Everything would have worked with that method but the *feel.* I wanted to immerse the reader in the feeling that he or she was in ancient Egypt.

Would you suggest actually going to Egypt? You went there once, didn't you?

Hated it. Climbed the pyramids, quite illegally, in seven minutes and ran down in five. The place has become a Third World country. It had nothing to do with ancient Egypt and so was terribly distracting to me. I understood that I could do my book only if I didn't go back there.

Have you talked to any Egyptians about Ancient Evenings?

I don't think it's relevant—any more than if I'd written a book about ancient Greece it would be relevant to talk to a Greek. Ancient Greece belongs to all of us.

As indeed Ancient Evenings *does.*

I would hope so.

Twelfth Round:
An Interview with Norman Mailer
Robert Begiebing/1983

From *Harvard Magazine*, 85 (1983), 40, 42-50. Copyright ©
1983 *Ha vard Magazine*. Reprinted by permission.

*"By the time you reach your sixties, you feel
as if you're in the twelfth round and you're
battered. . . . It may be that part of remaining
a writer is to ring yourself around more and
more with various protections. The price of
that, of course, is that inspiration enters the
door much less often. But at the same time
you can carry out your projects."*

Ten years in the writing, Ancient Evenings will be published in May.
For Norman Mailer, who turned sixty in January, this new book
marks an important transitional point. After more than a decade of
nonfiction, a big novel—the first of a planned trilogy—brings Mailer
back to the literary genre in which he made his name.

Pulitzer prizes in 1969 and 1980 for *The Armies of the Night* and
The Executioner's Song (not to mention additional awards for these
and other books) have affirmed Mailer's standing in contemporary
American letters. His public posturings and activist politics have
colored his reputation, but two dozen books, three films, a play, and
countless articles bear witness to his energy and resourcefulness.

Born in Long Branch, New Jersey, in 1923, Mailer grew up in
Brooklyn, graduated from Boys High School, and entered Harvard at
sixteen. Although he took his degree with honors in engineering
sciences, he was already bent on becoming a writer. In college his
output had included more than thirty short stories and two
unpublished novels and plays; "The Greatest Thing in the World,"

written under Professor Robert Gorham Davis, had won *Story* magazine's annual award.

Mailer was drafted in January 1944. He ultimately served in the Philippines as a headquarters clerk and an infantryman. Based on his war experience and published in 1948, his novel *The Naked and the Dead* made him suddenly famous at 25. So began one of the most important, notorious, and mercurial careers in postwar American literature.

Mailer appears to date himself from that 1948 success. (Of an unpublished novel—set in an insane asylum—which he began at Harvard, he later stated: "I do not know the young man who wrote this book. I do not like him very much.") Indeed, it would be hard to imagine a more extreme personality shift. The amiable, bright Jewish boy from Brooklyn was to become the ranting, hallucinating, brawling "General Marijuana" of the *Village Voice* in the Fifties. The next decades would bring Mailer's televised invective against the Vietnam War and General Westmoreland, his skirmishes with radical feminists, his wrangles with fellow authors Gore Vidal and William Styron. Thus embattled, the self-appointed Jeremiah got himself in trouble with his literary audience as well as the general public. But it was trouble Mailer wanted. He is nothing if not a disturber of bland uniformity, convention, and complacency—of what he sees as the "cancer," the totalitarianism, the spiritual death of our times.

Yet Mailer today is a gray and courteous eminence. Meeting him— a stoutish, five-foot-eight man who looks at first glance as if he might be vacationing in safari suit from regular stints on "Wall Street Week"—one is taken aback. Can this be the bold excursionist who has struggled with the nature of existentialism, sexuality, the unconscious, God, and the devil?

The conversation that follows suggests that the appearance does indeed deceive, perhaps as much as Mailer's "media image." It also offers fresh background on the first 25 years of Mailer's life, and clues to his current work—about which Mailer has been reticent since the mid Seventies, when he made his much-publicized million-dollar contract with Little, Brown to complete "a certain big novel."

Talking with Mailer, one sees that the journalist, revolutionary, and holy fool are still alive in the man—but that other, and older, personae have returned. For his capacious personality now seems to accommodate the disciplined worker, the self-effacing novelist, and the scholar. There is even a wink from the earnest young man from Brooklyn who got good grades and went to Harvard to study engineering.

You once said you started writing at about seven—a long, 300-page story about a trip to Mars. Then you quit. You began again about the time you were at Harvard. If your high-school interests weren't particulaly literary, what were they?
I built model airplanes all through high school. I wanted to be an aeronautical engineer—that was my prevailing interest. The books I read in high school were certainly not literary. I wasn't a literary man in any way. My idea of good writers was Jeffrey Farnol, Rafael Sabatini. My favorite book was probably *Captain Blood.*
I assumed I'd go to M.I.T. The only reason I applied to Harvard was that my cousin had gone there. I thought, well, it might be nice. And then, I lived in a very simple part of Brooklyn. It wasn't ethnic on the grand scale. You didn't have to fight your way to the candy store—we didn't have gangs. We were just quiet, middle-class kids. In those days there was so little traffic we used to play touch football and roller hockey in the street. Just a quiet street with small, what the British call "semiattached villas," which meant *real* small, two-family homes. And small lawns in front, so small that when you were playing roller hockey, if you bodychecked somebody hard they'd go flying across the sidewalk, and you had to go scrambling up a lawn that was banked. If that *ever* happened to you you'd come out with fire in your eyes and your skates full of dirt.

So street sports and engineering were your early interests?
Right. . . . very conventional. And in my senior year the girls would ask, "Where did you apply to college?" I'd say M.I.T. and it wouldn't register at all. Then I'd say Harvard and they'd look at me, "Whew!" So I thought, well, there must be something wonderful about Harvard.

You've mentioned that rather than the summit of your experience, high school was not a good time. And you felt deprived for thirty years thereafter. Why?
I went to Boys High School in Brooklyn, which is very much a boys' school. I was a year and a half younger than the average

student. High school went by in a blur of work and doing one's homework as quickly as possibly and getting out in the street to play. And there was no high-school life as such. Later I began to realize that for many people high school was the prime experience in their lives. It was the dating period and all that. In Brooklyn one went out with dates however one could. I felt straddled between my friends who were my age at home and were two years behind me at school. So I didn't feel I belonged particularly in one life or another. I'd say high school was really the equivalent of college for somebody who was working at a job and going to night school, and was bitter afterwards because he felt he never had any college life.

You've never written about that stage of your life. Is it something you can't deal with in writing?

I've always had the feeling that it doesn't make much sense to write about something when you know that others can write about it at least as well as you can or maybe better. I never felt I had that much to say about my childhood that was so special it was worth recording. It may mean that writers do play games with themselves— it may mean there is something I'm concealing from myself. I find over and over again that I hide what I can write about because it's risky to know that you can write about something. You can plunge into it before you're ready to give it proper commitment. This sounds very odd to people who never write, to see the unconscious as a vast area where military campaigns go on. I think it's the only metaphor that works because I discover over and over again that the unconscious will disclose to me what it chooses and when it chooses to. When I am working on a long book, for instance, I almost never have a thought about it when I'm not working. And I've come to recognize every year that it's highly impractical to think about it because you can lose it. I happen to have one of those memories that's virtually psychopathic in its halflife. I forget half of everything I think unless instantly, in about four seconds, I write it down. It's overspecialization for about thirty or forty years.

You were close to your parents? You felt no sense of needing to break away?

I didn't have a problem trying to break away in the manner that so many writers do. I didn't have to convince my parents that I should be a writer. It often takes up half of a young writer's energy. They were soon pleased that I wanted to be a writer. They loved reading my work, as only parents can.

How did you find being at Harvard? Did you feel like an outsider?
Harvard, I think at least in those days, had solved more delicate social situations than any other institution that could call itself truly part of the establishment. For instance, my freshman year, I'd say that eighty percent of the people that I was close to were from the same background I was from—they were Jewish, middle class, from small towns, some were from the city. But we all grouped together very much as young black students would today. The difference being that it never occurred to us that we were in an incredibly subtle ghetto. Over the four years at Harvard I don't think I ever once felt it.

Part of this was my innocence. But Myron Kaufmann was a classmate of mine—he wrote a marvelous novel called *Remember Me to God,* and in it the young man is Jewish and he is acutely aware of every social discrimination. That passed blissfully over me. I had no idea at all that I really was very much a part of an outgroup, in fact the word didn't exist to me. I had the experience of sitting next to a young man who was dressed in a particular way. I might have sat next to him a whole year. We might have exchanged as much as three lines of conversation such as, "My God, isn't old so-and-so stuffy today?" There was that sense that there was this other world, but I think that part of the brilliance of the way Harvard solved that problem was not having fraternities. Fraternities really burn it into you just which little group you belong to because the fraternities all have their status. Everyone in the college is aware of it. The Dekes are better than the Upsilons. You are acutely aware of where you belong in that scheme. If you don't get into any fraternity, you're down at the bottom—it breeds such misery.

At Harvard the opposite was done. A few people got in the clubs. Somehow after your first week at Harvard it was clear to you that certain people never get into clubs, and that you were one of them didn't matter. There was a certain scorn for the clubs, which was not certainly well founded, but we scorned the clubs. Who'd be so sleazy as to get into a club and get three C's and a D and all that? But we never thought of ourselves as being out of it. That was marvelous. That's the way the establishment should work. Never got a chance socially speaking, and never ached once. That takes three centuries of careful elaboration of the study of people's feelings.

Were you aware of anti-Semitism at Harvard?
No. I never felt it directly. The nearest example I could find—I couldn't even say it was anti-Semitism. I remember I went up to Harvard wearing this jacket and pants I bought of my own assistance. My mother didn't know a great deal about all this . . . I bought a gold and brown jacket and had green and blue vertical striped pants and saddle shoes. I saw my faculty adviser in the engineering department. He was a crusty old man. He didn't think too much of a lot of things, and he immediately told me that I should take a speech course. I said something about wanting to take German and he said, no, you'll pick it up, you don't need it. And I remember getting just salty enough to say to him, "Well, sir, if I can pick up German in the course of a year or two, I don't see why I can't learn to speak English." He was very aware that I had come from Brooklyn. I'd say that was the strongest single example I can think of. If people were anti-Semitic at Harvard in those days, and I'm sure some were, they were incredibly well bred about it. I didn't feel it was something that impinged on me. The way I felt it was only by comparing that comfortable, middle-class world I had been in—somehow I hadn't taken enough things in, it just wasn't a wide enough horizon. There was a tremendous amount to learn.

But it came to you at Harvard that there was an "establishment"? That's a theme that comes up again and again in your work.
In the part of Brooklyn I came from . . . in the public school I went to, even at Boys High, there was no feeling at all of an establishment. But by the time I got to Harvard I had to realize that an establishment was immense, was subtle, did not have a face, you couldn't even feel it particularly. The only way you were aware of it was that people were terribly serious about their education. And in Brooklyn I was always a little ashamed of being smart—somehow you weren't manly if you were smart. At Harvard it was the other way around. You were ashamed because you were maybe not smart enough. There were always people who were more brilliant than you, and that was admired, vastly admired.

I have to separate the Harvard establishment from other establishments. I'm not so sure that you shouldn't have an establishment, that establishment isn't necessary. That question is one of my obsessions, if we define obsession as a matter to which one always returns. And each time one returns to it with a different point of view about it. When we speak about something being obsessive it's because we don't end up with a fixed opinion. We could argue that certain obsessions are filled with hatred, but they are the exact opposite of what I'm saying—in such obsessions one always goes back to hate in the same way. I'm talking about the other kind of obsession, where one can't make up one's mind. I've pondered the question of establishment all the time. Is it good? Is it bad? Should we have an establishment as such? After all, what you are talking about is the manipulation of people by other people. That's the side which you have to question, the manipulation. Is it finally an absolute evil or a partial evil or a human necessity?

If we accept the idea of an establishment, then no question Harvard has the best establishment I've ever encountered, certainly better than the military establishment, better than the Washington establishment, better than the New York publishing establishment.

What teachers influenced you? You've mentioned Robert Gorham Davis in English A—you became a friend of sorts.

Yes, we're friendly to this day. Theodore Morrison was another who had a certain influence. I remember Dr. [Henry A.] Murray in abnormal psychology. . . . for his geniality, for the charm he brought to a subject normally considered charmless. Robert Hillyer was kind of marvelous—I'm one of the few people who ever took four years of writing courses at Harvard. . . . Hillyer I remember for his exquisite manners. That was probably a crucial part of my education at that point. If you're talking about shockers, the shock was simple. One grew up with rough and ready manners, and you just never measured people by their manners. You measured them by their athletic ability, their loyalties. You considered your parents and their evaluation of people by how much money they made, how good they were as providers. These measures were strong, crude, and serviceable.

At Harvard you ran into the spectrum of manners, and it was as if the manners were the morphology that revealed to you the social pattern behind. In other words, the degree to which one had social imagination, one could begin to conceive whole areas of society by the manners. That's a lifework. After all . . . it takes a life to know how a third or a half or even a fraction of the country works, socially speaking. But through others' manners you can imagine projections into what these people's lives are really like. It enlivens literature. I think the rich appreciation of literature is difficult without having some sense of the style of the people who go through the books. In that sense the professors I tend to remember are not necessarily the ones I studied with, but the ones who had manners that were memorable. I never took a course with F.O. Matthiessen, but I heard him give a few lectures, and they were memorable because there was something in his manner that was tragic. He had one of the most grave and dignified manners.

How about students? Any friends that particularly influenced you?
Thirty or forty or fifty, but I think just to name them would distort the reality of it. We influenced each other a lot.

As I think of it, meeting Bowden Broadwater was an extraordinary experience. Because Bowden had more style than anyone I'd ever met. He dominated the *Advocate,* his personality. When I came on as a sophomore, I think he was then a junior or a senior—he was Pegasus and he had high style. I remember when I read *Brideshead Revisited,* I kept clucking as I read it. It wasn't that Bowden looked in any way like Sebastian Flyte or that we were close friends. On the contrary, we were on opposite sides. There were two factions.

Would you say that was a high point of your Harvard years?
Oh, yes. The *Advocate* was probably what I enjoyed most about Harvard. I think it comes through in that article I wrote for *Esquire.*

What was your worst experience at Harvard?
There wasn't anything terribly onerous, nothing that makes me writhe with anger. There were a few silly experiences. Mostly my first year. Going up to Harvard, I managed to go over all the literature that was sent to us. Phillips Brooks House sent something that said when you get here, please drop in and visit us. Somehow I had the idea that the first thing you did when you got to Harvard, before you even went looking for your dorm, was to go to the Phillips Brooks House. As I was driving up with my future roommate, Martin Lubin, and his father, I said when we get there, we've got to find the Phillips Brooks House. We were looking at the map of the Yard, and I directed the car through traffic, and I went in with Marty. It was deserted, of course. It was Freshman Week, a few juniors and seniors had come up to work, and there was one fellow there. He was a very

tall senior and handsome—handsome as a Princeton man—literally smoking a pipe behind a desk, and he hadn't seen anyone in two hours. I realized I had made an error. I remember looking at him and saying, "Well, we're here." It just changed his day. He had to come up out of whatever he was thinking about . . . probably something pleasant. The moment I said it, all I wanted to do was get out of there. Of course he was feeling he wasn't doing his duty, so he was pulling us in and we were pulling away. Finally, we got out and I was perspiring behind my ears. So that was an embarrassment.

Once we were trying to get into the Old Howard. And they asked us how old we were. The others all said eighteen, and I, without thinking, said seventeen, and I was sixteen then. I thought I had to lie, so I said seventeen, and the guy said you can't get in, you have to be eighteen! I'm a freshman at Harvard, here's my identity card, you've got to be eighteen to be a freshman at Harvard. The guy looked at me at the door and said: "All right, kid, go in." And so all through freshman year whenever I would be winning an argument with my roommates, they'd jump up and start waving their identity cards yelling: "I'm eighteen! You've got to be eighteen to go to Harvard!"

And probably the bitterest blow freshman year was going out for crew, and working and working at it and realizing at a certain point that far from not making the team, the coach never even looked at me. And then I realized why. Someone took me aside and told me, look, you could be good but it wouldn't matter, your arms are too short. You throw off the entire rest of the crew. That experience of working one's manful best each day at those oars and never being looked at by the coach. . . .

As you see, I just don't have memories of real unpleasantness. I doubt if there have been four less painful years of my life.

What happened that you went to Harvard an aspiring aeronautical engineer and came out heading for the Pacific and wanting to write a great American war novel?

I think really the main influence was English A, because we were given *Studs Lonigan* to read. And that turned me on my head because Studs Lonigan grew up in a much tougher environment than I did, but there was still a similarity. He talked the way my friends and I talked in Brooklyn. And I realized you could write about those kinds of experiences and that was almost endlessly exciting. Dos Passos, Hemingway, Fitzgerald I also read in my freshman year. By the time that year was over I wanted to be a writer. It just took another year before I was so certain I wanted to be a writer that I knew I'd never be an engineer.

There wasn't anything in particular that was acting on you from outside, influencing you, changing you? It was a process of self-discovery?

Yes. That is not at all an unnatural development for writers. Certain books stimulate them and make them know that they want to become writers. I did take a course, now that I think of it, with Howard Mumford Jones in American literature that meant a lot. In fact, I still remember one of his phrases. He was talking about Dreiser. Howard Mumford Jones used to talk with great bombast, and I'm not deriding it. People use bombast and it's dreadful, but he made it great. He said, "You know Dreiser was a great writer, but when it came to style, he was abominable. His style read like a streetcar wheel with one flat side. It goes KA-BLUNK, KA-BLUNK, KA-BLUNK." He'd walk up and down the classroom doing that and we'd roar. But we'd be interested in Dreiser.

When I think of Harvard I don't think of it really in terms of influences. I think of it more as a matter of nuances and moods and modes, as if everything were connected with everything else. There was a fine filigree to one's stimulation. The art of it was you couldn't trace it out afterwards. Harvard changed me profoundly, but I couldn't say this was the reason or that was the reason. It was all of it.

And after you got out of Harvard?

I went into the Army nine months after I graduated. I think my draft card fell to the back of a file. There is no explanation for it because I should have been drafted after two months. And I didn't go to the draft board to ask because I was working on a novel and kept hoping that I'd have that much more time to finish it.

You mean Transit to Narcissus?

Yes. That got written in the nine months before I went into the Army. But then there were two years in the Army and that was a great change. And so was the success of *The Naked and the Dead*. In effect I encountered three sizable shocks during a period from 1939 to 1949. In those ten years my life was transplanted three times. It was really not a shock of brutality or tragedy. There was nothing designedly cruel about it. It was the kind of shock that a plant would feel if lifted up from one bed and put into another.

Are there things that you are aware of that happened to you that would help explain the dramatic change from your studious, disciplined boyhood self to what, starting in the early and mid Fifties, is your infamous self, the "General Marijuana," the renegade, the ranting critic of American institutions—that self?

We're getting into questions now that I can't answer short of writing a novel. To talk about it in an interview wouldn't work. It would just be confessional. I think the change that took place around '53, '54, '55 was so drastic and so thoroughgoing that we'd really have to pursue it to all the roots I have. Not only the biographical roots, but even, if you will, the karmic roots. I'm a great believer in karma. I do believe that we're not here just one time, and I don't have any highly organized theology behind that—it's just a passing conviction that keeps returning. Karma tends to make more sense than a world conceived without it, because when you think of the incredible elaborations that go into any one human being, it does seem wasteful of the cosmos to send us out just once to learn all those things, and then molder forever in the weeds. It doesn't make as much sense as the idea that we are part of some continual process that uses us over and over again, and indeed uses the universe over and over again. There is some sort of divine collaboration going on. So in that sense, since I believe in it and for me it's psychologically true, it's hard to give an explanation. But if I were to give one, the roots are also karmic. There are arguments that can't be accounted for by one life.

Did the 1949-50 screenwriter period produce shocks that caused change also?

We're giving a picture here of someone who is not terribly adaptable. My father was a terribly fussy, punctilious man. A marvelous man. A lot more of a gentleman than his son turned out to be. I remember one point when he was unemployed during the Depression and looking for work. He went out every day wearing spats in the heart of the Depression. He had marvelous manners—he came from South Africa, was very English as only a South African

can be. I think that probably some of his rigidity is in me. That's why each of these occasions came as a great shock.

Hollywood must have made a pretty big impact, because you were writing Barbary Shore *there and later* The Deer Park, *and in those books your political vision seems to change. What was it about Hollywood?*

Well, it wasn't Hollywood as such. I'm not one of the champions of Los Angeles. It's not a place I'd enjoy living that much. I suppose there are two recurring subjects in my life that just fascinate me over and over again. One of them is what we've already discussed, the establishment. The other is identity. And movies fascinate me inordinately because the question of identity is so vivid in them. Movie stars fascinate me. Their lives are so unlike anyone else's. You could almost postulate they come from another planet. The way of life of the movie star speaks of another order of existence. The lack of connection between a movie star's life and our lives is greater than the points of view we have in common.

Does that work into The Deer Park *at all?*

In *The Deer Park* I'm just beginning to contemplate the problem. Think of the character Lulu Meyers, the movie star. She's my first attempt to deal with that question. Of course I go at it hammer and tongs with Marilyn Monroe. But my Egyptian novel is also a study of identity. You see, I think there have been periods in history when no one has contemplated the problem of identity. Because we weren't necessarily far enough removed from the animals. We reacted to things that impinged upon us in the way a beast does. We fled, we attacked, we ate, we went to sleep. I think generations went by of that sort—and then there were periods where no question was more critical to anyone alive. Certainly in my early years at Harvard the question of my identity was paramount. The most interesting question to many of us in those days was, what do you really think of me. I remember once having a long talk with my roommate Marty Lubin, and I primed him—I wanted to come back with some fish. So I talked for about half an hour, analyzed his character in great detail. He listened, and when I got all done I said, "Marty, what do you think of me?" He paused and then he said. "Ah, gee, Norm, you're just a good guy." At which point I was ready to throw him out the window from the fifth floor of Dunster.

Speaking of identity—do you think the notorious publicity, the People *side, the* Enquirer *side of your identity has hurt the public or critical acceptance of your work?*

Well, it certainly hasn't done it any good. . . . I do believe that when people buy a hardcover book these days, to a slight extent it's a sacramental act. Very often the price of the book is such that people are making a choice between that or getting something else. To be crude about it, between the book or getting the baby a pair of new shoes. So you have to respect the author. If the author is somehow unsavory—and I don't see how anyone could run through People five times and not be wholly unsavory—then they may not buy your book. And there's a crude notion that if you get a lot of publicity, you sell books. Nothing could be more untrue. The authors who sell well, that is the good authors who sell well, get very little personal publicity. We don't read much about Saul Bellow, John Updike. We didn't used to read much about John Cheever. . . . But my image can't be changed. So I've just said the hell with it. I'll go ahead and do what I want to do. I don't think there is any way I could change that media point of view about me because of the mechanics of the media. When they run a story about somebody, they go to the clips. There's no way I'm going to get those clips out of all the media organs.

Let's talk about artistic identity. I see an apparent change toward more self-effacement in your writing, in narrative technique, in the last five years. Do you see a new maturity in your writing?

Maturity comes of its own accord. You don't ever say to yourself, well, now I'm going to be more mature. You get older, so your point of view shifts and compromise takes on more luster. A fixed point of view begins to seem harsh. The result is a greater maturity in the writing. But I may well go back to writing in the first person. I don't have any feeling about it as such. I just don't like to be bored when I'm writing. I often think by now I have much in common with a dentist who's been working for forty years. I'm sure he looks for a new way to make a hole in a tooth. Because otherwise he'd go mad.

It's interesting that the two books that you got the Pulitzer for, Armies *and* Executioner's Song, *are two extremes—the presentation*

*of the self on the one hand, and the reduction of self on the other. So
the reaction has been positive to either side of your artistic identity.*

Well, I think they are also two of the best books I've written. If I
had five favorite books those would be two of them. I don't think
there was any larger point of view in the choice of those two. I think it
just happened that *The Armies of the Night* was a pretty good book,
and it came along in a year when let's say the Pulitzer Committee
was sympathetic to that sort of book. *The Executioner's Song,* in its
period, probably, well . . . that sentence concludes itself.

*In Joseph McElroy's writing class at Columbia, you were talking
about* Why Are We In Vietnam? *and you said that if there are any
forces in the cosmos that "step in and give a writer a helping hand, I
got it right there." Do you find there are such moments of
inspiration?*

I can lay out a speculation for you.

All right, lay out a speculation.

If a god or a devil or some demiurge is looking for a writer or has
need of one . . . or an angel or an ogre or whatever . . . if there's
anything up there or out there or down there that is looking for an
agent to express its notion of things, then, of course, why wouldn't
they visit us in our sleep? Why wouldn't we serve as a transmission
belt? Just in the same sense, although this is gross, that a coach might
look for a wide receiver who really has great speed of foot because he
has designed some very long passes via a quarterback with a
particularly powerful arm. So it might be that your own abilities
would be one of the factors behind the ogre's choice of you. That's a
possibility. The only book I truly felt that on was *Why Are We in
Vietnam?*

Did it play any role at all in the Egyptian book?

No, that was just hard work, every step of the way.

*Do you have any desire at this point in your life to nurture another
side of yourself?*

If my eyes hold up, I think I would like to start reading seriously
again. There have been years when I've had a great deal of eyestrain
and I couldn't read as much as I wanted to. And then there were
years when I didn't feel like reading. I was too unsettled to read. I

think twenty years have gone by where I haven't been reading as much as I've wanted to read.

Do you see any young writers coming up that you admire? Any who might take the place you've talked about so many times, and maybe at one time tried to fill yourself, as "the champ"?

I have a confession to make. In the course of not reading enough in the last twenty years, I've not read the young writers. I've read them hardly at all. I remember when I came along, I thought, oh boy, now I'll be able to talk to Hemingway and Dos Passos, Farrell, all the writers I care about. They'll read my book and we'll be able to talk about it. My dreams will be realized. But I never met Dos Passos or Hemingway. I met Farrell once for lunch. I never met J.P. Marquand or Steinbeck. I sent Hemingway *The Deer Park* but it came back marked "Addressee unknown." I always felt he gave it to somebody at the post office to stamp it that way and send it back. It seemed to me that would be his sense of humor. At any rate I corresponded with Hemingway ten years after *The Naked and the Dead* came out.

At the time I was shocked that older authors didn't read younger authors. And I didn't understand it. I was furious. And I'm sure young authors feel that way now. You know—why doesn't Mailer read me? I grew up reading him and he influenced me in part and he owes it to me to read me. Why doesn't he? The reason is simple. I know now why they weren't reading me, and I know that because I don't read the young authors. One gets locked into one's own continuing concerns. I haven't used any prize-fighting images up till now, so I guess I had better use one. Whether you're fighting for the championship or not, you're fighting a fifteen-round fight. And by the time you reach your sixties, you feel as if you're in the twelfth round and you're battered. I don't say this self-pityingly—you're just not as good as you used to be in an awful lot of ways. . . . And your powers to protect yourself from distraction are much smaller. You really have to concentrate on those last few rounds. And so there's much less loose generosity in you. . . . You tend to isolate yourself because the odds that a young writer would come along and write something that can teach you something is not likely, although it might delight you, and you might say, gee, what talent. . . .

I've seen young writers that I think are good, some are damn good, and there seems to be more and more felicity all the time. Each year there seem to be more people who can really write stunning prose. And technique gets more and more elaborated. But I can't think offhand of any young writers who are philosophically disturbing at this point.

Czeslaw Milosz, in Bells of Winter, *writes about poetic inspiration as if the poet were a living room with its doors wide open, visitors come and go—all he can hope for is that the visitors are forces of good rather than evil.*

I think to the degree that you dare the prevailing winds you set yourself up for some incredible psychic gusts.

It may be that part of remaining a writer is to learn how to expose yourself less and less over the years and ring yourself around more and more with various protections. The price of that, of course, is that inspiration enters the door much less often. But at the same time you can carry out your projects. It seems to me that if there is any lesson I can draw from my working, it is that it has taken me close to forty years to learn how to write long books. *The Naked and the Dead* came early and that was to a certain extent a gift. I was a simple young man and I didn't understand the difficulties. If I had known the difficulties, I wouldn't have gotten into it. It would have taken me ten years.

You said in 1981 that things are sinister but not in the way you used to think they were sinister. What did you mean by that?

In the Sixties I used to see it as the FBI, the CIA being sinister. I had a sort of paranoid vision of the invisible government. Now I suppose it has moved over to the idea that such things as television and plastics are probably doing us much more harm, and getting us much closer to totalitarianism than the FBI or the CIA ever would.

What's the force behind that?

Well, there you get into dreamland, don't you? I sometimes think that there is a malign force loose in the universe that is the social equivalent of cancer, and it's plastic. It infiltrates everything. It's metastasis. It gets into every single pore of productive life. I mean there won't be anything that isn't made of plastic before long. They'll be paving the roads with plastic before they're done. Our bodies, our skeletons, will be replaced with plastic. It's some absolute vanity. It's

human vanity that I might assume is devil inspired, but it doesn't
have to be. It could come right out of man . . .

On the one hand we, all of us, consciously or unconsciously,
contain an adoration of the universe. We also have this great animus
toward the universe. It's larger than we are and that's intolerable to
us. The ego, or the twentieth-century manifestation of it, flames up in
us. We have to do something to that universe. We have to *score* it.
We have to literally score on it, and plastic is a wonderful way to do
that because we create something that the universe can't digest. We
literally make these carbon chains, these protein chains, that are put
together in a way that they just won't break down—
"nonbiodegradable"—that marvelous little new word.

The artifacts of this civilization will go on forever.
They'll go on forever, some of us hope and some of us don't hope.
But those who do are capturing the world. You say, well, where does
it all come from? What's the origin of it? And then, of course, one's
past philosophy runs out in outer speculation . . .

But I do think that plastic tends to deaden people. It deadens their
nerve ends. And when the nerve ends are dead, the mind is much
more susceptible to manipulation. Because, finally, the senses are
always our objective correction against having our minds manipulated
too far in a direction that's not natural.

So plastic becomes an effect as well as a cause?
Well, put it this way. If you wanted to convince someone of
something that would be very hard for him to swallow, wouldn't it be
a good idea to half anesthetize him first? And plastic does that. It just
deadens us. Now we get it from infancy on. I think one of the reasons
cocaine is so widespread now is that people's nerve ends are so
deadened they need something to absolutely jack up those nerve
ends. So that's one thing. And of course television is another. It's as if
a great dragon called entropy has come into aesthetics. And
television is the final reduction of all art into fifteen-minute slugs of
pap. The natural tendency of television is to reduce all entertainment
to the level of a commercial. When the commercial is as interesting as
the television, then you've got perfect television . . .

*Robert Frost once said there was something immodest in a man
who believes that he is about to go down—or that we are about to go
down—before the worst forces ever marshaled against us in the*

universe. In your work the point seems to be that we may very well be going down before just such forces.

Well, I never said that Robert Frost was going to approve of me.

But do you think we may be at such a crisis?

I don't think I'm the only one who thinks that. An awful lot of people are worried. . . . The world is now going through an apocalyptic time—I think the Eighties are going to be an incredible decade, with more surrealistic, fantastic, incredible change even than in the Sixties. . . . There are certainly signs that we are in a period that's not like other periods. One of them, and I think this is incredible, is that in the last twenty or certainly the last ten years, we've come to a point in this country where people no longer believe that the president knows the answers. I think part of Reagan's vast popularity in the media is because he's probably the most relaxed president we've had since Lord knows when. Maybe there was never a president as relaxed as Ronald Reagan. So people feel, well, he seems secure. Maybe he does know the answers. You know there's nothing more disconcerting to the average American than the thought that the president doesn't know the answers, doesn't really know where we're going.

Maybe that's why he's so relaxed, because he knows he doesn't know.

That could well be. Maybe you've come up with the first explanation of Ronald Reagan. That makes sense. It makes him rather a nice man. There is this humility before the imponderables that is a mark of grace.

Let's turn to the work you've been doing recently—your Egyptian novel, Ancient Evenings. *Do you feel good about the completed work at this point? You announced the book as early as '72, in* Existential Errands, *so it's been a long, probably difficult road.*

If I say I feel good about it, it's like saying my child is wonderful. It's not seemly. I will say it's the most ambitious book I ever worked on. It's by far the most unusual work I've done, and it's out of category. I can't think of any other novel that's remotely like it. . . . My hope is that it's very good indeed. But how good I don't have a clue. I think when it comes out, it will be the usual story. I hope it will get some wonderful reviews, and I'm certain it will get some terrible reviews.

If I were an unknown author, the book could be read a little more easily. But the trouble is everybody is going to be reading it and saying, "How the devil does Norman Mailer get himself up to start writing about Egyptian pharaohs? I mean that's really going too far." But it has nothing to do with the fact that that's my name. I'm an author. I have a right to imagine a work, and to write a work of the imagination. If I had any name but my own, people could read the book without too much suffering.

If it is indeed good in the artistic sense, maybe it would not have been published. It's not a blockbuster, a bestseller sort of book.
I certainly think it's good enough that no matter who had written it, it would have been published. And I think it's good enough that no matter who had written it, it would have received attention. Because if you spend ten years writing a book it should be good. Spending ten years on a book is like being married to someone for ten years. You wouldn't want to say at the end of those ten years that half of the time was worthless.

There were a lot of expectations, and at times earlier on you seemed to feed those expectations—that this would be your masterpiece. If that was ever a goal, did the process of writing the book change the goal?
Well, it deepened. It started as an excursion into Egypt. I was going to dip into Egypt for a chapter or two, then get out, move on to Greece and Rome, then the Middle Ages. I was thinking of sort of a picaresque novel. That was in the first half year of working on it. But I began to realize at the end of that half year that I was in Egypt for a long haul. So I started studying, and I've learned about ancient Egypt these ten years.

Was there any fear of the risk? You've used the word risk yourself several times.
Well, there is always fear in writing a book. If I had tried to write the book in a year, the fear would have been so great it couldn't have been written. But over ten years, you can carry the fear. *Writing* a book is the fear. That's why there are many more people who can write well than who do.

And there are other reasons for it. Some people can't take the meanness of the occupation. There's nothing very attractive about going into a room by yourself every day and looking at a piece of paper and making scratch marks on it. Doing that day after day, year after year, decade after decade, is punishing through the very monotony of the physical process. . . . Just the act of writing as a physical act is less interesting than painting. I never felt sorry for painters. I feel sorry for writers.

Obviously the emoluments of a profession and the spiritual satisfactions are quite different from the mean daily details of the work. In that mean sense, writing is not a comfortable or attractive profession day to day. Then you add to it the fear. There is always fear in writing. Most people take pride in the fears they can endure. It's obvious that you can't be a professional writer for as many years as I have been without taking a certain pride that I can endure those fears. I would say that writing is like all occupations that have some real element of risk. In the case of a writer the risk is to his ego. You really don't want to write a book in which you're not taking some risk . . . especially a long book. You can write a book quickly in two months, six months, or a year in which the risks are minimal. But to do a long book, you would want to take risks. Why not? How dignify it if large risks aren't being taken? And I will say I've taken more risks with the Egyptian novel than any book I've ever written. It's the most, dare I say it, audacious of the books I've done.

You've said all we can ever know is whether we have worked as hard as we can. Do you believe you've done that on this book?

Yes. I think I've used up every bit of inspiration I've had on this book. If the book is not good enough, then I'm not good enough. I feel that kind of peace about it.

Did it take you places you have never been before? Creating new ideas?

Yes. It also gave me an understanding of certain things. I think people are going to be immensely confused by the book. They are going to say, why did Mailer write it? What is he saying that means something to him? The man we know. What is in this?

Well, I think I've come to an understanding of the wealthy I've never had before, dealing with Egypt, it's gold, and its pharaohs. . . . There's that marvelous remark of Fitzgerald's that the rich are not like you and me, and Hemingway's answer, which was much applauded, but which I've always thought churlish, you know, yeah, they have more money, and everybody roars like crazy. The fact of the matter is Fitzgerald was trying to say something, and Hemingway was trying to keep him from saying it. The very rich are not like you and me. Just as movie stars are not like you and me. In fact the very rich and movie stars have much in common. They no longer have a trustworthy relation to the society around them. In the most umbilical sense, they can't trust anyone.

That's a good partial answer to my next question. Why Egypt? You've mentioned elsewhere that the beginning of scientific technique is a perversion of primitive magic, and you've also said that we went astray when we separated ourselves from the "dire discipline of magic," which might enable us to communicate with the cosmos. Is Egypt your subject because it represents a turning point from primitive dread, from magic, toward technology and the abuses of technology?

I don't know enough about history to be able to answer that, and I don't know if that's the point. I don't have a clue. Egypt was one of the places—I think it was definitely one of the places where magic was being converted into social equivalence, in effect used as an exchange.

That's what interested you, at least in part?

What interested me was that I made one assumption that certain people will argue with and others will find natural. The assumption is that the Egyptians had minds that are easily as complex and interesting as our minds. They had an intellectual discipline that was highly unscientific from our point of view. But I suspect no farther off the mark than ours. Now these are assumptions. So the book has an immense preoccupation with magic as such. I tend to end up writing the best novel on subjects no other good writer has ever written about. I can name a number of subjects that I've written the best work on, where there's no competition, subjects that no other writer would tackle. For instance, I'd say I've written the best biography of a movie star that's ever been written—*Marilyn*. Again there's no competition. I've written the best book about a heavyweight prize fighter that's ever been written, *The Fight*. Again, no competition. Now I think I've written the best novel about magic that's ever been written. But where are the others who have been writing about it? I don't know of a serious writer who's devoted himself to writing about magic. I mean, Aleister Crowley has written a novel about magic. Dion Fortune has written about magic. Other people have written magical novels, but they are not writers who are highly regarded. But I will say once again, that I've taken a field—I'm a bully—where there's no competition.

Are you writing about the rich? What we know of Egypt is mostly the testament of the rich, isn't it?
Yes. Of course, that's always your problem. There are very few characters in the novel who are not well born. Most of them are nobles of the highest rank.

Do you think that these people whom you are writing about, that in some way God's will was not kept from them? That they had a sense of what God's will was? Unlike as you've said, we may have lost touch with whatever God's will might be?
One has to keep reminding oneself that this is before the Judeo-Christian era. We're dealing with pagans. The pagan mind is fascinating, but I found while I was writing the book that when I went through it I had to keep making certain that there wasn't a single Judeo-Christian idea in it. Actually I think the Egyptians had a tremendous influence over the Hebrews. Much of the Old Testament you find in Egyptian prayers. Some of it's startling. The early pages of Genesis, the first page of Genesis could be taken from certain prayers to Ammon and the ways in which he created the universe.

Is it safe to look at Hebrew culture as a competing minor culture at the time?
It wasn't even quite a minor culture at the time. They were still a race of tribes and barbarians. They weren't taken seriously. Not at this period. Later they were. This is 1100 B.C. In fact, Moses appears in my book for about a page. He's seen as some sort of minor guerrilla who kills some Egyptian guards, and takes the Hebrews to a certain town with him across the desert to escape. The idea is to immerse yourself in another point of view when you are writing. Because when you do a lot of things come to you.

You said you wished nothing in the book to be contemporary. In what sense is there a connection between ancient Egypt and today? In other words, what's in it for modern readers?
Well, I've failed if we start reading the book that way. And I think that's going to be one of the difficulties for people, because most historical novels perform a service or pretend to teach us something

about today. And I will have failed if that's the way people react to my book.

The attraction then is not that there is a connection—the attraction is the lack of connection?

The lack of connection. I want people to realize, my God, there are wholly different points of view that can be as interesting as our own. And as thoroughgoing as our own. In other words, probably a social evening in Egypt—and this is one of the reasons I ended up calling the book *Ancient Evenings*—in that period three thousand years ago was as interesting as an evening in New York today. Not more interesting, necessarily, but as interesting . . . for altogether different reasons.

Not much happens in the sense of action, I believe you've said, in the sense of a typical wide-canvas, panoramic, historical novel.

Well, no, a lot does happen, but it doesn't happen immediately. The book certainly has the most complete architecture of any book I've written. It's in seven parts. Each of its parts, I would say, has a separate existence. The book continues from part to part, most definitely. But the nature of the book discloses itself part by part. When you've read part one and part two, you won't have any clue at all what part six and seven are going to be like. It's as if the book moves in a spiral.

You've said you're planning a trilogy. Will the other books be ten-year projects?

My hope is to do the next two books in three or four years each. If they each take ten years, I'd be celebrating my eightieth birthday.

My last question—people criticize you for presenting your existence, your life, your work, in a way that seems you want other people to believe as you do or be like you or live like you. How do you respond to that criticism?

I think I'm truly misunderstood there. I'm right and I'm wrong so often, so many times of the day, that I have no interest in having people think the way I think. What I'm interested in is that however people think they get better at it. That's what's important about one's work. In the work of good authors, if a book is good enough, you cannot predict how people are going to react to it. You shouldn't be able to. If it's good enough, it means it's not manipulative. If it's not

manipulative, everybody sort of goes off in a different direction. One
of my own favorite remarks is that it's not that I'm for the cops and
not that I'm for the crooks, but that I'm for the cops getting better
and the crooks getting better. I have a notion of society as an oven
where some fabulous dishes are being cooked, and in order for the
banquet to take place, every ingredient has to be in it.

I don't think it's an accident that I'm a novelist. Novelists have a
wicked point of view—wicked as opposed to evil. They are interested
in upping the ante. They're interested in more happening, not less.
One of the reasons that I detest television is that it reduces our
possibilities. Television was welcomed as something that would help
us understand the world. But I think, quite the contrary, it takes away
from us any possibility of ever comprehending the world because it
deadens our senses and because it gives us false notions, periodically,
systematically, and intensively.

*So presenting your ideas with force is a way of saying these are my
beliefs and this is my life and they are meant to stimulate you into
whatever it is that will be your ideas and your life.*

Yes. Once Ralph Ellison and I were out in Iowa together many
years ago, back in 1959, and we worked like crazy. We had a lively
audience, and the symposium went on for three or four days, for
Esquire. At the end of it, it suddenly seemed a little absurd to me that
we really worked that hard, got in so many arguments with students,
talked back and forth, and even argued with each other as lively as
hell. But then when it was over, there was a little bit of sadness that
something that had been truly exceptional was over. So I said to him,
"Why the hell did we do it?" He said, "Ah, shit, man, we're
expendable." I've always loved that remark. Because in a certain
sense one's ideas are expendable. If the best of my ideas succeed in
changing the mind of someone who's more intelligent than myself,
then that's fine. I'm a great believer in the idea that if you advance an
idea as far as you can and it's overtaken by someone who argues the
opposite of you, in effect you've improved your enemy's mind. Then
someone will come along on your side who will take your enemy's
improvement of your idea and convert it back again. I'm nothing if
I'm not a believer in the dialectic. And to that extent one does the
best one can. And that's the end of it. The thought of everyone
thinking the way I do is as bad as any other form of totalitarianism.

The Essential Mailer
Eugene Kennedy/1984

From *Sunday: The Chicago Tribune Magazine,* 9 September 1984, 23-25, 28-29. Reprinted by permission of Eugene Kennedy.

The grin carries a charge of exuberance, like that of an overdue explorer just out of the jungle savoring the hearty taste of survival after a bold and dark adventure that confirmed old hunches and delivered new knowledge of secret places. In short, Norman Mailer *looks* like a man who has just finished his twenty-third book and sixth novel, *Tough Guys Don't Dance,* and who hopes that people will enjoy reading this murder mystery set on the curled tip of Cape Cod as much as he enjoyed writing it.

"Let readers discover deeper meanings slowly, at their leisure," he says, still smiling. "I'll be happy if they find the book readable and enjoyable."

Mailer greets a neighbor as we walk down the gently curving block on which he lives in Brooklyn Heights, its brownstones inlaid with sun and quiet like fine old china cabinets. It might be Charleston afloat on summer but for Manhattan's hazy mass just across the East River.

"I always wanted," he continues easily, "to write a detective story with a hero a little braver—just a little—than thee or me. We see ourselves in the shoes of the private detective, and he usually gives a sense of confidence. People read such novels to let themselves dream of the strong side they might have had; they find it in the authoritative figure of the detective. Take that away and you're taking a big chance to test the theory that a man of average bravery will have sufficient magnetism to attract and interest the reader."

Another neighbor waves as we turn into a short, deeply shaded street. "The voice of Jake Barnes in *The Sun Also Rises* could have been that of a private eye in a detective story," he says. "Hemingway,

James Cain, and Dashiell Hammett understood that special world in which gesture has enormous importance."

Mailer pauses, sturdy as the century-old tree just beyond him, speaks softly, intensely: "One of the things that is always fascinating about violent people—about those living in crime, or the cops, is the intimacy of their relationships. They may be mortal enemies but they nevertheless have a great appreciation, a deep understanding of each other. That is the world in which gesture is so significant, and this canon of gesture is crucial to the tough-guy murder mystery."

He chuckles. "You not only dodge a bullet but you make a wry remark at the same time."

We pause outside a dry cleaning shop. "When I wrote *Ancient Evenings,* I was exploring power relationships among males, the way they seek and exercise power in relationship to each other. In this book I wanted to deal with the spectrum of male motivation leading from homosexuality to machismo. On the other side of this is socialized man. These are not altogether different kinds of personality." Mailer steps into the shop to pick up a just-pressed suit and safari jacket. "I have some things here for your son, too," the stooped merchant says. "No, no," Mailer replies genially, a father who has learned a thing or two over the years. "We'll let him take care of those himself."

Mailer speaks of Dostoyevsky as we return to his home. *Crime and Punishment* was "much more than a book about life and death and spiritual values," he contends, balancing the cleaning on his shoulder. "It was also a detective story." He continues amiably as we climb the four flights to the warning-flag-red door of his apartment: "There's a reason why writers with a literary reputation don't move to the detective novel. A detective novel depends on plot, and good plot works at the expense of characters. You cannot expect your characters to act with the uniformity of a *corps de ballet.* But the characters in the typical detective story *have* to behave for the sake of the plot."

The celebrated writer, who has won two Pulitzer Prizes as well as the National Book Award, enters the high-ceilinged apartment decorated with ship's rigging and hardware. From it one sights the humpbacked whale of Manhattan nosing into New York Harbor. "I have always been more interested in character than in plot, so I will hang onto my characters and not let them be sacrificed to plot. I wanted a murder mystery that was recognizable as such, that had characters as complex as those in non-murder books. This created a tension in writing it that was helpful to me."

While Mailer changes clothes, I step out onto his balcony. Below, graceful locust trees stand like Southern ladies rustling their dresses along a broad, picket-fenced promenade looking out at the Statue of Liberty, blurred in a web of scaffolding, and the bunched skyline of Manhattan.

"When I wrote *Ancient Evenings,*" Mailer says as he buttons his safari jacket, "I came to have a feeling for the very wealthy and their sense that real wealth and real power *do* buy you influence in the next world. Through their acquisitions in this world they are steadying their grip on eternity. That is their purpose in fortifying the family vault. No family of great wealth also has great love." He interrupts himself, chewing on a sweet distraction: "The Kennedys may be one rich and powerful family that is not devoid of love."

Mailer picks up his theme, speaking rapidly: "In *Tough Guys* I carry this theme of the rich forward. The character of Wardley is typical. He is the poor little rich boy who is hideously spoiled and perverse to the point of virtual evil. But, at the same time, there is something about him . . ." the writer's tone turns sympathetic, ". . . as if he never had a chance." It is filled with the chill of experienced appraisal as we descend the stairs. "These poor little rich boys, by the way, aren't so ineffectual. They can be terribly winsome but terribly nasty in the use of their power, too. They like to debase and humiliate others."

As we climb into the car to drive into Manhattan, he turns to the subject of the book's narrator, Timothy Madden, a writer in Provincetown, where Mailer himself has spent some part of 30 of the last 40 years, and with whose voice, manner, and existential concerns some critics have identified him. Mailer's blue eyes twinkle as he denies the similarity. "There are portentous differences between me and Madden in age, size, and background," he says. "Madden speaks for something like the collective consciousness of people who have lived through the last generation. They have certain values, not necessarily conventional ones. Madden has certain serious questions about himself. Is he a good man or not? He is sophisticated enough to know that he could be mad and not know it. He also wishes to regain his self-respect because he is ashamed of his life up until now."

A veil of shadow falls across the car as we approach the fortress-like base of the Brooklyn Bridge. "There is the question of his relationship with his full-blooded Irish father, and his striving to be honorable. And he has that Irish need to be classy."

Mailer seems delighted, playful, as I ask him about that and the half-Irish lineage of his hero. "Tim Madden," he responds enthusiastically, "is something else. He has the machismo of the sensitive Irishman. I made him half-Irish for comfort. I didn't want to project myself across the universe to enter the Irish mind! Besides, the New York Irish are not so Irish anymore. They have become, in later generations, more cosmopolitan. I made Tim that kind of Irishman. The pure ethnic is his father, Dougie Madden. I wanted him to be a real Irishman marked by that special kind of probity that they can possess along with powerful, murderous emotions."

The car rumbles over temporary planking just below the main thrust of the hundred-year-old bridge. "A prime characteristic of this kind of Irishman is loyalty. They are truly loyal to the point that they could be killed because of it. It is a death loyalty. These Irishmen also usually have a slightly embattled relationship with the Catholic Church. And a certain strain of hypocrisy may show up, as with Dougie's having an affair with the wife of a best friend. In these Irish you find a kind of sexual Puritanism side by side with broth-of-a-boy lust."

Mailer's tone is affectionate as he continues. "That's the kind of Irish I remember from growing up in Brooklyn, those who would be half-old enough now to be my father. They were fascinating because they were so completely different from the Jews. The Jews are so completely family-oriented, whereas many of these Irish tended to be solitary and to be heavy drinkers. We also had a sense of not being as tough as the Irish. . . ."

Manhattan, like a science-fiction monster waiting to swallow us, suddenly fills the frame of the bridge's west towers.

"There's a certain tightness about the Irish in some aspects," Mailer says, "and yet a great generosity about them in others. In the book you see it in the father's niggardly relationship to his son. But it's a dignified kind of meanness because being classy is his objective. I mean the kind of show of class you see in the Irishman who only has $10 in his pocket, has mouths to feed and bills to pay at home, and yet buys a round of drinks for everybody at the bar. . . ."

Mailer's massive brow crinkles in concentration below an aureole of silver hair as curly as wood shavings. "James Farrell reacted against that kind of Irish in his Studs Lonigan books. His early work is a repudiation of the kind of Irishman who could be a fool wasting the lives of those around him." He gestures as he continues animatedly. "Now, in an age in which personalities have begun to disappear and everybody is becoming like everybody else, in this special triumph of the age of plastic, these rock-ribbed kind of characters give us nourishment. They are like a great reef in the sea which, in the fog, is terribly feared. In a bad storm, however, that same reef gives you something to hold on to and protects you. A modest, indecisive man, on the other hand, is a negative energy center. Such a person takes something away from life."

He smiles, nods agreeably as I tell him of St. Thomas Aquinas' preference for a proud man over a pusillanimous man because the former will at least do something while the other may end up not doing anything at all. "Precisely," he adds, his profile outlined against New York's collection of cluttered towers as we head north along the East Side Drive.

"Farrell," he continues, "was an immense influence on me." *The Naked and the Dead* owes much to him, as does *The Executioner's Song*. Debts to authors is a notion difficult to explain. It resembles the way in which one painter can show another painter a direction, as Picasso did, showing other artists ways they might pursue even if he himself did not. Farrell showed me what you could do with the ordinary simple conditions of people's lives. I wondered if I could write *The Executioner's Song* in a simple, flat style. And because Farrell had done that already, I felt relieved about doing it.

"Nelson Algren was more popular in that he anticipated the present, whereas Farrell looked back at the past. In Algren you find the gestures and the gamesmanship, the zaniness and fun of the 1960s, '70s, and '80s. His world is one of practical jokes, of some people destroyed for too little, and of others rewarded for too little, and Algren deals with the absurdity and irony of it all. Farrell, on the other hand, was concerned with the measure of life. Algren, incidentally, didn't like Farrell and frequently criticized him."

We turn into a side street clogged with traffic. Mailer seems oblivious to the beeping horns, the riot of shouts, and the groan of construction equipment. "Mike Royko, one of the very best columnists in the country, catches the flavor of Algren's Chicago. They both reject delicacy, but they do so with great delicacy." He turns with a grin. "City life produces—I believe it is a phenomenon of the modern city—caustic wit. It is one of the essences of a city. If you lived in the country, this kind of wit would kill you. In New York and Chicago, it is a tonic. This wit serves as a bridge. It is a reaction to all these people around us. Once you've expressed the bottom line of caustic wit, you are able to like them and to get along in their midst."

Mailer laughs as I ask him how he would compare Irishmen as different as John F. Kennedy and Ronald Reagan. "It's really hard to compare them. You could see that Kennedy was Irish. And Ivy League as well. You could feel the Irishness in him and in his family. They were finely tuned representatives of the upper-class American Irish. With Reagan, it's hard to know whether he looked on himself as Irish earlier in life. Did he know that he was Irish before he was elected President and started telling stories with Tip O'Neill?"

He chuckles again as we climb out of the car into the glaring heat of 3d Avenue. "Reagan has Irish wit, the best of any President since Kennedy. He has the kind of wit that would make him a great host on a late-night TV show." He smiles at a pleasing notion. "He could be looked on as a right-wing Johnny Carson. . . ."

Mailer moves through the crowds into the cool fastness of his publisher's building lobby, nodding and speaking briefly with people who greet him, and then returns to a comparison of America's public Irishmen. "Jack Kennedy's personality was more formed, I think, than his brother Bobby's. Jack was cool, detached, witty. Bobby was trying on personalities. You could meet different Bobbies. There was the compassionate Bobby, the tough Bobby, Bobby the non-stop talker. Buried in Bobby was something of an artist. That's why he was trying on these different personalities. An artist, but *buried*, as I say, inside him. . . ."

The elevator doors open, and we walk through the maze of partitioned cubicles that leads to the editor's office, in which he will autograph 1,000 copies of *Tough Guys Don't Dance*. He smiles, raises a pen above the first opened volume. "You know, some books, like people, make you feel good, the way even a con man can. You're actually glad to see him come along. *Tough Guys* is one of my favorites. It may or may not be one of my best books, but I enjoy picking it up and reading it."

Mailer good-naturedly refuses to speak about his next book. "Bad luck to talk about it. I would just say that there are a couple of orphans in my unconscious." Here is the artist in an Irish mood of his own, standing guard over his own creative energies, as charming in changing the subject as a poet nursing his secret at midnight in a Dublin pub.

"Chicago, of course, is a very feisty city," he continues. "I have always loved it. I sort of like New Orleans, and I have a special feeling for Boston, where I went to school, and I also love San Francisco.

"But if I lived in some other city, it would be Chicago. I like its guttiness. It's like Brooklyn."

He signs his name, looks up with a smile that would give grace to a leprechaun. "If Chicagoans realize how deeply people feel about Brooklyn, they'll understand what a truly great compliment that is!"

Mailer on Mailer
Jennifer L. Farbar/1986

From *Esquire*, 105 (June 1986), 238, 240, 243-44, 247-49.
Reprinted with permission from *Esquire*. Copyright © 1986 by
Jennifer L. Farbar.

There are all the images: Mailer at the podium, Mailer at the
Pentagon, Mailer on screen, in jail, in bed. His writing is hard to
separate from the wild topography of his life. He has seen to that. For
nearly forty years, his career has blended literary celebration and
cultural celebrity. But the real power of Mailer has been his mind.
Without it, his search for sensation would have been not only
unknown, but occasionally unforgivable. It is Mailer's ideas that have
turned his exploits into statements—ideas about strength, sex, race,
war, crime, death—and perhaps most of all, his idea of himself:
belligerent prophet, bad boy, man's man. Through the campaigns,
the debates, the wives, the lectures, the postures—even the poems—
the critical Mailer idea has been that in speaking, he spoke for most
men. Remarkably, he usually did. Mailer said what we thought before
we had time, or talent, to see it ourselves. As a result, he could be
renounced and disputed, but never entirely dismissed. Since 1948,
he has given a voice to our worst and best selves, insisting the two
are often the same.

Mailer's career began with the kind of success that most writers just
imagine. At twenty-five, he published *The Naked and the Dead*, an
instant best seller that has been called the finest novel to come out of
World War II. The book was a stunning exploration of the
contradictions of power: its greatness in strong men, its corruption in
strong institutions. To later generations, those themes were the heart
of pacifism. In 1948, they were new. War, at that time, had just been
transformed into victory, and while other writers saw victory as a
justification of violence, Mailer saw violence as a justification for

dread. His view touched a broad, if tacit, fear of war with Russia. He became a kind of hero—with his own tough act to follow.

By the time the hype had died down, Mailer found himself in a decade far less vivid than the Forties. America had settled into a Cold War and a colder conscience. Mailer's instinct was to keep things hot. In *Barbary Shore* (1951), he wrote about socialism; in *The Deer Park* (1955), he wrote about sex and Hollywood. Neither novel was the hit he wanted; both had problems with publishers. But Mailer responded by showing that he had a genius for self-preservation. In a sense, that genius was conflict: finding or making a villain and a hero. Often the hero would be himself, and thus the enfant terrible was born.

The Fifties was Mailer's time to wail: grass, Seconal, alcohol, jazz, Harlem, sex, four-letter words. The Establishment was his villain; its rejection of him was oppression, and Mailer sensed—again correctly—that he wasn't its only victim. In 1955, he helped found *The Village Voice*, where he wrote an intentionally provocative column about, among other things, censorship, obscenity, Wilhelm Reich, Hip, and the limited intelligence of his readers. At the same time, Mailer was living a bohemian life, nurturing a fascination with what his body and his friends could take. The result—apart from hostility, outrage, and the charge that he was wasting his talent—was the brilliantly prophetic essay "The White Negro." It was a synthesis of a hundred untapped feelings that he'd found in himself and sensed were everywhere. "The White Negro" described the hipster as an American existentialist who responded to the threat of annihilation (both atomic and cultural) by becoming a modern outlaw. The essay introduced subjects that the Sixties counterculture would later drive into the ground: rebellion, race, mysticism, sex. But in 1957, Mailer had walked up to a mirror and seen an entire generation where there might have been one man.

Critics still wondered what had happened to his fiction. But with the exception of some poems and two novels (*An American Dream* and *Why Are We in Vietnam?*) Mailer used the Sixties to develop his reporting. In 1960, he covered the Democratic Convention for *Esquire,* creating a hero of JFK, another kind of outlaw. In his piece for *Esquire* on the Patterson-Liston fight, he did much the same for Floyd Patterson, and he showed a growing talent for discovering metaphor. Mailer was also exploring a different kind of reporting.

New Journalism is today about as new as modern art is modern, but putting oneself in the story was almost unheard of twenty years ago. That approach reached its height in 1968 with *The Armies of the Night*, Mailer's autobiographical account of the march on the Pentagon, a distillation of the country in a single, moving event. The book captured the fear and, again, the conflict of the Sixties—the hero was rebellion, and the villain Washington. It won him the National Book Award and the first of two Pulitzer Prizes. After three divorces, two mayoral bids, two arrests, and countless examples of how he'd avoided "the totalitarianism of the totally pleasant," Mailer was suddenly a hero.

It didn't last long. When, in 1970, he published a fifty-thousand-word piece in *Harper's* in response to attacks from the women's movement, Mailer was asking for it. "The Prisoner of Sex" was as outrageous to most women as his *Voice* columns had been to most readers. But a lot of men cheered him, finding a new model for macho. In March 1971, Mailer stood up in Town Hall, baiting and debating Germaine Greer and other feminists. He spoke of women's biological imperative to have children, he suggested that ignoring it changed the natural order of things, he condemned homosexuals for much the same reason—and he grinned most of the time. Gore Vidal was among the many critics of the book, and the two appeared together on *The Dick Cavett Show*. They hashed out many of the issues that had pervaded Mailer's career, and Vidal said: "What I detest in you . . . [is] your violence, your love of murder, your celebration of rage, of hate."

All that was the subject of *The Executioner's Song*, Mailer's 1979 "true-life novel" about Gary Gilmore. Addressing questions of cause and karma, it embodied the ethical confusion of the Seventies, just as *The Armies of the Night* had caught the convictions of the Sixties. The book won Mailer a second Pulitzer Prize and terrific reviews. Again, he had seen the future enough to find America's passion— even when it seemed that the passion had disappeared. As Wilfrid Sheed once put it: "So goes Mailer, so goes the nation. This is the form his genius takes."

Some things remain the same. When his novel *Ancient Evenings* was panned in 1983, Mailer put together an ad that quoted the worst reviews, just as he'd done for *The Deer Park* almost thirty years before. When Mailer spoke as PEN's president this year, he quoted at length, from "The White Negro," then faced off again with Gore Vidal.

Some things remain the same. But what has changed in Mailer's mind? Forty years after the war that he recounted in his first book, *Esquire* asked Norman Mailer to reflect on his idea.

Esquire: When you wrote *The Naked and the Dead*, America was still rejoicing in its triumph in World War II. But your novel focused on a character who showed what a lust for victory at any cost could do to a man. Sergeant Croft was a pretty radical concept for those times. Where do you think a guy like him would fit into the Army today?

Mailer: Croft? Croft would probably be cashiered out of the Army as psychologically unstable. I mean, the Army now has counseling services. Don't forget, we have a peacetime Army, and they try to make it agreeable. They have to compete with TV commercials and gracious hog-living. It's "Wear a tropical shirt, have a cooler for your beer, keep a beautiful broad on the diving board." The Army is trying to give some pale reflection of that—you know, "Join the Army, come to Hawaii." They forget that Jim Jones wrote a book called *From Here to Eternity.*

Croft would probably be running dope today. Or else he'd be in the CIA, working with the contras against the Sandinistas. But they wouldn't take him in the Army. No, he'd be too intense. He'd be too much of an Army man. One of the ironies of modern-day life is you can't be too much of the thing you do, it's insanity to be the thing you're doing.

Esquire: You have a lot of theories about what modern-day life has done to men's characters. In your essay on Kennedy, you said that "the twentieth century may yet be seen as that era when civilized man and underprivileged man were melted together into mass man . . . their extremes of personality singed out of existence by the psychic fields of force the communicators would impose." Where would you say that leaves us today?

Mailer: I think it has taken place. I think MTV is an example of it. Those guys in the audience who take off their shirts at pro-football games—thinking thereby they've entered the domain of the gods— are part of this. Maybe some of them would do it *without* a TV camera on them, but the idea first came because the cameras were looking at them. So they're in the field of electronic circuits.

Esquire: Do you think that to a certain extent this field has made men less male, diminished their masculinity?

Mailer: If masculinity is individuality, it's made them less male.

Esquire: Is it?

Mailer: Yes, I think so, to a degree. I mean, it's not enough to be a *man*, to be strong, to be physical, to be macho. It's worthless to be macho unless you're individual as well. And very few are. To the degree that machismo is a predictable code, then I would say one is not complete. You may be 90 percent a man, but the last 10 percent is walled off from you. Anyway, most people, myself most certainly included, are not 90-percent macho.

Esquire: You've applied the idea of being macho, of acting like a man, to virtually every aspect of a man's life. In an interview in 1962, you said that "our best hope for no atomic war is that the complexities of political life at the summit remain complex. . . . So I say create complexities, let art deepen sophistication . . . let us try to make *them* more complex. That is a manly activity. It offers more hope for saving the world than a gaggle of pacifists and vegetarians." Obviously, you were never pro-war, but you seemed to have a very specific idea of how it was that a man should respond to the war and the bomb.

Mailer: Well, I wouldn't support this paragraph today. Because, how does one create complexities? At that time, I thought maybe we could, but by now I've given up. I think the communications Establishment has succeeded in creating an ability to send out vast clouds of intellectual smog and so, far from creating complexities, we're creating ambiguities and dull obsessions.

Esquire: Later in that same interview you said that "one has to assume such men as Kennedy and Khrushchev are *halfway* decent, are not *necessarily* going to blow up the world, that indeed if everything else is equal they would just as soon *not* blow up the world." Do you think we could say the same about Reagan and Gorbachev?

Mailer: Yes. Yes, I would assume that. It doesn't mean that the man who gets to the top of the greasy pole, as Disraeli once put it, is decent when he starts. I don't think Khrushchev was a decent man when he began; I think he was probably a butcher and a brute. But success mellows bad men. I've been reading a lot about gangsters lately and it's just incredible how they get somewhat more civilized as they get older, less of a danger to society. I think people like Reagan and Gorbachev are probably nicer today than they were when they started. Now, there are exceptions. Hitler is, of course, the exception that keeps us from ever becoming complacent about this process. There are very odd people who gain power occasionally, who get worse and worse with power.

Esquire: You were really the first person to anticipate the importance of John Kennedy. In the essay "Superman Comes to the Supermarket," you wrote: "I knew if he became President it would be an existential event . . . America's tortured psychotic search for security would finally be torn loose from the feverish ghosts of its old generals, its MacArthurs and Eisenhowers."

Mailer: Well, in the Sixties there was a feeling that we were finally coming out of the Eisenhower era, and that there was an *army* of us who were sort of young, or *still* young, still at least in our mid-thirties, who were passionate and who were infuriated at the way we'd been held down and felt there was a world to gain. Now, since then we've *gained* that world, and lost it, and it's deteriorated completely, at least if that world centered at all upon the Democratic party, and in a very general way, it did. The Democratic party in 1960 was the party of the future, and that's all been lost. The romantic identification we made with the future then tends now to be romantic identification with the past, with better days behind us. Today's adventurous generation is now on the periphery; they become heroes on *Miami Vice*. Beer commercials now convey the romantic spirit. It's absurd, when you stop to think about it, because there was a time when there was a feeling that maybe brave men would run the country.

Esquire: As JFK did?

Mailer: Well, he represented something not predictable. He was so young, so handsome, that it meant that our national life had become a little like an adventure movie. That was exciting. Looking back on it, people complained about the presidency as much then as they do today, myself included, but we had a feeling there was more to complain about. The heart of the loss, with Jack Kennedy's assassination, is that we lost a chance to see him mature. If he'd been President for eight years, and if the people following had been like him in one way or another, we might have learned what happens

when a man like that *does* get older. Does he get wiser? Jimmy
Carter was a wholly developed man, to the degree that he could
develop, at the time he became President, so there was nothing to
look forward to. The same is true of Reagan. The same was
absolutely true with Jerry Ford. To a lesser extent, it was true with
Nixon, but unfortunately, if Nixon had a capacity for development
when he was elected in '68, he also had all that unhappy side of him,
also undeveloped, and it developed at an equal rate with his good
side, so we ended up with détente in China and Watergate.

Great leaders give their country an education. That is, since we live
with their lives, they enter our dreams, we think about them. What
we've always wanted are role models.

Esquire: Which JFK provided . . .

Mailer: The way Clint Eastwood provides a role model, the way
Sylvester Stallone does, and Warren Beatty, and Jack Nicholson.
These are people with a style that's nifty, for their own people. The
ranks who think Stallone's nifty might not necessarily include me, but
JFK had that for a lot of us, and it was marvelous, or at least the
presidency was a little more interesting than it is now.

Esquire: You called JFK an existential hero. To a certain extent,
you had done the same thing for the hipster in "The White Negro."
You said that the only answer for the hipster was to "accept the terms
of death, to live with death as immediate danger, to divorce oneself
from society, to exist without roots, to set out on that uncharted
journey into the rebellious imperatives of the self." Is there a modern-
day hipster?

Mailer: I think there is one, and just as the heroes of our day have
ended up in television commercials, so the hipsters of our day have
ended up being drug smugglers. Again a fall from grace. You know,
who now lives with death as immediate danger? *Who* divorces
himself from society? *Who* sets out on an uncharted journey into the
rebellious imperatives of the self? *Who?* The cocaine dealer. And
that's sad. Society itself has gotten more secure than ever, and more
people are going to college, but the education they get is the
equivalent of what a good high school education was in 1900. In
1900, a kid got out of high school and knew Latin. Now he knows
domestic engineering, which is how to work your Cuisinart.

Esquire: In "The White Negro" and later in *The Armies of the
Night,* you advance the idea of society as something that seeks to

undermine the strength of the individual, sometimes in strange ways. In *Armies* you said that society was designed to drive men deep into onanism and homosexuality, that "one defied such a fate by sweeping up the psychic profit which derived from the existential assertion of yourself—which was a way of saying that nobody was born a man; you earned manhood provided you were good enough." What *about* society is designed to drive men into homosexuality?

Mailer: You know, we had this abortive theme at the PEN Congress about the imagination of the state. If we'd gotten into it, I would probably have gone so far as to argue that the imagination of the state is not only conservative but reductive. It wishes people to become mediocrities, and its function, if we can talk of such things, is to *produce* mediocrities. And I think one of the ways in which you produce mediocrity is you take people who have a lot of natural stuff and you get them desperately obsessed with themselves. Matters like homosexuality and onanism are obsessive. The homosexual spends every day of his life saying, "Have I found a new pleasure principle or am I really out of the biological chain and a doomed man?" The onanist says, "Do I pay a price for my onanism or am I getting it for free?" That's an obsession. To the degree that society can make people who have a lot of stuff on the ball become obsessive, then they end up as mediocrities. Because finally obsessions are unendurable, so we settle for the mediocre, we settle for no thought, we settle for no self-stimulation. We settle for tried-and-true answers, to get a little security, to stop that endless angst which is consuming us.

Esquire: In "Ten Thousand Words a Minute," you cited Sartre: "A homosexual is a man who practices homosexuality. A man who does not, is not homosexual—he is entitled to the dignity of his choice. He is entitled to the fact that he chose not to become homosexual and is paying presumably his price." What appealed to you about that statement?

Mailer: I do think that if one feels no shame about being a homosexual, it's considerably easier to be a homosexual than a heterosexual. Because you are separated from society, the weight of society bears upon you far less, and promiscuity is far simpler. It seems to me it's much harder to be promiscuous with a great many women than it is to be promiscuous with a great many men. Because there's this biological center in women, no getting around it. Finally, women are located closer to the center of the universe than men. They procreate, they carry the future. Men don't. I mean, you could remove men from earth and for a hundred, two hundred years, new creatures could be created, men and women, because you'd have semen banks.

Esquire: Not a cheerful scenario.

Mailer: It goes into the core of human biology. Just think of it—suppose women got all the power. Let's talk in terms of science fiction: What would there be to keep women from killing all but enough men to be raised as slaves and to provide semen banks for the future, then killing them? I know there are women's liberationists who would get a light in their eyes if I ever proposed this to them.

Esquire: What's to say that men couldn't do the reverse?

Mailer: *History.* History's there to prove it. Men haven't done it. No matter what brutalities men have exercised upon women, they've obviously lived in sufficient awe of women. They didn't destroy women. But if you ever reversed it, if women had all the power, there would be very little to keep men safely on earth, I can tell you that.

That's probably why men are so desperate about maintaining their position. Beneath this comedy of New York middle-class women screaming at every outrage that's perpetrated upon them, these little privileged creatures, there's a real biological drama going on, a sense of biological superiority that women feel.

Esquire: How can a man rise above mediocrity?

Mailer: Well, you don't have to be the strongest guy on the block; you just have to end up being a little better than most people thought you'd be. That's being a man. A homosexual who surprises everybody with how artful he is in running his life, is a man. Being a man is a style rather than a sexual centrality; if you end up being just a little better than the prevailing acumen would guess you're going to be, then you're a man. Finally, being a man is an assertion. I work on the principle that nobody's born a man, you have to assert yourself to become a man, which is why it's so difficult. In a society that becomes more and more conformist and machine oriented and computer organized, separate notions of male and female become unpleasant. What women's liberation never contemplated is they may be working for the computer: about the time men and women become more alike, they'll fit into the computer more easily. You won't need two bytes to describe them, just one.

Esquire: You dealt with this in *The Prisoner of Sex.* But even back in 1962 you called Planned Parenthood an "abomination."

Mailer: Well, that goes back to the notion I had that great children come out of great fucks. It was the most sentimental of my ideas, and probably untrue, in that the world can't depend upon something so delicate as great fucks. I'm sure there have been periods in history when the number of great fucks became reduced so drastically that there'd be very few great people born, if that were the only thing that produced great people.

Esquire: You've always been adamantly opposed to birth control.

Mailer: If you're really contemptuous of religion, you shouldn't go to church every day and pretend that you're serious about it, because you'll pollute the air for those who are. By the same token, I don't think people should keep making love systematically, with no possible chance of making a child. They are further away from the biological chain than homosexuals at that point, because their option is open, and they're not exercising it. Until recently, the idea that you made love and therefore you got a child wasn't really conceived too seriously; I mean, thousands of years went by where people just didn't get children every time they made love. I'm willing to bet that in the days when there were no contraceptives women didn't get pregnant any more than they do now. I believe our biology can take care of it. I mean, my God, with the number of new chemicals they discover every day in the bloodstream, you're going to tell me that we don't have our own contraceptives built in? That a man can't take the edge off his semen? Or a woman refuse a host of sperm cells?

Esquire: That's a very romantic notion.

Mailer: No, I don't believe it's romantic. I think it's romantic to conceive of human nature as actually going forward these thousands of years, considering how bad we all are. *God* had a very romantic idea, which was that these miserable, messed-up creatures would continue. *That's* romantic.

Esquire: What about that sentence in *The Prisoner of Sex:* "The prime responsibility of a woman is to be on earth long enough to find the best mate for herself, and conceive children who will improve the species"?

Mailer: That sentence has gotten me into more trouble than any sentence I've ever written. It comes at the end of the book, which goes in and out of this question. Finally I come up with this as a 51–49 decision, that *maybe* this is the prime responsibility of a woman. I go back to the fact that if the race is going to go on, there is a certain responsibility that women have to respect the continuation. If they abdicate that responsibility, we're doomed. So in the place of all the other balancing factors on both sides, probably this is a responsibility for women. I think that one ineradicable aspect of universal despair is a woman married to the wrong mate; if she feels deep within herself that she's conceiving with the wrong man, I believe that's a terrible world for the particular woman.

Esquire: What do you think of the women's movement now?

Mailer: I don't think that women have done much in developing their ideas. Can you tell me some new ones that have come out of women's liberation in the last decade or so? What are they saying now they weren't saying fifteen years ago? What astonishing new theses has *Ms.* magazine come up with lately?

Many people respond supinely to totalitarian force. The women's movement at its worst is totalitarian—unforgiving, unfair, incapable of quoting accurately, and quick to distort the deeds of its adversaries.

Esquire: You said in your 1957 essay "A Public Notice on Waiting for Godot" that "the only revolution that will be meaningful and natural for the twentieth century will be the sexual revolution." In light of all you've just said, do you think it's taken place?

Mailer: I think we've had the sexual revolution, and it bears about as much relation to the ideal of free and happy and essentially healthy relations between men and women . . . yes, has had as much relation to that as the Soviet Union today has to Lenin's notion of what the communist world would be like.

Esquire: So why do you still say it's taken place? Maybe it hasn't.

Mailer: Oh, it's definitely taken place, I think there's no argument about that. I mean, just to bring matters close to home, you can write anything you want now, and you can get it published by a reputable publisher. You can print "fuck" and "piss" and so forth in *Esquire* when fifteen years, twenty years ago, I had to fight like a maniac to get the word "shit" in. That's just the surface of it, but people aren't shocked that much anymore by sexual behavior as such, indeed they're indifferent to it. There used to be a great excitement in writing about anything sexual because you felt as if you were striking a blow for freedom. Now it's so permissive that you feel conformist if you do portray anything sexually bizarre. In that sense, it's all gone sour. I think one reason is the huge amount of technology that's accompanied the sexual revolution. We haven't had free spirits cavorting on the beach; this has been people making love with vibrators and mood music, mood sound, all the crap and crapola of modern life. I once made the remark that people couldn't make love in front of a TV set; now, to prove me wrong, we've got video pornies.

Esquire: So are you saying it's taken place, but not with the end you'd anticipated?

Mailer: Like all revolutions, it went off the rails. It was a hook shot.

Esquire: Do you think there's room for anything else to happen?

Mailer: Well, I don't have a clue at this point. Thirty years ago, I was pretty sure I knew what was going to happen; on a few things I was right, and on many wrong, but I had certainty then that I don't have now. It seems to me a good many good and bad things are going on at once. It's as if all the consciousness that was liberated in the Sixties has been flying around like fallout, and hits people in odd ways.

Esquire: The hero and the outlaw are two ways that you've explored how people respond to that "fallout." Is someone like Gary Gilmore the antithesis of the hero?

Mailer: Why does he have to be the antithesis? He was a man. If you want to go in for the categories, he was a failed movie star. He took himself as seriously as a movie star, and toward the end of his life, one of the reasons he died the way he did, is he wanted to be a role model. I think in some odd way he succeeded for a few people. He was also a man who was so drenched in unpleasant reflexes that he could never have been a leader.

When I started *The Executioner's Song*, I thought I would like him more than I did. As I got to know him, I thought, if I was *ever* a cellmate with this guy I would've disliked him intensely. He had a lot of meanness in him, a lot of small-mindedness. He also had an extraordinary imagination. He proved to me that genius can also find a home in mediocrity. That was incredible. He was a very brave man too; that has to be said. The press called him a punk, which was an inaccurate name for him, because he would've died before he allowed anyone to call him punk to his face. He was a bad man, a dull man, a mediocre man, but he had heroic elements.

Esquire: Where does a man like Gilmore come from?

Mailer: I couldn't answer that. I lived in my mind with him for two years while writing *The Executioner's Song*, and finally decided I was not going to try to give an explanation of his personality. He was too complex for that. People who are always looking for a solution to everybody's personality are what I would call second-rate citizens. It's very easy to understand second-rate people, they function through simple governing principles. They like to dominate all experience with language, like to put everything in its place, label everything. Whereas first-rate people are impossible to understand. And very often, it's impossible to understand second-rate people with first-rate qualities, like Gilmore. Then you recognize you're confronting a mystery. But it's very easy to comprehend people who offer no mystery, because they've killed all of that mystery in themselves, which, to go back to what I've been saying all my life, is an expression of cowardice. The coward in ourselves kills the mystery in ourselves. We're all guilty of that in varying fashion.

Esquire: It seems that in *your* life, you certainly haven't avoided making waves; if anything you've fought life, in a sense. It makes one think of your piece about the Liston-Patterson fight. You talked about boxing as "a human activity, it showed part of what a man was like, it belonged to his ability to create art and artful movement on the edge of death or pain or danger or attack, and it had much to say about the subtleties of human style."

Mailer: Well, boxing *is* something that's specifically male, it's one sport that I don't think women are *ever* going to get into for the simplest reason, which is that they have breasts to lose. If I were a woman, I wouldn't want to suffer that.

I still feel the same way about boxing, but I despair of being able to argue about it. Most people don't like the idea of boxing because they feel, well, here are people degrading each other's brains and it's awful. They can't see beyond that. They don't understand that all of life is attrition, that we all get our brains beaten out in one fashion or another. We can get our brains dulled working at a nine-to-five clerical job, we get our brains beaten out drinking all night. The alternative to boxing is that a lot of tough kids with a lot of violence will be out on the street looking for action, and no one faces up to

that. Nobody can bear the idea that society is a compromise between
virtually unbalanceable impulses in human beings. If it's going to
work, there has to be a lot of behavior that makes no sense at all to a
rational mind. As, for instance, bullfighting, which gave a sense of the
deep to people who were very often, at least by their behavior in a
bullfighting crowd, vulgar, noisy, and ready to rain urine down on the
expensive seats.

Esquire: Do you think that's something particularly male, this
need to define oneself by going to the edge of death?

Mailer: Well, I still say yes. It's difficult to be a man. That's one
thing women never understand; they say, "There he is, he was given
that phallus. How dare God be that unfair, and not give me one?!
There must be something unjust at the very center of things." They
never think it through, they never try to. Which is, that in return for
that phallus, man is also given a state of prodigious instability vis-à-vis
women. Women are much more sure of themselves than men,
because a man can never rest, can never say to himself, "I've become
a man." When I was younger, I used to feel I wasn't enough of a
man, and then after many years I began to realize that all men felt
that way. It didn't matter how good you were, you were never good
enough. There's always some guy who can do something that you
can't do. But women keep thinking. Oh, if I had that phallus, I could
do it all. Well, they couldn't. They'd discover for themselves, they just
couldn't. They simply can't accept the idea that disproportion is
God's vision, not symmetry. So you see, I'm more of a bigot than
ever.

"Tough Guy" Mailer Shows He Can Dance with the Big Boys

Roger Ebert/1986

From the *Chicago Sun-Times*, 23 November, 1986, 6-8. Copyright © 1987, Roger Ebert. Reprinted with permission.

PROVINCETOWN, MASS.—Not far down the street there has been a bloody fist fight, two men pounding each other senseless over a woman, blood on the sidewalk, the police involved, but Norman Mailer hardly hears of it, he is so engrossed in the movie he is directing.

Mailer, who has had his share of fights in Provincetown and spent at least a few nights in its jail, is watching the way Ryan O'Neal puts down a telephone and turns to the window of a saloon to see a white Rolls-Royce speed down Commercial Street, the village's one-way main drag. Mailer is concerned that the car may disappear before his camera can see it. The shot is finally made to his liking, and then he sits down while the crew moves the lights for the next shot, and perhaps the bench next to the window feels familiar, because, he observes, "I've been coming to this bar for 40 years."

He is all bundled up in a goose-down jacket too small for him and leans against the wall at an angle, his tennis shoes braced against the floor. Before he speaks six words, I recognize that he is in a good mood; he has been shooting nights and sleeping days, keeping a punishing schedule for the first three weeks of the first big-budget Hollywood movie he has ever directed, and he is not tired; the experience seems to exhilarate him.

"If you are leading a life that has certain elements of risk in it, you have more energy," he explains. "I would decompose quickly in a deck chair. When I started the movie, I didn't know how good my energy was anymore, but I found it takes over everything."

He explains that the happiest week of his life was spent 16 years ago when he directed "Maidstone," a low-budget 1968 underground film starring Mailer's family and friends in a violent crime allegory. He says he believes film directing satisfies a side of his personality never touched by writing.

"When you write a novel," Mailer says, "it's all yours, but you can only use one part of yourself. When you direct, you use every last part of yourself—especially a practical side that's been frustrated all of my life. Moviemaking is a punctilious activity. In novel writing, you can get by with a lot of fire and smoke. In the movies, there is less margin for error."

For years, Mailer has been fighting for the title of America's foremost man of letters, and he has a good claim with his 20 or more books, including *The Naked and the Dead, The Armies of the Night,* and *The Executioner's Song.* But now he wants to be a movie director too. He is directing a thriller based on his 1984 novel *Tough Guys Don't Dance,* and he has a budget of some $5 million—modest by Hollywood standards, but still substantial—and a cast including Ryan O'Neal, Isabella Rossellini and a host of character actors. Cannon Films is financing the production, and Tom Luddy, who is teamed with Francis Coppola as the executive producer, observes with quiet wonder that after three weeks Mailer is on schedule and budget.

Cannon is run by Menahem Golan and Yoram Globus, the Israelis who are shaking up Hollywood with the biggest production slate of any American studio. They are known for taking chances. Still, you might ask, not unreasonably, why have they decided that Norman Mailer, at 63, is ready for his first try at big-time movie directing?

The answer to that question lies, perhaps, in a luncheon that Golan attended two years ago at the Cannes Film Festival, where his guest was the legendary French director Jean-Luc Godard. During the course of the meal, which was long and celebratory, Golan and Godard wrote a famous contract on a napkin, a contract committing Godard to direct a new film of Shakespeare's "King Lear."

A few hours later, Golan unfurled the napkin for the world's press, boasting that not only would Godard direct the film, but that Norman Mailer would write the screenplay, Woody Allen would play the Fool, and so on. There were those who doubted Golan's grand announcement, but now here is Mailer directing a Cannon film. Is there any connection?

"The two deals were set up together," Mailer recalls, smiling to himself. "I wrote the screenplay. Woody Allen is indeed set to play some sort of role, perhaps not the Fool. I wrote an adaptation of King Lear, a translation from Shakespeare to modern Mafia. I made Lear a Mafia lord. His name is Don Learo, and he's an old Mafia godfather who's become demented with his power. I felt only a Mafioso would be believable, going insane as Lear does. I couldn't take a modern oil millionaire; they're as circumspect as dentists, and appallingly well-balanced. Of course, I knew that writing a screenplay for Godard is like putting a message in a bottle and sending it out to sea. But perhaps there will be traces of 'Don Learo' in his movie."

Did you simply agree to write the screenplay so that Cannon would let you direct this movie?

"I had a conscience about it. I think 'Don Learo' is worth doing. What comes through is the parallel to 'Lear' when passion becomes so intense, it levitates—it lifts above reality. You can no longer measure what is sane or insane, the intensity of the passion creates a new state of being and the fun of the script was precisely translating that passion from Shakespeare's English to Mafia English. I found that it still held, that it was the equivalent of these marvelous transpositions that good mathematicians can make."

Mailer actually talks this way. He has been up all night for days, and has been working for hours and has stolen this moment to sit in the corner of a favorite bar, and the words and ideas come tumbling out, connections made between Shakespeare, the Mafia and mathematics. I listen, fascinated, until I remind myself that he has not answered the question.

So in other words, you agreed to write the Godard screenplay in order to get Cannon to let you direct this film?

"I've been waiting to direct this film for a couple of years. At one point I was offered $43 million to make it, but then I discovered the money was coming from people I'd never met and I didn't have a good feeling about it. I began to have the suspicion it was a laundering operation. I thought, to hell with that; it's one thing if an unknown director made a movie that way. Nobody would notice. But if I appeared with $43 million, it would demand some scrutiny."

And then Menahem Golan came along?

"In a funny way, he feels like family," Mailer says. "I feel as if I understand him.

"He is easy to caricature, because he always says what he thinks. He's shrewd, he has sound judgement. The big question is whether he will really make the move from exploitation films to serious ones. The real concern at Cannon is they like movies brought in on budget. They hate excess expenditure. That fits in with my own ideas; America is a study in waste right now, prodigious waste and shoddy work everywhere. Hollywood is particularly wasteful. So far, we've held to our budget. I want to go on and direct more films, and that will only happen if this one is successful. If it fails, I won't get another job until another 20 years, and by then I'll be 83."

And so Mailer marches out to direct another shot, this one of Ryan O'Neal running after the fleeing Rolls-Royce, while all the bar windows on both sides of the street are jammed with fans who have come to see the movie being made. They probably are more interested in O'Neal and his girlfriend, Farrah Fawcett, than in Mailer—who is a familiar sight on these streets. He summers here and spends much time in the winter, his favorite season for writing, when the population drops from 150,000 to 4,000 (mostly Portuguese fishermen).

Mailer's novel takes place in the winter, when an alcoholic writer broods over his bourbon about the loss of his lovely blond wife. The story is set in some of Provincetown's most familiar landmarks—the hero remembers trying to climb the Pilgrim Memorial, and does his drinking in a favorite corner of the historic Red Inn—but Mailer claims the movie will be a thriller that is not much about the real Provincetown.

"If you were at war and you had to pass through a town where you drank a lot," he explains, returning to his corner after the next shot is finished, "the war would be so much on your mind that the town would be incidental. This movie is not about Provincetown; it is a murder mystery, and the town gives it a certain air. If I were to make a movie about the town, it would be much slower, and have less plot, and be about two people living here in the winter. Provincetown is the last democratic town left in America. Everybody is absolutely equal here."

The town, it appears, does not necessarily have the same high opinion of Mailer. The owner of one restaurant told me he hoped Provincetown came out looking better in the movie than in the book, which painted a bleak wintertime picture of lonely drunks and addicts, preying on each other after a severed blond head is found hidden in the hero's secret marijuana stash. He is likely to be disappointed; Mailer has rewritten much of the plot for the screenplay, and added a cocaine scam as an important story element.

"I thought, what's interesting with cocaine is that it is the door to crime for yuppies," Mailer explains, with the detachment of a sociologist. "There was a lot of worry out of Hollywood that cocaine was all used up as a movie subject, people were bored with it. But it has an allure for middle-class people, and the movie is not about drug-dealing, but about how middle-class people get led into crime. The original novel didn't have a screenplay in it—the plot concerns who gets control of a hotel—and now, for better or worse, we have a murder mystery, a horror tale, perhaps a black comedy."

Will this be a "Norman Mailer Film" or just a film that you happened to have directed?

"It will be three-quarters my film. It has my script, and I have a talent for working with actors. Ninety percent of what the actors do will be, if not my creation, at least with my consent."

One of those actors is O'Neal, who for this role, cultivates a dissipated look, as if he had been drinking for days on end, as his character has. Mailer wonders how audiences will accept O'Neal: "They're used to seeing him in comedies. But he is a good actor—I loved him in 'Barry Lyndon'—and he is quick, exceptionally witty, his choices are nimble. The fact that he is a serious actor in this film will irritate some people, but I am happy to oblige them."

In casting Isabella Rossellini as a local femme fatale, Mailer changes the character to fit the actress. "In the novel, she is a truly sardonic Italian-American girl, tough and funny. But Isabella brought something else to it altogether, so I made her an Italian girl who came over here and stayed. I made her gentler and more romantic. I gave up humor and got a love story in return."

I was at the Telluride Film Festival two years ago, I say, when you brought your movie "Maidstone." That didn't go so well, did it?

Mailer shakes his head wonderingly. "I witnessed the death of my film," he says. "The audience left very steadily, throughout the film. Every scene lost one or two people. I was left with 40 out of 300. I could see the moments that were turning them off.

"I had said before the screening that only three people in the whole world understood and loved 'Maidstone.' After it was over, I told the famous story of Darryl Zanuck. At the wrap party for 'The Longest Day,' he said there were only three people who could do an unassisted one-arm chin-up, and he was one of them.

"He started to chin himself, and got almost up to the bar, and the drums rolled, but then he could go no farther, and finally he dropped to the ground, and said, 'Now there are only two people.' "

I ask Mailer what he thinks about the three films made from his books: "The Naked and the Dead," "An American Dream" and "The Executioner's Song."

"I didn't see 'An American Dream.' Friends took me aside and said it would make me violent. 'The Naked and the Dead'—Charles Laughton was going to direct it, he loved the novel, but then his 'Night of the Hunter' came out and failed, and that took away his enthusiasm. They got Raoul Walsh off his deathbed to direct it, and he directed his worst film, and died soon after.

"Now 'The Executioner's Song,' I thought, got better as it went on. I begged Larry Schiller [the man who supplied Mailer with the original research and transcripts of the story of convicted killer Gary Gilmore] not to direct it, but he said he had spent more time on it than I had, his life was in it, and before such passion one stands by and observes. Tommy Lee Jones was wonderful in it, even though he was all wrong for the script. He had too much energy; a man who has been in prison for 15 years is flattened out, and doesn't have much personality left. Tommy Lee was more like a biker caught on a drunken bust. But he skewed the script toward his energy, and it worked."

By now it is late at night in Provincetown, halfway through a shooting schedule that will last until three or four in the morning, and yet Mailer talks on, filled with ideas, with memories. I sit at his side, like a student. I remember reading his *Advertisements for Myself* when I was in high school and being impressed by the subtext of the book, a collection of his short fiction and journalism interspersed with autobiographical essays on how and why he came to write what he did, and be what he was. That book was one of the first documents of the New Journalism. And lurking beneath every sentence was another one that insisted that this man must be paid attention to. There was no pose of indifference in his work. He was a man who worked very hard because he thought it important to be listened to, to make his mark, to be remembered.

And so now I ask him about that drive, the same drive that has led him to write 20 books, and run for office, and be married six times, and organize an international congress of writers, and direct movies, and talk so passionately into the night.

"Two formative currents of personality came together to make my nature," he says, placing an emphasis on the word "my," which sounds almost musical. "One of them is being Jewish. I'm not a Holocaust hustler, I'm not asking for pity, but every Jew alive feels his relationship to the world is somehow more tenuous than other people's, and so to affirm his own existence is somehow more important. The second current was that I had a mother who spoiled me out of sight, with all that's good and bad about that, so I was accustomed to having attention paid to me, and that is probably the key to my personality.

"Of course, by the time you're 63, you change a great deal. You get more serious. I have, what, 10, 15, 20 years to work. I'm a believer in the theory that we have a navigator, and this navigator receives information the conscious mind is not aware of, saying *Do this now!* If I have a lot of energy while I'm doing something, I'm doing the right thing. My life's very simple that way."

But does it make a difference? Is it worth writing, worth making the effort, worth carrying on at such expense of personal effort?

"I think the greatest revelation one can find, is to go ahead and do something with the greatest purpose in the world, and the highest sincerity, and be dead wrong. But I cannot believe that this huge elaborate stage show of our world is bent for fire and disaster in the third act. I believe God has his or her own purpose, and may succeed or fail."

Mailer wraps his arms around his sides and rocks gently back and forth on his perch, his eyes focused on the middle distance. What do you mean? I ask. . . . That God is also contending against adversaries, and faces possible defeat?

"The idea of an omnipotent God leaves me apathetic, at best, and cold with anger, at worst," he says, "because if God is all-powerful, then there is a rather ugly show going on. I would rather think God is doing his or her best, against considerable adversity."

Your name used to be on the front pages, I say, remembering all the headlines about Mailer's brawls, Mailer's trials, Mailer's busts, Mailer's binges, Mailer's fights with wives. Now you are on the book pages.

"Well, I stopped drinking for a year and a half, and enjoyed having

my system clear of the stuff. When I went back I didn't enjoy the
hangovers so much, so now I drink in moderation, of all damn
things."

There is a certain detachment in his voice that perhaps wasn't
there years ago.

"A man who says he is happily married is a fool, but I will take a
chance and say that I am. I stopped getting into trouble years ago. I
think as you get older you make peace with who and what you are,
or you grow ill. And as I grow older, there are certain narcisstic
pleasures I no longer take. It doesn't help my day to see a good
photograph of myself in the paper, because there are no good
photographs any longer. There are such things as aging male
beauties, and I'm afraid I come under that category. That's all right. I
simply don't think about myself as much as I used to."

A Conversation with Norman Mailer

Barry H. Leeds/1987

Barry Leeds: May I call you Norman?

Norman Mailer: Sure, no problem.

Leeds: I asked you that years ago, but I didn't know if you remembered or not. I don't like just taking those liberties. One of the things that impressed me very much was when I saw you on TV with Henry Miller. You were no kid at the time, but you said, "May I call you Henry, Mr. Miller?" in an era when aluminum siding salesman call up and say, "Hey, Barry boy, how you doin'." [laughter] . . . I was rereading *The Fight* just the other day, and I enjoyed yet again that scene where you're running with Ali, especially when you're coming back by yourself and the lion roars. I love that part. I've quoted that to about fifty people.

Mailer: Yeah. I remember George Plimpton wrote about it and got it all wrong.

Leeds: Well, I hope you got everything right about him in *The Fight*. By the way, now that it's pretty well documented that Ali has been damaged by boxing, do you love the sport as much as you did?

Mailer: Well, I don't think I love it as much as I used to. One reason is because he's out of it.

Leeds: Right.

Mailer: Not because I don't care about the fight, but the week you spend waiting is boring. It degenerates into sitting around . . .

Leeds: With all the same guys, too.

Mailer: In the beginning it's dull drunks with fight reporters, who are pretty simple-minded people, and you chew the fight to bits before it takes place, and everybody's got a theory, and of course half the theories automatically end up being wrong, and even the half that

359

are right are usually misplaced to a degree, and then two out of three fights aren't that good, so you end up saying how many weeks do I have to do this? And you have to write about it afterward. The fight itself, a big championship fight, can still be about the most exciting spectacle in all the world. But the odds are poor. Maybe you get one out of four.

Leeds: One of the things that struck me the other day, for what it's worth, is something out of my own life. About a hundred years ago, when I was a sixteen-year-old merchant seaman and high school dropout, I worked under a bosun who had an interesting set of literary criteria. He said, "I read a lot of books, but not unless they got fightin' and fuckin' in them," and that seemed reasonable to me at the time. I didn't ask him if he read your books because who was I—I couldn't spell Norman Mailer at the time. But in a sense, it's this violence and sex in your work for which it's been attacked by some critics that in a way led me back into the world of literature and education and really changed my life.

Mailer: Well, I grew up on that: fighting and fucking was what made a good book. But you're doomed if you write about it.

Leeds: Yeah, but the important thing for me was that things happened in your books, yours and Hemingway's. Obviously you're not the only two authors, but you were the only two for me at the time I started growing up again in literature, and I was so grateful that people didn't just sit around eating cucumber sandwiches and drinking tea. And then I read this in your introduction to *A Transit to Narcissus*. You said, "I do not recognize the young man who wrote this book, I do not even like him very much, and yet I know that he must be me because his themes are mine, his ambition is as large for his age as my ambition would ever become, and I am not even without an odd regard for him. If I understand what he is trying to say, then he is close to saying the unsayable. The most terrible themes of my own life: the nearness of violence to creation, and the whiff of murder just beyond every embrace of love are his themes also." It occurs to me that although you're obviously evolving over these forty-odd years into a different kind of writer all the time, these thematic preoccupations really have remained constant—not static but constant—and I wonder if you feel that being thus preoccupied has hurt you, in that so many critics have been shortsighted about roundly attacking your work for those reasons.

Mailer: At the least it's made me hard to read for a number of people. They approach my books with anxiety, precisely the anxiety that street people feel when they're walking down the street and expect trouble. Most people who read books are—tend to be, at least—superficially gentle and reflective and civilized. They read books to avoid the street. While books about violence are exotic to such readers, they are also disturbing. And I think mine are doubly disturbing because what I'm saying is: look, I'm not asking you to read about violence so you can have a good read, I'm saying there's a lot of meaning in violence. That it's one aspect of a world-wide violence which appropriates us. You know I've been saying from the beginning, of course, there's individual violence versus the violence of the State. It takes a thousand forms. You could say that the spread of social programs is a very subtle form of violence. The scare right now about AIDS is an example of that. One thing doctors are famous for, over the centuries, is that their statistical forecasts are always off. We're being told now that a world-wide AIDS plague is coming. The statistics, oddly enough, I don't think necessarily bear it out. For one thing, the rate of AIDS in New York has not been doubling every year as they said it would. The rate of increase has been lowering each year; it's still on the increase, but it's been lowering. There's an inability of doctors to think intimately about these problems. I have a theory on AIDS for what it's worth. The question I raise is which kinds of homosexuals are decimated by AIDS? It seems to me that there are a great many homosexuals who have two practices. They're not only promiscuous in sex, but they're promiscuous in their use of antibiotics. The literature's just filled with cases of people who go to Turkish baths and make love with ten men and then go home and inject themselves with penicillin. I think they should make one simple study which is to try to find out how much in the way of antibiotics AIDS victims have taken in relation to the general population. My guess is that four or five times as much antibiotics has entered their blood streams before they got the AIDS. People have been promiscuous before and after Christ. Why does AIDS strike now? That kind of promiscuity has been going on from the birth of time with certain people, so this plague, I think, is not a reflection of promiscuity, it's a reflection of antibiotics. I would say ultimately (and this sounds mad, but it has to be taken as just an example of the way I think) if you extend your concepts far enough, antibiotics are a form of violence, a very attenuated form of social violence practiced upon people. Nobody ever asks us; nobody ever laid it out for us when it first came along. Doctors just said, "Here, take this. It's good for you. It'll cure your illness." The notion that illness might not be there to be cured by external means but was supposed to be cured from within is a desperately conservative notion. It's never been explored.

Leeds: Your extra-medical theories are going to have to be way out before I don't take them seriously, because in 1965 in *An American Dream* and in 1966 in *Cannibals and Christians*, when you codified your visions about cancer, I called my brother who was in medical school at the time. I read him the passage about patients firing out of the windows from cancer wards at people in the streets and the possibility of miraculous cures, and I said, "Is this way out?" And he said, "We don't know." And since then, of course, it's become less and less outlandish an idea, as you're well aware; so I take these extra-medical theories you come up with quite seriously. One other thing you said earlier that I wanted to address, is that you've always felt that the institutionalized violence of the State is far more horrendous than individual acts of violence. I understand that entirely in terms of Gary Gilmore, but I wonder what you think about the Bernhard Goetz case?

Mailer: Oh, I think like everybody else I'm mired in confusion on that one. First of all, I don't know what really happened there. I'm not sure Goetz knows what happened. It's one thing to defend yourself; it's another to take advantage of having a gun. And I think the truth there lies somewhere in between, so I've got to waffle on that one. If we could talk about an ideal approach to these matters, I'd say no one should ever have a gun, and everyone should know how to fight.

Leeds: Right.

Mailer: If everyone knew how to fight, there would certainly be no more fights than there are now, probably fewer. When violent people hang out together they tend to balance each other out. It's even an aesthetic principle. *Prizzi's Honor* proves it; you can find an interesting love story between two killers for hire because they're equal in the same way that two gentle, civilized people are equal. That is, a love story between Virginia Woolf and Leonard Woolf is as interesting as a love story between Jack Nicholson and Kathleen Turner, because they're equals.

Leeds: This thing about balancing out is true. Sometimes, it seems to me that you're never as safe as you are in a bad bar where nobody knows what you know or how fast you are or how bad you are: that everybody pretty much leaves each other alone.

Mailer: Well, they know the price of violence. The most dangerous situation, always, is when you have one person who's violent among a great many people who are not. That's always an unstable situation—that's explosive.

Leeds: One of the things about your work and you is I can't get away from it, which is to say that I've obviously read and taught and written on other authors, but I'm always finding your name *every place* I turn, and I don't just mean in *Newsweek*. I was just reading Philip Roth's latest novel, *The Counterlife* . . .

Mailer: I heard about that.

Leeds: Would you like to see this quotation?

Mailer: I never saw the passage.

Leeds: You can keep this copy if you like. It's really interesting. Zuckerman, Roth's character, the novelist, is in Israel, and the wife of this Meyer Kahane type of political Rabbi says, "Let me ask you a question. You are a friend of Norman Mailer?" "Both of us write books." "Let me ask you a question about your colleague Mailer. Why is he so interested in murder and criminals and killing? When I was at Barnard, our English professor assigned those books to read— books by a Jew who cannot stop thinking about murder and criminals and killing. Sometimes when I think back to the innocence of that class and the idiotic nonsense that they said there, I think, Why didn't I ask, 'If this Jew is so exhilarated by violence, why doesn't he go to Israel?' " [laughter]

Mailer: That's funny.

Leeds: Of course, on the next page, he defends the nature of the creative experience and such, but I thought you'd get a kick out of that. In line with something else you were saying, in *Fools Die* you probably know that Mario Puzo's got a character called Osano who bears some resemblance to you . . .

Mailer: Well, very little in a funny way because he smokes cigars which I hate and anyone who knows anything at all about me will know . . . I can think of three things I don't like. Cigars are probably the first, and the other is he has me killing a poodle. I had a poodle for eighteen years, so I resented that directly. You know, if I were ever to kill a dog, a poodle would be the last one.

Leeds: Well, there may be aspects of Puzo himself there, because I think he's a cigar smoker, and maybe he hates poodles. But anyway, Osano is always taking penicillin. That's one of the reasons I brought it up. Every time he has a sexual encounter, which is frequently, he prophylactically takes penicillin which is why, ultimately, he dies of syphilis. But here's the thing that really fascinated me . . .

Mailer: It's interesting to do that kind of job on a guy. It's something Jackie Susann used to do which is to put you into a book so people say "Oh yes, that's Norman Mailer" and then give you all the things you never do and that's double punishment. Not only are you written about badly, but inaccurately, and people believe it. I'm sorry. You were saying . . .

Leeds: Well, the amazing thing is, I was rereading *Fools Die,* and Puzo's got a passage written by Osano, in which he's talking about women. He says, "I have plans for [the woman I love.] I have dark graves in caves to hide her head." I said, Jesus Christ, this was years before *Tough Guys Don't Dance* was written. What an amazing coincidence. Maybe I'm making too much of it.

Mailer: No. That's interesting. I think Puzo's a gambler, and gamblers are incredibly instinctive. They're always either right or wrong. People who tend to be either right or wrong become gamblers. It's a way of searching out that potentiality in oneself. So he obviously hit on a theme. I never read *Fools Die.* Directly of course, you know, the decapitations in *Tough Guys* come out of that case with Tony Costa up in Provincetown where he dismembered four women's bodies. Well, that thing haunted me for years, and you know one reason why, of course, is you're probably familiar with that introduction to *Why Are We in Vietnam?*

Leeds: Yes, right.

Mailer: I was going to write about a group of people hiding out in the sand dunes of Provincetown who were making raids and killing and then along came Manson. That freaked me. And then Tony Costa a few years later.

Leeds: Was there a reason—this is fascinating to me personally— that in *Tough Guys Don't Dance* you returned to writing about a middle-aged character? I know that in *Armies* you said that there were parts of yourself that were nineteen and seventy-three and forty-four, and of course in *Ancient Evenings* Menenhetet is all ages, but it fascinates me, being middle-aged now myself . . .

Mailer: Listen, you look in great shape.

Leeds: Thank you. It intrigues me when I go back and look at *An American Dream,* which is really my favorite among the works; I know there are greater books, but it's the one that speaks to me most personally. And I was looking at the preface to *Deaths for the Ladies,* a book which I think I understood too quickly, and then here you went back again to writing about a middle-aged protagonist. Was there a reason that you revisited not only those haunts but that period?

Mailer: Yeah. One thing that literary critics don't pay enough attention to is the practicality of writers' themes. That is, you take a theme that you can handle. I had a set of objective circumstances. I had to write a book in two months and I had been unable to write this novel for a long time. For about a year I'd been trying to start it. I couldn't find my protagonist and I knew I was down to two months. So, I took one who would be comfortable. The only way to do a book quickly, I think, is to write in the first person, but you've got to have someone who's near enough to yourself so that he's comfortable. I chose a man who was not at all me in any real way, but was near enough so that his style wouldn't seem false to me. In other words, I wouldn't have to stretch for a style. I tried someone who could conceivably have read my work and argued with it, liked one book, not liked another. I would have been one of fifty-eight authors who made up his—what can I say—the dome of his aesthetic purview; and that was crucial. A lot comes out of that. In other words, I took someone who was middle-aged because to write about someone who was young would have been too great a stretch and my own age would have interfered in other ways. I didn't want to write about someone too near to me. Then I'd get involved with myself while writing the book. All these things were determined by the fact that the book had to be written quickly. You know, in movie-making, parenthetically, they have a wonderful phrase: "Do what is necessary." In other words, if you have to get a scene in before dark, the director will say "Do what is necessary," and what that means is, we'll get the shot in whether it's good or it's bad. We'll have it by dark because otherwise we're lost. *Tough Guys* is an example of what happens when you have to do what is necessary. The book took two months to write. If I'd had more time, it might have taken a year because I would have had time to go off on excursions that I couldn't afford any longer. Once you can only afford the task before you, you work quickly provided you've gotten yourself into a simple frame of mind. Most of writing consists of getting into that simple frame of mind; it's very, very hard to do. You know there's so much to write about and you've chosen a little and that's always irksome, and one's always rebelling against how little there is to write about in the particular book you've chosen.

Leeds: Speaking of the movie version, after doing those three movies in the late '60's that were so relatively unstructured, was it an interesting challenge, and were there any particular problems working from a structured script?

Mailer: It was altogether different. It was as different as boxing and wrestling. The movies I made all those years ago were great fun, wonderful fun. Making *Maidstone* was probably the most interesting week of my life. But now I had a budget, an expensive budget for me—small for a mainstream film—but still it was five million dollars. I had a schedule to keep to. I had movie stars; I had a script, a most detailed script. So it was different. I had to function with that. I wouldn't have dreamed of improvising much.

Leeds: Did you enjoy it?

Mailer: Oh, I enjoyed it a lot. The trouble is, I like making movies more than writing now. I'm tired of writing. I've been doing it for forty years, and there's not much fun left. I get a hold of myself in the morning and go into that room and dig more stuff out of that old gut. The gut rebels. It's tired of being called on to perform these yeoman duties. Whereas in making a movie you're really not an artist, more an aesthetic engineer. You've got a lot of talented people working under you and they come up to you and you've got to make instantaneous decisions about matters you know very little about. Like hairdo, costume. And so it's kind of fun. You're using everything you've ever learned to the best of your ability. It kept reminding me about being at war but in a good way. It was like the ideal war. Nobody got killed, but you ate in a different place every day, usually standing up. There were vehicles. The biggest problem, just as it was in the army, was where do you put the vehicles. You know when you pick a location shot, you pick it by its availability to a road. You could be in the deepest forest you ever saw, but it's got to be 100 yards from the road because that's where the trucks are parked. So there's a reverse logic in film making. You start with the costs and work toward the art.

Leeds: Did you enjoy working with Ryan O'Neal?

Mailer: Ohwell, that was heaven in a crazy way. Heaven is the wrong word. Ryan is a very, very bright guy. Word for word, sentence for sentence, he's smarter than I am. He's very quick. He's that way as a boxer. He's a very fast boxer and you can't win exchanges with him. He's terribly funny on the set. He's very generous. And the reason he's difficult is he's too generous, so he gives and gives and gives of himself and then at a certain point he's given too much. Then he gets into a black Irish mood and woe to the first person who crosses him at that point.

Leeds: He sounds like Tim Madden.

Mailer: No, he's different from Tim Madden, but I think he's done an incredible performance in the film. I think maybe it's the best thing he's ever done.

Leeds: When's it going to be out?

Mailer: October, if everything holds together.

Leeds: I loved your interview with Clint Eastwood in *Parade* a few years ago. I'm a big Clint Eastwood fan and I agree with you that *Honky Tonk Man* is his best film. But do you get the idea as I do that he's a bright guy who . . . Here's my theory: that he got really mad at the American public when *Honky Tonk Man* didn't go well; it's such a sensitive film. So in the next one, *Sudden Impact,* he gets the .44 magnum automatic that takes a shell the size of a beer can and blows up buildings. It seemed to me that this was intentional self-parody, that he said, "You want Dirty Harry, you're gonna get Dirty Harry."

Mailer: Well, I think so. You know it's very hard to understand the psychology of these big stars. Take guys like Burt Reynolds and Clint Eastwood and Stallone. I think they're enormously competitive people or they wouldn't be where they are. I think they see themselves as champs in what they do. And they hate losing. They hate losing the way a heavyweight champion hates losing a fight, and so if they make a movie and it doesn't do well at the box office, they can't get it out of their systems. It eats at them. It terrifies them. It terrifies them the way a heavyweight champion is terrified if he loses a fight, or even if a sparring partner makes him look bad on a given day. Their ego has the same . . . I once made the remark that heavyweight champions always verge on the edge of being insane. Because conceivably they were the toughest guys in the world and conceivably they weren't. There could always be some guy waiting for them in an alley, some maniac who one way or another could take them in a street fight. They just didn't know. They couldn't know if they were the toughest guy around or weren't and this has to eat at a man's stability. In the same way, movie stars have to feel: what are they made of, what are their ingredients? I'd hate to be a movie star on a bad day, waking up with a hangover and a dull fight with one's woman and feeling unattractive. That's a tough combination to contend with. I guess that's one reason they're so health conscious. The few I've known take enormous care of themselves, eat very properly. Eastwood's that way. He really watches his diet. Warren Beatty's that way. Beatty, who's a sensitive and very intelligent man, is a little off to the side. He won't put himself in the movies the way the others do. I mean, I think Burt Reynolds is just full of rage if a film doesn't score. You know, one of my favorite teasing notions—I'm absolutely serious about it, but no one will ever believe it—is (I would hope by '88 or '92; it probably won't be until 1996) that the best presidential contest we could have would be between Warren Beatty for the Democrats and Clint Eastwood for the Republicans.

Leeds: This is a question I've wanted to ask you since 1983. Do you still have the same master plan for the *Ancient Evenings* trilogy?

Mailer: No. And the reason I gave it up is the second book was going to be science fiction. And I just came to a sobering estimate of my ability to retain difficult material. First of all, I don't think the economics will ever come together because I'd need a year of serious reading to catch up on all the scientific material because if I were going to do a book on science fiction I'd want to do it so I'd become a sort of master of the medium, and that would take an awful lot of thinking, and I don't think well scientifically. I can tell because I've subscribed to *Scientific American* for fifteen years now, and I find more and more difficulty keeping up with the articles, which is a measure of your ability to understand those concepts. The concepts of science are getting more and more difficult for me all the time so I thought, what's the sense of writing such a book? I can't if I'm going to end up faking it.

Leeds: It really surprises me that you say that about yourself and science because I thought that in *Of a Fire on the Moon* your training in aeronautical engineering obviously shows through.

Mailer: It was a help. No, that was not a bad book, and I think that if I was going to write that trilogy which was already in my mind then, I think in a funny way I blew it by writing *Of a Fire on the Moon.* I was very depressed the entire time I was writing that book, and usually when you're very depressed writing a book it's because you're not writing the book you should have been writing. You're using up something that should have gone into another book, and I think that's exactly what I got into there. The excitement I felt about writing about science went into that book, and there was very little left over to do the science fiction book and I've been dawdling on it. So that's one reason why I don't think the trilogy will ever be fulfilled, and the other is that I've lost the feeling that it counts. I think there are very few people anymore who really care whether you do a trilogy like that. So you'd be the weekend sensation in *The New York Times Book Review* and then that'd be it. No one would ever read it. One of the things that startled me was how few people ever made any attempt to read *Ancient Evenings.* Even people who love my work just said, "Well, gee, I couldn't get into it," so . . .

Leeds: It drives me crazy when I hear that.

Mailer: Well, I do think there's a crisis in literature that's profound. It eats at everyone including me. I've lost some of my sense of high purpose and I think readers of literature have also lost it. TV is the true AIDS of our time. There's no mental immunology left for culture. Culture is totally infected by TV.

Leeds: One of my students came up to me. I always assign *The Naked and the Dead* the first week of classes. I get a lot of dropouts because of that, but the ones that stick with it love it. And this young girl (remember when we used to be able to call them girls?) came up to me . . .

Mailer: What do you have to say? This *person* came up?

Leeds: Well, woman, even if they're thirteen. Of course, my students are all over eighteen. I think that the eighteen-year old girls today are not militant about that; they don't care if you call them girls anymore. I think it's the people who came up during the movement that still take that seriously. But, anyway, this young woman came up to me (she's holding the Rinehart edition that you need a wheelbarrow to bring to class) and she said, "Is there a video on this?" [laughter] I love that.

Mailer: Is it that they read *The Naked and the Dead* and they drop out, why? Too long a book?

Leeds: No: they *don't* read it and they drop out. They see how big it is, and they say, "Have I got to read this? Wow!" And I say to them, if you don't like reading and talking about books and writing about them, then drop out. So a lot of them drop out and the ones I keep are great kids and they usually love the book. After forty years . . . Here's a quotation that's always intrigued me out of *An American Dream:* "No, men were afraid of murder, but not from a terror of justice so much as the knowledge that a killer attracted the attention of the gods; then your mind was not your own, your anxiety ceased to be neurotic, your dread was real. Omens were as tangible as bread. There was an architecture to eternity" . . . That's the line that rings for me. I wanted that to be the full title of my first book about you: *An Architecture to Eternity: The Structured Vision of Norman Mailer.* "There was an architecture to eternity which housed us as we dreamed, and when there was murder, a cry went through the market places of sleep. Eternity had been deprived of a room. Somewhere the divine rage met a fury." This sense of the cosmic order and an embattled God is something that obviously has pervaded your work, but do you feel that in recent years it's been expanded, refined, changed in any way?

Mailer: I think it has. You know if I end up writing a few more good books then those refinements ideally will find their way into that. I still would subscribe to every single thing that's said there. That hasn't changed a bit. Henry Kissinger once said to me, "I haven't had a new idea since I've been in government. You see, I'm working with all old ideas." And he's a very bright man obviously, a man who prides himself in his ability to think and to have new thoughts. That's the joy of life to many people and certainly to him, and I feel that way. But I find that idea you've just quoted is the key of all my ideas. There are little variations on it all the time, but to attempt to talk to you about it now, how it's changed, all I can say is it hasn't really changed that much. I'm still trying to find a way to embody all that in a book where it truly works for a reader who's never encountered these notions before.

Leeds: Yeah—who hasn't been a charter subscriber all along.

Mailer: Another reason why I was so drawn to writing about Gary Gilmore is I had the feeling deep down he believed the same thing. I found him a funny man and parts of him I understand perfectly; other parts of him to this day I don't have a clue. He had a quirky dull streak that I've never gotten near, but the side of him that wanted to die I understand perfectly. It was almost like he was dramatizing one of my favorite notions, that the soul can die before the body, and was quite aware of that and was determined not to let that happen and in that sense was heroic.

Leeds: I understand that. Speaking of criminals and of cops, too, I'd like to talk to you about Dougy "Big Mac" Madden [in *Tough Guys Don't Dance.*] One thing about Dougy is that he looks like a detective but he hates cops, and I think that a lot of people have been attracted or repelled by your interest in the criminal mentality, but they forget that you deal almost as much with the psychology of cops. You played a criminal in *Wild 90,* but a cop, a lieutenant, in *Beyond the Law,* and obviously it's the other side of the same coin. Do you know a lot of cops? My dad was a cop for twenty-one years in New York City and we had cops around the house all the time.

Mailer: I have a friend who's a detective on the police force and he gave me this.

Leeds: It's a miniature detective shield.

Mailer: Yeah. I'm fascinated with cops. I love good cops. I really think that it's such an extraordinary thing to be a good cop, it's so difficult, and a good cop probably has more temptations than any man in any profession you could name. And to keep their balance in the middle of all those conflicting forces . . . so I have two fondnesses. One's for a good cop; the other's for a good crook.

Leeds: I knew the latter but I didn't know if I should mention cops because for the most part in the books and even in the nonfiction, you're pretty negative about them. But I have to come clean, that while my dad probably would share a lot of the same views—he's in his seventies now—that you have about crooked cops, there were cops around in my life as I was growing up and in fact I used to impersonate one when we went to police conventions after I got big enough to look like I might be a young cop.

Mailer: Casting would always put you in as a cop.

Leeds: Thanks, I hope that's positive. Anyway, the thing is, those guys are really fun to be around. They're crazy in a weird way. All those Wambaugh novels . . .

Mailer: They have the most powerful dirty minds. A sense of motive . . . so mean and strong. I think it would be a marvelous novel to write about a good cop, but the only reason I've never been drawn toward it is because it's been so abused. I mean you can't turn on the television without finding a good cop. I'm so sick of that theme. I think it's been so abused. It's always used for ulterior motives. The worst forces of law and order are always used in the portrait of the good cop so I tend not to get into that, not much. But it would make a marvelous novel if you could find a way to do it.

Leeds: I started talking about Dougy. The thing about Dougy that fascinates me is that there's very little about fathers in your earlier works. Mikey Lovett is an amnesiac and Sergius' father throws him into an orphanage, and then suddenly here's this very positive, massive father figure. Could I ask . . .

Mailer: Nothing to do with my father. My father was small . . . a smaller man.

Leeds: I didn't assume that . . .

Mailer: You mean, why? Why did I get into it? I think it's the sort of thing you get into when you get into it. I've never written about childhood. I don't want to until the day I can really write about childhood. I don't want to write about anything unless I can do something with it that hasn't quite been done before. So that's all I ever ask of a book is that I have something new to say. I don't really want to write the same book other people are writing and so I've never found that moment when I could write about childhood. I may before I'm done. I've never really written about a father and a son until *Tough Guys.* I think it's the best thing in the book probably.

Leeds: There are some touching scenes there.

Mailer: In the movie it gets lost to a degree because there's no room for it. You know who played Dougy Madden? Larry Tierney. Remember, who did Dillinger? I think people are going to like him a lot.

Leeds: I'm really looking forward to that movie. By the way, are the three earlier movies available on cassettes?

Mailer: No, it's too expensive. It would cost seven hundred bucks to make one of them into a cassette, but I can't afford it.

Leeds: You know, there'd be a market. This pal of mine teaches a movie course, and he got *Wild 90* and I came in and gave a guest lecture. And then he got *Beyond the Law,* and then we couldn't get *Maidstone* and they said at the rental place that you had the only copy. Apparently you had taken it out of circulation.

Mailer: I might have taken it back at a certain point because what had happened was there are very few left and there was no income from them and I just thought they'd get chewed up, there would be nothing left at all, so I took them out of circulation.

Leeds: You were talking about dogs earlier and I'm struck by "Stunts" in *Tough Guys.* When you mentioned owning a poodle for eighteen years, was that by any chance the dog that you got in a fight about with a sailor in a bar because he called your dog a fag?

Mailer: Yeah. It was on the street actually. I had two dogs at the time. At that point Tibo had a wife who we later gave away because we came back from the country with Tibo and the wife and a pup and walking three dogs on a New York street got to be hilarious. I couldn't handle it. With three leashes. So we gave away two of them.

Leeds: That's a scene worthy of Charlie Chaplin. And I also like the story about Karl the German Shepherd and Dorothy Parker's dog. . . . I was thinking about other writers. I'm certainly not going to get into the Farrell, Dos Passos, Steinbeck thing that people ask you about all the time, but I just have to tell you that in terms of Hemingway, I keep finding you saying new things about him that always warm me because he's been so central to my life. I thought that in *Advertisements,* first of all, that capsule criticism of *The Old Man and the Sea* said more about that book than many long essays did. But I really was pleased that you said in a recent interview, "after *The Executioner's Song* I realized how very talented he was." I found that very heartwarming. I thought it was a very gracious thing to say.

Mailer: Well, he is, he was. Did you read that attack on Scribner's in *The New Republic* by Barbara Probst Solomon? Look for it in the library. Barbara Probst Solomon is a good writer who went and read the original Hemingway manuscript which is over at the Kennedy Library. And she says it's a great miscarriage of literary justice. *The Garden of Eden* as published is a total misrepresentation of the work that Hemingway was doing. The people in that book pass through many years; they're not just young. The thing's totally distorted.

Leeds: Well, I gather from what Baker said in his biography, purportedly it was in horrendous shape. But I wouldn't presume to know.

Mailer: What she said was that it wasn't in that bad shape, that the work would have been more interesting printed the way it was, sprawling all over the place with all the false starts but that finally what we would have seen is half the body of a giant book and that this thing is not Hemingway, that it's been so altered . . .

Leeds: It would be more interesting to guys like me. That's sad to hear. Another guy with large ambitions and big books is James Jones, who I know was a friend of yours. And I've always admired that trilogy (or tetralogy if you count *The Pistol*). People used to ask me, "Is *The Naked and the Dead* the great novel of WWII?" and I said "sure," and then eventually I had to say maybe not, if you take Jones's books as one massive work.

Mailer: I always thought *Eternity* was a bigger book.

Leeds: Not just *Eternity* itself, but *Eternity* and *The Pistol* and *The Thin Red Line* and *Whistle* put together, because in a sense he made World War II his Yoknapatawpha County; and I wonder if you feel, because you don't want to keep writing essentially the same book about the same things, that this return to the same central setting and preoccupations is artistically stultifying? Do you think that it shows too much limitation on the part of a writer like Jones?

Mailer: To begin with, a novelist writes the books that he or she can write and this is more true of serious novelists than commercial novelists. But a novelist does the kind of book that they can do until it gets distorted by their ambitions and by their idea of the kind of book to make them immortal. If you're reasonably young when you arrive and you start taking yourself seriously long before you've developed your metier then you tend to be very self-conscious. Jones was self-conscious. Styron and I are, to a degree, even to this day still a bit self-conscious because very early in life we were handed a role. We were young major novelists and it's a terribly funny role. You have to live up to it. You tend to think that way. I think Jones probably wrestled with the idea: Is this good or bad for my career to do a tetralogy on the war? He may have lost energy in thinking about it too much. I've tried to avoid those traps. I may have set myself a trap with the three big books, you see, and spent an awful lot of time thinking will I do it, should I do it, is it worth doing, can I do it? All those questions. And finally, writing novels at this point in my life is a little bit like falling in love: it isn't automatic. You know, one may never fall in love again with someone new and one may never get another novel, or one may; one may get five novels. You just don't know. You don't know if you're going to have a thrill-filled old age with five novels yet to be written or whether you'll dry up slowly and fall off the tree.

Leeds: I know which way I'm betting.

Mailer: Well, I was struck when I started making this movie about how much I was enjoying it, compared to the way I felt about writing for the last fifteen years. Something had gone out of the writing, maybe the belief that it makes a difference. I can't tell you what that does to effort. How vitiating to feel it just doesn't matter that much.

Leeds: Fitzgerald said something very similar when movies were in their infancy, and Kesey said something very similar last fall at Town Hall. He said, "If Chekhov were alive today, he'd be using a video recorder," and he said that's why the Alaskan novel or whatever the next one may eventually be isn't getting written. But Kesey showed so much promise. I don't know if you ever read *Sometimes a Great Notion,* but it's about fifty times greater than *Cuckoo's Nest.*

Mailer: Really.

Leeds: Yeah. It's a wonderful novel and I wonder if you're willing to say something about the kind of novelist who only tells us one or two stories and then stops. I guess we're lucky to get what we do but we don't get any more.

Mailer: Kesey certainly has an enormous amount to write about. Writers who write just a few books . . . I think nobody knows how much damage a book does to you except another writer. It's hell writing a novel; you really poison your body doing it. It's an unnatural physical activity to sit at a desk and squeeze words out of yourself. It means that you secrete various kinds of fatigues and poisons through your system that you don't get rid of easily. As you get older, it's worse. The other reason why I've been so obsessed with prize fighters is the idea of the aging prize fighter who has to get into shape for one more fight and knows the damage that fight is going to do to his body, which is already beginning to worsen; it puts him in a gloom. One of the things that characterizes almost every older fighter I've ever seen training for a fight is the depression that hangs over him and his camp because the only thing good that can

come out of it is money. The rest is all a foregone conclusion. Even if
he wins the fight—even if he wins it well—he's not going to get a new
purchase on life out of the fight the way a young fighter can by a
decisive victory. And that's true in writing. Writers will often make
grave decisions—am I going to write this book or not? And at a
certain point you have to believe that the book can be enormously
important or you won't suffer that kind of self-destruction. Because it
is self-destruction, it's quiet self-destruction, civilized self-destruction.
Let's say in writing a novel over two or three years of the hardest
work, that the damage it does to the body is equal to someone who
has never smoked before taking on two or three packs a day for a
few years. And I think if you could weigh those things you'd find it's
accurate. I think one reason I've always been such an amateur about
medicine and so interested in it at a great remove is because when
you're a writer, in a certain sense you're a doctor to yourself. You're
always feeling these various tensions and ailments creep into you.
From an early age writers become hypochondriacs. It goes with the
territory. Your factory is yourself. You're always examining the factory
for potential breakdowns, anticipating troubles, and so you get to be
awfully alert to the relation not only between yourself and the world
but the relationship between yourself and your body. And writing
impinges on your body.

Leeds: One of my favorite quotations about you is the opening of
Joan Didion's review in *The New York Times Book Review* of *The
Executioner's Song,* where she said so many people read you only
within their own limitations. I just wanted to ask you, do you like her
work?

Mailer: I have a lot of respect for her work. I once said that if there
were a particular woman writer today in America who you could
compare to Hemingway, it'd probably be Joan Didion.

Leeds: Absolutely.

Mailer: She has that same sense of the power of the sentence
sitting by itself and the power of the next sentence. There's no
accident that she writes movies and lives with film because her work,
like Hemingway's, is montage. That is, there's an assumption that the
reader's going to pay enough attention to each sentence so they'll
feel the next sentence come into place. It's very much like cuts in a
film. Sentences don't have to exist entirely by themselves; they exist
by their relation to the next sentence and the echo of the sentence

that just passed. She writes marvelous prose. Another thing about Hemingway that I liked so much after I finished *The Executioner's Song* is . . . I was doing that a little bit in *The Executioner's Song* but it just didn't compare. Pick up Hemingway and read him and boy, you feel that montage. People who write in a simple style, like Raymond Carver, depend on montage. You can't write in a simple style and get away with it unless you can do that . . . Those choices have to be exquisite—what goes next to what.

Leeds: I wanted to ask you about a guy that I'm interested in, Harry Crews, whom you mention in *Tough Guys Don't Dance*. Spider Nissen and Tim are always going through this list of writers and he's one of the guys they rip up once in a while. But here's a quotation that I like from an essay he wrote. He says, "I'm sick and tired of women in my face and on my case and I'm sick and tired of being sick and tired." [laughter] I thought that's something that might interest you. I know you gave him a blurb for *A Feast of Snakes*.

Mailer: Yeah. I think he's very funny and very tough and kind of incorruptible. Like he's set his course and if storms came across, then they come, it's all right, but he's staying on that course. He knows what he knows and he's going to write about it. He has a clarity of purpose in his writing that I like.

Leeds: Yeah, you can see it in his face.

Mailer: I've never met him.

Leeds: No, I haven't met him but on every book jacket his face gets fiercer; he's got lines on lines and this forceful scowl and you can just see that he's an uncompromising guy.

[Perhaps fifteen minutes of informal chat and amenities ensue.]

Leeds: Thanks for inviting me, Norman; and good luck on the movie.

Mailer: Thank you, Barry.

Dance of A Tough Guy
Michael Ventura/1987

From *L.A. Weekly,* 18-24 September 1987, 14-19, 22. Reprinted by permission of Michael Ventura.

I had seen him once before, in Berkeley in the fall of '72, in a hall filled to bursting with the shrillest of feminists, the gayest of gays, fringes left and right, and literature professors leading packs of profs-to-be, all eager to bait a writer whose work was too forceful to ignore and too paradoxical to embrace. They were after something very like blood—its literary equivalent, some greenish substance, part pus and part sperm, that would surely flow all over the stage if *one* of them could get this guy where he lived, shame him in front of the crowd. It was like a denful of Daniels lusting to leap upon one middle-aged lion.

Make that bear. When Mailer strode from the wings to center-stage, he walked from the shoulders on down, his chest out before him, looking at the crowd with a greedy smile. No stew of emotions would be too rank for *him,* that smile said. They booed, they hissed, they applauded all at once, and he inhaled it as if to say, "Is that the best you can do? You don't stink enough!" They got louder. His smile got sly. They finally subsided into a vaguely hostile yet appreciative murmur. Everybody was having a good time.

The Sex Pistols were still six years away, so none of us knew that this atmosphere of mutually excited antagonism between audience and performer was pure punk. Norman Mailer was even more Out There than he knew.

I'd come early to secure a center seat off the aisle on the third or fourth row. To my knowledge no American writer had yet been assassinated or kicked half to death—not, at any rate, for his writing—but if it was going to happen that year it was going to be

Mailer. At every level and in every niche of America, from Nixon to the Underground, *somebody* was pissed at him.

So that night I had a Maileresque idea of being a hero. I was skinny, unpublished, trembling with rages I could not yet name and stupidly eager for a fight. So I sat three steps and a leap from the stage, thinking that if it came to a rumble I was on Mailer's side.

The Presidential Papers, Advertisements for Myself, Cannibals and Christians and *The Prisoner of Sex* had been intellectually crucial to any vision of America I was ever going to have, and Mailer's intensity as an essayist had shown us all what was possible in that form; *The Deer Park* and *An American Dream* were novels that taught me that I wasn't crazy, or if I was crazy, I wasn't alone in how I felt my magic; so I figured I owed Mailer. I'm sure my fantasy went something like: We'd fight side by side, get the shit kicked out of us, and later he'd read my stuff and introduce me to Mr. Simon, Mr. Schuster, Mr. Scribner and whoever else published masterpieces. (The inner life of a serious unpublished writer is humid with such fantasies—they fog his eyes from the inside.)

But, alas, I had underestimated Mailer's ability to defuse a crowd.

He opened by announcing that he'd come with important tidings and that he didn't want to be interrupted every other line, so would the feminists and gays please do their hissing and booing now. They hissed and booed to a fare-thee-well. When the last hiss faded he peered over the podium, waited a beat and said:

"O-*beeeed*-iant little *bitches*, aren't you?"

It was a ploy that had to work beautifully or start a riot, and it worked beautifully. This was a house that could appreciate a masterstroke when it saw one, and it applauded accordingly. There would be a couple of demonstrations—gays dressed as pricks dancing onto the stage, that sort of thing; there would be arguments; there would be cat-calls and boos at various pronouncements; but the crowd was in his hands that night. It was clear that my desperate assistance would not be needed.

Fifteen years later, early last month . . . I finally met Mr. Norman Mailer, or whoever that was, walking across the patio of the Sunset Marquis—a different walk, a sailor's walk, and an old sailor's at that, an easy roll from the hips. Mid-60ish, gray, and a little shorter than me, robustly affable, a sweet sparkle in his blue eyes (as blue as Paul

Newman's, as blue as Bob Dylan's), his voice richly modulated and
gentle. His manner was courtly, in a sense that you almost never see
in this country, that of a man whose manners are absolutely right for
him. The presence of a man, in short, with nothing to prove.

Norman *who?*

I'd never met anyone so different in private from what he had
appeared to be, for so long, in public. He had the humility of one
who has found the limits of his rage. Twenty or so books, six
marriages, umpteen "newsworthy" hassles, thousands of public
appearances, each met (if we are to believe the writing, and I do) as
an exploration, a test, an attempt "to take an existential turn, to walk
into the nightmare" . . . seemed to have produced a radiant, Zenlike
air.

Of course, I was meeting Mailer in his capacity as film director, and
directors (considering the demands of their business) are a
suspiciously calm lot. It is a calm achieved by enacting one's excesses
through others. And while, as a dynamic, it is not all that different
from many marriages and nearly all child-rearing, it is certainly one of
the dirty little pleasures of directing.

But no, Mailer had lived enough of his excesses for one to feel that
he'd come by this surprising presence honestly. Two hours of movie
talk will solve no mysteries, and yet . . . for anyone to whom he's
been important, either as a teacher or as an antagonist, it's worth
reporting that Mailer's attentive, interested calm (which in contrast to
the public persona was just this side of eerie) seemed finally to be the
signature of that rarest creature of all: one who has gone his distance
and can look in his mirrors without shame, artifice, or surprise.

"Cinema—that river enema of the sins . . ." is how Norman Mailer
once defined the art that has obsessed him for so long. (*The Deer
Park*, his best novel, is also the best of the Hollywod novels.) He
meant for *Tough Guys Don't Dance* to live up to that definition, and
it does.

It was the least of his novels, an overworked rehash of the critically
savaged, badly underrated *An American Dream. Tough Guys'* prose
feels forced and its tone is strained. It's the only Mailer book in which
the writing itself—the life within the sentences—is flat. So it was the
obvious choice for Mailer's first "mainstream" film, because it could
make a better movie than a novel. Years ago he'd written why:
"Great novels invariably make the most disappointing movies, and

modest novels (like *The Asphalt Jungle*) sometimes make very good movies. It is because the original conception in modest novels is less special and so more capable of being worked upon by any number of other writers, directors and actors."

As a screenwriter, Mailer has cut his own novel to ribbons, thrown out most of what was warmed-over from *An American Dream,* condensed and improved the dialogue to an extraordinary degree, then gone on to rethink the accepted form of film as well.

"Somebody said, 'You know, you only see one policeman in the entire film,' " Mailer explained. "It isn't really true. You do see a couple of other cops once, but there isn't any of the paraphernalia of the policeman. A policeman is a member of a team. You never see a crime movie that has just one cop, like this one has. You have five cops, you have eight cops, you have people working at typewriters when you come to police headquarters. And my thing was, cut all that out. That's all part of the crap. We *know* there's a guy typing in a police station. Just show *our* cop. Don't get into the paraphernalia of things, because the awful, awful thing is that movies have become nothing *but* paraphernalia. You start getting into props, and there's no end to the props, and every prop has to be researched, and you have to photograph it properly, because if you don't photograph a prop properly it's a detriment to your film, it's a squashed fly on the wall. So I ended up abstracting the story in this way. My feeling was: abstract, abstract, abstract, get down to the ultimate core and see what happens."

He does this with scene structure and character development as well, so from the first to the last nearly every scene is either a climax or a tense prelude to a climax. In the film's first conversation, Tim Madden (Ryan O'Neal, in his finest performance in a long time) is trying to tell his father, or *not* tell his father, that he may have killed a woman, but he can't remember. At the same time his father, Dougy (Lawrence Tierny), is telling Tim that he has cancer. Deaths are talking to deaths.

In most Hollywood films both of these speeches would be tearful, climactic scenes. But for Mailer, they are an underplayed prelude. The purpose is to let in the Spirits. Dougy says that now that the doctors say he's terminal, "the Spirits circle around my bed and they tell me to dance. I tell 'em, 'Tough guys don't dance.' They tell me, 'Keep dancin'.' "

Cut from that conversation to:

Dancing. A party. The cop, Regency (superbly played by Wings
Hauser), has as deft and juicy an entrance as I've seen. He, Tim, and
Tim's witchy wife Patty Lareine (Debra Sandlund) are standing on a
stair landing, hovering above the dancers, talking good trash.

> **Tim:** You trying to wake up all the ghosts in Helltown?
> **Patti Lareine:** That is the idea—don't let the motherfuckers sleep.
> **Regency:** Lady, you sound like a witch.
> **Patti Lareine:** All good blondes are.
> **Tim:** You're not a real blonde.
> **Patti Lareine:** My pussy hair was yellow in high school till I went
> out and scorched it on a date with the football team.

A line she knows enough to exit on.

(At this point, the movie is still holding its most inventive character
in reserve, one Wardley Meeks III, played by a brilliant young actor
named John Bedford Lloyd, who gets to say, so mournfully and
wistfully, "I see such odd things when I pull a trigger.")

So however centered Mailer may have become, he still has livid
things to say. Or to put it another way, unlike Updike and Bellow,
Mailer won't comfort his readers by couching his meanings in that
upscale world they aspire both to achieve and protect. There are no
hiding places in a Mailer story, nowhere to retreat to. For Mailer,
comfort can cause cancer, and every plot resolution leads his
characters willy-nilly toward the next abyss—for the abyss is the only
place where tough guys *can* dance.

Most Hollywod movies start with their characters in relative safety,
take them into jeopardy, then pull them back. Safety at the beginning
is crucial to the form, otherwise there can be no reassuring and/or
tragic ending. Mailer's aesthetic is too stringent for that. He knows,
and we know, that people who start off talking to each other like
these do are already incapable of taking refuge in normalcy. They
begin in jeopardy, and any meaning they come to will have to leave
them in jeopardy as well.

When this aesthetically orgiastic commitment to a movie of
climaxes doesn't quite come off, it's laughable. Ryan O'Neal, having
just found out the worst about his wife, stands by the sea and
hysterically repeats, "Oh man! Oh God! Oh man! Oh God! Oh man!
Oh God! . . . "

Oh man. Awful.

Yet a couple of beats later there's a riveting speech by Regency that throws you back on the murderer in yourself—if you're the least bit turned on by what's turned him on.

In other words: Norman Mailer is a good director, with an inspired sense of casting, and blessed by the tense and beautiful cinematography of "visual consultant" John Bailey. In fact, Mailer's a director who's strung together enough memorable scenes for a dozen movies, and strung them on a precisely convoluted plot. Which is to say, a plot intentionally hard to follow in order that the essence of each scene can be experienced without the distraction of story. And yet, the story is there, strong, if that's what you want to pay attention to.

It adds up to: Mailer's filmmaking is as adventurous as his writing.

Aside from that, *Tough Guys* is what in America we've come to call "entertainment": Everyone gets laid, and most everyone gets killed. It's a juicy film, and well-made to boot, but it's not a great film, and has no grand meaning. Yet its intentions are not small. For it draws us into that netherworld between the masturbation fantasy and the declaration of love—into that place where need and fear meld into what passes, in the good old USA, for sex.

Michael Ventura: You once said that movies are more primitive than literature. What did you mean?

Norman Mailer: I think movies go deeper into the psyche. That's what I meant by more primitive. Years ago I said that if you were to set up a spectrum of sex, memory, dream and death, you could put film between memory and dream and have no trouble at all. There's a psychic artifact that exists there.

Ventura: I think that's what Josef Von Sternberg must have been referring to when he said, "I think the cinema has been here since the beginning of the world." That the fact of cinema seems to leap ready-made from some depth of the psyche, as though it has been waiting there all along.

Mailer: Whereas literature calls on many other factors. Literature is really much more social than film. Film is tribal. When you read a book, it involves the room you're sitting in, whether you're happy in that room, whether your social situation in life is appealed to by this book, or depressed by this book. If we read Hemingway, we're depressed by the fact that we're sedentary in relation to his heroes,

that they're having more exciting lives than we're having, and that
depresses us. If we read Henry James, we're wistful that we don't
know the nuances of society the way his people do. But when we're
in a movie, if the movie's good enough, we don't know whether
we're perceiving something about life or entering something deeper,
in the nature of dreams—those mysterious transactions that go on in
dreams.

So what I love about film is that it's spooky. Film is viscerally
spooky. A film that's not spooky is, by this arrogant definition, a bad
film. To the degree that a film has nothing spooky in it, it's
meretricious, wholly meretricious, it's a money machine, it's filmed
theater of a low sort. So you can imagine the directors I love. I love
Bunuel, I love Bergman, I love Coppola—he always had a touch of
the spooky in everything he does. I love Fellini, because in the middle
of all that gaity it's so spooky.

Ventura: The obvious question: Why moviemaking now, again,
instead of another novel, say? Have you become bored with writing?

Mailer: I didn't go to movie direction because I was bored with
writing. I wasn't bored with it, but I felt burnt out to a degree. I
thought I needed a change, a big change, in my life for a year or two.
Because I'd got to a point where I really hated the process of going
in every day and facing an empty page and having to contend with
the essential unhealthiness of writing. We sit there, we grind our guts
and squeeze them to get a few words—at least I do. And I'm always
in worse physical shape when I finish a book than when I start.
Always. So I just needed to do something that was altogether
different.

What I love about movie-directing is that it has *nothing* to do with
writing. On a day-to-day basis it's the exact opposite. When you
direct you use *every* part of your experience that you can't put into
writing, all the little things that you've learned over the years that you
can't use when you're writing a book. Particularly when you're
writing a novel, you tend to focus on what belongs to that novel, and
all sorts of things that you're also interested in never get into that
novel. They really have no occupational life for a couple of years.
They hang around in you, collecting psychic fat.

Suddenly when you're making a movie you're making decisions
on a hundred different things in a day. You're making the decision on
whether the food's good enough. Some of the people have been

complaining lately about the food—and morale *is* everything on a movie set. One of the ways in which a movie set is like a military campaign is morale: If you have bad morale in your troops, you're in a lot of trouble. So you've got to ask yourself the question, "Is this just ordinary grousing about the food, or is the food really getting a little sub par?" That's a serious question, and you've got to answer it for yourself.

Then the hairdresser comes up with the actress who's playing that day. "What do you think of the hairdo, Mr. Mailer?" Now, I've been married six times, and through six marriages I've said to my wife, "Uh, honey, I'd like a little curl there, uh . . ." "Get lost, will you! You don't know anything about hair!" But the hairdresser comes up, and I say, "I think you need a little curl there," and he says, "Yes, sir!" and he goes away. You're not only making decisions, you're being *obeyed.*

Shooting a film is so *practical,* so matter-of-fact and down-to-earth. The average good director is not really so much an artist as an aesthetic engineer. Movie directors bear the same relation to art as engineers do to physics. They're using the principles of aesthetics and mixing them with a great many other matters. You know, an engineer not only has to know the theory of bridge-building, he also has to know about the strength of the materials that go into that bridge, and he has to know about the reliability of the people who bring him the materials. If you're working with a crooked contractor you have to incorporate that in your estimate of the difficulties. So, in the same way, when you're making a movie, the strengths and frailties of all the people around you make demands on your sense of management, so you're almost never thinking theoretically.

Or you're doing a scene with a couple of actors, and it's a good scene, you've got some pretty good results. You can get better results, maybe; maybe you can't. Do you want to gamble time? Time is your money in a film—literally, it's your money. If you don't get done with this scene by lunch, then you're going to come back in that stupor after lunch, and still be doing that scene, and you're going to lose not half an hour or an hour, but *two* hours. So you're gambling. And that's exciting. And not only are you gambling, you're getting immediate results. Because you learn in the next hour or two whether your gamble won or lost. And then the next day in the dailies you see if it *really* came out.

Making movies, you're absolutely *in the world,* in the existential
sense. Whereas in literature, you withdraw from the world in order to
perceive the world. So they really use opposite sides of you. It's as
though I've been using one of my two sides for 40 years, and now I
can just leave that side alone for a year—wondering, of course, will I
ever go back to it, or will I not? Nonetheless I can leave it alone for a
year. And if it really still wants to write, that side, then it'll come
back—and maybe I'll write better than ever, maybe I won't. But at
least I'll give it that rest that it's been *yelling* for . . . 10 years now.

Ventura: You've written a lot about the soul, and about how the
act of writing brings you closer to the nature of your soul. Is it more or
less so with a film, or is the issue completely different?

Mailer: I think you get closer to your soul with a book, but you
get closer to the functioning of your psyche with a movie. Let me see
if I can amplify that a little. I think when you're writing a book there
are moments when you feel as if you're beaming a torch down into
the abyss, and you see the lineaments of your soul down there. You
don't travel down there in your soul, but you do perceive it. Because
in the course of writing a book you get out to some very astonishing
places, and you do have the light of your intuition, and it does throw
a long light.

When you're making a film, particularly after you've shot it and
you start editing it, you look at the same scene over and over and
over to take all the little dead spots out. Makes you feel like a
surgeon. What it also does is it involves your taste, and your
concentration. Seeing it over and over and over again you have to
keep your taste alive; you have to exercise your ability to concentrate
upon the same material over and over and over. And I'm the guy
who wrote, "Repetition kills the soul," which I thought of many times
when I was editing. But it doesn't kill it in this case, because it's not
absolute repetition; you're chasing down repetition in order to alter it
slightly. And as you do that, you're tuning your psyche.

When it's over, you have a sense not of how you think, but of how
you move thematically within your unconscious. And one of the
things you get is you end up with this lovely relationship with an
editor. I had a fine young editor, Deborah McDermott. We really had
a funny, sweet relation because the ultimate word was always mine,
but the art of it was that we'd never get to that point. Either she

would give in or I would give in, but we never wanted to get to the point where it was, "I don't care what you say, it's going to be this way and that's that." So *that* involved not only a sense of your own taste, but of someone else's taste. And because taste is the most graceful part of us, of our psyche, it was almost like a dance of tastes.

Ventura: I don't want to presume that I know what distinction you make between "psyche" and "soul."

Mailer: The soul, to me, is one's purchase on eternity. The reason I got into that 11-year stint writing *Ancient Evenings* was because I was so fascinated with the Egyptians—I had come across their notion of the hereafter, and it was close to my own: that the soul could die before the body. The Egyptians believed that after you die either your soul passes through the underworld and becomes eternal, or it perishes. So there was the second death within death, and that was the crucial death.

In that sense the soul is or is not eternal, but it's our purchase on eternity. The psyche—I mean, I wouldn't begin to know what its relation is, precisely, to the soul—but I think you could almost conceive of the soul perishing in life while the psyche would still function. The psyche is, among other things, that computer within one that takes account of all the factors of one's life and adjusts them and navigates through the obstacle course. The prime function of the psyche is to navigate through life. The soul could function with the psyche, but could be inimical to it also. It can feel that what the psyche wants to do is too mundane, too practical, too materialistic, too world-oriented. The soul may decide, "Oh, no, no, no, I'm in danger of dying if we go on with this course; I've really got to do something absolutely mad now in order to stay alive. Let the damn body die before me—then I keep my purchase on eternity." Which I think accounts for most irrational behavior in people. That's why certain guys will go out and drink themselves to death rather than do something reasonable, because at that point the soul really does want to die. Not all suicides are silly.

Ventura: *Tough Guys Don't Dance* doesn't go five frames without what most people would call "irrational behavior." So by your definition its characters are, in spite of some hideous acts and motivations, trying to save their souls. Maybe that's always been the great appeal of film noir? I've often thought that you could throw out every other sort of film (except maybe the Western) and still have its equivalent in the other arts, but not film noir. Film noir does something that nothing else has done, and *Tough Guys Don't Dance,* like *Blue Velvet,* is a contemporary film noir.

Mailer: You know, every dream is a film noir if you think about it. Because every dream is utterly unsentimental. A film like any of Bergman's films . . . They're not film noir, but they have that implacable, impervious edge of the dream. No mercy in the dream. So that's why you make that remark, "If you throw everything else out, you've got to keep film noir," because that's the closest to *film as an entity.* The farthest away from film as an entity is *The Sound of Music.*

Ventura: But film noir has a persistent convention which I get off on while I'm watching, but which afterwards makes me mad, and that is: If people can fuck great, then they have to be capable of murder. They have to kill. From *Double Indemnity* to *Body Heat,* from *Gilda* to *Tough Guys Don't Dance,* if people are good fuckers, then they're killers.

Mailer: But again I say it's the logic of the dream. Dream logic is strong and central: Fucking is penetration, murder is penetration, they're equal. That doesn't mean that they're equal to us in the way we lead our lives. If you want to approach it from the psychological side, apart from film for the moment, it can probably be argued that great fucking has to touch on our murderous impulses. The charm of *Prizzi's Honor* is that it proved a law which I'm sure that not only Huston lived with for many years, but that he adored, which is that the only time you have true love is between people who are equally murderous.

Great fucking engages. What makes copulation great is that you express the best and the worst in yourself. One of my favorite notions is that we only work with great energy when our best and our worst motive find an identity of interest in the event. They both come in together. So when we're working for God and the devil at once we have huge energy—Ollie North! So in the transcendental fuck, the deepest parts of ourself are engaged. Well, I would just submit the deepest part of almost everyone alive has murder in it, because civilization is built on the notion that we *don't* murder one another. That means that the murderer is piped into the deeper regions of the unconscious, and is there to be called upon when we have deep experiences. What makes for great fucking, among other elements, is that the murder is equal between the two people. When one person is more murderous than the other in the act of love, they are left, male or female, with an intolerable tension that keeps one from real satisfaction . . .

. . . he talked on, and it's on the tape, and it's pretty good, but my ability to listen stopped with that thought. For me, it's one of those thoughts that slits your life open top to bottom and makes you contemplate your unpleasantly palpitating liver.

And all the while, as he talked and as my street sense strained for confirmation of the genuineness of this peace, this calm I had sensed in him—all the while another current of words pulled at me, an undertow to our mood. Not that I thought of the exact quotes at the time. Still, they were present. (I had, after all, spent the last two days rereading pages of his work from the 13 titles—a number he'd appreciate—on my shelves.)

"The years pass into the years and we count our time in lonely private rhythms that have little to do with number judgment or the uncertain shifting memory of friends." (*The Deer Park*) "For there was that law of life so cruel and so just which demanded that one must grow or else pay more for remaining the same." (*The Deer Park*) Because "the core of life cannot be cheated. Every moment of one's existence one is growing into more or retreating into less. One is always living a little more or dying a little bit . . . The choice is not to live a little more or to not live a little more, it is to live a little more or to die a little more." (*Advertisements for Myself*)

"Not everyone can discharge their furies on an analyst's couch, for some angers can be relaxed only by winning power, some rages are sufficiently monumental to demand that one try to become a hero or else fall back on that death which is already within the cells." (*The Presidential Papers*) "We learn the truth by giving away pieces of our tongue. When we know it all, there is no tongue left." (*The Presidential Papers*) "And [I] had that knowledge which falls like rain, for now I understood that love was not a gift but a vow. Only the brave could keep it for more than a little while . . . It had always been the same, love was love, one could find it with anyone, one could find it anywhere. It was just that you could never keep it. Not unless you were ready to die for it, dear friend." (*An American Dream*)

Those aren't so much thoughts as bones, what they find when they cut you open. The bones of his body of thought. The rest—his politics, his notions of God, devil and soul, his sexual theories, his aesthetics, this movie—are flesh and features on those bones.

In the two hours we spent talking, what can I say but that I felt the trueness of those bones?

All his failures (Where, where, where is the novel of Marion Faye, the great character of *The Deer Park,* announced so long ago and which some of us have waited 25 years for?); all his excesses (Why were the bastards so important to you that you had to pose for them all the time, for all those years, until you ended up reacting to their reactions, so that their very mediocrity controlled you more than you knew, turning you into a dancing bear by the time the posing was done?); all his compromises (I mean the careful way you cozied up to the literary Mafia in the two years before the publication of *Ancient Evenings,* those cleverly polite interviews that made nice-nice to the world you had spent your best years rightly insulting); all the prices he had paid (for it had to cost him to tell me that *The Deer Park,* published 30 years ago, was probably his best novel) . . . hadn't been able to break those bones.

Or so I felt in my own bones.

His prices had been paid; the distance from his first books to that Berkeley lecture to the Sunset Marquis had been traversed; and here was Norman Mailer, gentle, wise, yet still dangerous, and growing in a way that was utterly unexpected. For hadn't he just done a good job directing his first "mainstream" movie—if a movie with a line like "Did she ever give you a rim job?" could be called mainstream.

Faulkner and Hemingway are, in many ways, far greater, but both diminished by the day after about age 50—frightening examples for young American writers. Maybe Mailer is going down slow, like the old blues says, but he is going down smart. Once in danger of becoming a parody of himself, he is defying expectations, escaping the role that has trapped him for so long. How many ever escape their traps so artfully?

And as I thought this, he was saying, "It's a spooky business, making films."

Index